Writing Research Papers

A Complete Guide

Fifteenth Edition

James D. Lester

James D. Lester, Jr.
Austin Peay State University

PEARSON

Boston   Columbus   Indianapolis   New York   San Francisco   Upper Saddle River
Amsterdam   Cape Town   Dubai   London   Madrid   Milan   Munich   Paris   Montréal   Toronto
Delhi   Mexico City   São Paulo   Sydney   Hong Kong   Seoul   Singapore   Taipei   Tokyo

Senior Vice President & Editorial Director: Joseph Opiela
Senior Sponsoring Editor: Katharine Glynn
Executive Marketing Manager: Roxanne McCarley
Senior Supplements Editor: Donna Campion
Executive Digital Producer: Stefanie A. Snajder
Digital Media Editor: Sara Gordus
Content Specialist: Erin Jenkins
Project Manager: Savoula Amanatidis
Project Coordination and Text Design: Electronic Publishing Services Inc., NYC
Page Makeup: SPi Global
Cover Designer/Manager: John Callahan
Cover Image: Alamy
Photo Researcher: Integra
Senior Manufacturing Buyer: Dennis J. Para
Printer and Binder: R. R. Donnelley and Sons Company–Crawfordsville
Cover Printer: Lehigh-Phoenix Color Corporation–Hagerstown

For permission to use copyrighted material, grateful acknowledgment is made to
the copyright holders on p. 383, which is hereby made part of this copyright page.

Library of Congress Cataloging-in-Publication Data
Lester, James D., (date).
   Writing Research Papers : A Complete Guide / James D. Lester, James D. Lester, Jr.
— 15th Edition.
      pages   cm
   Includes bibliographical references and index.
   ISBN-13: 978-0-321-95295-0
   ISBN-10: 0-321-95295-2
   ISBN-13: 978-0-321-95294-3
   ISBN-10: 0-321-95294-4
   1. Report writing—Handbooks, manuals, etc.   2. Research—Handbooks, manuals, etc.
I. Lester, James D., (date)   II. Title.
   LB2369.L4 2015
   371.30281—dc23

                                                                              2013036786

10 9 8 7 6 5 4 3 2—DOC—17 16 15 14

www.pearsonhighered.com

Paperbound Edition:
ISBN-10: 0-321-95295-2
ISBN-13: 978-0-321-95295-0

Contents

Chapter 10 Drafting the Paper in an Academic Style 156

Chapter 12   Writing the Introduction, Body, and Conclusion   200

Preface to the Instructor

For decades, this text has been the leader in offering current, detailed guidance about academic research, writing, and documentation. Over the last two decades, the world of academic research has changed dramatically. Most research is now done online, and this new universe of information has not only put an almost unimaginable wealth of new sources at our fingertips, but it has also brought challenges in evaluating the credibility and usefulness of those sources. Questions of academic integrity and unintentional plagiarism have arisen around the integration of electronic sources. This new fifteenth edition of *Writing Research Papers: A Complete Guide* confronts these new challenges and offers clear, detailed guidance to assist student researchers as they struggle to keep pace with online research, electronic publishing, and new documentation formats.

What Is New in This Edition?

- **New "Clear Targets" at the beginning of each chapter** provide students with a list of learning objectives that serve as a ready guide for finding documentation information quickly and that provide students with the key goals of the chapter.
- **New explanations of research techniques** in Chapter 4 show students how to apply cutting-edge tools and strategies in their research, including keyword searches with expanded Boolean operators and social networking sites.
- **Three new student papers** plus a new annotated bibliography provide fresh models of student research work.
- **Updated coverage of APA documentation style** brings students up to speed with the latest revisions especially how to handle electronic source documentation.

Key Features

The world of academic research is changing rapidly, especially with the ascendance of online research. Virtually every college student now writes on a computer and researches online. The fifteenth edition of *Writing Research Papers* continues to offer a wide array of resources to help students successfully plan and execute their research papers.

Help with Digital Research

The digital revolution is so pervasive in research writing today that a single chapter cannot properly encompass the topic. Instead, every chapter of this text has been updated to reflect the current context for academic writing, including the impact of technology on searching for appropriate topics, finding and evaluating source material, gathering notes and drafting the paper, avoiding plagiarism and embracing academic integrity, and, of course, documenting sources. Students are directed step by step through the various formats for documenting online sources and are offered clear, detailed guidance on blending electronic citations into their writing. The most extensive updated content is included in Chapter 4, where explanations are provided about new research techniques using social networking sites and keyword searches with expanded Boolean operators.

Current Documentation Guidelines

Since discipline-specific style guides offer very different methods for documenting sources—particularly electronic sources—depending on the academic field of research, a guide of this sort is vital to students who are responding to writing assignments in a variety of disciplines. To enable students to document sources correctly, this edition includes updated guidelines for the most important documentation formats.

- **Up-to-date coverage of MLA documentation style.** The Modern Language Association (MLA) significantly revised its documentation style for both print and electronic sources in the most recent edition of the *MLA Style Manual and Guide to Scholarly Publishing,* and the *MLA Handbook for Writers of Research Papers.* All sample citations and student papers in Chapters 1 to 14 reflect the current MLA style guides.
- **Revised APA documentation coverage.** The American Psychological Association (APA) also revised its documentation guidelines in the *APA Publication Manual.* All sample citations and student papers in Chapter 15 follow current APA documentation standards.
- **Current standards for CMS style.** The most recent edition of the University of Chicago Press' *Chicago Manual of Style* emphasizes the role of electronic research. All sample citations and student papers in Chapter 16 follow current CMS documentation standards.

Research Tips for Avoiding the Pitfalls of Plagiarism

Chapters 1 to 10 provide at least one "Research Tip," a feature that offers instruction and examples for citing sources appropriately and ethically, and avoiding plagiarism. Beginning with the section "Understanding and Avoiding Plagiarism," in Chapter 1, *Writing Research Papers* clearly explains what plagiarism is and presents strategies students can use to avoid unintentional plagiarism. Moreover, there is a special emphasis on how to blend quotations into academic writing and document Internet sources.

Guidelines for Evaluating Online Sources

Understanding what constitutes an appropriate source for an academic paper is more and more challenging for students, as more and more sources become instantly available online. *Writing Research Papers* assists student researchers in deciding if and when to use familiar search engines such as Google or Yahoo!, and also offers detailed advice on how to find respected scholarly sources—and how to determine whether a source is in fact credible. A checklist, "Evaluating Online Sources," helps students gauge the quality of online articles.

Student Papers

Student writing examples provide models for student writers of how other students have researched and drafted papers on a wide range of topics. With seven annotated sample papers, more than any other text of this kind, *Writing Research Papers* demonstrates format, documentation, and the different academic styles. Student papers include:

Ashley Irwin, "Sylvia Plath and Her 'Daddy'" (MLA Style)

Kaci Holz, "Gender Communication" (MLA style)

Caitlin Kelley, "More Academics for the Cost of Less Engaged Children" (APA style)

Clare Grady, "The Space Race: One Small Step—One Giant Leap" (CMS style)

Sarah Bemis, "Diabetes Management: A Delicate Balance" (CSE style)

Sarah Morrison, "Annotated Bibliography: Media Ethics" (MLA style)

Sarah Morrison, "Media Ethics: A Review of the Literature" (MLA style)

Sample abstracts in MLA and APA style are also displayed. Additional sample research papers are available in the *Instructor's Manual, Model Research Papers from across the Curriculum,* and on the MyWritingLab.

Reference Works by Topic

The list of references in the Appendix, "Finding Reference Works for Your General Topic," provides a user-friendly list of sources for launching your research project. Arranged into ten general categories, as listed on pages 375–382, the Appendix allows a researcher to have quick access to relevant library books, library databases, and Internet sites.

Accessible, Navigable Design

As in previous editions, *Writing Research Papers* is printed in full color, making information and features easier to find and more pleasing to read, and bringing strong, visual elements to the instruction. Icons identify special features, like the "Where to Look" boxes signaling cross-references. The spiral-bound version of *Writing Research Papers* also includes tab dividers to make information easier to find. The tabs include additional websites, as well as tables of contents for the following sections.

Additional Resources for Instructors and Students

MyWritingLab™ **Now Available for Composition.** MyWritingLab is an online homework, tutorial, and assessment program that provides engaging experiences to today's instructors and students. By incorporating rubrics into the writing assignments, faculty can create meaningful assignments, grade them based on their desired criteria, and analyze class performance through advanced reporting. For students who enter the course under-prepared, MyWritingLab offers a diagnostic test and personalized remediation so that students see improved results and instructors spend less time in class reviewing the basics. Rich multimedia resources are built in to engage students and support faculty throughout the course. Visit www.mywritinglab.com for more information.

Interactive Pearson eText. An eText version of *Writing Research Papers*, Fifteenth Edition, is also available in MyWritingLab. This dynamic, online version of the text is integrated into MyWritingLab to create an enriched, interactive learning experience for students.

CourseSmart. Students can subscribe to *Writing Research Papers*, Fifteenth Edition, as a CourseSmart eText (at CourseSmart.com). The site includes all of the book's content in a format that enables students to search the text, bookmark passages, save their own notes, and print assignments that incorporate lecture notes.

Instructor's Manual

This extensive guide contains chapter-by-chapter classroom exercises, research assignments, quizzes, and duplication masters. Instructors can visit http://www.pearsonhighered.com/IRC to download a copy of this valuable resource.

Acknowledgments

Many key people supported the development of *Writing Research Papers: A Complete Guide,* Fifteenth Edition. I am grateful to the following students for their help and for allowing me to use their work as models in this book: Kaci Holz, Caitlin Kelley, Ashley Irwin, Clare Grady, Sarah Morrison, and Sarah Bemis.

I am of course grateful to the reviewers who provided helpful suggestions for this revision, including Emory Reginald Abbott, Georgia Perimeter College; Stevens R. Amidon, Indiana University-Purdue University Fort Wayne; Crystal Bacon, Community College of Philadelphia; John Christopher Ervin, Western Kentucky University; Morgan Halstead, Malcolm X Community College; Candy A. Henry, Westmoreland County Community College; Joseph Kenyon, Community College of Philadelphia; Mark M. Kessler, Washington State Community College; Paulette Longmore, Essex County College; Anna Maheshwari, Schoolcraft College; Andrew J. Pegman, Cuyahoga Community College, Eastern Campus; Sylvia Y. S. Rippel, Lincoln University; Jeffrey Roessner, Mercyhurst University; and Carrie Tomberlin, Bellevue College.

For editorial assistance that kept us focused, special thanks are extended to the Pearson group, in particular Joe Opiela, Vice President and Publisher for English; Katharine Glynn, Senior Sponsoring Editor; Rebecca Gilpin, Assistant Editor; and Savoula Amanatidis, Project Manager; as well as Electronic Publishing Services Inc.

Heartfelt appreciation is also extended to the members of my family: Martha, Mark, Caleb, Jessica, Peyton, Sarah, and Logan. Their love and patience made this project possible.

JAMES D. LESTER, JR.

james.lester@cmcss.net

1   Writing from Research

Chapter 1 Clear Targets

Communication begins when we make an initial choice to speak or to record our ideas in writing. Regardless of the writer's experience, writing is a demanding process that requires commitment. This chapter charts a direction for your research project:

- Understanding why research is an important method of discovery
- Learning the conventions of academic writing
- Overcoming the pitfalls of plagiarism with proper documentation
- Understanding the terminology of a research assignment
- Establishing a schedule for your research project

The written word—whether it is a history paper, a field report, or a research project—creates a public record of our knowledge, our opinions, and our skill with language; hence, we must strive to make our writing accurate, forceful, and honest.

Discovering a well-focused topic, and more importantly a reason for writing about it, begins the process. Choosing a format, exploring sources through critical reading, and then completing the writing task with grace and style are daunting tasks.

Despite this, writing is an outlet for the inquisitive and creative nature in each of us. Our writing is affected by the richness of our language, by our background and experiences, by our targeted audience, and by the form of expression that we choose. With perceptive enthusiasm for relating detailed concepts and honest insights, we discover the power of our own words. The satisfaction of writing well and relating our understanding to others provides intellectual stimulation and insight into our own beliefs and values.

As a college student, you will find that your writing assignments will extend past personal thoughts and ideas to explore more complex topics. Writing will make you confident in your ability to find information and present it effectively in all kinds of ways and for all sorts of projects, such as:

- A theme in a first-year composition course on the dangers of social networking sites.
- A paper in history on Herbert Hoover's ineffectual policies for coping with the Great Depression of the early 1930s.
- A report for a physical fitness class on the benefits of ballroom dancing as exercise.
- A sociological field report on free and reduced-cost lunches for school-aged children.
- A brief biographical study of a famous person, such as American agrarian labor leader César Chávez.

All of these papers require some type of "researched writing." Papers similar to these will be assigned during your first two years of college and increase in frequency in upper-division courses. This book eases the pressure—it shows you how to research "online discussion groups" or "the Great Depression," and it demonstrates the correct methods for documenting the sources.

We conduct informal research all the time. We examine various models and their options before buying a car, and we check out another person informally before proposing or accepting a first date. We sometimes search online for job listings to find a summer job, or we roam the mall to find a new tennis racket, the right pair of sports shoes, or the latest DVD. Research, then, is not foreign to us. It has become commonplace to use a search engine to explore the Internet for information on any subject—from personal concerns, such as the likely side effects of a prescribed drug, to complex issues, like robotics or acupuncture.

In the classroom, we begin thinking about a serious and systematic activity, one that involves the library, the Internet, or field research. A research paper, like a personal essay, requires you to choose a topic you care about and are willing to invest many hours in thinking about. However, unlike a personal essay, a research paper requires you to develop your ideas by gathering an array of information, reading sources critically, and collecting notes. As you pull your project together, you will continue to express personal ideas, but now they are supported by and based on the collective evidence and opinions of experts on the topic.

Each classroom and each instructor will make different demands on your talents, yet all stipulate *researched writing*. Your research project will advance your theme and provide convincing proof for your inquiry.

- *Researched writing* grows from investigation.
- *Researched writing* establishes a clear purpose.
- *Researched writing* develops analysis for a variety of topics.

Writing Research Papers introduces research as an engaging, sometimes exciting pursuit on several fronts—your personal knowledge, ideas gleaned from printed and electronic sources, and research in the field.

1a   Why Do Research?

Instructors ask you to write a research paper for several reasons:

Research Teaches Methods of Discovery. Explanation on a topic prompts you to discover what you know on a topic and what others can teach you. Beyond reading, it often expects you to venture into the field for interviews, observation, and experimentation. The process tests your curiosity as you probe a complex subject. You may not arrive at any final answers or solutions, but you will come to understand the different views on a subject. In your final paper, you will synthesize your ideas and discoveries with the knowledge and opinions of others.

Research Teaches Investigative Skills. A research project requires you to investigate a subject, gain a grasp of its essentials, and disclose your findings. Your success will depend on your negotiating the various sources of information, from reference books in the library to computer databases and from special archival collections to the most recent articles in printed periodicals. The Internet, with its vast quantity of information, will challenge you to find reliable sources. If you conduct research by observation, interviews, surveys, and laboratory experiments, you will discover additional methods of investigation.

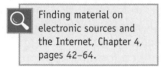
Finding material on electronic sources and the Internet, Chapter 4, pages 42–64.

Research Develops Inquiry-Based Techniques. With the guidance of your instructor, you are making inquiry to advance your own knowledge as well as increase the data available for future research by others.

Research Builds Career Skills. Many career fields rely on investigation and inquiry for fact-finding purposes. Researchers work across a broad spectrum of disciplines, including the physical and life sciences of biology, chemistry, and physics. Engineering sciences in the aerospace, computer science, and automotive production fields must rely on past research while forging new manufacturing trends. Social scientists in the fields of economics, sociology, psychology, and political science foster advancements in society through investigative studies. Research professionals are on the cutting edge of scientific and technological developments, and their work leads to new medicines, consumer products, industrial processes, and numerous other developments.

Research Teaches Critical Thinking. As you wade through the evidence on your subject, you will learn to discriminate between useful information and unfounded or ill-conceived comments. Some sources, such as the Internet, will provide timely, reliable material but may also entice you with worthless and undocumented opinions.

Research Teaches Logic. Like a judge in the courtroom, you must make perceptive judgments about the issues surrounding a specific topic. Your decisions, in effect, will be based on the wisdom gained from research of the subject. Your paper and your readers will rely on your logical response to your reading, observation, interviews, and testing.

Research Teaches the Basic Ingredients of Argument. In most cases, a research paper requires you to make a claim and support it with reasons and evidence. For example, if you argue that "urban sprawl has invited

> Making a claim and establishing a thesis, 2f, pages 24–27.

wild animals into our backyards," you will learn to anticipate challenges to your theory and to defend your assertion with evidence.

1b Learning the Conventions of Academic Writing

Researched writing in each discipline follows certain conventions—that is, special forms are required for citing sources and designing pages. These rules make uniform the numerous articles written internationally by millions of scholars. The society of language and literature scholars, the Modern Language Association, has a set of guidelines generally known as MLA style. Similarly, the American Psychological Association has its own APA style. Other groups of scholars prefer a footnote system, while still others use a numbering system. These variations are not meant to confuse; they have evolved within disciplines as the preferred style.

What is important for you, right now, is to determine which documentation style to use. Many composition instructors will ask you to

> MLA Style, pages 250–258
> APA Style, pages 289–317
> Chicago (CMS) Style, pages 318–336
> CSE Style, pages 337–356

use MLA style, as explained in Chapters 11–14, but they are just as likely to ask for APA style (Chapter 15) if your topic concerns one of the social sciences. In a like manner, your art history instructor might expect the footnote style but could just as easily request the

APA style. Ask your instructor early which style to use and organize accordingly.

Regardless of the research style that you employ, your writing should advance substantive issues and inquiry. Keep in mind three key investigative conventions:

Analysis	Classify the major issues of your study and provide detailed analysis of each in defense of your thesis.
Evidence	Provide well-reasoned propositions and statements that are supported by facts, details, and evidence with proper documentation.
Discussion	Relate the implications of your findings and the merits of the study, whether an author's poetic techniques, a historical movement, or a social issue.

1c   Understanding and Avoiding Plagiarism

The most important convention of academic writing is the principle of giving proper credit to the work of others. **Plagiarism is defined as the act of claiming the words or ideas of another person as your own.** Plagiarism is a serious violation of the ethical standards of academic writing, and most colleges and universities have strict penalties, including academic probation or expulsion, for students who are guilty of plagiarism. Most schools publish an official code of student conduct (sometimes called an academic integrity policy), and you should be familiar with this document as it applies to your research and writing.

Some students will knowingly copy whole passages from outside sources into their work without documentation. Others will buy research papers from online sources or friends. These intentional acts of academic dishonesty are the most blatant forms of plagiarism. *Unintentional plagiarism,* however, is still a violation of academic integrity.

Understanding and Avoiding Plagiarism, Chapter 7, pages 95–108.

Unacknowledged use of another person's sentences, phrases, or terminology is plagiarism, so provide a citation and use quotation marks to show exactly where you are drawing on others' work. Similarly, unacknowledged use of another person's ideas, research, or approach is also plagiarism, so write careful paraphrases.

CHECKLIST

Avoiding Unintentional Plagiarism

The following guidelines will help you avoid unintentional plagiarism.

- **Citation.** Let readers know when you borrow from a source by introducing a quotation or paraphrase with the name of its author.

- **Quotation marks.** Enclose within quotation marks all quoted words, phrases, and sentences.

- **Paraphrase.** Provide a citation to indicate the source of a paraphrase just as you do for quotations.

- **Parenthetical citations and notes.** Use one of the academic documentation styles (MLA, APA, CMS, or CSE) to provide specific in-text citations for each source according to the conventions of the discipline in which you are writing.

- **Works cited or references pages.** Provide a complete bibliography entry at the end of your paper for every source you use, conforming to the standards of the documentation style you are using.

1d Understanding a Research Assignment

Beyond selecting an effective subject, you will need a reason for writing the paper. Literature instructors might expect you to make judgments about the structure and poetic techniques of Walt Whitman. Education instructors might ask you to examine the merits of a balanced curriculum for secondary students. History instructors might want you to explore an event—perhaps the tactics and strategies of the abolitionist movement leading up to the American Civil War.

Understanding the Terminology

Assignments in literature, history, and the fine arts will often require you to *evaluate, interpret,* and *perform causal analysis.* Assignments in education, psychology, political science, and other social science disciplines will usually require *analysis, definition, comparison,* or a search for *precedents* leading to a *proposal.* In the sciences, your experiments and testing will usually require a discussion of the *implications* of your findings. The next few pages explain these assignments.

Evaluation

To evaluate, you first need to establish clear criteria of judgment and then explain how the subject meets these criteria. For example, student evaluations of faculty members are based on a set of expressed criteria—an interest in student progress, a thorough knowledge of the subject, and so forth. Similarly, you may be asked to judge the merits of a poem, an art exhibit, or the newest trends in touchscreen cameras. Your first step should be to create your criteria. What makes a good movie? How important is a poem's form and structure? Is space a special factor in architecture? You cannot expect the sources to provide the final answers; you need to experience the work and make your final judgments on it.

Let's see how evaluation develops with one student, Sarah Bemis, who was asked to examine diabetes. At first, Sarah worked to define the disease and its basic attack on the human system. However, as she read the literature she shifted her focus from a basic definition to evaluate and examine the methods for controlling diabetes. Her paper, "Diabetes Management: A Delicate Balance," appears on pages 346–356.

In many ways, every research paper is an evaluation.

Interpretation

To interpret, you must usually answer, "What does it mean?" You may be asked to explain the symbolism in a piece of literature, examine a point of law, or make sense of test results. Questions often point toward interpretation:

What does this passage mean?
What are the implications of these results?
What does this data tell us?
Can you explain your reading of the problem to others?

For example, your instructor might ask you to interpret the 1954 Supreme Court ruling in *Brown v. Board of Education*; interpret results on pond water testing at site A, in a secluded country setting, and site B, near a petrochemical plant; or interpret a scene from Henrik Ibsen's *An Enemy of the People.*

In a paper on Internet dating, one student found herself asking two interpretive questions: What are the social implications of computer dating? and What are the psychological implications?

Definition

Sometimes you will need to provide an extended definition to show that your subject fits into a selected and well-defined category. Note these examples:

1. A low-fat diet reduces the risk of coronary disease.

   You will need to define "low-fat" by describing foods that make up a low-fat diet and naming the benefits from this type of diet.

2. Title IX has brought positive changes to college athletic programs.

   You will need to define the law in detail and specify the changes.

3. The root cause of breakups in relationships is selfishness.

   This topic will require a definition of selfishness and examples of how it weakens relationships.

A good definition usually includes three elements: the subject (low-fat diet); the class to which the subject belongs (diets in general); and the differences between others in this class (low-carb or Atkins). Definition will almost always become a part of your work when some of the terminology is subjective. If you argue, for example, that medical experiments on animals are cruel and inhumane, you may need to define what you mean by *cruel* and explain why *humane* standards should be applied to animals that are not human. Thus, definition might serve as your major thesis.

Definition is also necessary with technical and scientific terminology, as shown by Sarah Bemis in her paper on diabetes. The paper needed a careful, detailed definition of the medical disorder in addition to the methods for managing it. By her inquiry, she reached her conclusion that medication in harmony with diet and exercise were necessary for victims of the disease. Her research paper appears on pages 346–356.

Proposal

A proposal says to the reader, "We should do something." It often has practical applications, as shown by these examples:

- To maintain academic integrity, college administrators must enact stringent policies and punishments for cheating and plagiarism.
- A chipping mill should not be allowed in our town because its insatiable demand for timber will strip our local forests and ruin the environment.

A proposal calls for action—a change in policy, a change in the law, and, sometimes, an alteration of accepted procedures. Again, the writer must advance the thesis and support it with reasons and evidence.

In addition, a proposal demands special considerations. First, writers should convince readers that a problem exists and is serious enough to merit action. In the previous example about chipping mills, the writer will need to establish that, indeed, chipping mills have been proposed and perhaps even approved for the area. Then the writer will need to argue that they endanger the environment: They grind vast amounts of timber of any size and shave it into chips that are reprocessed in various ways. As a result, lumberjacks cut even the immature trees, stripping forests into barren wastelands. The writer presumes that clear-cutting damages the land.

Second, the writer must explain the consequences to convince the reader that the proposal has validity. The paper must defend the principle that clear-cutting damages the land, and it should show, if possible, how chipping mills in other parts of the country have damaged the environment.

Third, the writer will need to address any opposing positions, competing proposals, and alternative solutions. For example, chipping mills produce chip board for decking the floors of houses, thus saving trees that might be required for making expensive plywood boards. Without chipping mills, we might run short on paper and homebuilding products. The writer will need to note opposing views and consider them in the paper.

Causal Argument

Unlike proposals, which predict consequences, causal arguments show that a condition exists because of specific circumstances—that is, something has caused or created this situation, and we need to know why. For example, a student's investigation uncovered reasons why schools in one state benefit greatly from a lottery but do not in another.

Let's look at another student who asked the question, "Why do numerous students, like me, who otherwise score well on the ACT test, score poorly in the math section of the test and, consequently, enroll in developmental courses that offer no college credit?" This question merited his investigation, so he gathered evidence from his personal experience as well as data drawn from interviews, surveys, critical reading, and accumulated test results. Ultimately, he explored and wrote on a combination of related issues—students' poor study skills, bias in the testing program, and inadequate instruction in grade school and high school. He discovered something about himself and many details about the testing program.

Comparison, Including Analogy

An argument often compares and likens a subject to something else. You might be asked to compare a pair of poems or to compare stock markets—NASDAQ with the New York Stock Exchange. Comparison is seldom the focus of an entire paper, but it can be useful in a paragraph about the banking policy of Andrew Jackson and that of his congressional opponents.

An analogy is a figurative comparison that allows the writer to draw several parallels of similarity. For example, the human circulatory system is like a transportation system with a hub, a highway system, and a fleet of trucks to carry the cargo.

Precedence

Precedence refers to conventions or customs, usually well established. In judicial decisions, it is a standard set by previous cases, a *legal precedent.* Therefore, a thesis statement built on precedence requires a past event that establishes a rule of law or a point of procedure. As an example, let's return to the argument against the chipping mill. If the researcher can prove that another mill in another part of the country ruined the environment, then the researcher has a precedent for how damaging such an operation can be.

Implications

If you conduct any kind of test or observation, you will probably make field notes in a research journal and tabulate your results at regular intervals. At some point, however, you will be expected to explain your findings, arrive at conclusions, and discuss the implications of your scientific inquiry—what did you discover, and what does it mean?

For example, one student explored the world of drug testing before companies place the products on the market. His discussions had chilling implications for consumers. Another student examined the role of mice as carriers of Lyme disease. This work required reading as well as field research and testing to arrive at final judgments. In literature, a student examined the recurring images of birds in the poetry of Thomas Hardy to discuss the implications of the birds in terms of his basic themes.

1e   Establishing a Research Schedule

Setting a schedule at the beginning of a research project helps you stay on track and reminds you to follow the basic steps in the process. This book is organized to help you follow along with each step in the process. Write dates in the spaces on pages 9–10 next to each step and keep yourself on schedule.

____ **Finding and narrowing a topic.** Your topic must have a built-in question or argument so you can interpret an issue and cite the opinions found in your course materials.

____ **Drafting a thesis and research proposal.** Even if you are not required to create a formal research proposal, you need to draft some kind of plan to help direct and organize your research before you start reading in depth. See sections 2f and 2g and Chapter 3.

_____ **Reading and creating a working bibliography.** Preliminary reading establishes the basis for your research, helping you discover the quantity and quality of available sources. If you can't find much, your topic is too narrow. If you find too many sources, your topic is too broad and needs narrowing. Chapters 4 and 5 explain the processes for finding reliable sources online and in the library.

_____ **Creating notes.** Begin entering notes in a digital or printed research journal. Some notes will be summaries, others will be carefully selected quotations from the sources, and some will be paraphrases written in your own voice. Chapter 9 details the techniques for effective notetaking.

_____ **Organizing and outlining.** You may be required to create a formal outline; formal outlines and additional ideas for organizing your ideas are presented in sections 9h and 9i.

_____ **Drafting the paper.** During your writing, let your instructor scan the draft to give you feedback and guidance. He or she might see further complications for your exploration and also steer you clear of any simplistic conclusions. Drafting is also a stage for peer review, in which a classmate or two looks at your work. Section 13a, pages 219–221, gives more details on peer review. Chapters 10–12 explain matters of drafting the paper.

_____ **Formatting the paper.** Proper document design places your paper within the required format for your discipline, such as the number system for a scientific project or the APA style for an education paper. Chapters 14–17 provide the guidelines for the various disciplines.

_____ **Writing a list of your references.** You will need to list in the proper format the various sources used in your study. Chapters 14–17 provide documentation guidelines.

_____ **Revising and proofreading.** At the end of the project, you should be conscientious about examining the manuscript and making all necessary corrections. With the aid of computers, you can check spelling and some aspects of style. Chapter 13 gives tips on revision and editing. The Glossasry is a list of terms that explains aspects of form and style.

_____ **Submitting the manuscript.** Like all writers, you will need at some point to "publish" the paper and release it to the audience, which might be your instructor, your classmates, or perhaps a larger group. Plan well in advance to meet this final deadline. You may present the paper in a variety of ways—on paper, through e-mail to your instructor, on a USB flash drive, in a drop box, or on your own website.

Chapter 2 Clear Targets

M ost instructors allow students to find their own topics for major writing assignments. Therefore, your task is to choose a topic that will hold your interest throughout the entire research process. At the same time, your chosen topic will need a scholarly perspective. This chapter charts a direction for your research project:

- Relating personal ideas to a scholarly problem
- Talking with others to refine the topic
- Refining your topic through online sources
- Utilizing databases and electronic resources to perfect your topic
- Developing a thesis statement, enthymeme, or hypothesis
- Drafting a research proposal

As you make the connection between your interests and the inherent issues of the subject, keep in mind that a scholarly topic requires inquiry as well as problem solving. To clarify what we mean, let's take a look at how two students launched their projects.

- Valerie Nesbitt-Hall saw a cartoon about a young woman saying to a man, "Sorry—I only have relationships over the Internet. I'm cyber-sexual." Although laughing, Valerie knew she had discovered her topic—online romance. Upon investigation, she found her scholarly angle: Matching services and chat rooms are like the arranged marriages from years gone by.
- Norman Berkowitz, while watching a news update on the continuing struggles of service members in the Iraq War, noticed dry and barren land, yet history had taught him that this land between the Tigris and the Euphrates rivers was formerly a land of fruit and honey, perhaps even the Garden of Eden. What happened to it? His interest focused, thereafter, on the world's water supply, and his scholarly focus shifted to the ethics of distribution of water.

As these examples show, an informed choice of subject is crucial for fulfilling the research assignment. You might be tempted to write from a personal interest, such as "Fishing at Lake Cumberland"; however, the content and the context of the research task should drive you toward a serious, scholarly perspective: "The Effects of Toxic Chemicals on the Fish of Lake Cumberland." This topic would probably send you into the field for hands-on investigation (see Chapter 6 for more on field research).

In another example, you might be intrigued by the topic "Computer Games," but the research assignment requires an evaluation of issues, not a description. It also requires detailed definition. A better topic might be "Learned Dexterity with Video and Computer Games," which requires the definition of learned dexterity and how some video games promote increased hand and eye coordination. Even in a first-year composition class, your instructor may expect discipline-specific topics, such as:

Education	Differentiated Instruction: Options for Classroom Participation
Political Science	Conservative Republicans and the Religious Right
Literature	Kate Chopin's *The Awakening* and the Women's Movement
Health	The Effects of Smoking during Pregnancy
Sociology	Parents Who Lie to Their Children

A scholarly topic requires inquiry, like those above, and it sometimes requires problem solving. For example, Sarah Bemis has a problem—she has diabetes—and she went in search of ways to manage it. Her solution—a balance of medication, monitoring, diet, and exercise—gave her the heart and soul of a good research paper. (See pages 346–356 for "Diabetes Management: A Delicate Balance.")

CHECKLIST

Narrowing a General Subject into a Scholarly Topic

Unlike a general subject, a scholarly topic should:

- Examine one narrowed issue, not a broad subject.
- Address knowledgeable readers and carry them to another plateau of knowledge.
- Have a serious purpose—one that demands analysis of the issues, argues from a position, and explains complex details.
- Meet the expectations of the instructor and conform to the course requirements.

Thus, your inquiry into the issues or your effort to solve a problem will empower the research and the paper you produce. When your topic addresses such issues, you have a reason to:

- Examine with intellectual curiosity the evidence found.
- Share your investigation of the issues with readers, bringing them special perspectives and enlightening details.
- Present a meaningful discussion of the implications of your study rather than merely presenting a summary of ideas.

2a Relating Your Personal Ideas to a Scholarly Problem

Try to make a connection between your interests and the inherent issues of the subject. For instance, a student whose mother became seriously addicted to the Internet developed a paper from the personal experiences of her dysfunctional family. She worked within the discipline of sociology and consulted journals of that field. Another student, who worked at a volume discount store, developed a research project on bargain shopping and its effect on small-town shop owners. She worked within the discipline of marketing and business management, reading appropriate literature in those areas. Begin with two activities:

1. Relate your experiences to scholarly problems and academic disciplines.
2. Speculate about the subject by listing issues, asking questions, engaging in free writing, and using other idea-generating techniques.

Connecting Personal Experience to Scholarly Topics

You can't write a personal essay and call it a research paper, yet you can choose topics close to your life. Use one of the techniques described in the following list:

1. **Combine personal interests with an aspect of academic studies:**

   Personal interest: Skiing
   Academic subject: Sports medicine
   Possible topics: "Protecting the Knees"
                         "Therapy for Strained Muscles"
                         "Skin Treatments"

2. **Consider social issues that affect you and your family:**

   Personal interest: The education of my child
   Social issue: The behavior of my child in school
   Possible topics: "Children Who Are Hyperactive"
                         "Should Schoolchildren Take Medicine
                         to Calm Their Hyperactivity?"

3. **Consider scientific subjects, if appropriate:**

Personal interest:	The ponds and well water on the family farm
Scientific subject:	Chemical toxins in the water
Possible topic:	"The Poisoning of Underground Water Tables"

4. **Let your cultural background prompt you toward detailed research into your heritage, your culture, or the mythology of your ethnic background:**

Ethnic background:	Native American
Personal interest:	History of the Apache tribes
Possible topic:	"The Indian Wars from the Native American's Point of View"
Ethnic background:	Hispanic
Personal interest:	Struggles of the Mexican child in an American classroom
Possible topic:	"Bicultural Experiences of Hispanic Students: The Failures and Triumphs"

HINT: Learn the special language of the academic discipline and use it. Every field of study, whether sociology, geology, or literature, has words to describe its analytical approach to topics, such as the *demographics* of a target audience (marketing), the *function* of loops and arrays (computer science), the *symbolism* of Maya Angelou's poetry (literature), and *observation* of human subjects (psychology). Part of your task is learning the terminology and using it appropriately.

Speculating about Your Subject to Discover Ideas and to Focus on the Issues

At some point you may need to sit back, relax, and use your imagination to contemplate the issues and problems worthy of investigation. Ideas can be generated in the following ways:

Free Writing

To free write, merely focus on a topic and write whatever comes to mind. Do not worry about grammar, style, or penmanship, but keep writing nonstop for a page or so to develop valuable phrases, comparisons, personal anecdotes, and specific thoughts that help focus issues of concern. Below, Jamie Johnston comments on violence and, perhaps, finds his topic.

> The savagery of the recent hazing incident at Glenbrook North
> High School demonstrates that humans, both men and women, love a
> good fight. People want power over others, even in infancy. Just look
> at how siblings fight. And we fight vicariously, too, watching boxing
> and wrestling, cheering at fights during a hockey game, and on and on.
> So personally, I think human beings have always been blood thirsty
> and power hungry. The French philosopher Rousseau might claim a
> "noble savage" once existed, but personally I think we've always
> hated others.

This free writing set the path for this writer's investigation into the
role of war in human history.

Listing Keywords

Keep a list of words, the fundamental terms that you see in the literature. These can help focus the direction of your research. Jamie Johnston
built this list of terms as he began to explore research about war:

prehistoric wars	early weapons	noble savages
remains of early victims	early massacres	slaves
sacrificial victims	human nature	power
limited resources	religious sacrifices	honor

These keywords can help in writing the rough outline, as explained in
the following section.

Arranging Keywords into a Rough Outline

Writing a preliminary outline early in the project might help you see
if the topic has substance so you can sustain it for the length required. At
this point, the researcher needs to recognize the hierarchy of major and
minor issues.

> Prehistoric wars
>> Evidence of early brutality
>>> Mutilated skeletons
>> Evidence of early weapons
>>> Clubs, bows, slings, maces, etc.
>> Walled fortresses for defense

> Speculations on reasons for war
>
>> Resources
>>
>> Slaves
>>
>> Revenge
>>
>> Religion
>
>> Human nature and war
>>
>>> Quest for power
>>>
>>> Biological urge to conquer

This initial ranking of ideas would grow in length and mature in depth during the research process.

Clustering

Another method for discovering the hierarchy of your primary topics and subtopics is to cluster ideas around a central subject. The cluster of related topics can generate a multitude of interconnected ideas. Here's an example by Jamie Johnston:

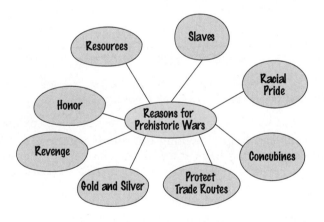

Narrowing by Comparison

Comparison limits a discussion to specific differences. Any two works, any two persons, any two groups may serve as the basis for a comparative study. Historians compare Civil War commanders Robert E. Lee and Ulysses S. Grant. Political scientists compare conservatives and liberals. Literary scholars compare the merits of free verse and those of formal verse. Jamie Johnston discovered a comparative study in his work, as expressed in this way:

> Ultimately, the key questions about the cause of war, whether
> ancient or current, center on one's choice between biology and

culture. One the one side, society as a whole wants to preserve its culture, in peace if possible. Yet the biological history of men and women suggests that we love a good fight.

That comparative choice became the capstone of Johnston's conclusion.

Asking Questions

Research is a process of seeking answers to questions. Hence, the most effective researchers are those who learn to ask questions and seek answers. Raising questions about the subject can provide clear boundaries for the paper. Stretch your imagination with questions to develop a clear theme.

1. **General questions examine terminology, issues, causes, and so on. For example, having read Henry Thoreau's essay "Civil Disobedience," one writer asked:**

   What is civil disobedience?
   Is dissent legal? Is it moral? Is it patriotic?
   Is dissent a liberal activity? Conservative?
   Should the government encourage or stifle dissent?
   Is passive resistance effective?
   Answering the questions can lead the writer to a central issue or argument, such as "Civil Disobedience: Shaping Our Nation by Confronting Unjust Laws."

2. **Rhetorical questions use the modes of writing as a basis. One student framed these questions:**

Comparison:	How does a state lottery compare with horse racing?
Definition:	What is a lottery in legal terms? in religious terms?
Cause/Effect:	What are the consequences of a state lottery on funding for education, highways, prisons, and social programs?
Process:	How are winnings distributed?
Classification:	What types of lotteries exist, and which are available in this state?
Evaluation:	What is the value of a lottery to the average citizen? What are the disadvantages?

3. **Academic disciplines across the curriculum provide questions, as framed by one student on the topic of sports gambling.**

Economics:	Does sports gambling benefit a college's athletic budget? Does it benefit the national economy?
Psychology:	What is the effect of gambling on the mental attitude of the college athlete who knows huge sums hang in the balance on his or her performance?

History: Does gambling on sporting events have an identifiable tradition?

Sociology: What compulsion in human nature prompts people to gamble on the prowess of an athlete or team?

4. **Journalism questions explore the basic elements of a subject: Who? What? Where? When? Why? and How? For example:**

Who? Athletes
What? Illegal drugs
When? During off-season training and also on game day
Where? Training rooms and elsewhere
Why? To enhance performance
How? By pills and injections

The journalist's questions direct you toward the issues, such as "win at all costs" or "damaging the body for immediate gratification."

5. **Kenneth Burke's *pentad* questions five aspects of a topic: act, agent, scene, agency, purpose.**

What happened (the act)?	Crucifixion scene in *The Old Man and the Sea*.
Who did it (agent)?	Santiago, the old fisherman.
Where and when (scene)?	At the novel's end.
How did it occur (the agency)?	Santiago carries the mast of his boat up the hill.
What is a possible motive for this event (purpose)?	Hemingway wanted to make a martyr of the old man.

This researcher can now search the novel with a purpose—to find other Christian images, rank and classify them, and determine if, indeed, the study has merit.

2b Talking with Others to Refine the Topic

Personal Interviews and Discussions

Like some researchers, you may need to consult formally with an expert on the topic or explore a subject informally while having coffee or a soda with a colleague, relative, or work associate. Ask people in your community for ideas and for their reactions to your general subject.

Nesbitt-Hall's interview can be found on pages 85–88.
For example, Valerie Nesbitt-Hall knew about a couple who married after having met initially in a chat room on the Internet. She requested an interview and got it.

Casual conversations that contribute to your understanding of the subject need not be documented. However, the conscientious writer will credit a formal interview if the person approves. The interviewed subjects on pages 85–86 preferred anonymity.

Online Discussion Groups

What are other people saying about your subject? You might share ideas and messages with other scholars interested in your subject. Somebody may answer a question or point to an interesting aspect that has not occurred to you. With discussion groups, you have a choice:

- Classroom e-mail groups that participate in online discussions of various issues.
- Online courses that feature a discussion room.
- Discussion groups on the Internet.
- Real-time chatting with participants online—even with audio and video, in some cases.

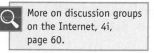
More on discussion groups on the Internet, 4i, page 60.

Many instructors may set up informal classroom discussion lists and expect you to participate online with fellow students. In other cases, the instructor might suggest that you investigate a specific site, such as Voice of the Shuttle, a website for humanities research. You can find many discussion groups, but the manner in which you use them is vital to your academic success. Rather than chatting, solicit ideas and get responses to your questions about your research topic.

CHECKLIST

Exploring Ideas with Others

- Consult with your instructor.
- Discuss your topic with three or four classmates.
- Listen to the concerns of others.
- Conduct a discussion or an interview (see pages 85–88).
- Join a computer discussion group.
- Take careful notes.
- Adjust your research accordingly.

2c   Using Online Searches to Refine Your Topic

The Internet provides a quick and easy way to find a topic and refine it to academic standards. Chapter 4 discusses these matters in greater detail. For now, use the subject directories and keyword searches.

Internet searches, 4c, pages 48–53.

Using an Online Subject Directory

Many search engines have a subject directory that organizes sources by topic. For example, **Yahoo! Directory** organizes online sources in broad categories like arts and humanities, education, social sciences, and so forth. If you started with a topic such as "alternative medicine," you would quickly realize that your topic was too broad: **Yahoo! Directory** lists more than forty subtopics for "alternative medicine." The directory might help to identify a narrower topic, such as aromatherapy or meditation, that you might be able to research more effectively.

Because you want to present an academic study about your topic, you might also conduct an online search using **Google Scholar.** This Web program can direct your search across many disciplines through articles, theses, books, and abstracts that are presented by academic publishers, professional societies, online repositories, universities, and other websites. Google Scholar helps you find relevant work across the world of scholarly research.

However, the Internet has made it difficult to apply traditional evaluations to an electronic article: Is it accurate, authoritative, objective, current, timely, and thorough in coverage? Some Internet sites are advocates to special interests, some sites market products or sprinkle the site with banners to commercial sites and sales items, some sites are personal home pages, and then many sites offer objective news and scholarly information. The answers:

1. Go to the reliable databases available through your library, such as InfoTrac, ERIC, ProQuest, and EBSCOhost. These are monitored sites that give information filtered by editorial boards and peer review. You can reach them from remote locations at home or the dorm by connecting electronically to your library.
2. Look for articles on the Internet that first appeared in a printed version. These will have been, in most cases, examined by an editorial board.
3. Look for a reputable sponsor, especially a university, museum, or professional organization.
4. Consult Chapter 4, which discusses the pros and cons of Internet searching.

Using an Internet Keyword Search

Using Google or a similar search engine allows you to search for keywords related to your topic. A keyword search for "American history manuscripts," for example, leads to the Library of Congress page shown in Figure 2.1. This page allows users to search the Library's manuscript collection by keyword, name and subject, date, or topic. Topic headings include military history, diplomacy and foreign policy, and women's history, all of which would help find sources leading to a more focused topic.

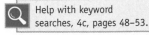
Help with keyword searches, 4c, pages 48–53.

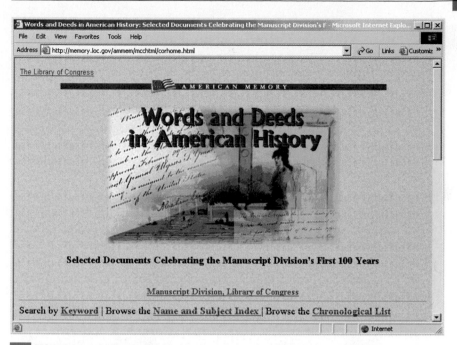

FIGURE 2.1   A Library of Congress site "Words and Deeds in American History," found by using a keyword search for American history manuscripts.

Boolean expressions let you focus your keyword search by stipulating which words and phrases *can* appear in the results, which words *must* appear, or which topics *must not* appear in the search results. Most online databases and Web search sites include the use of Boolean search terms, specifically *AND, OR,* and *NOT,* as well as the plus (+) or minus (−) signs. Placed between keywords, Boolean expressions instruct the search engine to display only those websites in which your research terms appear in certain combinations, and to ignore others.

Utilizing Boolean expressions in a keyword search will help to narrow your general subject. For example, one student entered "Internet + addiction," and the computer brought up thousands of sources. By tightening the request to the phrase "Internet addiction" enclosed within quotation marks, she cut the list considerably and discovered other keywords: cyber-wellness, weboholics, and netaddiction. She realized she had a workable topic. For more assistance with keyword searches using Boolean expressions, see pages 48–53.

2d   Using the Library's Electronic Databases to Find and Narrow a Topic

College libraries have academic databases not found on general search engines, such as InfoTrac, ERIC, and ProQuest. These database files are reliable because they refer you to thousands of articles that

Evaluating Online Sources, pages 45–46

have been peer reviewed by experts or filtered through editorial processes. For now, examine various titles as you search for your own topic. If you see one of interest, click on it for more information. Follow these steps:

1. **Select a database.** Some databases, such as InfoTrac and ProQuest, are general; use them to find a subject. Other databases focus on one discipline; for example, ERIC indexes search only specific educational sources. These databases will move you quickly to a list of articles on your topic.

2. **List keywords or a phrase to describe your topic, enclosed within quotation marks.** Avoid using just one general word. For example, the word *forestry* on the Electronic Library database produced over 5,000 possible sites. The two-word phrase "forest conservation" produced a more manageable number of sites. Here is one of the entries: "A New Year for Forest Policy." Jami Westerhold. *American Forests.* 118.4 (Winter 2013) p14.

3. **Examine the various entries for possible topics.** Look for relevant articles, browse the descriptions, read the abstracts, and—when you find something valuable—print the full text, if it is available.

2e Using the Library's Electronic Book Catalog to Find a Topic

Instructors expect you to cite information from a few books, and the library's book index will suggest topics and confirm that your subject has been treated with in-depth studies in book form, not just on the Internet or in magazines. Called by different names at each library (e.g., Acorn, Felix, Access), the electronic index lists all books housed in the library, as well as other helpful items. It does not index articles in magazines and journals, but it will tell you which periodicals are housed in the library and whether they are in printed form or on microforms. Like the electronic databases described in 2d, the index will help you find a workable topic by guiding you quickly from general subjects to subtopics and, finally, to specific books.

Section 5c, pages 67–68, describes the process in great detail with examples. For now, enter your subject, such as *food, nutrition, allergies,* to see what titles are available in the library. The titles, such as *Children and Food Allergies, Environmental Poisons in Our Food,* or *Living with Something in the Air,* will suggest a possible topic, perhaps "Special Diets to Control Allergic Reactions to Food." If you go into the stacks to find a book, take the time to examine nearby books on the same shelf, for they will likely treat the same subject.

With your working topic in hand, do some exploratory reading in books to enhance your understanding of the topic. Carefully read the **titles** of books and chapter titles, noting any key terms:

The Lessons of the French Revolution
Napoleon's Ambition and the Quest for Domination
"Perspectives: Napoleon's Relations with the Catholic Church"

These titles provide several keywords and possible topics for a research paper: *Napoleon's ambition, Napoleon and the Church, the French Revolution.*

Inspect a book's **table of contents** to find topics of interest. A typical history book might display these headings in the table of contents:

The French Revolution
The Era of Napoleon
Reaction to Napoleon and More Revolutions
The Second Empire of France

If any of these headings look interesting, go to the book's **index** for additional headings, such as this sample:

Napoleon
     becomes Emperor, 174–176
     becomes First Consul, 173
     becomes Life Consul, 174
     and the Catholic Church, 176–178
     character of, 168–176
     and codes of law, 178–179
     defeated by enemies, 192–197
     encounters opposition, 190–191
     extends empire in Europe, 180–189
     seizes power for "One Hundred Days," 198
     sent to Elba, 197
     sent to St. Helena, 199

If you see something that looks interesting, read the designated pages to consider the topic further.

HINT: Topic selection goes beyond choosing a general category (e.g., "single mothers"). It includes finding a research-provoking issue or question, such as "The foster parent program seems to have replaced the orphanage system. Has it been effective?" That is, you need to take a stand, adopt a belief, or begin asking questions.

2f   Developing a Thesis Statement, Enthymeme, or Hypothesis

One central statement will usually control an essay's direction and content, so as early as possible, begin thinking in terms of a controlling idea. Each has a separate mission:

- A **thesis statement** advances a conclusion the writer will defend: *Contrary to what some philosophers have advanced, human beings have always participated in wars.*
- An **enthymeme** uses a *because* clause to make a claim the writer will defend: *There has never been a "noble savage," as such, because even prehistoric human beings fought frequent wars for numerous reasons.*
- A **hypothesis** is a theory that must be tested in the lab, in the literature, and/or by field research to prove its validity: *Human beings are motivated by biological instincts toward the physical overthrow of perceived enemies.*

Let us look at each type in more detail.

Thesis

A thesis statement expands your topic into a scholarly proposal, one that you will try to prove and defend in your paper. It does not state the obvious, such as "Langston Hughes was a great poet from Harlem." That sentence will not provoke an academic discussion because your readers know that any published poet has talent. The writer must narrow and isolate one issue by finding a critical focus, such as this one that a student considered for her essay:

> Langston Hughes used a controversial vernacular language that paved the way for later artists, even today's rap musicians.

This thesis statement advances an idea the writer can develop fully and defend with evidence. The writer has made a connection between the subject, *Langston Hughes,* and the focusing agent, *vernacular language.* Look at two other writers' preliminary thesis statements:

THESIS: Chat rooms and online matching services enable people to meet only after a prearranged engagement by e-mail.

THESIS: Hamlet's character is shaped, in part, by Shakespeare's manipulation of the stage setting for Hamlet's soliloquies.

In the first, the writer will defend online romance as similar to prearranged marriages of the past. In the second, the writer will discuss how various shifts in dramatic setting can affect the message of the primary character.

Depending on the critical approach, one topic might produce several issues from which the writer might pick:

Biological approach: Functional foods may be a promising addition to the diet of those who wish to avoid certain diseases.

Economic approach: Functional foods can become an economic weapon in the battle against rising health care costs.

Historic approach: Other civilizations, including primitive tribes, have known about food's healing properties for centuries. Why did we let modern chemistry blind us to its benefits?

Each of the previous statements will provoke a response from the reader, who will demand a carefully structured defense in the body of the paper.

Your thesis anticipates your conclusion by setting in motion the examination of facts and pointing the reader toward the special idea of your paper. Note in the following examples how three writers developed different thesis statements even though they had the same topic, "Santiago in Hemingway's *The Old Man and the Sea*." (This novel narrates the toils of an old Cuban fisherman named Santiago, who desperately needs the money to be gained by returning with a good catch of fish. On this day he catches a marlin. After a long struggle, Santiago ties the huge marlin to the side of his small boat. However, during the return in the darkness, sharks attack the marlin so that he arrives home with only a skeleton of the fish. He removes his mast and carries it, like a cross, up the hill to his home.)

THESIS: Poverty forced Santiago to venture too far and struggle beyond reason in his attempt to land the marlin.

This writer will examine the economic conditions of Santiago's trade.

THESIS: The giant marlin is a symbol for all of life's obstacles and hurdles, and Santiago is a symbol for all suffering humans.

This writer will examine the religious and social symbolism of the novel.

THESIS: Hemingway's portrayal of Santiago demonstrates the author's deep respect for Cuba and its stoic heroes.

This writer takes a social approach in order to examine the Cuban culture and its influence on Hemingway.

Enthymeme

Your instructor might want the research paper to develop an argument expressed as an enthymeme, which is a claim supported with a *because* clause. Examples:

> ENTHYMEME: Hyperactive children need medication because ADHD
>
> is a medical disorder, not a behavioral problem.

The claim that children need medication is supported by the stated reason that the condition is a medical problem, not one of behavior. This writer will need to address any unstated assumptions—for example, that medication alone will solve the problem.

> ENTHYMEME: Because people are dying all around the globe from
>
> water shortages, the countries with an abundance of
>
> water have an ethical obligation to share it.

The claim that countries with water have an ethical obligation to share is, of course, the point of contention.

Hypothesis

A hypothesis proposes a theory or suggests an explanation for something. Here are the various types of hypotheses.

The Theoretical Hypothesis

> Discrimination against young women in the classroom, known
>
> as "shortchanging," harms the women academically, socially, and
>
> psychologically.

Here the student will produce a theoretical study by citing literature on "shortchanging."

The Conditional Hypothesis

> Diabetes can be controlled by medication, monitoring, diet, and
>
> exercise.

Certain conditions must be met. The control will depend on the patient's ability to perform the four tasks adequately to prove the hypothesis valid.

The Relational Hypothesis

> Class size affects the number of written assignments by writing
>
> instructors.

This type of hypothesis claims that as one variable changes, so does another, or it claims that something is more or less than another. It could be tested by examining and correlating class size and assignments, a type of field research (see pages 92–93).

The Causal Hypothesis

> A child's toy is determined by television commercials.

This causal hypothesis assumes the mutual occurrence of two factors and asserts that one factor is responsible for the other. The student who is a parent could conduct research to prove or disprove the supposition. A review of the literature might also serve the writer.

2g Drafting a Research Proposal

A research proposal is presented in one of two forms: (1) a short paragraph to identify the project for yourself and your instructor, or (2) a formal, multipage report that provides background information, your rationale for conducting the study, a review of the literature, your methods, and the conclusions you hope to prove.

The Short Proposal

A short proposal identifies five essential ingredients of your work:

- The specific topic
- The purpose of the paper (to explain, analyze, or argue)
- The intended audience (general or specialized)
- Your voice as the writer (informer or advocate)
- The preliminary thesis statement or opening hypothesis

For example, here is the proposal of Norman Berkowitz:

> The world is running out of fresh water while we sip our Evian. However, the bottled water craze signals something—we do not trust our fresh tap water. We have an emerging crisis on our hands, and some authorities forecast world wars over water rights. The issue of water touches almost every facet of our lives, from religious rituals and food supply to disease and political stability. We might frame this hypothesis: Water will soon replace oil as the economic resource most treasured by nations of the world. However, that assertion would prove difficult to defend and may not be true at all. Rather, we need to look elsewhere, at human behavior, and at human responsibility for preserving the environment for our children. Accordingly, this paper

---

CHECKLIST

Addressing the Reader

Identify your audience. Have you visualized your audience, its expertise, and its expectations? Your perception of the reader will affect your voice, style, and choice of words.

Identify your discipline. Readers in each discipline will bring differing expectations to your paper with regard to content, language, design, and documentation format.

Meet the needs of your readers. Are you saying something worthwhile? Something new? Do not bore the reader with known facts from an encyclopedia. (This latter danger is the reason many instructors discourage the use of an encyclopedia as a source.)

Engage and even challenge your readers. Find an interesting or different point of view. For example, a report on farm life can become a challenging examination of chemical contamination because of industrial sprawl into rural areas, and an interpretation of a novel can become an examination of the prison system rather than a routine discourse on theme or characterization.

---

will examine (1) the issues with regard to supply and demand, (2) the political power struggles that may emerge, and (3) the ethical implications for those who control the world's scattered supply of fresh water.

This writer has identified the basic nature of his project and can now go in search of evidence that will defend the argument.

The Long Proposal

Some instructors may assign the long proposal, which includes some or all of the following elements:

1. A *cover page* with the title of the project, your name, and the person or agency to whom you are submitting the proposal.

More Academics for the Cost of Less Engaged Children

Caitlin Kelley

Submitted to

Dr. Maxine Girdner

In fulfillment of course requirements for English 4010

2. If required, add an *abstract* that summarizes your project in 50 to 100 words (see page 309 for additional information).

The elimination of elementary school recess periods was investigated to examine the theoretical implications of depriving learners of these important mental and physical stimuli. The goal was to determine the effect of the modern trend to use recess time for longer academic periods. The social and psychological implications were determined by an examination of the literature, including comments from educational leaders. Results are mixed, as the end result of an increased emphasis on standardized testing will not be realized for several years. The social implications affect the mental and physical lives of school-aged children who are learning less about cooperation with their peers and more about remaining stagnant with little activity for lengthy periods of time.

3. Include a *purpose statement* with your *rationale* for the project. In essence, this is your thesis statement or hypothesis, along with your identification of the audience that your work will address and the role you will play as investigator and advocate.

This project was suggested by Dr. Maxine Girdner to fulfill the writing project for English 4010 and also to serve the University Committee on Strategies and Needs in Elementary Education, which has launched a project on Contemporary Student Needs, Grades K–12. This paper, if approved, would become part of the committee's findings and contribute to the final report booklet.

4. A *statement of qualification* that explains your experience and, perhaps, the special qualities you bring to the project. Caitlin Kelley included this comment in her proposal:

I bring firsthand experience to this study. I have completed my methods courses for my degree in elementary education. Moreover, I am nearing the end of my practicum for my student teaching requirement. Entering a classroom of third graders was exciting at first, but then I realized that teaching is truly a lot of work. It is work for me, but also requires a great attention to detail by my students. I was surprised to find that my learners were only allowed thirty minutes of recess three times during the week and a structured physical education class on only two days. This caused me to ponder whether the education that these children are receiving is developing the physical as well as the academic abilities of each learner.

5. A *review of the literature,* which surveys the articles and books that you have examined in your preliminary work (see pages 128–134 for an explanation and another example).

Limited research is being done concerning the role of recess in the development of elementary-aged children. My search of the literature produced several informative articles. According to Poynter, "40 percent of schools in the United States have cut recess or are considering dropping it." The question is why are nearly half of the elementary schools around the country dropping free play and expression from the daily lives of young children? Svensen outlines that the two prevailing reasons for the reduction and elimination of free play are to reduce the risk of accidents and to provide students more time in their day for academics, "mostly reading and math." Contradicting these arguments are parents and doctors who feel that recess provides children with the opportunity to strengthen "social connections and friendship skills" (Fisher). The research of Greg Toppo has revealed that the process of eliminating or limiting recess is the decision of the principal of the elementary school. "The principal of each school respectively decides whether his or her children need that extra time for play, or whether it would be better spent on academics" (Toppo). In the typical classroom, children sit in their seats for up to six hours each day. One source stated, "shortening recess by five minutes daily provides 25 minutes of additional instruction time each week" (Matthews). This lack of a break often proves to be a problem because the students are restless and fidgety (Bossenmeyer). In some schools, however, "with the principal's permission, a teacher can take his or her class outside for 15 minutes. For the kids, it's like a jailbreak" (DeGregory).

6. A *description of your research methods,* which is the design of the *materials* you will need, your *timetable,* and, where applicable, your *budget.* These elements are often a part of a scientific study, so see Chapters 15 and 17 for work in the social, physical, and biological sciences. Here is Kelley's description:

This paper will examine the problems associated with eliminating recess and the effect of an overemphasis on academics in elementary schools. Cutting out play time for young children affects their social skills and their physical skills. Students need to learn to make up their own rules and play their own games. With recess, students can experience uninstructed play in contrast to being constantly directed all day. On the playground, with adults serving only as supervisors, children learn to work through altercations, to make decisions, and also how to make friends. Because of the stagnant environment of school, too many children would rather play inside with electronics than go outside. It is essential to have physical contact with other children in a world of technology where students often play by themselves while staring at the video screen; additionally, children who are glued to their computers interact less with other children, become passive learners, and read less. Recess is a physical activity for most children, which is constructive toward their health and well-being. If children had recess as an outlet to run around and play, the rates of childhood obesity would be cut

CHECKLIST

Explaining Your Purpose in the Research Proposal

Research papers accomplish several tasks:

- They explain and define the topic.
- They analyze the specific issues.
- They persuade the reader with the weight of the evidence.

1. Use *explanation* to review and itemize factual data. Sarah Bemis explains how diabetes can be managed (see pages 346–356), and Clare Grady explains the pressures associated with the space race in the 1960s (see pages 331–336).
2. Use *analysis* to classify various parts of the subject and to investigate each one in depth. Ashley Irwin examines the emotions in poetry generated by tragic life events (pages 228–236), and Caitlin Kelley analyzes the importance of recess for elementary students (pages 310–317).
3. Use *persuasion* to question the general attitudes about a problem and then affirm new theories, advance a solution, recommend a course of action, or—at least—invite the reader into an intellectual dialog.

because the children would be burning calories. In addition, when children are taken outside for recess after lunch, they are exposed to and become used to playing outdoors, an activity that can be repeated in the home environment.

YOUR RESEARCH PROJECT

1. Make a list of your personal interests and items that affect your mental and physical activities, such as homework, hiking, or relations with your family. Examine each item on the list to see if you can find an academic angle that will make the topic fit the context of your research assignment. See section 2a, pages 13–18, for more help.

2. Ask questions about a possible subject, using the list on pages 17–18.

3. Look around your campus or community for subjects. Talk with your classmates and even your instructor about campus issues. Focus on your hometown community in search of a problem, such as the demise of the Main Street merchants. Investigate any environmental concerns in your area, from urban sprawl to beach erosion to waste disposal. Think seriously about a piece of literature you have read, perhaps Fitzgerald's *The Great Gatsby*. If you are a parent, consider issues related to children, such as finding adequate child care. When you have a subject of interest, apply to it some of the narrowing techniques described on pages 13–18, such as clustering, free writing, or listing keywords.

4. To determine if sufficient sources will be available and to narrow the subject even further, visit the Internet, investigate the library's databases (e.g., InfoTrac), and dip into the electronic book catalog at your library. Keep printouts of any interesting articles or book titles.

5. Consult your research schedule, pages 9–10, to determine the steps that you have completed in your preliminary steps for topic discovery and the next actions to take for moving forward with the research project.

3 Organizing Ideas and Setting Goals

Chapter 3 Clear Targets

The beginning steps in the research project can sometimes seem haphazard. After the initial search to narrow your topic and confirm the availability of sources, you should organize your ideas so that reading and notetaking will relate directly to your specific needs. This chapter provides ideas for charting the direction of your research:

- Using a clear order for the course of your research work
- Utilizing your research proposal to direct notetaking
- Listing key terms and phrases for taking notes
- Asking questions to identify issues
- Organizing ideas with modes of development
- Charting the direction of your research with your thesis

With scattered notes on sheets of photocopied material or printouts from the Internet, your initial work may seem jumbled and cluttered; therefore, carefully organize ideas with a preliminary plan to find your way through the research maze.

3a Using a Basic Order to Chart the Course of Your Work

Your finished paper should trace the issues, defend and support a thesis, and provide dynamic progression of issues and concepts that point forward to the conclusion. The paper should provide these elements:

Identification of the problem or issue
A review of the literature on the topic
Your thesis or hypothesis
Analysis of the issues
Presentation of evidence
Interpretation and discussion of the findings

In every case, you must generate the dynamics of the paper by (1) building anticipation in the introduction, (2) investigating the issues in the body, and (3) providing a final judgment. In this way, you will satisfy the demands of the academic reader, who will expect you to:

- Examine a problem
- Cite pertinent literature on it
- Offer your ideas and interpretation of it

All three are necessary in almost every instance. Consequently, your early organization will determine, in part, the success of your research paper.

3b Using Your Research Proposal to Direct Your Notetaking

Your research proposal, if you developed one, introduces issues worthy of research. For example, the last sentence of this research proposal names three topics:

> Everybody thinks water is plentiful and will always be here. I'm afraid that water might soon replace oil as an economic resource most treasured by nations. We already have legal battles about the sharing of water, and we may one day have wars over it. Preliminary reading has shown that a growing world population faces a global water supply that is shrinking. Accordingly, this paper will examine some of the issues with regard to supply and demand, the political power struggles that are emerging, and the ethical and perhaps even moral implications engulfing the world's scattered supply of fresh water.

This writer will search the literature and write notes to build an environmental examination of those who have good supplies of water and those who do not.

Note: For a discussion of and directions for completing the research proposal, see Chapter 2, pages 27–32.

Another writer sketched the following research proposal, which lists the types of evidence necessary to accomplish her project:

> Organ and tissue donation is a constant concern in our society. This paper will expose the myths that prevail in the public's imagination and, hopefully, dispel them. It will explore the serious need of and benefits derived from donated organs and tissue. It will also itemize the organs and their use to rehabilitate the diseased and wounded. It will evaluate, but it will also be a proposal: Sign the donor card!

3c Listing Key Terms and Phrases to Set Directions for Notetaking

Follow two fairly simple steps: (1) Jot down ideas or words in a rough list, and (2) expand the list to show a hierarchy of major and minor ideas. Student Norman Berkowitz started listing items that are affected by and depend on the world's water supply:

wildlife survival
sanitation and hygiene
irrigation of farms and the food supply
bioscience issues
water distribution
global warming
the Ogallala aquifer

Berkowitz could begin notetaking with this list and label each note with one of the phrases.

> **HINT:** What you are looking for at this point are terms that will speed your search on the Internet and in the library's indexes.

3d Writing a Rough Outline

As early as possible, organize your key terminology in a brief outline, arranging the words and phrases in an ordered sequence, as shown in this next example. Jamie Johnston began research in the matter of prehistoric wars. He soon jotted down this rough outline:

Prehistoric wars

Evidence of weapons

Evidence from skeletal remains

Evidence of soldiers and fortresses

Reasons for early fighting

Resources

Slaves, concubines, and sacrificial victims

Gold, silver, bronze, copper

Revenge

Defend honor

     Cause for human compulsion to fight

       Biology

       Culture

This outline, although sketchy, provides the terminology needed for key-word searches on the Internet and in your library's databases. Also, it's not too early to begin initial reading and writing notes for the items on the list.

RESEARCH TIP

Using a Direct Quotation to Avoid Plagiarism

In the early phases of his research, Jamie Johnston's Internet search located a useful site that provided the key idea for a thesis about prehistoric warfare. The Web article from *Musket, Sword and Paint* provided expert information:

> A small group of causeways have shown signs of warfare. These sites have a more continuous ditch and are placed on top of a hilltop or spur. "Organized warfare was not new; it had been practiced for a millennium in pre-historic times," Arthur Ferrill.

The temptation for Jamie Johnston was to incorporate the ideas of the source into his paper without giving credit for the original thought to the author:

> *Organized warfare had been practiced for a millennium in prehistoric times.*

To avoid this form of intentional plagiarism, and to add credibility to his own ideas, the student can add the name of the source and blend the direct quotation into his research:

> *According to Arthur Ferrill, "Organized warfare was not new; it had been practiced for a millennium in pre-historic times."*

3e   Using Questions to Identify Issues

Questions can invite you to develop answers in your notes. (See also section 2a, "Asking Questions," pages 17–18.) Early in her work, one student made this list of questions:

What is a functional food?

How does it serve the body in fighting disease?

Can healthy eating actually lower health care costs?

Can healthy eating truly prolong one's life?

Can we identify the components of nutritional foods that make
them work effectively?

What is an antioxidant? a carcinogen? a free radical? a triglyceride?

She then went in search of answers and built a body of notes. One question might lead to others, and an answer to a question, "Are nutritional foods new?" might produce a topic statement for a paragraph:

Although medical professionals are just beginning to open their
minds and eyes to the medicinal power of food, others have known
about food's healthful properties for centuries.

3f Setting Goals by Using Organizational Patterns

Try to anticipate the kinds of development, or organizational patterns, you will need to build effective paragraphs and to explore your topic fully. Then base your notes on the modes of development: *definition, comparison and contrast, process, illustration, cause and effect, classification, analysis,* and *description.* Here's a list by one student who studied the issues of organ and tissue donation:

Define tissue donation.

Contrast myths, religious views, and ethical considerations.

Illustrate organ and tissue donation with several examples.

Use statistics and scientific data.

Search out causes for a person's reluctance to sign a donor card.

Determine the consequences of donation with a focus on saving
the lives of children.

Read and use a case study on a child's death and organ donation
by the public.

Explore the step-by-step stages of the process of organ donation.

Classify the types and analyze the problem.

Give narrative examples of several people whose lives were saved.

With this list in hand, a writer can search for material to develop as *contrast, process, definition,* and so forth.

> ■ **HINT:** Try developing each important item on your list into a full
> paragraph. Write a definition paragraph. Write a paragraph to
> compare and contrast the attitudes expressed by people about
> organ donation. Then write another paragraph that gives four
> or five examples. By doing so, you will be well on your way to
> developing the paper.

One student recorded this note that describes the subject:

> Organ and tissue donation is the gift of life. Each year, many
> people confront health problems due to diseases or congenital birth
> defects. Organ transplants give these people the chance to live a
> somewhat normal life. Organs that can be successfully transplanted
> include the heart, lungs, liver, kidneys, and pancreas (Barnill 1).
> Tissues that can be transplanted successfully include bone, corneas,
> skin, heart valves, veins, cartilage, and other connective tissues
> (Taddonio 1).

3g Using Approaches across the Curriculum to Chart Your Ideas

Each scholarly field gives a special insight into any given topic.
Suppose, for example, that you want to examine an event from U.S.
history, such as the Battle of Little Bighorn. Different academic disciplines
will help you approach the topic in different ways.

Political Science:	Was Custer too hasty in his quest for political glory?
Economics:	Did the government want to open the western lands for development that would enrich the nation?
Military Science:	Was Custer's military strategy flawed?
Psychology:	Did General Custer's ego precipitate the massacre?
Geography:	Why did Custer stage a battle at this site?

These approaches can also produce valuable notes as the student searches
out answers in the literature, as shown in this example:

> The year 1876 stands as a monument to the western policies of
> Congress and the president, but Sitting Bull and Custer seized their
> share of glory. Custer's egotism and political ambitions overpowered

his military savvy (Lemming 6). Also, Sitting Bull's military tactics (he told his braves to kill rather than show off their bravery) proved devastating for Custer and his troops, who no longer had easy shots at "prancing, dancing Indians" (Potter 65).

3h Using Your Thesis to Chart the Direction of Your Research

Often, the thesis statement sets the direction of the paper's development.

Arrangement by Issues

The thesis statement might force the writer to address various issues and positions.

> **THESIS:** Misunderstandings about organ donation distort reality and set serious limits on the availability of those persons who need an eye, a liver, or a healthy heart.
>
> **ISSUE 1.** Many myths mislead people into believing that donation is unethical.
>
> **ISSUE 2.** Some fear that as a patient they might be terminated early for their body parts.
>
> **ISSUE 3.** Religious views sometimes get in the way of donation.

The outline above, though brief, gives this writer three categories that require detailed research in support of the thesis. The notetaking can be focused on these three issues.

Arrangement by Cause/Effect

In other cases, the thesis statement suggests development by cause/effect issues. Notice that the next writer's thesis on television's educational values points the way to four very different areas worthy of investigation.

Formulating an effective thesis, 2f, pages 24–27.

> **THESIS:** Television can have positive effects on a child's language development.
>
> **CONSEQUENCE 1.** Television introduces new words.
>
> **CONSEQUENCE 2.** Television reinforces word usage and proper syntax.
>
> **CONSEQUENCE 3.** Literary classics come alive verbally on television.
>
> **CONSEQUENCE 4.** Television provides the subtle rhythms and musical effects of accomplished speakers.

CHECKLIST

Evaluating Your Overall Plan

1. What is my thesis? Will my notes and records defend and illustrate my proposition? Is the evidence convincing?
2. Have I found the best plan for developing the thesis with elements of argument, evaluation, cause/effect, or comparison?
3. Should I use a combination of elements—that is, do I need to evaluate the subject, examine the causes and consequences, and then set out the argument?

This outline can help the writer produce a full discussion on television viewing.

Arrangement by Interpretation and Evaluation

Evaluation will evolve from thesis statements that judge a subject by a set of criteria, such as your analysis of a poem, movie, or museum display. Notice how the next student's thesis statement requires an interpretation of Hamlet's character.

THESIS: Shakespeare manipulates the stage settings for Hamlet's soliloquies to uncover his unstable nature and forecast his failure.

1. His soul is dark because of his mother's incest.

2. He appears impotent in comparison with the actor.

3. He is drawn by the magnetism of death.

4. He realizes he cannot perform cruel, unnatural acts.

5. He stands ashamed by his inactivity in comparison.

Arrangement by Comparison

Sometimes a thesis statement stipulates a comparison on the value of two sides of an issue, as shown in one student's preliminary outline:

THESIS: Discipline often involves punishment, but child abuse adds another element: the gratification of the adult.

COMPARISON 1.   A spanking has the interest of the child at heart but a beating or a caning has no redeeming value.

COMPARISON 2.   Time-outs remind the child that relationships are important and to be cherished, but lockouts in a closet only promote hysteria and fear.

COMPARISON 3.   The parent's ego and selfish interests often take precedence over the welfare of the child or children.

YOUR RESEARCH PROJECT

1. Make a list of key terms related to your topic (see section 3c for examples). When you have a list, try to group the terms into main ideas and subtopics. You can use this list as a rough working outline to guide your reading and notetaking.

2. Develop a list of questions about your topic. Try to generate a list of questions yourself and then follow up by asking some of your friends or classmates to suggest questions that they would like to know more about based on your initial topic. See section 3e.

3. Revisit your thesis statement to think about what kind of direction it sets for your paper's development. Consider some of the development patterns described in section 3h and experiment with applying one or more of these patterns to your topic and thesis statement.

4. Review the steps that you have taken in your research schedule, pages 9–10, to determine the focus of your research plan.

Gathering Sources Online

Chapter 4 Clear Targets

Digital sources are now a major source of research information. The Internet makes available millions of computer files relating to any subject—articles, illustrations, sound and video clips, and raw data. This chapter provides direction for online searches:

- Searching for viable academic information on the Web
- Accessing online sources
- Evaluating and filtering the complex web of Internet sites

Although the Internet cannot replace the references found in the library or field research, it offers the best and worst information, and requires careful evaluation. When reading an Internet article, always take time to judge its authority and veracity.

Most Internet sites meet basic academic standards, yet you should keep in mind that the best scholarly articles are found through the library's databases. With all online sources, you must filter personal opinion pieces that contain unsubstantiated information. Many commercial sites disguise their sales pitch with informative articles. In other cases you will encounter advocacy pages that have a predetermined bias that dismisses objective analysis of an issue in favor of the group's position on the topic—the environment, gun control laws, immigration, and so forth. This chapter will help you identify these sites. See specifically the Checklist, pages 45–46, "Evaluating Internet Sources."

You must also be wary of the pitfalls of plagiarism. **Plagiarism** involves downloading online material into your paper without citation and documentation, thereby making it appear to be your own work. Additionally, you can buy a canned research paper and submit it as your own. This is also plagiarism and can result in your failing the course or even being placed on academic probation.

For a full discussion of plagiarism, see pages 95–108.

Therefore, this chapter will help you with two tasks: (1) to become an efficient searcher for academic information on the Web; and (2) to become accomplished at evaluating and filtering the wealth of material available on Internet sites.

CHECKLIST

Using Online Rather Than Print Versions

Online versions of articles offer advantages, but they also present problems. On the plus side, you can view them almost instantly on the computer monitor. You can save or print an abstract or article without the hassle of photocopying, and you can even download material to your flash drive and, where appropriate, insert it into your paper. However, keep these issues in mind:

- The text may differ from the original printed version and may even be a digest. Therefore, cite the Internet source to avoid giving the appearance of citing from the printed version. There are often major differences between the print version of an article in *USA Today* and the one found on their companion website. Cite the correct one in your Works Cited.

- Online abstracts may not accurately represent the full article. In fact, some abstracts are not written by the author at all but by an editorial staff. Therefore, resist the desire to quote from the abstract and, instead, write a paraphrase of it—or, better, find the full text and cite from it (see also pages 71–72).

- You may need to subscribe (at a modest cost) to some sites. A company has the right to make demands before giving you access. However, your school library can often provide you with access to the sites most suitable for your research.

4a Beginning an Online Search

To trace the good and the bad, let's follow the trail of one student, Sherri James, who has decided, because she is a competitive swimmer, to investigate the use of drugs for enhancing one's athletic performance in the pool—not that she wants to try drugs but rather to educate herself and produce a research paper at the same time.

Probably the first thing most of you do, like Sherri James, is visit your favorite search engine, such as Ask, Bing, Google, Dogpile, or Yahoo!. At the search window, Sherri James typed "fitness and drugs." Among the listed sites, she was directed to a few commercial sites (*.com*). They each wanted to sell something—power supplements, a carb-electrolyte drink, and cybergenics nutritional products and instructional videos. One site advertised steroids for sale, such as Epogen and Erythropoietin. For Sherri

44 Gathering Sources Online

James, these Internet locations offered no information, except to suggest this note that she jotted into her research journal:

With supplements, drugs, and even steroids readily available on websites, it's no wonder so many athletes get caught in the "quick-fix" bodybuilding trap.

To refine her Internet search, Sherri James decided to try an online directory search. By entering her topic "fitness + drugs" into the browser for **Yahoo! Directory,** she found hyperlinks to the following websites:

Doping and Sports—collective expert assessment on doping by bicyclists

Drugs in Sport—provides information on performance-enhancing drugs in sport, the latest articles on the subject, reports, resources, and useful websites

RESEARCH TIP

Avoiding "Cut-and-Paste" Plagiarism

Here is information from a health website that Sherri James found in her online research:

> There is no reason a master swimmer with a busy schedule can't have a competitive training regimen. It requires some creativity and a change in attitude. Although we tend to think that training only occurs in the pool, that's just not the case. I've outlined a training program for master swimmers that recognizes that they have limited time. This program has three parts:
>
> In-pool training
>
> Out-of-pool training
>
> Nutrition
>
> Your in-pool training should have two components: technique development and aerobic conditioning.

Instead of pasting the content directly from the website, Sherri noted only the factual information contained on the site that was relevant to her paper, namely the valuable advice on in-pool and out-of-pool training techniques, training, stretching, and calisthenics, in addition to promoting particular supplements. By critically evaluating the source and noting only the particular facts that are relevant, you can avoid the common pitfall of "cut-and-paste" plagiarism.

Evaluating Online Sources

The Internet and other online sources supply huge amounts of material, some of it excellent and some not so good. You must make judgments about the validity and veracity of these materials. In addition to your commonsense judgment, here are a few guidelines:

1. Prefer the *.edu* and *.org* sites. Usually, these are domains developed by an educational institution, such as Ohio State University, or by a professional organization, such as the American Philosophical Association. Of course, *.edu* sites also include many student papers, which can include unreliable information.

2. The *.gov* (government) and *.mil* (military) sites are generally considered to be reliable, but look closely at any information that involves politically sensitive materials.

3. The *.com* (commercial) sites are generally developed by for-profit organizations. Keep in mind that (a) they are selling advertising space, (b) they often charge you for access to their files, (c) they can be ISP sites (Internet Service Provider) that people pay to use and to post their "material." Although some *.com* sites contain good information (for example, reputable newspaper and magazine sites), use these sites with caution unless you can verify their reliability.

4. Look for the *professional* affiliation of the writer, which you will find in the opening credits or an e-mail address. Search for the writer's home page: Type the writer's name into a search engine to see how many results are listed, including a list of his or her books. If you find no information on the writer, you will need to rely on a sponsored website. That is, if the site is not sponsored by an organization or institution, you should probably abandon the source and look elsewhere.

5. Look for a bibliography that accompanies the article, which will indicate the scholarly nature of this writer's work.

6. Usenet discussion groups offer valuable information at times, but some articles lack sound, fundamental reasoning, or evidence to support the opinions.

7. Look for the timeliness of the information on the site. Check dates of publication and how often the information is updated.

8. Treat e-mail messages as mail, not scholarly articles. A similar rule applies to chat.

9. Does the site contain hypertext links to other professional sites or to commercial sites? Links to other educational

> sites serve as a modern bibliography to more reliable sources. Links to commercial sites are often attempts to sell you something.
>
> 10. Learn to distinguish from among the different types of websites, such as advocacy pages, personal home pages, informational pages, and business and marketing pages.

    Findlaw: Drug Use in Sports—includes a story archive and background information on testing, prevention, policies, and commonly used drugs

    NCAA Drug Testing—information on the association's drug-testing policy

    PlayClean—promotes anti-doping policies and preventing youth drug use through sports; from the Office of National Drug Control Policy

Sherri had now found site domains other than commercial ones, such as *.org, .gov, .net,* and *.edu.* At the NCAA website, she was able to print out the NCAA (National Collegiate Athletic Association) Drug-Testing Program and use portions of the rules in her paper. Here is one of her notes:

The NCAA clearly forbids blood doping. It says, "The practice of blood doping (the intravenous injection of whole blood, packed red blood cells or blood substitutes) is prohibited and any evidence confirming use will be cause for action consistent with that taken for a positive drug test" (Bylaw 31.1.3.1.1).

Sherri also found an article entitled "Women and Drugs" by the Office of National Drug Control Policy. She was now finding material worthy of notetaking:

A study by scientists at Columbia University has found the signals and situations of risk are different for girls and that "girls and young women are more vulnerable to abuse and addiction: they get hooked faster and suffer the consequences sooner than boys and young men" ("Women and Drugs").

Sherri James has begun to find her way to better sources on the Internet, but she will still need to examine the academic databases by logging on at her college library (see Chapter 5). She will also need to consider doing field research, such as interviewing fellow athletes or developing a questionnaire (see pages 84–86 and 90–91).

4b Reading an Online Address

Following is some information to help you understand online addresses. In the library, you must employ a book's call number to find it. On the Internet, you employ a Uniform Resource Locator (URL), like this one for psychology from Pearson Higher Education: http://www.pearsonhighered.com/educator/discipline/Psychology/91000065.page

- The *protocol* (http://) transmits data.
- The *server* (www, for World Wide Web) is the global Internet service that connects the multitude of computers and the Internet files.

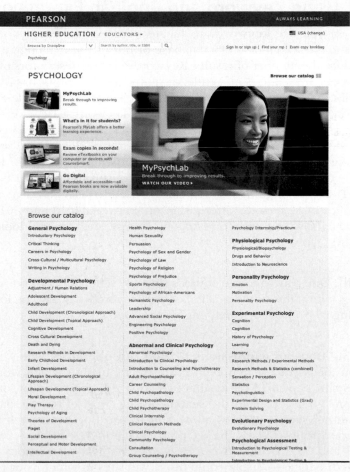

FIGURE 4.1   **Psychology website from Pearson Higher Education.**

- The *domain* (pearsonhighered.com) names the organization feeding information into the server with a *suffix* to label the type of organization: *.com* (commercial), *.edu* (educational), *.gov* (government), *.mil* (military), *.net* (network organization), and *.org* (organization).
- The *directory/file* (educator/discipline/psychology) finds one of the server's directories and then a specific file.
- The *hypertext markup language* (html) names the computer language used to write the file.

Often, knowing just the protocol and the server.domain will get you to a home site from which you can search deeper for files. The URL http://www.pearsonhighered.com/educator/discipline/Psychology/91000065.page will take you to the psychology page for Pearson Higher Education (see Figure 4.1), where you can examine a specific directory, such as theories of counseling or abnormal psychology.

4c   Using Keyword and Boolean Expressions

When you use **keywords** to locate sources, you enter words and phrases in the search field of a database or Internet search engine to help you reduce the number of results. Keywords are the descriptors or identifying words in a source's main title, or terms that the author has identified as significant. Selecting keywords that are relevant to your topic will help to narrow your search results. To make your keyword searches even more efficient, you can also use guided keyword search options to combine search elements, group terms, or select indexes or fields to be searched.

Using a search engine's **advanced** or **custom search** tool lets you narrow your keyword searches by answering prompts on an onscreen menu. This type of guided search can be used to select a range of dates for publications, such as "after 2011" or "between 2010 and 2014." You can also narrow your search results by format, such as only looking for certain file types.

> **HINT:** One way to locate sources that are scholarly is to search for sites within the *.edu* domain. Scholarly sources can also be located using a specialized search engine like Google Scholar.

Using **Boolean expressions** or **Boolean operators** with keywords lets you focus your search even more by stipulating which words and phrases *can* appear in the results, which words *must* appear, or which terms *must not* appear in the search results. Most electronic databases and Internet search engines allow you to use Boolean search expressions, specifically *AND* or the + ("plus") symbol, *NOT* or the – ("minus") symbol, and *OR*. Placed between keywords, Boolean expressions instruct the search engine to display only those websites in which your research terms appear in certain combinations, and to ignore others. Figure 4.2 shows the results of a keyword search using Boolean expressions.

- **AND (+):** This operator narrows the search by retrieving only records that contain all terms connected by it. Most search engines, such as Google and Yahoo!, will assume you want to enter AND or (+) between a string of terms even if you don't use the Boolean expression.

  Example: **food dye** is searched as **food + dye.**

  Example: **food + dye + ADHD** will only list websites that contain all three terms.

- **NOT(–):** This identifier excludes sites that contain the specified word or phrase. Using the term NOT or (–) finds sources that include one term but not the other. For example, if you want to eliminate "cancer" from your search about hyperactivity caused by food dye, add the word NOT before that term.

  Example: **food AND dye AND hyperactivity NOT cancer**

- **OR:** Using "OR" broadens your search boundaries to include records containing more than one keyword. For example, if you want to expand your search to include sources about food dye's connection

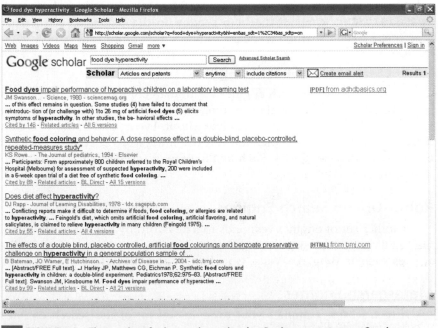

◼ **FIGURE 4.2   The results of a keyword search using Boolean operators on Google Scholar.**

to hyperactivity, or its relationship to allergies, use the expression "OR" in your search.

Example: **food AND dye AND hyperactivity OR allergy**

- **Quotation marks ("")**: Placing search terms inside quotation marks will signal the database or search engine to look for an exact phrase. Placing a phrase or term inside quotation marks will exclude sources that don't contain the exact phrase.

Example: **"food dye" AND "hyperactive children"**

Wildcard searches use symbols to search for the various forms of a basic, root word. Rather than conducting several searches for the same basic word—such as *child, children, childhood,* and so on—you can focus your keyword search to find a term with variant spelling or endings by using an asterisk (*) or a question mark (?) as the wildcard or truncation symbol.

The asterisk (*) usually takes the place of one or more characters at the end of a word.

Example: **diet*** Results: **diet, diets, dietary, dietician, dietetics**

The question mark (?) usually takes the place of a single character in a word.

Example: **ne?t** Results: **neat, nest, next**

Some databases and search engines use different wildcard symbols such as (!), ($), or (:). Consult the help section in the database or Internet search site to learn which wildcard symbols are supported.

Subject Directory Search Engines

Subject directory search engines are human compiled and indexed to guide you to general areas that are then subdivided to specific categories. Your choices control the list. Sites like About, Lycos, and Yahoo! contain directories arranged by topic. You can use a keyword search or click on one of the topic categories, such as **Finance,** to go deeper into the Web directories.

Robot-Driven Search Engines

Another set of engines responds to a keyword by electronically scanning millions of Web pages. Your keywords will control the size of the list at sites such as Bing, AltaVista, Google, Go, and HotBot.

Metasearch Engines

A metasearch examines your topic in several of the search engines listed previously. Thus, you need not search each engine separately. For example, when you enter a query at the Mamma website, the engine simultaneously queries about ten of the major robot-driven search engines. It then provides you with a short, relevant set of results. You will get fewer results than might appear at one of the major search engines. For example, the request for "chocolate + children" produced 170,000,000 results on AltaVista but only 100 on Mamma.com. A metasearch engine gives you a focused list of sites. The metasearch engine selects the first few listings from each of the other engines under the theory that each engine puts the most relevant sites at the top of its list; however, some commercial sites are able to buy their way to the top of various lists. Consider using a metasearch engine such as Dogpile, Mamma, Metacrawler, or Surfwax.

Specialized Search Engines

Other search engines specialize in one area, such as WWWomen (women's studies), TribalVoice (Native American studies), and Bizweb (business studies). In addition, many websites, such as the Library of Congress and New York Times Online, have search engines just for themselves. Even sites for local newspapers have search engines for their own archives (see pages 57–59).

Educational Search Engines

Educational search engines provide subject indexes for the various disciplines (humanities, sciences) and for subtopics under those headings (history, literature, biochemistry, and so on). Try several, because they will take you to academic material, not commercial sites with advertising banners popping up all over the screen:

English Server	Iseek
Internet Public Library	ERIC
ProQuest K–12	Scirus
Library of Congress	Intute
Discovery Channel	Voice of the Shuttle

Returning once again to Sherri James and her investigations, she entered the phrase "blood doping" at the Scirus search engine, which directed her to the United States Olympic Committee, where she found the following source:

What is doping?

Currently national anti-doping agencies around the world are working to harmonize the definition of doping. For USADA testing, each athlete is responsible for his/her International Federation's (IF) definition of doping since USADA looks to IF definitions. The Olympic Movement

Anti-Doping Code (OMADC), revised by the International Olympic Committee (IOC) in 2012, set forth one definition of doping as follows:

> "The presence of a substance, defined as a prohibited substance under the Olympic Movement Anti-Doping Code (OMADC), in a competitor's sample or the use of a prohibited method under OMADC."

Doping does not necessarily mean that performance is enhanced. The ethics of both sport and medical science are breached when someone dopes. It is important to remember that a doping violation can happen regardless of whether an athlete deliberately uses a prohibited substance, or unknowingly uses a product containing a prohibited substance. The presence of a prohibited substance or evidence of the use of prohibited method in your sample constitutes a doping violation, irrespective of how it got there.

The bottom line is that you are responsible for any substance that you ingest—it is your responsibility to ensure that any product you take does not contain a prohibited substance.

Why is doping prohibited?

Doping is prohibited to protect your rights to compete on a level playing field without the use of prohibited substances or prohibited methods. There are other reasons to prohibit doping, including the fact that doping can cause:

- **Harm to athletes who dope.** Most sports carry a certain amount of risk. Many prohibited substances and methods may add serious risks of harm to those that use them. Clean and ethical sport does not require that athletes take unnecessary risks.
- **Harm to athletes who do not dope.** Athletes who dope ruin fair sport for all athletes who do not dope. Clean athletes may perceive the need to dope in order to compete with other athletes they suspect are doping. This senseless cycle of doping can bring about personal devastation through health and safety risks, and the destruction of sport.

With this information, Sherri James can provide a clear definition of doping as well as draw several ideas from this source.

Avoiding Unintentional Plagiarism

The wording and language of many websites can be clear and straightforward, as in the example from the Olympic Movement Anti-Doping Code:

> **Harm to athletes who dope.** Most sports carry a certain amount of risk. Many prohibited substances and methods may add serious risks of harm to those that use them. Clean and ethical sport does not require that athletes take unnecessary risks.

The simplicity of the language used in this Internet file can lead to incorporating the idea into an essay without giving proper credit to the source:

> *Clean and ethical sport does not require that athletes take unnecessary risks.*

By borrowing the exact words without giving proper credit to the source, the student has committed plagiarism. Unacknowledged use of another person's sentences, phrases, or terminology is plagiarism, so provide a citation and use quotation marks to show exactly where you are borrowing ideas from a source. Proper documentation with a reference to the source can avoid unintentional plagiarism:

> *It is the view of the Olympic Movement Anti-Doping Code that "clean and ethical sport does not require that athletes take unnecessary risks."*

Educational Search Engines Maintained by Libraries

Here's a list of excellent sites that provide valuable academic information: BUBL Link, Internet Public Library, and Internet Scout.

HINT: Most Web browsers include a Bookmark or Favorites tool to save addresses for quick access. When you find a file you want to access later, create a bookmark so you can revisit it with just a click of the mouse. In Microsoft Internet Explorer, use the button bar marked Favorites to make your bookmarks. *Note*: If you are working at a university computer laboratory, do not add bookmarks to the hard drive. Instead, save the bookmarks to your flash drive or personal drop box by using Save As in the File menu.

4d Using RSS and Social Bookmarking

Searching the Internet opens a door to countless sources you can use for your research, including journals, periodicals, blogs, and wikis. After you have generated a list of useful sources, though, it can be difficult and time consuming to keep up with the latest news and developments related to your topic. One great way to simplify this part of your research is to use RSS (Rich Site Summary).

RSS Feeds

You can use RSS to set up a document called a *Web feed* using software known as a reader. There are many free online readers available, such as Google Reader, CNET, and Bloglines. These readers allow you to "subscribe" to the news feeds on your favorite sites and receive updated material from all of those sites on one Web page.

To subscribe to a particular website, look for a symbol like this one: 🔊 When you click on this icon, you will receive directions on how to subscribe to that site's RSS feed. After you have subscribed to all of the sites needed for your research, you can use the different features in the reader to focus your research more narrowly. For example, in Figure 4.3 you can see how one student used Boolean operators in the search box

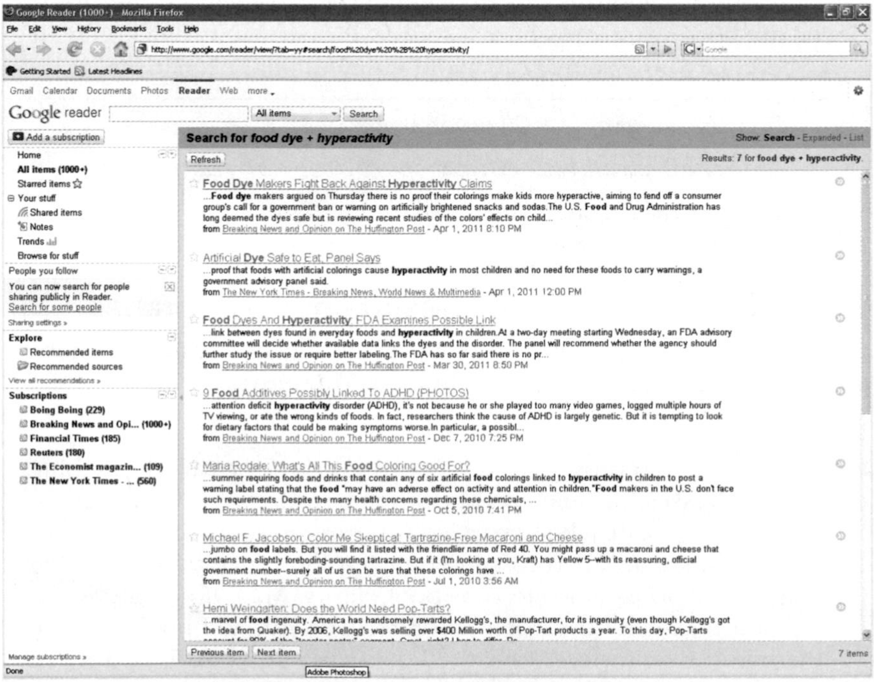

FIGURE 4.3 Google Reader RSS search using Boolean operators.

on Google Reader to find the latest news about how consuming food dyes might lead to hyperactivity in children.

Web 2.0 and Social Bookmarking

Web 2.0 refers to online tools or applications that facilitate the sharing of information through social networking sites, blogs, and "folksonomies" (simple shared vocabularies). These tools can help your research by linking you to a network of other individuals who have located sites relevant to your topic and marked them using "tags" that help you find and search within those sites. You can also use these tags to organize and manage the many different online sources that you use in your research.

"Social bookmarking" is an example of this kind of networked research. As you conduct your online research on a topic, you can use the tools available on a site like Delicious.com to save and organize your bookmarks. When you use a site such as Delicious.com to save your bookmarks instead of using your Web browser, you'll have the opportunity to list topic-specific keywords or "tags" that describe the site. In Figure 4.4, you can see the bookmarks one student has saved for his research on the link between food dyes and hyperactivity in children, as well as the tags he has assigned to each of those bookmarks.

As your list of saved bookmarks grows, you can use the list of tags on the right side of the Delicious.com screen to sort your bookmarks by

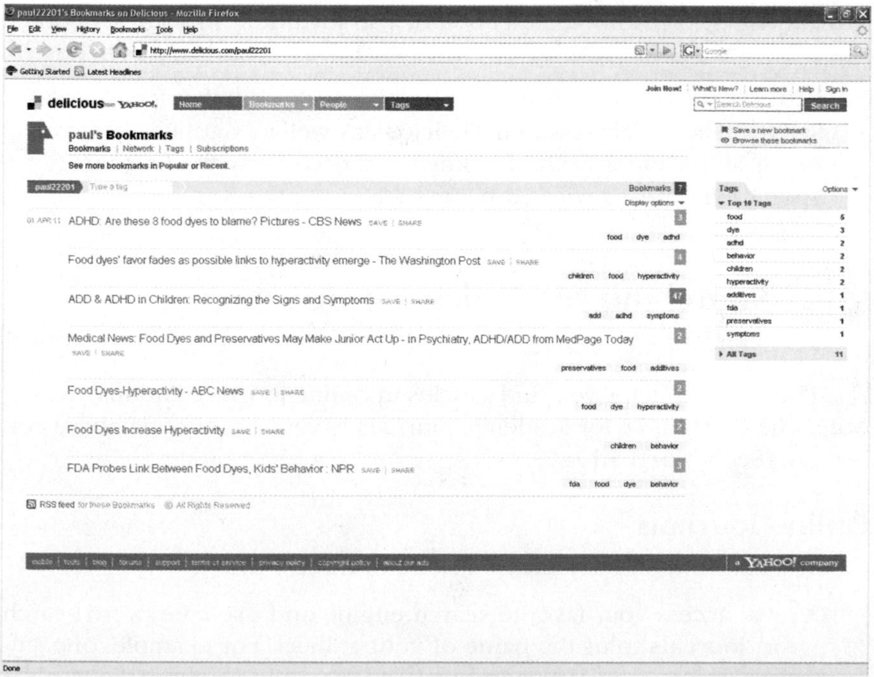

FIGURE 4.4   Delicious.com screen showing a student's selected bookmarks and tags.

a particular tag so that you can focus on a specific part of your online research. You can also group your existing tags into groups by organizing them into "bundles." Because this data is all stored within the Delicious .com site, you can access and work with your bookmarks from any computer or device that can connect to the Internet.

With "social bookmarking," all of your bookmarks are public, and other people can use your tags. You can create a network of other individuals who have bookmarked and tagged sites that are relevant to your research topic. This allows you to use other people's tags to find even more sources that you can use. You can also use the search tool to search the entire Delicious.com community for a particular tag.

Another social networking source you can include in your research involves using "microblogging" sites like Twitter. Twitter is generally used to connect individuals in a network and allow them to communicate and share information and links in short "tweets" limited to 140 characters. The key tool that can aid you in your research is the Twitter "hashtag," which users use to tag a particular word in their tweets. Other users can search by hashtag term, for example by entering "#hyperactivity" to find what others have written and linked to regarding this topic. It is also possible to set up an RSS feed for a Twitter hashtag search, allowing you to receive immediate updates on all related tweets.

As with all online search techniques, researching with Web 2.0 requires a critical eye in order to find reliable, appropriate sources. Be sure that you evaluate the credibility of each source you choose to add to your list of social bookmarks before you include it in your network.

HINT: There are specialized social networking sites that focus exclusively on academic research. Delicious as well as Citulike allow you to tag, store, and organize bookmarks for scholarly works, primarily spotlighting peer-reviewed papers.

4e Searching for Articles in Journals and Magazines

The Internet helps you find articles in online journals and magazines. *Note:* The *best* source for academic journals is your library's database collection. (See section 5d.)

Online Journals

You can find online journals in one of three ways:

- First, access your favorite search engine and use a keyword search for "journals" plus the name of your subject. For example, one student accessed AltaVista and used a keyword search for "journals + fitness." The search produced links to twenty online journals devoted to fitness, such as *Health Page, Excite Health,* and *Physical Education.* Another student's search for "women's studies + journals" produced a list of relevant journals, such as *Feminist Collections, Resources for Feminist Research,* and *Differences.* By accessing one of these links, the student can examine abstracts and articles.

* Second, access a search engine's subject directory. In Yahoo!, for example, one student selected Social Science from the key directory, then clicked "Sociology," and journals, to access links to several online journals, such as *Edge: The E-Journal of Intercultural Relations* and *Sociological Research Online.*

* Third, if you already know the name of a journal, go to your favorite search engine to make a keyword query, such as "Contemporary Sociology," which will link you to the social science journal of that name.

Online Magazines

Several directories exist for discovering articles in magazines.

Magazine-Directory lists magazine home pages where you can begin your free search in that magazine's archives. For example, you can search *The Atlantic, Harper's,* or *Newsweek.*

Highbeam Research has a good search engine, but it requires membership (which is free for one month). Remember to cancel your membership after you finish your research.

Pathfinder gives you free access to several popular online magazines such as *Time, People,* and *Fortune.*

ZD Net provides excellent access to industry-oriented articles in banking, electronics, computers, management, and so on. It offers two weeks of free access before charges begin to accrue.

4f   Searching for Articles in Newspapers and Media Sources

First, to find almost any newspaper in the United States, even the local weeklies, consult usnpl.com. This site takes you to the *Aspen Times* or the *Carbondale Valley Journal* or one of 800-plus other newspapers. In most cases, the online newspaper has its own internal search engine that enables you to examine articles from its archives. Figure 4.5 shows the opening page of the online site for a local newspaper in Memphis, Tennessee. Notice especially the **Archives** hyperlink, a feature that enables you to find articles from past issues.

Most major news organizations maintain Internet sites. Consult one of these:

The Chronicle of Higher Education presents news, information, and current issues in education.

FIGURE 4.5   Web page from the Memphis Commercial Appeal.

CNN Interactive maintains a good search engine that takes you quickly, without cost, to transcripts of its broadcasts. It's a good source for research in current events.

C-SPAN Online focuses on public affairs and offers both a directory and a search engine for research in public affairs, government, and political science.

Fox News provides articles from its own network and also from news services such as Reuters and the Associated Press.

National Public Radio Online shares audio articles via RealPlayer as well as print articles.

The **New York Times** is the largest metropolitan newspaper in the United States, with local and national content.

> *USA Today* has a fast search engine that provides information about current events.
>
> *U.S. News Online & World Report* has a fast search engine and provides free, in-depth articles on current political and social issues.
>
> *Wall Street Journal* is a business-oriented site has excellent information, but it requires a subscription.
>
> The *Washington Times* provides up-to-the-minute political news.

To find other newspapers and online media, search for "newspapers" in a search engine. Your college library may also provide Lexis-Nexis, which searches news sources for you.

4g Searching for Photographs and Other Visual Sources

For some topics, you may want to find photographs or other visual sources as part of your research. A paper on representations of women in World War II propaganda posters, for example, would require visual evidence to support its thesis. In disciplines like history and art, visual sources might be central to your paper. For topics in U.S. history and culture, the Library of Congress has a comprehensive archive of visual and multimedia sources in its American Memory collection. Because of their persuasive power, images need to be selected and used carefully in any research paper.

The best place to begin searching for photographs and other visual sources is through a website devoted specifically to online images, such as Picsearch, or through the "images" link on a search engine.

Remember that visual sources, like all other sources, need to be carefully incorporated into your paper and properly documented. See section 10e for more advice about using visuals effectively in your paper. Photographs and other visual sources are copyrighted works like any other published source, and need to be cited to give proper credit to their creators. See pages 168–170 for examples showing proper citation format for photographs, graphs, and other visual sources.

4h Accessing E-books

Access to books online simplifies and speeds up your research by allowing you Web access to novels and resource books. Some of the best sources of full-text, online books are Project Gutenberg, JSTOR, and the Online Books Page at the University of Pennsylvania. These sites index books by author, title, and subject. They also provide a search engine that will take you quickly, for example, to the full text of Thomas Hardy's *A Pair of Blue Eyes* or to Linnea Hendrickson's *Children's Literature: A Guide to the Criticism.* This site adds new textual material almost every day, so consult it first. Understand, however, that contemporary books, still under copyright protection, are not included. That is, you can freely download an Oscar Wilde novel but not one by Alice Walker. *Caution:* Other sites offer e-books, but they are commercial and require a subscription.

4i Using Listserv, Usenet, Blogs, and Chat Groups

E-mail discussion groups have legitimacy for the exchange of academic ideas when everybody in the group has the same purpose, project, or course of study. Chat rooms seldom have academic value. Let's look at each briefly.

E-mail News Groups

The word **listserv** is used to describe discussion groups that correspond via e-mail about a specific educational or technical subject. For example, your literature professor might ask everybody in the class to join a listserv group on Victorian literature. To participate, you must have an e-mail address and subscribe to the list as arranged by your instructor.

In like manner, online courses, which have grown in popularity, usually have a discussion area where students are expected to participate by responding to general questions for the group or corresponding with each other about assignments, issues, and other topics. On the Blackboard system, for example, online students have a Discussion Board with any number of Forums where they may participate or where they are required to participate. At some point you may wish to join a list, and each site will explain the procedure for subscribing and participating via e-mail in a discussion.

Real-Time Chatting

Blogs, Usenet, and chat groups use Internet sites with immediate messaging rather than e-mail. To access Usenet, go to a website such as Yahoo! Messenger or Google Chat to launch the search. Typing "fitness" might take you to a reasonable discussion, yet some dialogue may not apply to your specific topic. Another way to find discussion groups is through a keyword search for "List of online chat groups" at one of the search engines. If you want a commercial site that requires a monthly fee, try usenetserver.com. However, *you cannot cite from these anonymous sources,* so they are best avoided for your academic work.

4j Examining Library Holdings via Online Access

Most major libraries now offer online access to their library catalogs. This allows you to search their collections for books, videos, dissertations, audio tapes, special collections, and other items. However, you must open an account and use your identification to log in, just as you do with your college library. You may sometimes order books online through interlibrary loan. Additionally, some libraries now post full-text documents, downloadable bibliographies, databases, and links to other sites.

If you need identification of all books on a topic, as copyrighted and housed in Washington, DC, consult the Web page for the Library of Congress. This site allows you to search by word, phrase, name, title, series, and number. It provides special features, such as an American Memory Home Page, full-text legislative information, and exhibitions, such as Lincoln's "Emancipation Proclamation."

For an Internet overview of online libraries, their holdings, and addresses, you might consult LIBCAT or LIBWEB. These sites take you to home pages of academic, public, and state libraries. You will be prompted for a public-access login name, so follow the directions for entering and exiting the programs.

Another type of online library is IngentaConnect. This site provides a keyword search of 17,000 journals by author, title, or subject. Copies of the articles can be faxed to you, usually within the hour, for a small fee.

4k Finding an Internet Bibliography

You can quickly build a bibliography on the Internet in two ways: by using a search engine or by visiting an online bookstore.

Search Engine

At a search engine on the Internet, such as AltaVista, enter a descriptive phrase, such as "Child Abuse Bibliographies." You will get a list of bibliographies, and you can click on one of them, such as Child Abuse, Child Abuse Articles, or Child Abuse Reports.

Clicking on the hypertext address will carry you to a list:

Child Abuse Statistics
Child Abuse and Law
Child Sexual Abuse
Risk Assessment

Clicking on the first item will produce a set of hypertext links to articles you might find helpful, such as this one:

> Gustavsson, Nora, and Ann E. MacEachron. "Managing Child Welfare in Turbulent Times." *Social Work* 58.1 (Jan. 2013): 86. Print.

4l Conducting Archival Research on the Internet

The Internet has made possible all kinds of research in library and museum archives. You may have an interest in this type of work. If so, consider several ways to approach the study.

Go to the Library

Go into a library and ask about the archival material housed there, or use the library's electronic catalog. Most libraries have special collections. The Stanford University Library, for example, offers links to antiquarian books, old manuscripts, and other archives. It also provides ways to find material by subject, by title, and by collection number. It carries the researcher to a link, such as the London (Jack) Papers, 1897–1916, at the Online Archive of California. These can be accessed by Internet if the researcher has the proper credentials for entering and using the Stanford collection.

Go to an Edited Search Engine

An edited search engine, such as Yahoo!, may give you results quickly. For example, requesting "Native American literature + archives" produced such links as:

> **American Native Press Archives**
> **Native American History Archive**
> **Native Americans and the Environment**
> **Indigenous Peoples' Literature**
> **Sayings of Chief Joseph**

One or more of these collections might open the door to an interesting topic and enlightening research. You might also search the directory and subdirectories of a search engine to take you deeper into the files.

Go to a Metasearch Engine

A metasearch engine such as Dogpile offers a way to reach archival material. Make a keyword request, such as "Native American literature + archives." Dogpile will list such sites as Reference Works and Research

Material for Native American Studies. There, the Native American Studies Collections offer several valuable lists:

Native American Studies Encyclopedias and Handbooks
Native American Studies Bibliographies
Native American Studies Periodical Indexes
Native American Biography Resources
Native American Studies Statistical Resources
Links to other Native American sites on the Internet
Links to Usenet discussion groups related to Native Americans

Thus, the researcher would have a wealth of archival information to examine. One site, for example, carried a researcher to the Red Earth Museum (see Figure 4.6).

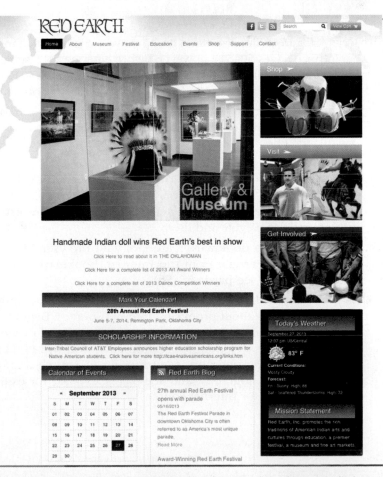

FIGURE 4.6 The home page of the Red Earth Museum, where a student might find archival information on Native Americans.

Go to a Listserv or Usenet Group

Using a search engine, simply join your topic with the word listserv: "Native American literature + listserv." The search engine will produce such links as **Native-L: Native Literature listserv and archives.** By following the proper procedures, you can log on and begin corresponding. Participants might quickly point you in the direction of good topics and sources for developing the paper.

Utilize Newspaper Archives

After you locate a newspaper of interest, use the newspaper's search engine to explore its archives of articles. See page 57 for more information on this valuable resource.

YOUR RESEARCH PROJECT

1. To look for an online discussion group on your topic, go to a metasearch engine (see pages 50–51); however, before entering your subject, select the button for searching newsgroups rather than the Web. Explore the choices. You may also search the lists described in section 4i, page 60.

2. Voice of the Shuttle is a large and powerful search engine for educational information. Enter this site and search for your topic. If unsuccessful, try one of the other educational search engines listed on page 51.

3. When you have found an Internet article directly devoted to your subject, apply to it an evaluation as described on pages 45–46. Ask yourself, "Does this site have merit?" Apply that same test to other Internet articles as you find them.

4. Practice using the Bookmark feature of your browser. That is, rather than printing an article from the Internet, bookmark it instead for future reference (see pages 55–56).

5. As you would with library sources, begin making bibliography entries and writing notes about promising Internet sources. Begin building a computer file of promising sources, develop a folder of printouts from the Internet, and save pertinent information you will need for your bibliography entries later on (see pages 66–67 for more information on a working bibliography, and see pages 256–262 for examples of the bibliography for Internet sources).

5 Gathering Sources in the Library

Chapter 5 Clear Targets

The library should be the center of your research, whether you access it electronically or visit in person. This chapter launches your research through scholarly publications:

- Accessing library sources to launch the search
- Developing a working bibliography
- Finding credible sources on your topic
- Utilizing indexes for topic development

As the repository of the best books and periodicals, the articles that you access through the library are, in the main, written by scholars and published in journals and books only after careful review by a board of like-minded scholars. Logged in at the library, you can download articles to your computer, print files, or read books online.

5a Launching the Search

Your research strategy in the library should include four steps, with adjustments for your individual needs.

1. **Conduct a preliminary search for relevant sources.** Scan the reference section of your library for its electronic sources as well as the abundance of printed indexes, abstracts, bibliographies, and reference books. Search the library's electronic book catalog and dip into the electronic databases, such as Academic Search Premier or InfoTrac. This preliminary work will serve several purposes:

   - It shows the availability of source materials with diverse opinions.
   - It provides a beginning set of reference citations, abstracts, and full-text articles.
   - It defines and restricts your subject while providing an overview of the subject.

2. **Refine the topic and evaluate the sources.** As soon as you refine the topic, you can spend valuable time reading abstracts, articles, and pertinent sections of books. Most instructors will expect you to reference and cite from scholarly sources, so a mix of journal articles and books should accompany your online articles or field research.

3. **Take shortcuts.** First, consult the Appendix of this book, "Finding Reference Works for Your General Topic" (pages 375–382), which lists appropriate electronic and printed sources. It sends you to key sources in historical, social, scientific, and philosophical disciplines.

   In addition, you will need to access a variety of computer sources in the library, such as the electronic book catalog (see pages 67–68) and the electronic services like InfoTrac (see pages 71–74). From the computer workstation in the library, you can develop a working bibliography, read abstracts and full-text articles, and, in general, make substantive advances in researching your topic.

4. **Read and take notes.** Examine books, articles, essays, reviews, computer printouts, and government documents. Whenever possible, create notes as you read so you can transcribe them or paste them into your text.

5. **Consult with a librarian.** If your topic does not initially generate a number of sources, confer with a librarian. A reference librarian may suggest more appropriate words or phrases for the subject; this can be a critical step when you feel that you might be stuck.

> **HINT:** Just as we learn proper Internet behavior, we learn basic library etiquette, such as talking softly out of respect for others and not bringing in food or drinks. At the computer station, you should analyze sources and then print; do not randomly print everything. (See pages 45–46 for methods of analyzing a source.)

5b   Developing a Working Bibliography

> More examples of bibliography format, Chapters 14–17.

Because the research paper is a major project involving many papers and notes, organization is crucial. That means keeping a copy of every abstract, article, and downloaded file with full publication information for all print and Internet materials. A working bibliography serves three purposes:

1. It locates articles and books for notetaking purposes.
2. It provides information for the in-text citations, as in this example in MLA style:

   The healing properties of certain foods have been noted by Milner (682–88) and Hasler (6–10).

3. It provides information for the final Works Cited or reference page (see Chapters 14–17). If you store your entries in a computer file, you can easily insert them into your Works Cited page at the end of your manuscript.

Your final manuscript will require a Works Cited page listing all of the sources you used in your paper, so now is the time to start developing a working bibliography.

Whether you keyboard your sources for easy access or make handwritten notes, each entry of your working bibliography entry should contain the following information—with variations, of course, for print and Internet sources:

1. Author's name
2. Title of the work
3. Publication information
4. Medium of publication (Web, Print)
5. Date of access (Web only)
6. (Optional) A personal note about the location or contents of the source

Works Cited Entry for a Book (MLA style):

Bry, Dave. *Public Apology*. New York: Grand Central, 2013. Print.

Works Cited Entry for a Journal Article (MLA style):

Williamson, Peter, Megan Mercurio, and Constance Walker. "Songs of
   the Caged Birds: Literacy and Learning with Incarcerated Youth."
   English Journal 102.4 (Mar. 2013): 31–37. Print.

Works Cited Entry for a Magazine Article (MLA style):

Petruzzi, J. David. "A Bloody Summer for Horsemen." *Civil War Times*.
   June 2013: 30–37. Print.

Works Cited Entry for an Article Found on an Academic Database (MLA style):

Cooper, Christopher A. and H. Gibbs Knotts. "Overlapping Identities
   in the American South." *Social Science Journal* 50.1 (Mar. 2013):
   6–12. *EBSCOHost*. Web. 19 Oct. 2013.

Bibliography Entry for an Internet Article (MLA style):

Werner, Erica. "Labor, Business Agree to Principles on Immigration."
   Denver Post Online. 21 Feb 2013. Web. 28 Mar. 2013.

5c   Finding Books on Your Topic

Much of your research will be conducted on the library's electronic network with call numbers to its own books and with links to sources around the world.

Using Your Library's Electronic Book Catalog

Your library's computerized catalog will, in theory, include every book in the library filed by subject, author, and title. Begin your research at the catalog by using a *keyword search* to a subject, such as "Health." You will get a list of books on the monitor, and you can click each one to gather more information. The list will look something like this:

Search Results

One for Another—Golden's Rules and Tools for Creating Healthy
    Relationships. Douglas B. Thich. 2013.

Marriage Matters. Cynthia Ellingsen. 2013.

Take Back Your Marriage: Sticking Together in a World That Pulls Us Apart.
    William Doherty. 2013.

In effect, the electronic book catalog has provided a bibliography that lists a variety of available books on a particular subject. The next procedure is to click on one, such as *Take Back Your Marriage: Sticking Together in a World That Pulls Us Apart,* to get the full details and access information.

HINT: Many college libraries as well as public libraries are now part of library networks. The network expands the holdings of every library because one library will loan books to another. Therefore, if a book you need is unavailable in your library, ask a librarian about an interlibrary loan. Understand, however, that you may have to wait several days for its delivery. Most periodical articles can be accessed online.

Using the Library's Bibliographies

You may need to supplement your working bibliography by searching reference guides, bibliographies, and indexes. When ordering its research databases, the library subscribes to electronic versions or print versions of bibliographies. These guides, such as *Bibliographic Index,* will give you a list of books relating to your subject. Figure 5.1 shows a bibliographic

---

Prehistoric War

LeBlanc, Steven A. *Constant Battles: The Myth of the Peaceful, Noble Savage.* New York: St. Martin's, 2003 p 247–64.

FIGURE 5.1 Example from *Bibliographic Index*, 2013.

list found in LeBlanc's book on pages 247–264. Such a list could be a valuable resource in the early stages of research.

If the book fits your research, you will probably want to write a Works Cited entry for this source. Then you can examine the text as well as the bibliography on pages 247–264 of LeBlanc's book, where you might find additional articles on this topic. Here is a student's bibliography notation:

> LeBlanc, Steven A. *Constant Battles: The Myth of the Peaceful, Noble Savage.*
>
> New York: St. Martin's, 2003. Print. Bibliography on pages 247–264.

Using the Trade Bibliographies

Trade bibliographies, intended primarily for use by booksellers and librarians, can help you in three ways:

1. Discover sources not listed in other bibliographies.
2. Locate facts of publication, such as place and date.
3. Determine if a book is in print.

Consult online or in printed version:

Subject Guide to Books in Print (New York: Bowker, 1957–date).

Note: Online, this source may appear as **Books in Print.**

Use this work for its subject classifications, any one of which will provide a ready-made bibliography to books. Figure 5.2 shows a sample found with the keyword "history."

FIGURE 5.2   From *Subject Guide to Books in Print,* Online.

1. Author 2. Title 3. Library of Congress number 4. Number of pages 5. Date of publication 6. International Standard Book Number (used when ordering) 7. Publisher

Using the Bibliographies in the Appendix

Go to the Appendix of this book, pages 375–382. It furnishes a guide to important reference works—some in print at the library, some online in the library's electronic network, and others available on the Internet. Reference sources are listed for ten major categories (see pages 375–382). Here are three examples of titles to reference works that you will find under the heading "Issues in the Arts, Literature, Music, and Language." The first is a printed source in the library, the second is available on the library's electronic network, and the third is available on the Internet.

> *Bibliographic Guide to Art and Architecture.* Boston: Hall, 1977–date. Published annually, this reference work provides bibliographies on most topics in art and architecture—an excellent place to begin research in this area.
>
> *Contemporary Literary Criticism (CLC)* This database provides an extensive collection of full-text critical essays about novelists, poets, playwrights, short story writers, and other creative writers.
>
> *Voice of the Shuttle* This site offers hundreds of links to major online resources for literature, art, history, philosophy, and studies in science.

Examining the Bibliography at the End of a Book

When you get into the stacks, look for bibliographies at the end of books. Jot down titles in your working bibliography or photocopy the list for further reference. An example is shown in Figure 5.3.

Searching for Bibliographies at the End of Journal Articles

Look for bibliographies at the end of articles in scholarly journals. For example, students of history depend on the bibliographies in various issues of *English Historical Review,* and students of literature find bibliographies in *Studies in Short Fiction.* In addition, the journals themselves provide subject indexes to their own contents. If your subject is "Adoption," you will discover that a majority of your sources are located in a

See also 8a, "Finding Reliable Sources."

SECONDARY SOURCES

Abbott, Edith. "The Civil War and the Crime Wave of 1865–70." *Social Service Review,* 1977.

Amis, Moses N. *Historical Raleigh,* 1913.

Andrews, Marietta M. *Scraps of Paper.* 1929.

Badeau, Adam. *Military History of U.S. Grant.* 1885.

Bailey, Mrs. Hugh. "Mobile's Tragedy: The Great Magazine Explosion of 1865."*Alabama Review,* 1968.

Bakeless, John. "The Mystery of Appomattox." *Civil War Times Illustrated,* 1970.

FIGURE 5.3   A portion of a bibliography list at the end of N. A. Trudeau's book *Out of the Storm.*

few key journals. In that instance, going straight to the annual index of one of those journals will be a shortcut.

5d Finding Articles in Magazines and Journals

An index furnishes the exact page number(s) of specific sections of books and of individual articles in magazines, journals, and newspapers. The library's online index of databases not only directs you to articles in magazines, it also gives an abstract of the article, and most often, it provides the full text.

Searching the General Indexes to Periodicals

The library network gives you access to electronic databases. Here are just a few of the many that will be available to you:

AGRICOLA	Agriculture, animal and plant sciences
America: History and Life	U.S. history
American Chemical Society Publications	Chemistry
BioOne	Biological, ecological, and environmental sciences
CINAHL	Nursing, public health, and allied health fields
ERIC	Education and mass communication
GPO	Government publications on all subjects
HighWire	Science, technology, and medicine
InfoTrac	All subjects
JSTOR	Social sciences
Lexis Nexis	News, business, law, medicine, reference
MLA Bibliography	Literature, linguistics, and folklore
Music-Index	Music
Project MUSE	Social sciences, arts, humanities
PsycINFO	Psychology, medicine, education, social work
Westlaw	Legal subjects, including laws and cases

One of these databases will usually guide you to several sources, provide an abstract, and often provide a full-text version of the article, as shown in Figure 5.4.

The Journal of Nutrition, April 2013, 143:486–492.

Dietary Supplement Use and Folate Status during Pregnancy in the United States.

Byline: Amy M. Branum, Regan Bailey, and Barbara J. Singer

Adequate folate and iron intake during pregnancy is critical for maternal and fetal health. No previous studies to our knowledge have reported dietary supplement use and folate status among pregnant women sampled in NHANES, a nationally representative, cross-sectional survey. We analyzed data on 1296 pregnant women who participated in NHANES from 1999 to 2006 to characterize overall supplement use, iron and folic acid use, and RBC folate status. The majority of pregnant women (77%) reported use of a supplement in the previous 30 d, most frequently a multivitamin/mineral containing folic acid (mean 817 µg/d) and iron (48 mg/d). Approximately 55–60% of women in their first trimester reported taking a folic acid- or iron-containing supplement compared with 76–78% in their second trimester and 89% in their third trimester. RBC folate was lowest in the first trimester and differed by supplement use across all trimesters. Median RBC folate was 1628 nmol/L among users and 1041 nmol/L among nonusers. Among all pregnant women, median RBC folate increased with trimester (1256 nmol/L in the first, 1527 mmol/L in the second, and 1773 nmol/L in the third). Given the role of folic acid in the prevention of neural tube defects, it is notable that supplement use and median RBC folate was lowest in the first trimester of pregnancy, with 55% of women taking a supplement containing folic acid. Future research is needed to determine the reasons for low compliance with supplement recommendations, particularly folic acid, in early pregnancy.

FIGURE 5.4   InfoTrac printout with abstract.

CHECKLIST

Using Databases

Library databases are the most effective way to locate and access scholarly journal articles. If you can, visit your library for a tutorial on using databases. Use the following steps to find articles in databases.

1. **Go to your library home page and find the links to the databases.**

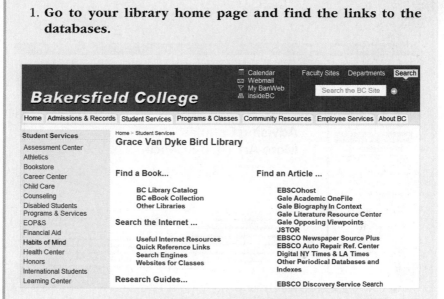

Every library's home page is different, but you can usually find a section that will link you to the database collections.

2. **Select a database and search by keyword for articles on your topic.**

A keyword search for "gender and communication" results in a list of articles like the one above. From your results list, you can preview article titles and publication information to select articles that look promising for your topic.

3. Locate the full text of the articles you need.

By clicking on the "PDF Full Text" link on the search results page, you can download the full text of this article. If the full text is not available online, you will need to copy the title and publication information and find the printed article in your library stacks.

Be sure to record the author, title, and publication information for your source, as well as the database you used to retrieve it. You'll need that information later for your works cited page. See pages 178–180 for information about citing sources retrieved from databases.

RESEARCH TIP

Paraphrasing a Passage to Avoid Plagiarism

A paraphrase requires you to restate in your own words the thought, meaning, and attitude of someone else. With interpretation, you act as a bridge between the source and the reader as you capture the wisdom of the source in approximately the same number of words.

Depending on the expertise of your audience, you might paraphrase passages like this one:

> This issue is concerned with clinical pharmacology of the tumescent technique for local anesthesia using large volumes of very dilute lidocaine and epinephrine. The tumescent technique produces profound local anesthesia of the skin and subcutaneous fat that lasts for many hours.
>
> —From **http://www.liposuction.com**

In the paraphrase below, notice how the writer uses everyday terms and places the technical words within parentheses. You can reverse this style as follows: "the use of lidocaine (a local anesthesia)."

The tumescent technique for liposuction is the use of a local anesthesia (lidocaine) and a constrictor of blood vessels (epinephrine). Injected into fatty tissue, the two drugs provide a local anesthesia for both the patient's skin and the underlying tissue to be withdrawn (www.liposuction.com).

This paraphrase shows how to recognize the source in a parenthetical citation, a technique that works well when you are citing from a work that does not identify the author.

Finding Indexes by Topic in the Appendix

The Appendix in this textbook, pages 375–382, lists many indexes to periodical articles. The list is organized by topic, so you can find the best references for your field. Shown below are three of the entries for music:

Bibliographic Guide to Music. Boston: Hall, 1976–present. Annually. This reference work provides an excellent subject index to almost every topic in the field of music. It will give you the bibliographic data to several articles on most topics in the field.

Music Index. Warren, MI: Information Coordinators, 1949–date. This reference work indexes music journals such as *American Music Teacher, Choral Journal, Journal of Band Research,* and *Journal of Music Therapy.*

RILM Abstracts of Music Literature. Online and in print. This massive collection provides you with brief descriptions to help you in selecting appropriate works for your bibliography.

Readers' Guide to Periodical Literature

The *Readers' Guide to Periodical Literature* (online and in print) indexes important reading for the early stages of research in magazines such as:

American Scholar	*Foreign Affairs*	*Psychology Today*
Astronomy	*Health*	*Scientific Review*
Business Week	*Oceans*	*Science Digest*
Earth Science	*Physics Today*	*Technology Review*

Social Sciences Index

The *Social Sciences Index* (online and in print) indexes journal articles for 263 periodicals in these fields:

Anthropology	Geography	Political science
Economics	Law and criminology	Psychology
Environmental science	Medical science	Sociology

Humanities Index

The *Humanities Index* (online and in print) catalogs 260 publications in several fields:

Archeology	Folklore	Performing arts
Classical studies	History	Philosophy
Language and literature	Literary	Religion
area studies	Political criticism	Theology

Other Indexes

Other indexes of importance include:

Applied Science and Technology Index for articles in chemistry, engineering, computer science, electronics, geology, mathematics, photography, physics, and related fields.

Biological and Agricultural Index for articles in biology, zoology, botany, agriculture, and related fields.

Business Periodicals Index for articles in business, marketing, accounting, advertising, and related fields.

Education Index for articles in education, physical education, and related fields.

In addition to these major indexes, you should examine the reference work for your topic as listed in the Appendix of this book, pages 375–382.

Searching for an Index to Abstracts

An abstract is a brief description of an article, usually written by the author. An index to abstracts can accelerate your work by allowing you to read the abstract before you assume the task of locating and reading the entire work. You may find them at the electronic book catalog by entering the keyword "abstracts," which will produce a list with great variety. It will look something like this:

show detail	Abstracts of current studies
show detail	Dissertation abstracts international

1 — DT: Article

2 — TI: Methamphetamine Laboratories: The Geography of Drug Production

3 — AU: Weisheit, Ralph A. and L. Edward Wells

4 — SO: Western Criminology Review; 11(2): 9–26. 17p. 5 figures/ 3 tables

5 — IS: 1096-4886

6 — AB: There has been considerable public concern and legislative activity surrounding the issue of domestic methamphetamine production. What has not been extensively examined is the broader context within which domestic methamphetamine production takes place. This study utilizes geographic location data on 14,448 seized methamphetamine laboratories to document the association between the presence of methamphetamine labs and economic factors, social factors, and crime. The study shows that laboratory seizures spiked upward immediately prior to the implementation of legislation restricting access to methamphetamine precursor drugs and declined immediately after the legislation was passed, remaining well below pre-regulation levels. However, more than a third of U.S. counties reported laboratory seizures after strict precursor regulations were in place, suggesting that while the problem of local methamphetamine lab production was diminished by precursor regulation, it was not eliminated. The study also examined factors most strongly associated with the seizure of methamphetamine laboratories at the county level. Economic instability was not a good predictor of the presence of methamphetamine labs, nor were spatial or geographic variables. In general, counties with higher lab seizure rates tended to have a predominantly White, English-speaking population with a substantial representation of evangelical churches. Methamphetamine laboratory counties also tended to have employment based on manufacturing, a larger farm population, single-female-headed households, a higher than average property crime rate, be more racially segregated, have a population that moved into the household within the past year, and have a higher percent of occupied housing. In sum, neither traditional measures of social disorganization nor measures of civic engagement consistently predict the presence of methamphetamine labs.

FIGURE 5.5   Sample entry from an abstract index search.

(1) DT = document type; (2) TI = title of the article; (3) AU = author; (4) SO = source; (5) IS = ISSN number; (6) AB = abstract of the article.

| show detail | Social work abstracts |
| show detail | Women studies abstracts |

A more specific keyword search will include your discipline, such as "psychology abstracts." This will produce a reference, most likely, to PsycINFO, the searchable database produced by the American Psychological Association. It will give you the type of entry shown in Figure 5.5.

Searching for Abstracts of Dissertations

You may also want to examine the abstracts to the dissertations of graduate students in *Dissertation Abstracts International,* which you can access from the Internet. For example, an online search of *ProQuest Dissertations & Theses* for 2011–2012 listed an entry shown in Figure 5.6 under the heading "American Novelists."

You may cite the abstract in your paper, but inform your readers you are citing from the abstract, not the actual dissertation.

American Novelists

1 —— From Hawthorne to History: The Mythologizing of John Endecott.
2 —— By Abigail F. Davis, PhD
3 —— UNIVERSITY OF MINNESOTA, 2011, 253 pages —— 4
5 —— AAT 543221

FIGURE 5.6   Example of an online search of *ProQuest Digital Dissertations.*
(1) Title of dissertation, (2) author, (3) affiliation, (4) number of pages, (5) publication number.

5e   Searching for a Biography

When you want to examine the life of a person, you will find biographies in both books and articles and in print versions as well electronic versions. The electronic book catalog will usually provide multiple sources if you enter the keywords "biography + index."

show detail	Literary Biography
show detail	Index to Artistic Biography
show detail	Biography Index

Several electronic indexes, like InfoTrac and ProQuest, will provide you with abstracts to some biographies and even full-text biographies, such as these:

Biography Reference Bank
Current Biography Illustrated
Wilson Biographies Plus Illustrated

Other indexes, in print and online, also have value for finding biographies.

Biography Index

The *Biography Index* in its printed form has long been a starting point for studies of famous persons. It will lead you to biographical information for people of all lands. See Figure 5.7 for the information provided in a biography search.

Summit, Pat, 1952–Present, Women's basketball coach
> Summit, Pat. *Sum It Up: One Thousand and Ninety-Eight Victories, a Couple of Irrelevant Losses, and a Life in Perspective.* New York: Crown. 2013.

■ **FIGURE 5.7** From *Biography Index.*

Current Biography Yearbook

Current Biography Yearbook provides a biographical sketch of important people. Most articles are three to four pages in length, and they include references to other sources at the end. It is current, thorough, and international in scope.

Contemporary Authors

Contemporary Authors provides a biographical guide for current writers in fiction, nonfiction, poetry, journalism, drama, motion pictures, television, and a few other fields. It provides a thorough overview of most contemporary writers, giving a list of writings, biographical facts (including a current address and agent), sidelights, and, in many cases, an interview by the editors of the guide with the author. Most entries include a bibliography of additional sources about the writer.

Dictionary of Literary Biography

The *Dictionary of Literary Biography* provides profiles of thousands of writers in more than 100 volumes under such titles as these:

American Humorists, 1800–1950
Victorian Novelists after 1885
American Newspaper Journalists, 1926–1950

5f Searching for Articles in Newspaper Indexes

Electronic networks enable you to find newspaper articles from across the nation. Your library may have a newspaper search engine on its network, or you may need to go to the Internet to access newspapers.com. It will take you quickly to more than 800 newspapers, from the *Aspen Times* to the *Carbondale Valley Journal.* In most cases, online newspapers have their own internal search engine that enables you to examine articles from

[🔍] More on newspapers on the Internet, 4e, pages 57–59.
the archives. See pages 57–59 for a full discussion and image of a hometown newspaper. In addition, several indexes are helpful:

Christian Science Monitor Historic Archive
The New York Times Index
London Times Index
Wall Street Journal Index

5g   Searching Special Subject Directories

Also important for developing a working bibliography are databases that feature articles on a common topic. For example, ProQuest provides archives of sources such as newspapers, periodicals, dissertations, and other aggregated databases. Content is accessed most commonly through library Internet gateways, with navigation through such search platforms as eLibrary, CultureGrams, or SIRS.

Social Issues Resources Series (SIRS)

Social Issues Resources Series (SIRS) collects articles on special topics and reprints them as one unit on a special subject, such as the influence of social media, prayer in schools, or pollution. With *SIRS,* you will have ten or twelve articles readily available. Figure 5.8 shows one of numerous sources on the topic of online privacy and social networking, as listed in *SIRS Researcher:*

"Toward of historical Sociology of Social Situations"

Diehl, David and Daniel McFarland.

American Journal of Sociology Vol. 115, No. 6

May 2010; Lexile Score: <u>1370</u>; 22K, SIRS Researcher

Summary: In recent years there has been a growing call to historicize sociology by paying more attention to the contextual importance of time and place as well as to issues of process and contingency. Meeting this goal requires bringing historical sociology and interactionism into greater conversation via a historical theory of social situations. Toward this end, the authors of this article draw on Erving Goffman's work in Frame Analysis to conceptualize experience in social situations as grounded in multilayered cognitive frames and to demonstrate how such a framework helps illuminate historical changes in situated interaction.

FIGURE 5.8   **An annotated bibliography from *THE SIRS Researcher*.**

The CQ Researcher

The CQ Researcher will have categorized articles, like *SIRS,* devoted to one topic, such as "Energy and the Environment." It will examine central issues on the topic, give background information, show a chronology of important events or processes, express an outlook, and provide an annotated bibliography. In one place you have material worthy of quotation and paraphrase as well as a list of additional sources.

> **HINT:** For the correct citation forms to articles found on ProQuest or *The CQ Researcher,* See section 14c, pages 262–264.

5h Searching for Government Documents

All branches of the government publish massive amounts of material. Many of these documents have great value for researchers, so investigate the following source if your topic is one that government agencies might have investigated:

GPOAccess is a site that will take you to the files of the Government Printing Office. The database list includes *Congressional Bills, Congressional Record, Economic Indicators, Public Laws,* the U.S. Constitution, and much more. Following is a Works Cited entry for a report from *GPO Access,* a catalog of U.S. government publication:

```
United States. Congress. House. Subcommittee on Economic Growth,

     Job Creation and Regulatory Affairs. "Unintended Consequences:

     Is Government Effectively Addressing the Unemployment Crisis."

     Hearing. 113th Cong., 1st sess. S Hearing 113-2. Washington: GPO,

     2013. Print.
```

Other works that provide valuable information on matters of the government are:

> *Monthly Catalog of the United State Government Publications.* The printed version of GPO.
> *Public Affairs Information Service Bulletin (PAIS),* online and in print. This work indexes articles and documents published by miscellaneous organizations. It's a good place to start because of its excellent index.
> *Congressional Record,* online and in print. This daily publication features Senate and House bills, documents, and committee reports.
> *Public Papers of the Presidents of the United States,* online and in print. This work is a publication of the Executive Branch, which includes not only the president but also all members of the cabinet and various agencies.

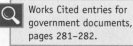
Works Cited entries for government documents, pages 281–282.

5i Searching for Essays within Books

Some essays get lost in collections and anthologies. You can find essays listed by subject on this database at your library:

Essay and General Literature Index

This reference work helps you find essays hidden in anthologies. It indexes material of both a biographical and a critical nature:

King, Martin Luther, 1929–1968
  Raboteau, A. J. Martin Luther King and the tradition of black religious protest. (*In* Religion and the life of the nation; ed. by R. A. Sherrill, p. 46–65).

Your electronic book catalog will give you the call number to Sherrill's book.

YOUR RESEARCH PROJECT

1. If you have not already done so with an orientation group, take the time to stroll through your library. Identify its various sections, special features, and the types of information available there.

2. At the library, sit down at one of the computer terminals and investigate its options. Make up a topic for the moment and search for books or articles at the terminal. Try to find an abstract or a full-text article and then print it.

3. Go to the reference desk and ask the librarian for a specialized bibliography on your topic—that is, say something like this: "Do you have a specialized bibliography on global warming?"

4. To test the resources of the library, go in search of information about the day you were born. Don't limit yourself to major events of the day; go also in search of hometown news. Look at the advertisements to see what people were wearing and what things cost back then.

The Library Search

When you start your research on a topic, you will need to switch between the computer terminals, the library stacks of books and periodicals, and the printed bibliographies and indexes, according to the resources in your library. Start, perhaps, with the sources on this list.

To find books:
    Electronic book catalog with keyword
    Online with keywords "bibliographies + [your discipline]"

To find periodical articles:
    An electronic database with a keyword
    Online with keywords "indexes + [your discipline]"
    The Wilson indexes

To find an abstract:
    Online with keywords "abstracts + [your discipline]"

To find biographies in books and periodicals:
    Online with keywords "biography + indexes"
    Biography Index, online or in print

To find newspaper articles:
    Internet at http://www.newspapers.com
    Electronic database under keyword "newspapers"

To find pamphlet files:
    Online with the library's network to *SIRS* and *The CQ Researcher*

To find government documents:
    Internet access to *GPOAccess*

To find essays within books:
    Essay and General Literature Index, online or in print

6 Conducting Field Research

Chapter 6 Clear Targets

Each discipline has different expectations in its methods of inquiry and presentation. This chapter provides a variety of field research techniques:

- Investigating local sources
- Investigating government documents
- Researching within a discipline
- Developing a survey or questionnaire
- Conducting experiments, tests, and observation

The human species is distinguished by its ability to examine the world systematically and to create pioneers for the millennium, such as computer technicians, microsurgeons, and nuclear engineers. Through field research you may become one of them.

Field research refers, in general, to any studies conducted outside the library, such as digging at an archeology site, measuring a sinkhole fault, observing student behavior at a parking lot, or surveying a selected group with a questionnaire. This type of work may provide valuable information, and you should consider it as a worthy ingredient in your research plans. Therefore, converse with people by letter or e-mail, and if time permits it, conduct personal one-on-one interviews or use a questionnaire. Watch television specials, visit the courthouse archives, and conduct research by observation under the guidance of an instructor (see pages 90–93).

Set up your field research in an objective manner in order to control subjective feelings. Although you may have strong personal feelings about your topic, look objectively for viable evidence. All writers get deeply involved in their subject, but they must couple that involvement with the skill of detachment. What are the facts? What conclusions do they support? Conduct the test, get results, and then discuss their implications.

6a   Investigating Local Sources

Interviewing Knowledgeable People

Talk to people who have experience with your subject. Personal interviews can elicit valuable in-depth information. Interviews provide information that few others will have. Look to organizations for knowledgeable experts. For example, if writing on folklore, you might contact the county historian, a senior citizens' organization, or the local historical society. If necessary, post a notice soliciting help: "I am writing a study of local folklore. Wanted: People who have a knowledge of regional tales." Another way to accomplish this task is to join an e-mail discussion group to invite commentary from a group interested in the same topic (see pages 18–19 for more details). Try using the discussion board if yours is an online class. For accuracy, save files or record the interview (with permission of the person interviewed, of course). When finished, make a bibliography entry just as you would for a book:

> Sedaris, Pamela. Message to the author. 13 Mar. 2014. E-mail.

Note: For a paper written in APA style, you should document an e-mail interview in the text only, not in the references. To maintain the anonymity of the source, write this in-text citation: (Anonymous interview, April 6, 2014). The APA style requires that you omit from the References items that are not retrievable, such as e-mail messages, interviews, personal letters, memos, or private papers.

In addition to the checklist of guidelines listed, on page 91, you need to remember several vital matters. First, be prepared for interviews, which means that you know your interviewee's professional background and that you have a set of pertinent questions, with followups. Second, keep your focus on the principal issue. Subjects may want to wander toward tangential ideas, so you need to bring them back to the central subject with an appropriate question. Third, maintain an ethical demeanor that honors with accuracy the statements of the subject.

Student Valerie Nesbitt-Hall researched the role of matching services and chat rooms in promoting online romance. Because she was acquainted with a couple that had met online and eventually married, she decided to request an interview—online, of course. These were her questions and, in brief form, the responses of the subjects, Stephen of Scotland and Jennifer of the United States.

1. **When did you first meet online?** Answer: *September of 2006*
2. **What prompted you to try an online matching service?** Answer: *We didn't really try online matching services. We chatted in a chat room, became friends there, and met in person later.*

3. **Who initiated the first contact?** Answer: *Stephen initiated the first online chat.*

4. **How long into the relationship did you correspond by e-mail before one of you gave an address and/or phone number? Who did it first, Steve or Jennifer?** Answer: *We chatted and corresponded by e-mail for nine months before Jennifer shared her phone number.*

5. **How long into the relationship did you go before sharing photographs?** Answer: *At nine months we began to share written correspondence and photographs.*

6. **Who initiated the first meeting in person? Where did you meet? How long were you into the relationship before you met in person?** Answer: *Stephen first requested the meeting, and Jennifer flew from the States to Glasgow, Scotland. This was about a year into the relationship.*

7. **How much time elapsed between your first online meeting and your marriage?** Answer: *One and a half years after our first chat, we were married.*

8. **Did you feel that online romance enabled you to prearrange things and protect your privacy before meeting in person?** Answer: *Yes. We were cautious and at times reluctant to continue, but we kept coming back to each other, online, until we knew the other well enough to trust in the relationship. Once we got offline into what we might call real-time dating, the love blossomed quickly.*

9. **Has the difference in nationalities been a problem?** Answer: *Yes, but only in relation to sorting out immigration matters. Also, Jennifer's parents were concerned that she was going to another country to see someone she had never met.*

10. **Finally, would you recommend online matching services or chat rooms to others who are seeking mates?** Answer: *Yes, in the right circumstances. We were lucky; others might not be.*

Writing Letters and Corresponding by E-mail

Correspondence provides a written record of research. As you would in an interview, ask pointed questions so correspondents respond directly to your central issues. Tell the person who you are, what you are attempting to do, and why you have chosen to write to this particular person or set of persons. If germane, explain why you have chosen this topic and what qualifies you to write about it.

Make your message a fairly specific request for a minimum amount of information. It should not require an expansive reply. If you use a quotation from the reply, provide a bibliography entry on the Works Cited page:

Casasola, Evelyn. Principal of Parkview Elementary School, Topeka, KS.

Message to the author. 5 Apr. 2014. E-mail.

RESEARCH TIP

Creating a Summary from Notes

The summary note describes the source material with quick, concise writing that pinpoints key facts and data. If its information is needed, you can rewrite it later in a clear, appropriate prose style, and if necessary, return to the source for revision. Use summary notes to preserve statistics, recall an interesting position, or record material. The following summary condenses the answers from the ten interview questions used by Valerie Nesbitt-Hall into a quick synopsis:

> *Research uncovered a match that resulted in marriage. The two subjects, Jennifer and Stephen, were interviewed on the matter of cyber romance. What follows is a brief summary of the interview, which is on file. The couple met online in September of 2006 in a chat room, not on a matching service. Stephen initiated the first contact, and they chatted anonymously for nine months before Jennifer initiated an exchange of phone numbers, addresses, and photographs. Stephen initiated the first meeting in person after 11 months, inviting Jennifer to travel from the United States to Glasgow, Scotland. Seven months later they married; it was 1.5 years from the time they met at the Internet newsgroup.*

Reading Personal Papers

Search out letters, diaries, manuscripts, family histories, and other personal materials that might contribute to your study. The city library may house private collections, and the city librarian can usually help you contact the county historian and other private citizens who have important documents. Obviously, handling private papers must be done with the utmost decorum and care. Again, make a bibliography entry for such materials:

Joplin, Lester. "Notes on my visits to the Robert Penn Warren family home and museum in Guthrie, Kentucky." October 13, 2013. MS. Nashville.

Attending Lectures and Public Addresses

Watch bulletin boards and the newspaper for featured speakers who might visit your campus. When you attend a lecture, take careful notes and, if it is available, request a copy of the lecture or speech. Remember, too, that many lectures, reproduced on video, will be available in the library or in departmental files. Always make a bibliography entry for any words or ideas you use.

Petty-Rathbone, Virginia. "Edgar Allan Poe and the Image of Ulalume."

Heard Library, Vanderbilt U., Nashville. 25 Jan. 2014. Address.

6b Investigating Government Documents

Local Government

Visit the courthouse or county clerk's office, where you can find facts on elections, censuses, marriages, births, and deaths. These archives include wills, tax rolls, military assignments, deeds to property, and much more.

State Government

Contact by phone or online a state office that relates to your research, such as Consumer Affairs (general information), the Public Service Commission (which regulates public utilities such as the telephone company), and the Department of Human Services (which administers social and welfare services). The agencies may vary by name in your state. Remember, too, that the state will have an archival storehouse whose records are available for public review.

Federal Government

The Government Printing Office (GPO) provides free access to a wealth of information produced by the federal government. Begin searching these resources at http://www.gpo.gov/. In addition, you can gain access to the National Archives Building in Washington, DC, or to one of the regional branches in Atlanta, Boston, Chicago, Denver, Fort Worth, Kansas City, Los Angeles, New York, Philadelphia, and Seattle. Their archives contain court records and government documents, which you can review in two books: *Guide to the National Archives of the United States* and *Select List of Publications of the National Archives and Record Service* (see http://www.archives.gov). You can view some documents on microfilm if you consult the *Catalog of National Archives Microfilm Publications*. One researcher, for example, found the information shown in Figure 6.1 while looking for information on the Articles of Confederation.

The researcher also made a bibliography entry to record the source of this information.

The Charters of Freedom. "The First Constitution—The Articles of

Confederation." Web. 12 Nov. 2013.

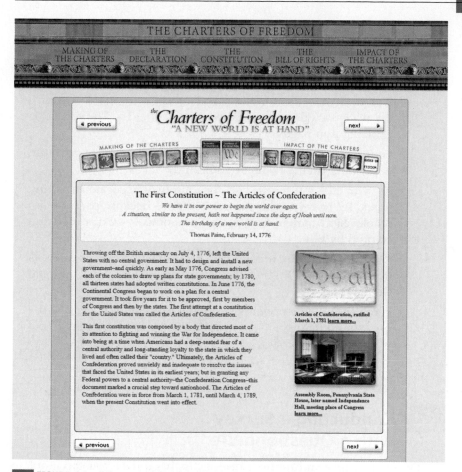

FIGURE 6.1 "Charters of Freedom" from the National Archives.

6c Examining Audiovisual Materials, Television, and Radio

Important data can be found in audiovisual materials: films, filmstrips, music, CDs, slides, audio cassettes, video cassettes, and DVDs. You will find these sources both on and off campus. Consult such guides as *Educators Guide* (film, filmstrips, and tapes), *Media Review Digest* (nonprint materials), *Video Source Book* (video catalog), *The Film File,* and *International Index to Recorded Poetry.* Television, with its many educational channels, such as The History Channel, offers invaluable data. With a DVR or VCR, you can record a program for detailed examination. Again, write bibliography entries for any materials that contribute to your paper:

Stout, Kristie Lu. "Experiencing a Potential Cyber Attack." Interview. CNN.

20 Mar. 2013. Television.

CHECKLIST

Using Media Sources

- Watch closely the opening and closing credits to capture the necessary data for your Works Cited entry. The format is explained on pages 282–288.

- Your citations may refer to a performer, director, or narrator, depending on the focus of your study.

- As with live interviews, be scrupulously accurate in taking notes. Try to write with direct quotations because paraphrases of television commentary can unintentionally be distorted and colored by bias.

- Consult online documentaries and other resources such as those found at PBS.org, the Discovery Channel, or National Geographic TV.

- Plan carefully the review of a media presentation, even to the point of preparing a list of questions or a set of criteria to help with your judgment.

6d Conducting a Survey with a Questionnaire

Questionnaires can produce current, firsthand data you can tabulate and analyze. Of course, to achieve meaningful results, you must survey a random sample—that is, each one must represent the whole population in terms of age, sex, race, education, income, residence, and other factors. Various degrees of bias can creep into the questionnaire unless you remain objective. Thus, use the formal survey only when you are experienced with tests and measurements as well as with statistical analysis or when you have an instructor who will help you with the instrument.

Online surveys have become an essential tool for a variety of research fields, including social and official statistics inquiries. Internet surveys offer capabilities beyond those available for any other type of self-administered questionnaire. Because the entire data collection period is significantly shortened, online surveys can collect and process data in a timely manner. Moreover, questions with long lists of answer choices can be used to provide immediate coding of answers to certain questions that are usually asked in an open-ended fashion in paper questionnaires. Popular online survey sites include Zoomerang, SurveyMonkey, Kwik-Surveys, and QuestionPro, among others. Since online surveys can be tailored to the situation, ease of use is enhanced for respondents as well

Interviews, Letters, Private Papers, Courthouse Documents

- Set up appointments in advance.
- Consult with experienced persons. If possible, talk to several people in order to weigh their different opinions. Telephone and e-mail interviews are acceptable.
- Be courteous and on time for interviews.
- Be prepared in advance with a set of focused, pertinent questions for initiating and conducting the interview.
- Handle private and public papers with great care.
- For accuracy, record the interview with a digital recorder (with permission of the person interviewed, of course).
- Double-check direct quotations with the interviewee or the tape.
- Get permission before citing a person by name or quoting his or her exact words.
- Send helpful people a copy of your report, along with a thank-you note.

as the compiler of the information. Provide a Works Cited entry for your survey information:

> Sanderson, Micah. "Study and Class Time vs. Leisure Time." Survey.
>
> Emporia, KS: Emporia State U. *QuestionPro*. Web. 11 Nov. 2013.

Be advised that most schools have a Human Subjects Committee that sets guidelines, draws up consent forms, and requires anonymity of participants for information gathering that might be intrusive. An informal survey gathered in the hallways of campus buildings lacks credibility in the research paper. If you build a table or graph from the results, see "Using Visuals Effectively in a Research Essay," pages 168–170, for examples and instructions. Label your survey in the Works Cited entry:

> Castor, Diego, and Carmen Aramide. "Child Care Arrangements of Parents
>
> Who Attend College." Questionnaire. Coeur d'Alene, Idaho: North
>
> Idaho College, 2014. Print.

Unlike interview questions (see pages 85–86), which are meant to elicit a response from one person or a couple, questionnaires are designed for multiple responses from many people, from twenty-five to thirty up to several thousand. Design them for ease of tabulation with results you can arrange in graphs and charts.

6e Conducting Experiments, Tests, and Observation

Empirical research, usually performed in a laboratory, can determine why and how things exist, function, or interact. Your paper will explain your methods and findings in pursuit of a hypothesis (your thesis). An experiment thereby becomes primary evidence for your paper.

Observation is field research that occurs outside the lab—"in the field"—which might be a child care center, a movie theater, a parking lot, or the counter of a fast-food restaurant. The field is anywhere you can observe, count, and record behavior, patterns, or systems. It might also include observing and testing the water in a stream, the growth of certain wildflowers, or the nesting patterns of deer.

Most experiments and observations begin with a *hypothesis,* which is similar to a thesis statement (see pages 24–27). The hypothesis is a statement assumed to be true for the purpose of investigation. *Hummingbirds live as extended families governed by a patriarch* is a hypothesis needing data to prove its validity. *The majority of people will not correct the poor grammar of a speaker* is a hypothesis that needs testing and observation to prove its validity.

However, you can begin observation without a hypothesis and let the results lead you to conclusions. Assignment 1, page 93, asks you to conduct a double-entry observation for one week and to write a short reflection about what you learned by keeping the field notes. This could be your introduction to field research.

CHECKLIST

Conducting a Survey

- Keep the questionnaire short, clear, and focused on your topic.
- Write unbiased questions. Let your professor review the instrument before using it.
- Design a quick response to a scale (Choose A, B, or C), to a ranking (first choice, second choice, and so on), or to fill in the blanks.
- Arrange for an easy return of the questionnaire, even to the point of providing a self-addressed, stamped envelope.
- Retain e-mail responses until the project is complete.
- Provide a sample questionnaire and your tabulations in an appendix.
- Tabulate the results objectively. Even negative results that deny your hypothesis have value.

Conducting an Experiment or Observation

- Express a clear hypothesis.
- Select the proper design for the study—lab experiment, observation, or the collection of raw data in the field.
- Include a review of the literature, if appropriate.
- Keep careful records and accurate data.
- Don't let your expectations influence the results.
- Maintain respect for human and animal subjects. In that regard, you may find it necessary to get approval for your research from a governing board. Read your college's rules and regulations on research that requires the use of humans and animals.

Generally, a report on an experiment or observation follows an expected format featuring four distinct parts: introduction, method, results, discussion. Understanding these elements will help you design your survey. Consult section 15e, "Formatting an APA Paper," for detailed guidelines for a report of empirical research or a theoretical paper.

YOUR RESEARCH PROJECT

1. Select an event or object from nature to observe daily for one week. Record field notes in a double-entry format by using the left side of the page to record and the right side of the page to comment and reflect on what you have observed. Afterward, write a brief paragraph discussing your findings.

Record:

Day 1
10-minute session at window, three hummingbirds fighting over the feeder

Day 2
10-minute session at window, saw eight single hummingbirds and one guarding feeder by chasing others away

Response:

Is the male chasing away the female, or is the female the aggressor?

I did some research, and the red-throated male is the one that's aggressive.

2. Look carefully at your subject to determine if research outside the library will be helpful for your project. If so, what kind of research: correspondence? local records? the news media? a questionnaire? an observation or experiment?

3. Work closely with your instructor to design an instrument that will affect your research and your findings. In fact, most instructors will want to examine any questionnaire that you will submit to others and will want to approve the design of your experiment or observation.

4. Follow university guidelines on testing with humans and animals.

7 Understanding and Avoiding Plagiarism

Chapter 7 Clear Targets

Intellectual property has value; hence, there are ethical standards for writing in an academic environment. The purpose of this chapter is to define and explore the ethics of research writing:

- Using sources to enhance your credibility
- Using sources to place a citation in its proper context
- Honoring property rights and crediting sources
- Properly documenting borrowed ideas and words
- Sharing credit and honoring it in collaborative projects
- Honoring and crediting sources in online classrooms
- Seeking permission to publish material on your website

By studying examples of careful documentation as well as plagiarism, we can discover the worst and best of research projects and citing borrowed material. Moreover, we must face the constant problem of the Internet, which makes it easy to copy and download material and paste it into a paper.

Plagiarism is defined as the act of claiming the words or ideas of another person as your own. Plagiarism is a serious violation of the ethical standards of academic writing, and most colleges and universities have strict penalties, including academic probation or expulsion, for students who are guilty of plagiarism. Most schools publish an official code of student conduct (sometimes called an academic integrity policy), and you should be familiar with these guidelines and how they apply to your research and writing.

Students who knowingly copy whole passages from outside sources into their work without documentation are committing the most blatant form of plagiarism. **Unintentional plagiarism,** however, is still a violation of academic integrity. Unacknowledged use of another person's sentences, phrases, or terminology is plagiarism, so provide a citation and use quotation marks to show exactly where you are drawing on others' work. Similarly, unacknowledged use of another person's ideas, research, or approach is also plagiarism, so write careful paraphrases. Review the checklist in Chapter 1 (page 5) for guidelines to help avoid unintentional plagiarism.

7a Using Sources to Enhance Your Credibility

Research is something you need to share, not hide. What some students fail to realize is that citing a source in their papers, even the short ones, signals something special and positive to your readers—that you have researched the topic, explored the literature about it, and have the talent to share it. Research writing exercises your critical thinking and your ability to collect ideas. You will discuss not only the subject matter, such as the degradation of prairie soil resources, but also the *literature* of the topic, such as articles from the Internet and current periodicals found at your library's databases. By announcing clearly the name of a source, you reveal the scope of your reading and thus your credibility, as in this student's notes:

> According to Mathers and Rodriguez, soil erosion reduces soil productivity through losses of nutrients, water storage capacity, and organic matter.
>
> Dumanski and others report that the estimated annual costs of erosion across the Great Plains "lie in the range of 155–177 million dollars in the case of water and between 213–271 million dollars in the case of wind" (208).
>
> "A new water era has begun," declares Postel (24). She indicates that the great prairies of the world will dry up, including America's. When Americans notice the drought, perhaps something will happen.

These notes, if transferred into the paper, will enable readers to identify the sources used. The notes give clear evidence of the writer's investigation into the subject, and they enhance the student's image as a researcher. You will get credit for displaying the sources properly. The opposite, plagiarism, presents the information as though it were your own:

> The great prairies of the world will soon dry up, and that includes America's, so a new water era has begun.

That sentence borrows too much. If in doubt, cite the source and place it within its proper context.

7b Placing Your Work in Its Proper Context

Your sources will reflect all kinds of special interests, even biases, so you need to position them within your paper as reliable sources. If you must use a biased or questionable source, tell your readers up front. For example, if you are writing about the dangers of cigarette smoke, you will find different opinions in a farmer's magazine, a health and fitness magazine, and a trade journal sponsored by a tobacco company. You owe it to your readers to scrutinize Internet sites closely and examine printed articles for:

- Special interests that might color the report
- Lack of credentials
- An unsponsored website
- Opinionated speculation, especially that found on blogs and in chat rooms
- Trade magazines that promote special interests
- Extremely liberal or extremely conservative positions

Here's an example: Norman Berkowitz, in researching articles on the world's water supply, found an article of interest but positioned it with a description of the source, as shown in this note

> *Earth First,* which describes itself as a radical environmental journal, features articles by an editorial staff that uses pseudonyms, such as Sky, Jade, Wedge, and Sprig. In his article "The End of Lake Powell," Sprig says, "The Colorado River may soon be unable to provide for the 25 million people plumbed into its system" (25). The danger, however, is not limited to Lake Powell. Sprig adds, "This overconsumption of water, compounded with a regional drought cycle of 25 years, could mean that Lake Powell and every other reservoir in the upper Colorado River area will be without water" (24–25).

Not only does Berkowitz recognize the source with name, quotation marks, and page numbers, he identifies the nature of the magazine for his readers.

7c Understanding Copyright

The principle behind copyright law is relatively simple. Copyright begins at the time a creative work is recorded in some tangible form—a written document, a drawing, a video recording. It does not depend on a legal registration with the copyright office in Washington, DC, although published works *are* usually registered. Thus, the moment you express yourself creatively on paper, in song, on a canvas, that expression is your intellectual property. You have a vested interest in any profits made from the distribution of the work. For that reason, songwriters, cartoonists, fiction writers, and other artists guard their work and do not want it disseminated without compensation.

Copyright law in the social networking context remains in flux because of rapid advancements and changes in online technology. The recent attempt to prevent the downloading of music onto private computers is a demonstration of this concern. The ease with which Internet users are able to distribute copyrighted information has dramatically increased the prevalence of copyright infringement. However, it is important for the student researcher to distinguish his or her classroom efforts from profit-generating websites.

Scholarly writing is not a profitmaking profession, but the writers certainly deserve recognition. We can give that recognition by providing in-text citations and bibliography entries. As a student, you may use copyrighted material in your research paper under a doctrine of *fair use* as described in the U.S. Code, which says:

> The fair use of a copyrighted work . . . for purposes such as criticism, comment, news reporting, teaching (including multiple copies for classroom use), scholarship, or research is not an infringement of copyright.

Thus, as long as you borrow for educational purposes, such as a paper to be read by your instructor, you should not be concerned. Just give the source the proper recognition and documentation, as explained next in section 7d. However, if you decide to *publish* your research paper on a website, then new considerations come into play (see section 7g, "Seeking Permission to Publish Material on Your Website").

7d Avoiding Plagiarism

There are a number of steps you can take to avoid plagiarizing. First, develop personal notes full of your own ideas on a topic. Discover how you feel about the issue. Then, rather than copy sources one after another onto your pages of text, try to express your own ideas while synthesizing the ideas of the authorities by using summary, paraphrase, or direct quotation, which are explained fully on pages 136–148. Rethink and reconsider ideas gathered during your reading, make meaningful connections, and, when you refer to the ideas or exact words of a source—as you inevitably will—give the other writer full credit.

To repeat, *plagiarism* is offering the words or ideas of another person as one's own. Major violations, which can bring failure in the course or expulsion from school, are:

- The use of another student's work
- The purchase of a "canned" research paper
- Copying whole passages into a paper without documentation
- Copying a key, well-worded phrase into a paper without documentation
- Putting specific ideas of others into your own words without documentation
- Inadequate or missing citation

- Missing quotation marks
- Incomplete or missing Works Cited entry

Whether deliberate or not, these instances all constitute forms of plagiarism.

Unintentional plagiarism is often a result of carelessness. For example:

- The writer fails to enclose quoted material within quotation marks, yet he or she provides an in-text citation with name and page number.
- The writer's paraphrase never quite becomes paraphrase—too much of the original is left intact—but he or she provides a full citation to name and page.

RESEARCH TIP

Documenting Borrowed Ideas and Words

As an academic writer, you must document fully any borrowed ideas and words. The academic citation—name, page number, and Works Cited entry—establishes two things beyond your reliability and credibility:

1. A clear trail for other researchers to follows if they also want to consult the source.
2. Information for other researchers who might need to replicate (*reproduce*) the project.

> *Vanessa Stillman states "a young teacher's ability to think about the future, to touch the future, and to develop life-long learners will eliminate first year jitters, worries, and pessimism."*

That's it—no page number and no reference to the title of the journal article. As a researcher, you must provide specific information so a reader could go in search of the full essay by Stillman. Following is a more complete use of source information:

> *Vanessa Stillman in her essay "Lessons for Future Educators" says "a young teacher's ability to think about the future, to touch the future, and to develop life-long learners will eliminate first year jitters, worries, and pessimism" (34).*

When you provide an academic citation, you have made it clear *whom* you have read, *how* you used it in your paper, and *where* others can find it.

> ### CHECKLIST
>
> ### *Documenting Your Sources*
>
> - Let the reader know when you begin borrowing from a source by introducing the quotation or paraphrase with the name of the authority.
> - Enclose within quotation marks all quoted materials—both key phrases and sentences.
> - Use an indented block for quotations of four lines or more.
> - Make certain that paraphrased material has been rewritten in your own style and language. The simple rearrangement of sentence patterns is unacceptable.
> - Provide specific in-text documentation for each borrowed item, but keep in mind that styles differ for MLA, APA, CSE, and CMS standards.
> - Provide a bibliography entry in the Works Cited for every source cited in the paper, including sources that appear only in content footnotes or an appendix.

In these situations, instructors must step in and help the beginning researcher, for although these cases are not flagrant instances of plagiarism, they can mar an otherwise fine piece of research.

Common Knowledge

You do not need to document information that is considered "common knowledge." But how do you know what is or is not common knowledge? Use the following criteria to determine whether or not a particular piece of information can be considered common knowledge.

1. **Local knowledge.** You and your reader might share local or regional knowledge on a subject. For example, if you attend Northern Illinois University, you need not cite the fact that Illinois is known as the Land of Lincoln, that Chicago is its largest city, or that Springfield is the capital city. Information of this sort requires *no* in-text citation, as shown in the following example.

   The flat rolling hills of Illinois form part of the great Midwestern

   Corn Belt. It stretches from its border with Wisconsin in the north to

   the Kentucky border in the south. Its political center is Springfield

   in the center of the state, but its industrial and commercial center

is Chicago, that great boisterous city camped on the shores of Lake
Michigan.

However, most writers would probably want to document the following passage:

Early Indian tribes on the plains called themselves *Illiniwek*
(which meant strong men), and French settlers pronounced the name
Illinois (Angle 44).

2. **Shared experiences.** Coursework and lectures will give you and
   members of your class a similar perspective on the subject. For example, students in a literary class studying African-American writers
   would share common information, so the student might write, without documentation, something like this:

   Langston Hughes, an important poet in the 1920s and 1930s,
   became a leader of the Harlem Renaissance, and like so many writers,
   he took great pride in his African-American heritage. He was not afraid
   to use the vernacular black dialect, and I would say that he is one of
   the fathers of today's rap music.

   If the student shifts to nongeneral information, then a citation is
   in order:

   Hughes has been described by Gerald Early as the major artistic
   link between the revolutionary poet Paul Lawrence Dunbar and the
   radical poet Amiri Baraka (246).

3. **Common Facts.** Common factual information that one might find in
   an almanac, fact book, or dictionary need not be cited. Here is an
   example:

   As an American "Founding Father," John Adams was a statesman,
   diplomat, and leading advocate of American independence from Great
   Britain. A lawyer and public figure in Boston, Adams was as a delegate
   from Massachusetts to the Continental Congress. He assisted Thomas
   Jefferson in drafting the Declaration of Independence in 1776 and
   served as its primary advocate in the Congress.

   The preceding passage needs no documentation; however, when
specific incidents are added, the more likely will be the need for documentation. Of course, provide a citation for analysis that goes beyond
common facts.

Common Knowledge That Does Not Need to Be Documented

- Do not document the source if an intelligent person would and should know the information, given the context of both writer and audience.
- Do not document terminology and information from a classroom environment that have become common knowledge to all members of the class.
- Do not document the source if you knew the information without reading it in an article or book.
- Do not document almanac-type information, such as date, place of birth, occupation, and so on.
- Do not document information that has become general knowledge by being reported repeatedly in many different sources (i.e., Michael Jordan holds several National Basketball Association [NBA] scoring records).

The achievements of John Adams have received greater recognition in modern times, though his contributions were not initially as celebrated as those of the other Founding Fathers (Hixson 86).

Correctly Borrowing from a Source

The next examples in MLA style demonstrate the differences between accurate use of a source and the dark shades of plagiarism. First is the original reference material; it is followed by the student versions that use the passage, along with discussions of their failures and merits.

Original Material:

Cyber attacks are the new normal. It seems each week a news outlet reports yet another high-profile data breach affecting businesses and consumers. Even so, many companies fail to realize the severity of the threat. In fact, a recent report from the Federation of European Risk Management Associations (FERMA) reveals that, surprisingly, only 16% of companies have designated a chief information security officer to oversee cyber-risk and privacy, and less than half have a strategy for communicating a cyber-risk incident to the public. The report, "Meeting the Cyber

Risk Challenge," reveals another disturbing statistic: Companies are failing to purchase coverage for a cyber-attack. Only 19% of respondents claimed they have purchased security and privacy insurance designed to cover exposures associated with information security and privacy issues. But preparing is about more than just insurance.

—Holbrook, Emily. "Cyber what?" *Risk Management,* (Mar. 2013): 45. *Academic OneFile.* Web. 26 Mar. 2013.

STUDENT VERSION A A case of rank plagiarism that is ethically and morally wrong:

> A recent report from the Federation of European Risk Management Associations (FERMA) reveals that, surprisingly, only 16% of companies have designated a chief information security officer to oversee cyber-risk and privacy, and less than half have a strategy for communicating a cyber-risk incident to the public. The report, "Meeting the Cyber Risk Challenge," reveals another disturbing statistic: Companies are failing to purchase coverage for a cyber-attack. Only 19% of respondents claimed they have purchased security and privacy insurance designed to cover exposures associated with information security and privacy issues. But preparing is about more than just insurance.

This passage reads well, and the unsuspecting reader will probably think so as well. However, the writer has borrowed almost the whole passage from Holbrook, so it is plagiarism of the first order. The writer implies to the reader that these sentences are an original creation when, in fact, the sentences are actually stolen from a source.

STUDENT VERSION B Plagiarism that steals the ideas directly from a source:

> Cyber attacks have become a normal occurrence in our society as data breaches affecting businesses and consumers occur each week. Far too few companies have a chief information security officer to oversee cyber-risk and privacy; moreover, most have no plan or strategy for communicating a cyber-risk incident to the public.

This version borrows extensively from the original with paraphrasing and reworking key phrases and clauses. The writer has stolen the main ideas of the original without credit of any sort. The words might belong to the student writer, but the ideas belong to Holbrook.

STUDENT VERSION C Plagiarism that paraphrases improperly and offers a vague citation:

> As reported by multiple news outlets, cyber attacks in which a data breach affects businesses and consumers have become commonplace in modern society. Few companies realize the severity of the threat. Most companies do not have a designated chief information security officer to oversee cyber-risk and privacy, nor do they have a strategy for communicating a cyber-risk incident to the public (Holbrook 45).

This version is somewhat better. It provides a reference to Holbrook, but readers cannot know that the paraphrase contains far too much of Holbrook's language—words that should be enclosed within quotation marks. Also, the citation to Holbrook is ambiguous; when does the borrowing begin? The next version handles these matters in a better fashion.

STUDENT VERSION D An acceptable version with a proper citation to a block quotation:

> According to Emily Holbrook, "each week news outlets report yet another high-profile data breach affecting businesses and consumers" (45). Sadly, cyber attacks have become the norm in the new millennium:
>
> > A recent report from the Federation of European Risk Management Associations (FERMA) reveals that, surprisingly, only 16% of companies have designated a chief information security officer to oversee cyber-risk and privacy, and less than half have a strategy for communicating a cyber-risk incident to the public.
> > (Holbrook 45)

This version represents a satisfactory handling of the source material. The source is acknowledged at the outset of the borrowing, the passage has been quoted as a block of material, and a page citation closes the material. Let's suppose, however, that the writer does not want to quote an entire passage. The following example shows a paraphrased version.

STUDENT VERSION E An acceptable version with a citation to the source:

> Cyber-risk attacks have become the norm in the new millennium. According to Emily Holbrook, editor of *Risk Management* magazine,

"Companies are failing to purchase coverage for a cyber-attack. Only 19% of respondents claimed they have purchased security and privacy insurance designed to cover exposures associated with information security and privacy issues" (45).

This version also represents a satisfactory handling of the source material. In this case, a direct quotation is employed, the author and the authority are acknowledged and credited, and an introduction presented in the student's own language precedes Holbrook's ideas.

7e Sharing Credit in Collaborative Projects

Joint authorship is seldom a problem in collaborative writing, especially if each member of the project understands his or her role. Normally, all members of the team receive equal credit. However, it might serve you well to predetermine certain issues with your peer group and the instructor:

- How will the project be judged and grades awarded?
- Will all members receive the same grade?
- Can a nonperformer be dismissed from the group?
- Should each member write a section of the work and everybody edit the whole?
- Should certain members write the draft and other members edit and publish it to the Web?
- Can the group work together via e-mail rather than meeting frequently for group sessions?

Resolving such issues at the beginning of a project can go a long way toward eliminating entanglements and disagreements later on. *Note*: Electronic publishing of your collaborative project on the Web raises other legal and ethical questions (see section 7g, pages 107–108).

7f Honoring and Crediting Sources in Online Classrooms

A continually growing trend in education is the Web-based course or online course via e-mail. In general, you should follow the fair use doctrine of printed sources (see pages 97–98)—that is, give proper credit and reproduce only limited portions of the original.

The rules are still emerging, and even faculty members are often in a quandary about how to transmit information. For educational purposes, the rules are pretty slack, and most publishers have made their texts or portions thereof available on the Web. Plus, the copyrights of many works have expired, are now in the public domain, and are therefore free. In addition, many magazines and newspapers have made online versions of their articles available for free.

CHECKLIST

Information That Must Be Documented

1. An original idea derived from a source, whether quoted or paraphrased. This next sentence requires an in-text citation and quotation marks around a key phrase:

   > Genetic engineering, by which a child's body shape and intellectual ability is predetermined, raises for one source "memories of Nazi attempts in eugenics" (Riddell 19).

2. Your summary of original ideas by a source:

   > Genetic engineering has been described as the rearrangement of the genetic structure in animals or in plants, which is a technique that takes a section of DNA and reattaches it to another section (Rosenthal 19–20).

3. Factual information that is not common knowledge within the context of the course:

   > Genetic engineering has its risks: A nonpathogenic organism might be converted into a pathogenic one or an undesirable trait might develop as a result of a mistake (Madigan 51).

4. Any exact wording copied from a source:

   > Kenneth Woodward asserts that genetic engineering is "a high-stakes moral rumble that involves billions of dollars and affects the future" (68).

What you send back and forth with classmates and the instructor(s) has little privacy and even less protection. When sharing electronic communication, abide by a few commonsense principles:

1. Credit sources in your online communications just as you would in a printed research paper, with some variations:
   • The author, creator, or webmaster of the site
   • The title of the electronic article
   • The title of the website
   • The date of publication on the Web

- The medium of publication (Web)
- The date you accessed the site

2. Download to your file only graphic images and text from sites that have specifically offered users the right to download them.
3. Non-free graphic images and text, especially an entire website, should be mentioned in your text, even paraphrased and quoted in a limited manner, but not downloaded into your file. Instead, link to them or point to them with URL addresses. In that way, your reader can find the material and count it as a supplement to your text.
4. Seek permission if you download substantive blocks of material. See section 7g if you wish to publish your work on the Web.
5. If in doubt, consult by e-mail with your instructor, the moderator of a listserv, or the author of an Internet site.

7g   Seeking Permission to Publish Material on Your Website

If you have your own home page and website, you might want to publish your research on the Web. However, the moment you do so, you are *publishing* the work and putting it into the public domain. That act carries responsibilities. In particular, the *fair use* doctrine of the U.S. Code refers to the personal educational purposes of your usage. When you load onto the Internet borrowed images, text, music, or artwork, you are making that intellectual property available to everybody all over the world.

Short quotations, a few graphics, and a small quantity of illustrations to support your argument are examples of fair use. Permission is needed, however, if the amount you borrow is substantial. The borrowing cannot affect the market for the original work, and you cannot misrepresent it in any way. The courts are still refining the law. For example, would your use of two comic strips related to your research topic be substantial? Yes, if you reproduce them in full. Would it affect the market for the comic strip? Perhaps. Follow these guidelines:

- Seek permission for copyrighted material you publish within your Web article. Most authors will grant you free permission. The problem is tracking down the copyright holder.
- If you make the attempt to get permission and if your motive for using the material is *not for profit,* it's unlikely you will have any problem with the copyright owner. The owner would have to prove that your use of the image or text caused him or her financial harm.
- You may publish without permission works that are in the public domain, such as a section of Hawthorne's *The Scarlet Letter* or a speech by the president from the White House.
- Document any and all sources that you feature on your website.

- If you provide hypertext links to other sites, you may need permission to do so. Some sites do not want their address clogged by inquiring students. However, right now the Internet rules on access are being freely interpreted.
- Be prepared for people to visit your website and even borrow from it. Decide beforehand how you will handle requests for use of your work, especially if it includes your creative efforts in poetry, art, music, or graphic design.

YOUR RESEARCH PROJECT

1. Begin now to maintain a systematic scrutiny of what you borrow from your sources. Remember that direct quotation reflects the voice of your source and that paraphrase reflects your voice. Just be certain, with paraphrase, that you don't borrow the exact wording of the original.

2. Look at your college bulletin and the student handbook. Do they say anything about plagiarism? Do they address the matter of copyright protection?

3. Consult your writing instructor whenever you have a question about your use of a source. Writing instructors at the freshman level are there to serve you and help you avoid plagiarising (among other responsibilities).

4. If you think you might publish your paper on the Web and if it contains substantial borrowing from a source, such as five or six cartoons from the *New Yorker* magazine, begin now to seek permission for reproducing the material. In your letter or e-mail, give your name, the name of your school, the subject of your research paper, the material you want to borrow, and how you will use it. You might copy or attach the page(s) of your paper in which the material appears.

8 Reading and Evaluating Sources

Chapter 8 Clear Targets

With your research and writing, you will enter the intellectual discussions found in numerous places, but questions will arise quickly during your reading:

- How do I find and evaluate the best, most appropriate sources?
- How can I evaluate a source by analyzing its parts or just part of a source?
- How do I respond to the source information?

One answer to all three questions is this: Be skeptical and cautious. Do not accept every printed word as being the truth. This chapter cuts to the heart of the matter:

- Finding and evaluating reliable sources
- Using a mix of primary and secondary sources
- Responding to the sources
- Preparing an annotated bibliography or review of literature

Constantly review and verify to your own satisfaction the words of your sources, especially in this age of electronic publication.

8a Finding Reliable Sources

Several resources are readily at hand to guide you in finding reliable sources.

Your instructors. Do not hesitate to ask your instructor for help in finding sources. Instructors know the field, know the best writers, and can provide a brief list to get you started. Sometimes instructors will even pull books from their office shelves to give you a starting point.

Librarians. Nobody knows the resources of the library like the professionals. They are evaluated on how well they meet your needs. If you ask for help, they will often walk into the stacks with you to find the appropriate reference books or relevant journal articles.

The library. The college library provides the scholarly sources—the best books, certainly, but also the appropriate databases and the important journals—in your field of study. As we discussed in Chapter 4, the library databases are grounded in scholarship and, in general, they are not available to the general public on the Web. You can access this information with your student identification. A public library may have, but seldom does have, the scholarly resources of an academic library.

The date. Try to use recent sources. A book may appear germane to your work, but if its copyright date is 1975, the content has probably been replaced by recent research and current developments. Scientific and technical topics *always* require up-to-date research. Learn to depend on monthly and quarterly journals as well as books.

Choices. An inverted pyramid shows you a progression from excellent sources to less reliable sources. The pyramid chart does not ask you to dismiss items at the bottom, but it indicates that sources at the top are generally more reliable and therefore preferred.

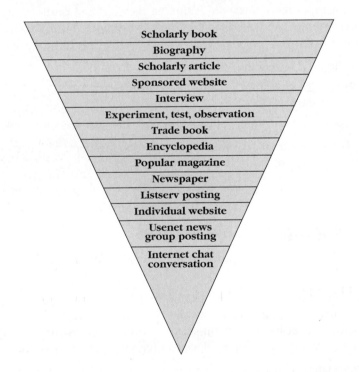

Scholarly Book

A college library is a repository for scholarly books—technical and scientific works, doctoral dissertations, publications of university presses, and textbooks. These sources offer in-depth discussions and careful documentation of the evidence.

A quick approach for reviewing a book is through an online database. American literature student Aurora Newberry used her library access to *Project Muse* to find a review about the southern author William Faulkner. Using the site's search mechanism, she found a listing and access link that took her to a book review by Joanna Davis-McElligatt on *William Faulkner: Seeing through the South* by John T. Matthews. A portion of the review is reproduced below to show that book reviews can provide penetration into the essence of a text.

William Faulkner: Seeing through the South (review)
Joanna Davis-McElligatt
From: *College Literature*
Volume 40, Number 1, Winter 2013
pp. 139–141 | 10.1353/lit.2013.0003
In lieu of an abstract, here is a brief excerpt of the content:

In his comprehensive introduction to Faulkner's authorship, *William Faulkner: Seeing through the South,* John T. Matthews argues that though the author was in many ways a provincial Mississippian who wrestled with the South's troubled past, he was also a cosmopolite and modern writer who dedicated himself to exploring the profound global, national, and regional shifts of his time. Through careful close reading of each of Faulkner's nineteen novels, as well as much of his lesser-known short fiction, Matthews reveals how Faulkner's art consistently asks how individuals process the massive upheavals associated with modernity, and how their varying reactions tell us about their distinct characters, backgrounds, and futures (20). Over five lengthy chapters, in which he largely follows the chronological trajectory of Faulkner's works, Matthews deftly and often brilliantly draws out the specific ways each of Faulkner's texts responds both aesthetically and thematically to pressing historical contingencies. In addition, Matthews is also interested in drawing out Faulkner's biography as it is related to his work. To that end, he examines Faulkner's time spent working as a Hollywood screenwriter, his affair with Meta Carpenter Wilde, and his marriage and life with Estelle Oldham Faulkner. The cumulative effect of the blending of history and Faulkner's biography is a fresh and utterly relevant reading of Faulkner's oeuvre, one that encourages readers to examine his life and work in ever more complicated ways.

Documenting Notes to Avoid Plagiarism

Aurora Newberry, a student in American literature, used her library access to explore the influence of modern society on the Southern tradition in the writings of William Faulkner. Using the review article by Joanna Davis-McElligatt for *William Faulkner: Seeing through the South,* she pulled a section of the source to use in her paper, but also wrote the full Works Cited entry for easy reference and documentation:

Joanna Davis-McElligatt reflects on Faulkner's art, which consistently asks "how individuals process the massive upheavals associated with modernity, and how their varying reactions tell us about their distinct characters, backgrounds, and futures" (139).

Works Cited Entry:

Davis-McElligatt, Joanna. Rev. of *William Faulkner: Seeing through the South,* by John T. Matthews. *College Literature.* 40.1 (Winter 2013): 139–41. Print.

By documenting the source information at this early discovery stage, the student Aurora Newberry has given herself a head start to creating the Works Cited page for the research project.

Biography

The librarian can help you find an appropriate printed biography from among the thousands available. Short biographies appear in such works as *Contemporary Authors, American National Biography,* and *Who's Who in Philosophy.* Longer critical biographies are devoted to the life of one person, such as Richard Ellmann's *Oscar Wilde,* a study of the Irish poet and playwright, and Alf Mapp's *Thomas Jefferson: A Strange Case of Mistaken Identity,* which interprets the life and times of the former president. To find a critical biography, use the electronic book catalog at the library. You can also find biographies online. Most notable figures have several websites devoted to them that include articles by and about them.

Reference works by topics and issues, Appendix, pages 375–382.

Refer to biography for these reasons:

1. To verify the standing and reputation of somebody you want to paraphrase or quote in your paper.
2. To provide biographical details in your introduction. For example, the primary topic may be Carl Jung's psychological theories of the unconscious, but information about Jung's career might be appropriate in the paper.
3. To discuss a creative writer's life in relation to his or her work. That is, Jamaica Kincaid's personal life may shed some light on your reading of her stories or novels.

Scholarly Article

A scholarly article usually appears in a journal you access through the library's databases. With a journal article, you may feel confident in its authenticity because the authors of journal articles write for academic honor, they document all sources, and they publish through university presses and academic organizations that use a jury to judge an article before its publication. Thus, a journal article about child abuse found in *Child Development* or in *Journal of Marriage and Family* should be reliable, but an article about child abuse in a popular magazine may be less reliable in its facts and opinions. Usually, but not in every case, you can identify a journal in these ways:

1. The journal does not have a colorful cover; in fact, the table of contents is often displayed on the cover.
2. No colorful drawings or photography introduce each journal article, just a title and the name of the author(s).
3. The word *journal* often appears in the title (e.g., *American Journal of Sociology*).
4. The yearly issues of a journal are bound into a book.
5. Usually, the pages of a journal are numbered continuously through all issues for a year (unlike magazines, which are paged anew with each issue).

Sometimes you may face a bewildering array of articles, and you will wonder which pieces are the best. One way to evaluate a set of articles is with *citation searching,* which will search for authors who have been cited repeatedly in the literature. For example, while researching for sources on the ecology of wetlands, one student saw repeated references to Paul Keddy, as shown in these three citations:

Keddy, Paul. *The Competition.* New York: Springer-Verlag, 2007. Print.
Keddy, Paul. *Water, Earth, Fire.* New York: Springer-Verlag, 2008. Print.
Keddy, Paul. *Wetland Ecology: Principles and Conservation.* New York: Cambridge UP, 2011. Print.

Common sense told the student to search out something by Keddy; it is apparent that he is respected in this field because of the numerous citations and references to his works in the literature.

Sponsored Website

The Internet supplies both excellent information and some that is questionable in value. You must make judgments about the validity of these materials. Ask yourself a few questions about any article from a website:

> Online article, annotated by a student, page 119.

Is it appropriate to my work?
Is it reliable and authoritative?
Is it sponsored by an institution or organization?

Consult section 4b for a set of guidelines.

Interview

Interviews with knowledgeable people provide excellent information for a research paper. Whether conducted in person or by e-mail, the interview brings a personal, expert perspective to your work. The key element, of course, is the expertise of the person.

Experiment, Test, or Observation

Gathering your own data for research is a staple in many fields, especially the sciences. An experiment will bring primary evidence to your paper as you explain your hypothesis, give the test results, and discuss the implications of your findings. For a full discussion on conducting scientific investigation, with guidelines and details on format, see section 6e, pages 92–93.

Trade Book

CNC Robotics: Build Your Own Workshop Bot and *A Field Guide to Industrial Landscapes* are typical titles of nonfiction trade books found in bookstores and some public libraries, but not usually in a college library. Designed for commercial consumption, trade books seldom treat with depth a scholarly subject. Trade books have specific targets—the cook, the gardener, the antique dealer. In addition, trade books, in general, receive no rigorous prepublication scrutiny like scholarly books and textbooks do. For example, if your topic is "dieting" with a focus on "fad diets," you will find plenty of diet books at the local bookstore and on commercial websites. However, pass them by in favor of serious discussions backed by careful research that you will find by searching your library's databases.

Encyclopedia

By design, encyclopedias contain brief surveys of well-known persons, events, places, and accomplishments. They will serve you well during preliminary investigation, but most instructors prefer that you go beyond encyclopedias in order to cite from scholarly books and journal articles. Encyclopedias seldom have the critical perspective you can gain from books and journal articles.

Magazine

Like trade books, magazines have a targeted audience—young women, wrestling fans, computer connoisseurs, travelers. The articles are written rather quickly and seldom face critical review by a panel of experts. Therefore, exercise caution when reading a popular commercial magazine.

However, some magazines target an intellectual audience and thereby have a superior quality with academic merit; these include *Atlantic Monthly, Scientific Review, Astronomy, Smithsonian, Discover, Harper's,* and the *New Yorker.* In general, college libraries house the intellectual magazines, but they can also be found at most chain bookstores.

Newspaper

Some newspaper articles are not carefully researched or peer reviewed, but major newspapers such as the *New York Times,* the *Los Angeles Times,* and the *Wall Street Journal* offer carefully fact-checked information and rigorously researched stories. Generally, newspapers offer an excellent source of information, especially of local information that may not be found elsewhere.

Listserv

E-mail information via listserv deserves consideration when it focuses on an academic issue, such as British Romantic literature or, more specifically, the poetry of Robert Browning. In many cases, listservs originate from a college or scholarly organization. In fact, many instructors establish their own listserv sites for individual classes. Online courses usually feature a listserv site for exchange of ideas and peer review. These listservs can be a great way to seek out possible topics and learn what literature teachers or sociologists are talking about these days. *Caution:* Use the listserv to generate ideas, not as a source for facts to use in quotations.

Individual Website

A person's home page provides a publication medium for anybody who presumes to a knowledge he or she does or does not possess. You can't avoid home pages because they pop up on search engines, but you *can* approach them with caution. For example, one student, investigating the topic "fad diets," searched the Web, only to find mostly commercial sites that were blatant in their commercial attempts to sell something and home pages that described personal battles with weight loss. Caution is vital. On this point see section 4a, pages 45–46.

Usenet

Usenet newsgroups post information on a site. Like call-in radio shows, they invite opinions from a vast cross section of people, some reliable and some not. In most cases, participants employ an anonymous username, rendering their ideas useless for a documented paper.

Internet Chat Conversations

Chat rooms have almost no value for academic research. In most cases, you don't even know who you are chatting with, and the conversations are seldom about scholarly issues.

8b Selecting a Mix of Primary and Secondary Sources

Primary sources include novels, speeches, eyewitness accounts, interviews, letters, autobiographies, and the results of original research. Feel free to quote often from a primary source if it has direct relevance to your discussion. If you examine a poem by Percy Bysshe Shelley, you must quote the poem. If you examine President Barack Obama's domestic policies on health care, you must quote from White House documents.

Secondary sources are writings *about* the primary sources, *about* an author, or *about* somebody's accomplishments. Examples of secondary sources are a report on a presidential speech, a review of new scientific findings, and an analysis of a poem. A biography provides a second-hand view of the life of a notable person. A history book interprets events. These evaluations, analyses, or interpretations provide ways of looking at primary works, events, and lives.

For information about reading a key part of a book, article, or Internet site see pages 116–123.

Do not quote liberally from secondary sources. Be selective. Use a well-worded sentence, not the entire paragraph. Incorporate a key phrase into your text, not eight or nine lines.

The subject area of a research paper determines in part the nature of the source materials. Use the chart on the next page as a guide.

8c Evaluating Sources

Evaluating the Key Parts of an Article

Look closely at these parts of any article that looks promising:

Citing from Primary and Secondary Sources

	Primary Sources	*Secondary Sources*
Literature	Novels, poems, plays, short stories, letters, diaries, manuscripts, autobiographies, films, videos of live performances	Journal articles, reviews, biographies, critical books about writers and their works
Government, Political Science, History	Speeches, writings by presidents and others, the *Congressional Record,* reports of agencies and departments, documents written by historic figures	Newspaper reports, news magazines, political journals and newsletters, journal articles, history books
Social Sciences	Case studies, findings from surveys and questionnaires, reports of social workers, psychiatrists, and lab technicians	Commentary and evaluations in reports, documents, journal articles, and books
Sciences	Tools and methods, experiments, findings from tests and experiments, observations, discoveries, and test patterns	Interpretations and discussions of test data as found in journals and books (scientific books, which are quickly dated, are less valuable than up-to-date journals)
Fine Arts	Films, paintings, music, sculptures, as well as reproductions and synopses of these designed for research purposes	Evaluations in journal articles, critical reviews, biographies, and critical books about the authors and their works
Business	Market research and testing, technical studies and investigations, drawings, designs, models, memorandums and letters, computer data	Discussion of the business world in newspappers, business magazines, journals, government documents, and books
Education	Pilot studies, term projects, sampling results, tests and test data, surveys, interviews, observations, statistics, and computer data	Analysis and evaluation of educational experimentation in journals, pamplets, books, and reports

1. The **title**. Look for the words that have relevance to your topic before you start reading the article. For example, "Children and Parents" may look ideal for child abuse research until you read the subtitle: "Children and Parents: Growing Up in New Guinea."

2. An **abstract**. Reading an abstract is the best way to ascertain if an essay or a book will serve your specific needs. Some are available at the beginning of printed articles; others are provided by abstracting services (e.g., *Psychological Abstracts*). Most articles found through the library's databases will feature an abstract that you should read before printing or downloading the entire article. Save a tree, read before printing.

3. The **opening paragraphs**. If the opening of an article shows no relevance to your study, abandon it.

4. The **topic sentence** of each paragraph of the body. These first sentences, even if you scan them hastily, will give you a digest of the author's main points.

5. The **closing paragraph(s)**. If the opening of an article seems promising, skim the closing for relevance.

6. **Author credits**. Learn something about the credentials of the writer. Magazine articles often provide brief biographical profiles of authors. Journal articles and Internet home pages generally include the author's academic affiliation and credentials.

Read an entire article only if a quick survey encourages you to further investigation. Student Joe Matthews, an environmental engineering major, scanned an article for his paper on global warming. Figure 8.1 shows how he wrote marginal notes and comments that were germane to his study.

Evaluating the Key Parts of a Book

A **book** requires you to survey several items beyond those listed previously for articles:

1. The **table of contents**. A book's table of contents may reveal chapters that pertain to your topic. Often, only one chapter is useful. For example, Richard Ellmann's book *Oscar Wilde* devotes one chapter, "The Age of Dorian," to Wilde's *The Picture of Dorian Gray*. If your research focuses on this novel, then the chapter, not the entire book, will demand your attention.

2. The **book jacket,** if one is available. For example, the jacket to Richard Ellmann's *Oscar Wilde* says:

> Ellmann's *Oscar Wilde* has been almost twenty years in the work, and it will stand, like his universally admired *James Joyce,* as the definitive life. The book's emotional resonance, its riches of authentic color and conversation, and the subtlety of its critical illuminations give dazzling life to this portrait of the complex

Moderate Climate Warming Could Melt Permafrost

Puneet Kollipara

A stalagmite's past may help reveal Earth's future. By studying Siberian cave formations as old as 500,000 years, researchers have found that even moderate climate warming may set off significant thawing of permafrost.

If such extensive thawing of frozen soil occurred today, it could trigger a massive release of greenhouse gases, scientists report online February 21 in *Science*. Permafrost locks in huge amounts of carbon, so if the frozen ground thaws, much of the carbon could convert to carbon dioxide and methane and boost global warming.

During an era with average temperatures just 1.5 degrees Celsius warmer than preindustrial times, permafrost melted in areas that today are frozen year-round, the researchers report. Alarmingly, this melting came with a change in climate less than the 2 degrees that the United Nations has set as a target for averting catastrophic effects of warming, says Ted Schuur of the University of Florida, Gainesville, who was not involved in the study. The new research, he says, is the first to shed light on permafrost from hundreds of thousands of years ago. "It's nice to look back in the past and see what's already happened on the Earth, and that gives us some confidence about our future predictions," Schuur says.

Mineral deposits in Siberian caves add layers much like trees add rings. Researchers searched in the formations for clues on permafrost's history and found that just a 1.5° Celsius rise could thaw permafrost in areas that are completely frozen now. Researchers can use soil and ice to calculate the age of existing—but not past—permafrost.

In nearly all of the warm periods studied, layers grew on speleothems in areas that today have partial permafrost cover, the researchers found. During the warmest period studied, some 400,000 years ago, global temperature was 1.5 degrees higher than in preindustrial times. Only during that period did speleothems grow in the cave farthest to the north.

That suggests that 1.5 degrees of warming was enough to thaw permafrost even in areas that are fully covered today. And the finding implies the same could happen in the future, says George Kling of the University of Michigan in Ann Arbor. "Our challenge is to predict how much and how fast the carbon currently frozen in permafrost will enter the atmosphere," he says. Vladimir Romanovsky of the University of Alaska Fairbanks praises the study but warns against generalizing its findings to permafrost in other regions of the globe, noting that the method has some uncertainty. "Permafrost could be only one of the possible causes of growing or not growing of

The writer addresses climate change on frozen soil and the damaging effects of greenhouse gases.

A review of past effects reveals the need for environmental preservation.

Researchers can calculate current permafrost levels based on soil and ice samples.

Significant thawing and environmental damage could occur with as small as a 1.5 degree fluctuation.

The challenge for researchers is to predict the speed at which thawing might occur and the measure of greenhouse gases.

(continued)

FIGURE 8.1   Article with marginal comments on items that the student considered important to his thesis.

Source: Science News, 183.7, 6 Apr. 2013, p. 10.

speleothems." One possibility is that fractures in still-frozen permafrost could allow water to seep through, he says.

Another concern is that the method the researchers used might not detect partial thawing. If that had happened, water may not have reached caves, and speleothems would not have grown, Romanovsky says. But even partial thawing could change the climate, he warns, by turning previously locked-up carbon into greenhouse gases.

◼ **FIGURE 8.1** *(continued)*

RESEARCH TIP

Using a Direct Quotation to Avoid Plagiarism

Looking for source information for his research project on the environmental concerns of climate change, environmental engineering student Joe Matthews examined and incorporated ideas from the article in Figure 8.1 from *Science News*. The section of the text that he plans to use is blended into his ideas below with a clear reference to the author and the page number of the article:

> Climate change is slowly but steadily ruining our environment. Although it might seem insignificant, one example of this drastic shift is the release of greenhouse gases during the thawing of permafrost. It is the view of author Puneet Kollipara that an increase of just 1.5 degrees Celsius would liquefy carbon deposits "that could be converted by melting into carbon dioxide and methane, boosting global warming" (10).

Matthews has provided a reference to the source, quotation marks around the borrowed information, and a page number for reference. In this manner he has properly borrowed from a source and avoided the pitfall of plagiarism.

man, the charmer, the great playwright, the daring champion of the primacy of art.

Such information can stimulate the reading and notetaking from this important book.

3. The **foreword, preface,** or **introduction.** An author's *preface* or *introduction* serves as a critical overview of the book, pinpointing

the primary subject of the text and the particular approach taken. For example, Ellmann opens his book *Oscar Wilde* by saying:

> Oscar Wilde: we have only to hear the great name to anticipate that what will be quoted as his will surprise and delight us. Among the writers identified with the 1890s, Wilde is the only one whom everyone still reads. The various labels that have been applied to the age—Aestheticism, Decadence, the Beardsley period—ought not to conceal the fact that our first association with it is Wilde, refulgent, majestic, ready to fall.

This introduction describes the nature of the book: Ellmann will portray Wilde as the dominating literary figure of the 1890s. A *foreword* is often written by somebody other than the author. It is often insightful and worthy of quotation.

4. The **index**. A book's index lists names and terms with the page on which they are mentioned within the text. For example, the index to *Oscar Wilde* lists about eighty items under *The Picture of Dorian Gray*, among them:

homosexuality and, 312, 318
literature and painting in, 312–13
magazine publication of, 312, 319, 320
possible sources for, 311
underlying legend of, 314–315
W's Preface to, 311, 315, 322, 335
W's self-image in, 312, 319
writing of, 310–314

An index, by its detailed listing, can determine the relevance of the book to your research.

Guidelines for evaluating Internet sources, 4a, pages 45–46.

Evaluating the Key Parts of an Internet Article

The techniques listed previously for evaluating periodical articles (pages 116–118) apply also to Internet articles. In addition, examine:

1. The **home page,** if there is one. Prefer sites sponsored by universities and professional organizations. You may have to truncate the URL to find the home page where such information is featured.
2. Look for **hypertext links** to other sites whose quality can again be determined by the domain tags *.edu, .org,* or *.gov.* Be wary of sites that have the tag *.com.*

Figure 8.2 displays a sponsored website that student researcher Danny Ortiz discovered in his search of sources about the deterioration of dams in the water-deprived areas. It shows an online article by

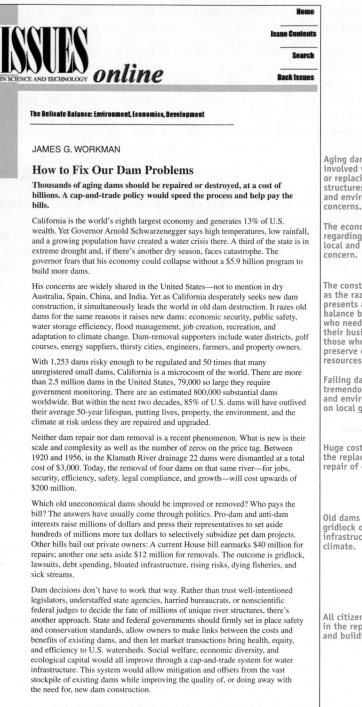

Home
Issue Contents
Search
Back Issues

ISSUES *online*
IN SCIENCE AND TECHNOLOGY

The Delicate Balance: Environment, Economics, Development

JAMES G. WORKMAN

How to Fix Our Dam Problems

Thousands of aging dams should be repaired or destroyed, at a cost of billions. A cap-and-trade policy would speed the process and help pay the bills.

California is the world's eighth largest economy and generates 13% of U.S. wealth. Yet Governor Arnold Schwarzenegger says high temperatures, low rainfall, and a growing population have created a water crisis there. A third of the state is in extreme drought and, if there's another dry season, faces catastrophe. The governor fears that his economy could collapse without a $5.9 billion program to build more dams.

His concerns are widely shared in the United States—not to mention in dry Australia, Spain, China, and India. Yet as California desperately seeks new dam construction, it simultaneously leads the world in old dam destruction. It razes old dams for the same reasons it raises new dams: economic security, public safety, water storage efficiency, flood management, job creation, recreation, and adaptation to climate change. Dam-removal supporters include water districts, golf courses, energy suppliers, thirsty cities, engineers, farmers, and property owners.

With 1,253 dams risky enough to be regulated and 50 times that many unregistered small dams, California is a microcosm of the world. There are more than 2.5 million dams in the United States, 79,000 so large they require government monitoring. There are an estimated 800,000 substantial dams worldwide. But within the next two decades, 85% of U.S. dams will have outlived their average 50-year lifespan, putting lives, property, the environment, and the climate at risk unless they are repaired and upgraded.

Neither dam repair nor dam removal is a recent phenomenon. What is new is their scale and complexity as well as the number of zeros on the price tag. Between 1920 and 1956, in the Klamath River drainage 22 dams were dismantled at a total cost of $3,000. Today, the removal of four dams on that same river—for jobs, security, efficiency, safety, legal compliance, and growth—will cost upwards of $200 million.

Which old uneconomical dams should be improved or removed? Who pays the bill? The answers have usually come through politics. Pro-dam and anti-dam interests raise millions of dollars and press their representatives to set aside hundreds of millions more tax dollars to selectively subsidize pet dam projects. Other bills bail out private owners: A current House bill earmarks $40 million for repairs; another one sets aside $12 million for removals. The outcome is gridlock, lawsuits, debt spending, bloated infrastructure, rising risks, dying fisheries, and sick streams.

Dam decisions don't have to work that way. Rather than trust well-intentioned legislators, understaffed state agencies, harried bureaucrats, or nonscientific federal judges to decide the fate of millions of unique river structures, there's another approach. State and federal governments should firmly set in place safety and conservation standards, allow owners to make links between the costs and benefits of existing dams, and then let market transactions bring health, equity, and efficiency to U.S. watersheds. Social welfare, economic diversity, and ecological capital would all improve through a cap-and-trade system for water infrastructure. This system would allow mitigation and offsets from the vast stockpile of existing dams while improving the quality of, or doing away with the need for, new dam construction.

Aging dams and the cost involved with repairing or replacing the structures are economic and environmental concerns.

The economics regarding old dams is a local and national concern.

The construction as well as the razing of dams presents a difficult balance between those who need the water for their businesses and those who want to preserve our natural resources.

Failing dams can put a tremendous economic and environmental strain on local governments.

Huge costs accompany the replacement and repair of old dams.

Old dams cause a gridlock over spending, infrastructure, and local climate.

All citizens have a stake in the repair, removal, and building of dams.

■ **FIGURE 8.2   Internet article from *Issues in Science and Technology Online*.**

James G. Workman accompanied by his marginal notes to key ideas. Examine your Internet articles in like manner.

8d Outlining a Source

You can frame an outline to capture an author's primary themes by listing statements that reveal the major issues and any supporting ideas. A quick outline of the Workman article, page 122, might look like this:

> Aging dams and the cost involved with repairing or replacing the structures.
>
> We must think globally, for the need for more dams is vital to the economy of the state of California as well as the economy of the nation.
>
> The construction as well as the razing of dams present a difficult balance between those who need the water for their businesses and those who want to preserve our natural resources.
>
> Because they only have a lifespan of fifty years, failing dams can put a tremendous economic and environmental strain on local governments.
>
> Astronomical costs accompany the replacement and repair of old dams.
>
> Added to the tremendous cost of dam improvements and removal is the gridlock over spending, infrastructure, and local climate.
>
> In truth, all citizens have a stake in the repair, removal, and building of dams.

This quickly drawn outline by Danny Ortiz provides an overview of the article with the issues clearly labeled. Ortiz can go in search of other sources that address these issues.

8e Summarizing a Source

A summary condenses into a brief note the general nature of a source. Writing a summary forces you to grasp the essence of the material. You might even use it in your paper with your evaluation and comments. The summary could serve as the heart of an annotated bibliography, which is a citation with a summary attached (see pages 125–127). Here is Danny Ortiz's summary of the Workman article (see page 122).

James Workman offers his views on environmental and economic

cost involved with repairing or replacing the structures. Because they

only have a lifespan of fifty years, failing dams can put a tremendous

economic and environmental strain on local governments. Workman

encourages us to think globally, for the need for more dams is vital

to the economy of the state of California as well as the economy of

the nation. The construction as well as the razing of dams presents

a difficult balance between those who need the water for their

businesses and those who want to preserve our natural resources.

Added to the tremendous cost of dam improvements and removal is

the gridlock over spending, infrastructure, and local climate. Workman

wants to make all citizens aware of the tremendous costs involved with

the repair, removal, and building of dams.

This summary can serve the researcher as he develops the paper, and it can become a part of the paper as part of the review of the literature (see pages 128–134).

CHECKLIST

Responding to a Source

- Read and make marginal notes on your sources. See pages 117–123 for details and examples.
- Search out scholarly materials—books and journals—by accessing your college library's resources. Do not depend entirely on the Internet.
- If appropiate, use a mix of quotations from primary sources, such as a novel, as well as paraphrases and quotations from secondary sources. See page 116 for a list of both types.
- Assess the nature of the source for any bias it might contain. See pages 109–110 and pages 171–173 for details.
- Read and highlight the key parts of the source, whether it is an article, book, or Internet site. See pages 117–123 for further details.
- Outline key ideas to identify the issues. See page 123 for an example.
- Write a summary that captures the essence of the article. See pages 123–124 for an example.

8f Preparing an Annotated Bibliography

An *annotation* is a summary of the contents of a book or article. A *bibliography* is a list of sources on a selected topic. Thus, an annotated bibliography does two important things: (1) It gives a bibliographic list of a selection of sources; and (2) it summarizes the contents of each book or article. Writing an annotated bibliography may at first appear to be busywork, but it will help you evaluate the strength of your sources.

Following are the characteristics for four forms of annotated bibliographies:

Indicative Defines the scope of the source, lists the significant topics included, and tells what the source is about.

Informative/Summative Summarizes the source. To write it, begin by writing the thesis before developing it with the argument or hypothesis.

Evaluative Weighs the strengths and weaknesses of the source to gauge its relevance and usefulness with advancing your thesis.

Combination Most annotated bibliographies follow this form by using one or two sentences to summarize or describe content and one or two sentences providing an evaluation.

The annotated bibliography that follows summarizes a selection of sources on the topic of media ethics.

Morrison 1

Sarah Morrison

Dr. Gotcher

Communications 4600

October 26, 2013

Media Ethics: An Annotated Bibliography

Ess, Charles. *Digital Media Ethics*. New York: Wiley, 2009. Print.

Charles Ess is a professor of Interdisciplinary Studies at Drury
University. In his book *Digital Media Ethics*, he emphasizes the
ethical difficulty faced by journalists in the 21st century. Ess
provides a clear perspective for writers and reporters of the digital
age. "Because our communications can quickly and easily reach
very large numbers of people around the globe, our use of digital
communication technologies thus makes us cosmopolitans (citizens
of the world) in striking new ways" (Ess 16). Ess goes on to describe
how people from all around the world can view any story, video, or

image at the touch of a fingertip (17). Central to views of Ess is the ethical decision that a journalist must make when covering a news story.

Good, Howard. "Teaching Ethics in a Dark World." *The Chronicle of Higher Education* 59.23 (11 Feb. 2013): 83. Print.

Good ponders whether it is irresponsible to teach students to take democratic ideals and ethical principles seriously and then send them out into a world that has little respect for either. Similarly, it is a challenge to take democratic ideals and ethical principles seriously when our world has little respect for either. Underlying everything is a belief that "freedom of the press exists so that controversies can be resolved honorably, through informed dialogue, rather than through intimidation or brute force" (Good 83).

Kovach, Bill, and Tom Rosenstiel. "The Elements of Journalism: What Newspeople Should Know and the Public Should Expect— Introduction." *Journalism.org.* 19 June 2006. Web. 25 Oct. 2013.

Kovach and Rosenstiel studied the perceived flaws in modern media. They barely recognized what they considered journalism in much of the work of their colleagues, for "instead of serving a larger public interest, they feared, their profession was damaging it." They go on to explain that because journalism is the system that societies use to supply information, we thereby "care about the character of news we get: they influence the quality of our lives, our thoughts, and our culture."

Miller, Ron. "Journalistic Responsibility in the Digital Age." *EContent* 36.2 (Mar. 2013): 32. Web. 21 Oct. 2013.

In this article Miller relates the power of online media and social networking. He regards social networks, such as Twitter and Facebook, as outlets that "exacerbate the problem by perpetuating the rumors and spreading misinformation" (32). He goes on to state that "In times of such obvious confusion, journalists should be the ones confirming the facts" (32). Added to this concern is the

question of how much incorrect information is generated as users
share and expound upon individual stories.

Slattery, Karen, and Erik Ugland. "The Ethics of Staging." *The Digital
Journalist*. Feb. 2005. Web. 22 Oct. 2013.

According to the authors of *"The Ethics of Staging,"* "Staging
is a particularity knotty problem for both print and television
photojournalists. Some argue that staging should never occur. But
others argue that, as a practical matter, photographers routinely
interfere with reality before shooting a scene." They go on to say
that "this issue is especially important for photojournalists because
it speaks to truth-telling." According to Slattery and Ugland,
staging may occur for three reasons. The first involves staging for
the purpose of editing, which relates to conventions of lighting,
reverse angle shots, interviews, and cutaways. The second reason for
staging is for the purpose of time when a subject is asked to repeat
or recreate an action. The third act of staging involves manipulating
the action in front of the camera to cause the story "to develop in a
certain way, when there is no reason to believe it would develop in
that way otherwise."

Wolper, Allan. "Pictures of Pain: Outcry against *The Journal News'* Gun Map
Paints Hypocritical Portrait of Media Critics." *Editor & Publisher* Mar.
2013: 28+. Web. 24 Oct. 2013.

This author raised the issue of privacy regarding "over-the-top"
news coverage. He took issue with the coverage of the December 14,
2012, school shootings at Sandy Hook Elementary School in rural
Newtown, Connecticut, where twenty small children and six school
officials were gunned down. According to Wolper, the press and
photographers "stole some of the most private moments from friends
and relatives of the victims without worrying whether those pictures
would haunt them forever." Calling attention to this form of local
terrorism is good, yet it is difficult to support the "hard-edged"
version of many reporters.

8g Preparing a Review of the Literature on a Topic

The *review of literature* presents a set of summaries in essay form for two purposes:

1. It helps you investigate the topic because it forces you to examine and then describe how each source addresses the problem.
2. It organizes and classifies the sources in some reasonable manner for the benefit of the reader.

Thus, you should relate each source to your central subject, and you should group the sources according to their support of your thesis. For example, the brief review that follows explores the literature on the subject of media ethics. It classifies the sources under a progression of headings: the issues, the causes, the consequences, and possible solutions.

Like Sarah Morrison in the following paper, you may want to use headings that identify your various sections.

Sarah Morrison

Dr. Gotcher

Communications 4600

October 26, 2013

Media Ethics: A Review of the Literature

Communication professionals often face the dilemma of whether to intervene or become involved in their own news stories. Some may think that it is the media's responsibility to act as a concerned citizen to protect the individuals who are being physically injured and hurt. Others view the media's responsibility simply as observers who are capturing the moment and not intervening into the scene. These ideas have been categorized here to establish the issues, show reasons for this media dilemma, and suggest possible solutions.

The Issues

Charles Ess, professor of Interdisciplinary Studies at Drury University, emphasizes the ethical difficulty faced by journalists in *Digital Media Ethics*. With the varied media outlets come a variety of ethical views. He states, "Because our communications can quickly and easily reach very large numbers of people around the globe, our use of digital communication technologies thus makes us cosmopolitans (citizens of the world) in striking new ways" (Ess 16). Ess goes on to describe how people from all around the world can view any story, video, or image at the touch of a fingertip (17). The scrutiny that writers and reporters of the digital age will face can cause far more caution when debating what ethical approach to take when intervening in a news story.

Nowhere has this opinion been more magnified than when photographer Kevin Carter captured the image of a starving child in the Sudan being approached by a vulture. While the scene paints a truthful image of how awful the lives are of those who are starving in third world countries, Carter faced severe scrutiny about waiting to capture the image rather than helping the poor child find nourishment ("On a Wing").

In similar fashion, the powerful presence of online media also poses a fast-paced dilemma. Ron Miller in "Journalistic Responsibility in the Digital Age," regards social networks, such as Twitter and Facebook, as outlets that "exacerbate the problem by perpetuating the rumors and spreading misinformation" (32). He goes on to state that "In times of such obvious confusion, journalists should be the ones confirming the facts" (32). Sadly, the opposite is usually true as journalists, driven by pressure to outdo one another, report flawed information. Noël Merino states that "a large percentage of online news comes from social networks." One must question how much misinformation is generated as users recommend and share individual stories, rather than individual publications, with each other. "Social networks have also replaced online news sites as destinations for news and allow audiences to shape and filter the news that reaches them" (Merino).

Similarly, it is a challenge to take democratic ideals and ethical principles seriously when our world has little respect for either. Underlying everything is a belief that "freedom of the press exists so that controversies can be resolved honorably, through informed dialogue, rather than through intimidation or brute force" (Good 83).

There is a fine line that the media is responsible for following. Should they capture their story at all costs? Or should they stop capturing the moment and become a part of the event when someone's life is in danger? CNN's Anderson Cooper was one of the first major news reporters to arrive on the scene after the 2010 Haiti earthquake. While reporting, Cooper noticed a young boy who was bleeding from the head. He dropped his story and began to aid the child in need. He made the decision to no longer be just an observer; instead, Cooper jumped into the story immediately when he noticed that someone was in danger ("Anderson Cooper"). Anderson Cooper became a part of the news story in itself and was no longer just a journalist. The bleeding boy was helped immediately, and ethically. This act by Anderson Cooper is the definition of a global citizen; the correct actions were taken at the right time. Deciding to be an observer, volunteer, or good citizen must be made by the journalist in each situation.

Causes

The questions that come to mind regarding media ethics include the following: What is the media's responsibility? When should the reporter or photographer intervene? How far can ethics be pushed so that the communications professional can get their story? Further complicating the matter are two concerns—the "need to know" influence of live news coverage and the staging of media events.

Cause 1: The "Need to Know" Factor

The media possesses the key and the power to learn about information that the viewer would ordinarily not know; hence, the media is constantly in question and under considerable stress regarding "live" television.

Gene Policinski states, "A free press never should agree automatically to withhold information for anything less than the most compelling of arguments, certainly not for political expediency or convenience." Policinski writes of situations in which the media has been asked to hold off on running a story for political or security reasons. On the other side of Policinski's article, the issue of leaking information from the CIA about a bombing threat is addressed. The CIA intercepted a plan to blow up an America-bound airliner. As the article states, "The news service also confirmed that it had learned about the plot , but agreed to White House requests not to publish because the CIA operation was still under way." During this instance, the "need to know" side of reporting was used because of the security threat that this news could cause. The balance between "need to know" and "want to know" should cause any media savvy individual to think about the repercussions of issuing their report.

Cecilia Vega expounds on the issue of "need to know" versus the "want to know." After Hurricane Katrina hit New Orleans, and recovery teams were sent into the area, the viewpoint of the Federal Emergency Management Agency was that no reporters should have been allowed to film or report as the rescue teams were pulling bodies from homes. The media practitioners would only be satisfied with the "want to know" for the viewers; however, pictures of dead bodies were something that many citizens realized was not a "need to know."

Like Vega, Allan Wolper raised the issue of privacy regarding the "over-the-top" news coverage of the December 14, 2012, school shootings at Sandy Hook Elementary School in rural Newtown, Connecticut, where twenty small children and six school officials were gunned down. The media trucks that swamped the Sandy Hook area "stole some of the most private moments from friends and relatives of the victims without worrying whether those pictures, posted online across the Internet, would haunt them forever" (Wolper). The free press is supposed to call attention to this kind of local terrorism, yet it is difficult to support this "hard-edged" version of journalism just to fulfill the "want to know" of viewers and readers.

The ethical principle that should be followed when deciding what is right or wrong with regard to sharing information with the public should be: Is it "need to know" or is it "want to know"? Figuring out if the information will give the public a clear and concise news story or if the information will be too graphic and gory for live television are choices that have to be made by journalists in all branches of the media.

Cause 2: The Staging of Media Events

There are numerous articles, news clips, and interviews that are posted each day in the media, yet many of these events are staged. Letting the interviewee know the questions ahead of time and coaching them on their responses happens more often than the public knows. As the writers of *The Ethics of Staging* emphasize, "Staging is a particularity knotty problem for both print and television photojournalists. Some argue that staging should never occur. But others argue that, as a practical matter, photographers routinely interfere with reality before shooting a scene" (Slattery & Ugland).

The article entitled "Soldiers' Chat with Bush Choreographed in Advance," demonstrates staging for a political cause. Deb Riechmann discusses how staging can be used to aid the president with reinforcing his agenda in the form of an interview. "It was billed as a conversation with US troops, but the questions President Bush asked on a teleconference call Thursday were choreographed to match his goals for the war in Iraq and Saturday's vote on a new Iraqi constitution" (Riechmann).

Staged news stories and photos surface during times of natural disaster. The U.S. news blog "The Guardian" said that during Hurricane Sandy, many people relied on social media to get their information, yet there were many misleading stories that circulated. According to news account, "before Hurricane Sandy made landfall, doctored photos of sharks in New York streets and outdated images of East Coast landmarks made the rounds" (Holpunch).

Consequences and Solutions

Every story has a different circumstance, but the responsibility of the media is to be the eyes and ears for the public. Many rely on the media as their only source of information about the world around them. If the media professionals are not ethically and morally good citizens, then public viewers will not want to listen or read their stories. They will find another journalist who always does the right thing, even if it means not getting the best angle on your story.

Kovach and Rosenstiel have concluded that we need news to live our lives, "to protect ourselves, bond with each other, identify friends and enemies." They go on to explain that because journalism is the system that societies use to supply information, we thereby "care about the character of news we get: they influence the quality of our lives, our thoughts, and our culture."

Due to this concerned outlook, we expect members of the media to take action when necessary. If a life is in danger, then there is a call to action. If there are others who are helping the situation, then the reporter may be able to be an observer. In any instance, the decision lies in each journalist's hands.

Whether in print, during a live broadcast, or posted online, a journalist must follow standards and guidelines. Reporting news that is moving and interesting can be very difficult; however, getting a story no matter what the cost only hurts those involved. Knowing when to step in and help others is essential in any walk of life, but media professionals who act as observers owe it to the public to step in as volunteers when they see someone in desperate need.

Works Cited

"Anderson Cooper Carries Bloody Child to Safety in Haiti." 20 Mar. 2010.
    Web. 22 Oct. 2013.

Ess, Charles. *Digital Media Ethics.* New York: Wiley, 2009. Print.

Good, Howard. "Teaching Ethics in a Dark World." *The Chronicle of Higher
    Education* 59.23 (11 Feb. 2013): 83. Print.

Holpuch, Amanda. "Hurricane Sandy Brings Storm of Fake News and Photos
    to New York." *U.S. News Blog.* 30 Oct. 2012. Web. 24 Oct. 2013.

Kovach, Bill, and Tom Rosenstiel. "The Elements of Journalism:
    What Newspeople Should Know and the Public Should Expect—
    Introduction." *Journalism.org.* 19 June 2006. Web. 25 Oct. 2013.

Miller, Ron. "Journalistic Responsibility in the Digital Age." *EContent* 36.2
    (Mar. 2013): 32. Web. 21 Oct. 2013.

"On a Wing and a Prayer." *Down to Earth* 15 Mar. 2013. *General OneFile.*
    Web. 13 Apr. 2013.

Policinski, Gene. "Tricky Call: Deciding When News Should Be Withheld."
    The Leaf Chronicle [Clarksville, TN]. 15 May 2012. Web. 20 Oct. 2013.

Morrison 7

"Preface to 'How Have New Technologies Affected Media Ethics?'." *Media Ethics*. Ed. Noël Merino. Detroit: Greenhaven Press, 2013. Current Controversies. *Opposing Viewpoints in Context*. Web. 23 Oct. 2013.

Riechmann, Deb. "Soldiers' chat with Bush choreographed in advance." *The Leaf Chronicle* [Clarksville, TN]. 14 Oct 2005. Web. 22 Oct. 2013.

Slattery, Karen, and Erik Ugland. "The Ethics of Staging." *The Digital Journalist*. Feb. 2005. Web. 22 Oct. 2013.

Vega, Cecilia M. "As Bodies Recovered, Reporters Are Told 'No Photos, No Stories'." *San Francisco Chronicle*. 13 Sept. 2005. Web. 23 Oct. 2013.

Wolper, Allan. "Pictures of Pain: Outcry against *The Journal News'* Gun Map Paints Hypocritical Portrait of Media Critics." *Editor & Publisher*. Mar. 2013: 28+. Web. 24 Oct. 2013.

YOUR RESEARCH PROJECT

1. Examine your sources to test the validity of the list against the inverted pyramid on page 110. Do you have enough sources from the upper tier of scholarly works? If not, go in search of journal articles and scholarly books to beef up the list. Do not depend on Internet articles entirely, even if every one is from a sponsored website.

2. Conduct a citation search (see pages 113–114 for details) on your topic, which will help you identify key people who have written on the subject several times and for several publications.

3. Examine the chart of primary and secondary sources on page 117. Look for your discipline—literature, government, history—and then determine if you are using a mix of primary and secondary sources.

4. Respond to one of your sources by writing two items: (1) a rough outline of the contents of the source (see page 123); and (2) a brief summary of the source (see pages 123–124).

5. Consult the research schedule from section 1e, pages 9–10, to reflect upon your analysis of the research topic. Through careful consideration of your narrowed topic and notes, you can move toward organizing and drafting your paper.

Writing Effective Notes
and Creating Outlines

Chapter 9 Clear Targets

Notetaking is the heart of research. If you write high-quality notes, they may
need only minor editing to fit the appropriate places in your first draft.
Prepare yourself to write different types of notes—quotations for well-phrased
passages by authorities but also paraphrased or summarized notes to maintain
your voice. This chapter explains the following types of notes:

- *Personal notes* that express your own ideas or record field research.
- *Quotation notes* that preserve any distinguished syntax of an authority.
- *Paraphrase notes* that interpret and restate what the authority has said.
- *Summary notes* that capture in capsule form a writer's ideas.
- *Field notes* that record interviews, tabulate questionnaires, and maintain
  records of laboratory experiments and other types of field research.

To present your examination of the topic, the accurate notes from your
personal research will join with your carefully paraphrased notes from
experts on the topic to form the support for your thesis. As a researcher,
your goal is to share verifiable information, but others can verify your
work only if good records are kept and reported.

Gathering Printouts, Photocopies, Scanned Images, and Downloaded Data

Today's technology makes it fairly easy to collect material quickly
and in volume. You can print online articles or save them to a file. You
can use a scanner to make digital images of graphics as well as text. Plus,
photocopy machines enable you to carry home a few sheets of paper
instead of an entire book.

All this material will gradually make sense as you arrange it and use
it. *Warning:* Document *everything*. Keep *everything*. You will need to cite
the source in the text and in a bibliography entry, so don't throw away a
note, printout, or photocopy.

9a Creating Effective Notes

Whether you write notes on a computer or by hand, you should keep in mind some basic rules, summarized in the checklist.

Honoring the Conventions of Research Style

Your notetaking will be more effective from the start if you practice the conventions of style for citing a source, as directed by your instructor and advocated by the Modern Language Association (MLA), American Psychological Association (APA), Chicago Manual of Style (CMS), or Council of Science Editors (CSE), and as shown briefly below and explained later in this book.

MLA: Dalton Forney states, "Like a modern day 'Siege Perilous,' the presidency is a tenuous hot seat, ever besieged by the next national issue or global crisis" (19).

APA: Forney (2014) has commented, "Like a modern day 'Siege Perilous,' the presidency is a tenuous hot seat, ever besieged by the next national issue or global crisis" (p. 19).

CMS footnote: Dalton Forney states, "Like a modern day 'Siege Perilous,' the presidency is a tenuous hot seat, ever besieged by the next national issue or global crisis."[4]

CSE number: Forney has commented, "Like a modern day 'Siege Perilous,' the presidency is a tenuous hot seat, ever besieged by the next national issue or global crisis"[5].

Using a Computer for Notetaking

1. Record notes and save them using one of two methods:
   a. Write each note as a separate temporary file in a common directory so each can be moved later into the appropriate section of your draft via the Copy and Paste commands.
   b. Write all notes in a single file. Begin each new note with a code word or phrase. When you begin the actual writing of the paper, you can begin writing at the top of the file, which will push the notes down as you write.
2. You can record the bibliography information for each source you encounter by listing it in a BIBLIO file so that you build the necessary list of references in one alphabetical file. Chapters 14, 15, 16, and 17 will assist with the correct style and formatting.

9b Writing Personal Notes

The content of a research paper is not a collection of ideas transmitted by experts in books and articles; it is an expression of your own ideas as supported by the scholarly evidence. Readers are primarily interested in *your* thesis statement, *your* topic sentences, and *your* personal view and analysis of the issues. Therefore, during your research, record your thoughts on the

CHECKLIST

Writing Effective Notes

1. Write one item per note to facilitate the shuffling and rearranging of the data as you develop your paper during all stages of organization. Several notes can be kept in a computer file if each is labeled clearly.
2. List the source with name, year, and page to prepare for in-text citations and/or bibliographic entries.
3. Label each note with a descriptive word or term (for example, "objectivity on television").
4. Write a full note in well-developed sentences to speed the writing of your first draft.
5. Keep everything (photocopy, scribbled note, or computer file) in order to authenticate dates, page numbers, and full names of authors and publication information.
6. Label your personal notes with "my idea" or "personal note" to distinguish them from the sources.

Identifying sources, 174–177

In his third volume of *American Literature*,

Italics, 370

Darrel Abel narrates the hardships of the Samuel Clemens

family in Hannibal, yet Abel asserts that "despite such

Using lowercase after *that,* 194

hardships and domestic grief, which included the deaths

of a brother and sister, young Sam Clemens [Mark Twain]

Interpolations, 197–199

had a happy and reasonably carefree boyhood" (11–12).

Single quotation marks, 189

Page citations, 174–176

Abel acknowledges the value of Clemens's "rambling

reminiscences dictated as an 'Autobiography' in his old

Punctuation with quotations, 189–193

age" (12). Of those days Clemens says, "In the small

Ellipses points, 194–197

town . . . *everybody* [my emphasis] was poor, but didn't

know it; and everybody was comfortable, and did know it"

Signaling your emphasis of another's words, 197–199

(qtd. in Abel 12). Clemens felt at home in Hannibal with

One source quotes another, 180–182

everybody at the same level of poverty.

FIGURE 9.1 Conventions of style for writing notes.

issues by writing plenty of personal notes in your research journal or in your computer files. Personal notes are essential because they allow you to:

- Record your discoveries.
- Reflect on the findings.
- Make connections.
- Explore another point of view.
- Identify prevailing views and patterns of thought.

Personal notes should conform to these three standards:

1. The idea on the note is yours.
2. The note is labeled with "my idea," "mine," or "personal thought" so that later you can be certain it has not been borrowed.
3. The note is a rough summary, a sketch of ideas, or, preferably, a complete sentence or two.

A sample of a personal note follows:

Personal Thought

For me, organ donation is a gift of life, so I have signed my donor card. At least a part of me will continue to live if an accident claims my life. My boyfriend says I'm gruesome, but I consider it practical. Besides, he might be the one who benefits, and then what will he say?

9c   Writing Direct Quotation Notes

Quoting the words of another person is the easiest type of note to write. Quotation notes are essential because they allow you to:

- Capture the authoritative voice of the experts on the topic.
- Feature essential statements.
- Provide proof that you have researched the subject carefully.
- Offer conflicting points of view.
- Show the dialog that exists about the topic.

In the process, you will need to follow basic conventions:

1. Select quoted material that is important and well-phrased, not something trivial or something that is common knowledge. NOT "John F. Kennedy was a Democrat from Massachusetts" (Rupert 233) BUT "John F. Kennedy's Peace Corps left a legacy of lasting compassion for the downtrodden" (Rupert 233).
2. Use quotation marks. Do not copy the words of a source into your paper in such a way that readers will think *you* wrote the material.

3. Use the exact words of the source.
4. Provide an in-text citation to author and page number, like this (Henson 34–35), or give the author's name at the beginning of the quotation and put the page number after the quotation, like this example in MLA style:

> Barnill says, "More than 400 people each month receive the gift of sight through yet another type of tissue donation—corneal transplants. In many cases, donors unsuitable for organ donation are eligible for tissue donation" (2).

5. The in-text citation goes *outside* the final quotation mark but *inside* the period.
6. Try to quote key sentences and short passages, not entire paragraphs. Find the essential statement and feature it; do not force your reader to fumble through a long quoted passage in search of the relevant statement. Make the brief quotation a part of your sentence, in this way:

> Trying to mend their past eating habits, many Americans adopt functional foods as an essential step toward a more health-conscious future. This group of believers spends "an estimated $29 billion a year" on functional foods (Nelson 755).

7. Quote from both primary sources (the original words by a writer or speaker) and secondary sources (the comments after the fact about original works). The two types are discussed immediately following.

Quoting Primary Sources

Quote from primary sources for four specific reasons:

1. To draw on the wisdom of the original author
2. To let readers hear the precise words of the author
3. To copy exact lines of poetry and drama
4. To reproduce graphs, charts, and statistical data

Selecting a mix of primary and secondary sources, pages 116–117.

Cite poetry, fiction, drama, letters, and interviews. In other cases, you may want to quote liberally from a presidential speech, cite the words of a businessman, or reproduce original data. As shown in the next example, quote exactly, retain spacing and margins, and spell words as in the original.

The brevity of life in Percy Bysshe Shelley's "Mutability":

We are as clouds that veil the midnight moon;

How restlessly they speed, and gleam, and quiver,

Streaking the darkness radiantly!—yet soon

Night closes round, and they are lost forever:

Or like forgotten lyres, whose dissonant strings

Give various response to each varying blast,

To whose frail frame no second motion brings

One mood or modulation like the last.

Quoting Secondary Sources

Quote from secondary sources for three specific reasons:

1. To display excellence in ideas and expression by experts on the topic
2. To explain complex material
3. To set up a statement of your own, especially if it spins off, adds to, or takes exception to the source as quoted

The overuse of direct quotation from secondary sources indicates either (1) that you did not have a clear focus and copied almost everything related to the subject verbatim, or (2) that you had inadequate evidence and used numerous quotations as padding. Therefore, limit quotations from secondary sources by using only a phrase or a sentence, as shown here:

The geographical changes in Russia require "intensive political

analysis" (Herman 611).

If you quote an entire sentence, make the quotation a direct object. It tells *what* the authority says. Headings on your notes will help you arrange them.

Geographic Changes in Russia

In response to the changes in Russia, one critic notes, "The American

government must exercise caution and conduct intensive political

analysis" (Herman 611).

More examples of handling quoted materials, Chapter 11, pages 174–199.

Blend two or more quotations from different sources to build strong paragraphs, as shown here:

Functional foods are helping fight an economic battle against

rising health care costs. Clare Hasler notes, "The U.S. population is

getting older," which means more people are being diagnosed and

treated for disease (68). These individuals are putting a huge financial

strain on the health care system with their need for expensive

antibiotics and hospital procedures. Dr. Herbert Pierson, director of

the National Cancer Institute's $20 million functional food program, states, "The future is prevention, and looking for preventive agents in foods is more cost effective than looking for new drugs" (qtd. in Carper xxii).

9d Writing Paraphrased Notes

A paraphrase is the most difficult note to write. It requires you to restate, in your own words, the thought, meaning, and attitude of someone else. With *interpretation,* you act as a bridge between the source and the reader as you capture the wisdom of the source in approximately the same number of words. Use paraphrase for these reasons:

- To maintain your voice in the paper
- To sustain your style
- To avoid an endless string of direct quotations
- To interpret the source as you rewrite it

Keep in mind these five rules for paraphrasing a source:

1. Rewrite the original in about the same number of words.
2. Provide an in-text citation of the source (the author and page number in MLA style).
3. Retain exceptional words and phrases from the original by enclosing them within quotation marks.
4. Preserve the tone of the original by suggesting moods of satire, anger, humor, doubt, and so on. Show the author's attitude with appropriate verbs: "Edward Zigler condemns . . . defends . . . argues . . . explains . . . observes . . . defines."
5. To avoid unintended plagiarism, put the original aside while paraphrasing to avoid copying word for word. Compare the finished paraphrase with the original source to be certain the paraphrase truly restates the original and uses quotation marks with any phrasing or standout words retained from the original.

HINT: When instructors see an in-text citation but no quotation marks, they will assume that you are paraphrasing, not quoting. Be sure their assumption is true.

Here are examples that show the differences between a quotation note and a paraphrased one:

Original Quotation:

Bullying   Colvin 211

_ _ _ _ _

Dr. Delaney Colvin explains, "Cyberbullying is increasing at a disturbing rate. While most bullying in the past happened primarily at school, social cruelty can now occur with the ease of a keystroke." (211).

Paraphrase of the Original Quotation:

Cyberbullying   Colvin 211

Dr. Delaney Colvin explains that bullying has moved past the school setting, for online harassment through social media sites continues to increase at an alarming rate (211).

Original Quotation (more than four lines):

Cyberbullying   Colvin 211

Dr. Delaney Colvin clarifies the trend:

> While the Internet is a tool that benefits the individual
> as well as society, online bullying has increased the
> power imbalance between victims and perpetrators.
> Serious problems arise when screen names are stolen
> and used to send malicious messages with racist or
> sexist content as well as compromising photographs to
> unlimited audiences. (211)

As shown above, MLA style requires a ten-space (two tabs) indention.

Paraphrase of the Original Quotation:

Cyberbullying   Colvin 211

Online resources and social sites can enhance society, yet Colvin pinpoints the imbalance between cyberbullies and their victims. Hurtful and harmful attacks can occur "when screen names are stolen and used to send malicious messages." Through racial and sexual attacks as well as inappropriate images, online bullying plunges the victim into a web of lies and insinuation (211).

As shown in the example above, place any key wording of the source within quotation marks.

Original Quotation:

Bullying   Colvin 211

—————

"Cyberbullying is the most problematic yet least-studied form of bullying that adolescents face today" (Colvin 211).

Paraphrase of the Original Quotation:

Cyberbullying   Colvin 211

—————

Dr. Delaney Colvin encourages further research to address the broad spectrum of hurtful, online dangers faced by today's teenagers (211).

9e Writing Summary Notes

The *summary note* describes and rewrites the source material without great concern for style or expression. Your purpose at the moment will be quick, concise writing without careful wording. If the information is needed, you can rewrite it later in a clear, appropriate prose style and, if necessary, return to the source for revision. Use summary notes for these reasons:

- To record material that has marginal value
- To preserve statistics that have questionable value for your study
- To note an interesting position of a source speaking on a closely related subject but not on your specific topic
- To reference several works that address the same issue, as shown in this example:

The logistics and cost of implementing a recycling program have been examined in books by West and Loveless and in articles by Jones et al., Coffee and Street, and Abernathy.

Success with the summary requires the following:

1. Keep it short. It has marginal value, so don't waste time fine-tuning it.
2. Mark with quotation marks any key phrasing you cannot paraphrase.

RESEARCH TIP

Paraphrasing a Passage to Avoid Plagiarism

When you paraphrase, keep in mind that it is not sufficient to alter only a few words or to change the order of words in the sentences. Paraphrasing requires that you completely rewrite the passage. The paraphrase requires you to restate in your own words the thought, meaning, and attitude of someone else. Following is an original source along with an unacceptable paraphrase:

> America needs a new vision of itself and its destiny. We fall too much under the influence of men who encourage us to keep what we have and deny it to those seeking a new and better life. Our task is to be the servant nation bringing encouragement to all peoples who are struggling to attain a better society.
>
> —From Gerald Kennedy's *Fresh Every Morning,* page 77.

Unacceptable Paraphrase

A new vision is needed for America to fulfill its destiny. We feel the need to be encouragers and helpers to those who are struggling to attain a better society, but Americans are influenced by a leadership that is content with holding on to what we have while denying a better life for others.

This unacceptable version has made some token changes by using a few synonyms and altering the sentences slightly. Otherwise, this is a word-for-word copy of the original, and if the note were to be placed into the research paper in this form, the writer would be guilty of plagiarism.

Acceptable Paraphrase

The strength of our country and its providence is to assist those who are less fortunate. In this sense, America acts as the caretaker for those who long for a strengthened culture filled with humanity and prosperity. Whether led by political icons or by our neighbors, America's role in the modern world is to enable those less fortunate to help themselves (Kennedy 77).

The second version restructures the sentences and changes the vocabulary of the original passage while maintaining the essence of the original passage.

3. Provide documentation to the author and page number. However, a page number is unnecessary when the note summarizes the entire article or book, not a specific passage.

> TV & reality   Epstein's book
>
> -----
>
> Now dated but cited by various sources, Epstein's work in
> 1973 seems to lay the groundwork for criticism in case after case of
> distorted news broadcasts.

This sort of summary might find its way into the final draft, as shown here:

> Television viewers, engulfed in the world of communication,
> participate in the construction of symbolic reality by their perception
> of and belief in the presentation. Edward Jay Epstein laid the
> groundwork for such investigation in 1973 by showing in case after
> case how the networks distorted the news and did not, perhaps could
> not, represent reality.

9f Writing Précis Notes

A précis note differs from a quick summary note. It serves a specific purpose, so it deserves a polished style for transfer into the paper. It requires you to capture in just a few words the ideas of an entire paragraph, section, or chapter. Use the précis for these reasons:

- To review an article or book
- To annotate a bibliography entry
- To provide a plot summary
- To create an abstract

Success with the précis requires the following:

1. Condense the original with precision and directness. Reduce a long paragraph to a sentence, tighten an article to a brief paragraph, and summarize a book in one page.
2. Preserve the tone of the original. If the original is serious, suggest that tone in the précis. In the same way, retain moods of doubt, skepticism, optimism, and so forth.
3. Write the précis in your own language. However, retain exceptional phrases from the original, enclosing them in quotation marks. Guard against taking material out of context.
4. Provide documentation.

Use the Précis to Review Briefly an Article or Book

Note this example of the short review:

On the "Donor Initiative"   2014 Website

The National Community of Organ and Tissue Sharing has a
website devoted to its initiatives. Its goal is to communicate the
problem—for example, more than 55,000 people are on the waiting
lists. It seeks a greater participation from the public.

With three sentences, the writer has made a précis of the entire article.

Use the Précis to Write an Annotated Bibliography

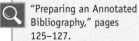
Preparing a review of lit-
erature, pages 128–134.

An annotation is a sentence or paragraph
that offers explanatory or critical commentary on an article or book. It seldom extends
beyond two or three sentences. The difficulty of this task is to capture
the main idea of the source.

"Top Ten Myths about Organ Donation." Web. 10 Feb. 2014. This
informative site from the National Kidney Foundation dispels the many
myths surrounding organ donation, showing that selling organs is
illegal, that matching donor and recipient is highly complicated, and
secret back room operations are almost impossible.

Use the Précis in a Plot Summary Note

"Preparing an Annotated
Bibliography," pages
125–127.

In just a few sentences, a précis summarizes a novel, short story, drama, or similar literary work, as shown by this next note:

Great Expectations by Charles Dickens describes young Pip, who
inherits money and can live the life of a gentleman. But he discovers
that his "great expectations" have come from a criminal. With
that knowledge, his attitude changes from one of vanity to one of
compassion.

Furnish a plot summary in your paper as a courtesy to your readers to
cue them about the contents of a work. The précis helps you avoid a full-
blown retelling of the whole plot.

Use the Précis As the Form for an Abstract

An abstract is a brief description that appears at the beginning of an article to summarize the contents. It is, in truth, a précis. Usually, it is written by the article's author, and it helps readers

Abstract using APA style, pages 309–310.

make decisions about reading or skipping the article. You can find entire volumes devoted to abstracts, such as *Psychological Abstracts* and *Abstracts of English Studies*. An abstract is required for most papers in the social and natural sciences. Here's a sample:

Abstract

The functional food revolution has begun! Functional foods, products that provide benefits beyond basic nutrition, are adding billions to the nation's economy each year. So what is their secret? Why are functional foods a hit? Functional foods are suspected to be a form of preventive medicine. This news has made the public swarm and food nutritionists salivate. Consumers hope that functional foods can calm some of their medical anxieties. Many researchers believe that functional foods may be the answer to the nation's prayers for lower health care costs. This paper goes behind the scenes, behind all the hype, in its attempt to determine if functional foods are an effective form of preventive medicine. The paper identifies several functional foods, locates the components that make them work, and explains the role that each plays in the body.

RESEARCH TIP

Documenting to Avoid Plagiarism

Careful attention to the rules of documentation will help to avoid plagiarism—the unacknowledged use of someone else's words or ideas. Avoid these pitfalls when creating notes for your research topic:

- Omitting quotation marks when citing the exact language of a source
- Failing to revise all ideas in a source that you are paraphrasing
- Providing no documentation for a quotation or paraphrase
- Omitting the correct name, page number, and source information from a note

The proper use of source material enhances your credibility as a researcher. At the same time, it ensures that you will not be guilty of plagiarism.

9g Writing Notes from Field Research

Depending on the focus and scope of your project, you might be expected to conduct field research. This work requires different kinds of notes kept on charts, cards, notepads, laboratory notebooks, a research journal, or the computer.

> The report of empirical research, 6e, pages 92–93.

If you **interview** knowledgeable people, make careful notes during the interview and transcribe those notes to your draft in a polished form. A digital recorder can serve as a backup to your notetaking.

If you conduct a **questionnaire,** the results will become valuable data for developing notes and graphs and charts for your research paper.

If you conduct **experiments, tests,** and **measurements,** the findings serve as your notes for the results section of the report and will give you the basis for the discussion section.

9h Creating Outlines Using Academic Models

A General All-Purpose Model

If you are uncertain about the design of your paper, start with this bare-bones model and expand it with your material. Readers, including your instructor, are accustomed to this sequence for research papers. It offers plenty of leeway.

Identify the subject.
Explain the problem.
Provide background information.
Frame a thesis statement.

Analyze the subject.
Examine the first major issue.
Examine the second major issue.
Examine the third major issue.

Discuss your findings.
Restate your thesis and point beyond it.
Interpret the findings.
Provide answers, solutions, or a final opinion.

To the introduction you can add a quotation, an anecdote, a definition, or comments from your source materials. Within the body, you can

> Developing introductions, bodies, and conclusions, Chapter 12.

compare, analyze, give evidence, trace historical events, and handle other matters. In the conclusion, you can challenge an assumption, take exception to a prevailing point of view, and reaffirm your thesis. Flesh out each section, adding subheadings as necessary, to create an outline.

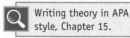 Writing theory in APA style, Chapter 15.

Model for Advancing Your Ideas and Theories

If you want to advance a theory in your paper, use this next design, but adjust it to eliminate some items and add new elements as necessary.

Introduction:
> Establish the problem or question.
> Discuss its significance.
> Provide the necessary background information.
> Introduce experts who have addressed the problem.
> Provide a thesis statement that addresses the problem from a fresh perspective, if at all possible.

Body:
> Evaluate the issues involved in the problem.
> Develop a past-to-present examination.
> Compare and analyze the details and minor issues.
> Cite experts who have addressed the same problem.

Conclusion:
> Advance and defend your theory as it grows out of evidence in the body.
> Offer directives or a plan of action.
> Suggest additional work and research that is needed.

Model for the Analysis of Creative Works

If you plan to analyze musical, artistic, or literary works, such as an opera, a set of paintings, or a novel, adjust this next model to your subject and purpose.

Introduction:
> Identify the work.
> Give a brief summary in one sentence.
> Provide background information that relates to the thesis.
> Offer biographical facts about the artist that relate to the specific issues.
> Quote and paraphrase authorities to establish the scholarly traditions.
> Write a thesis statement that establishes your particular views of the literary work.

Body:
> Provide evaluative analysis divided according to such elements as imagery, theme, character development, structure, symbolism, narration, and language.

Conclusion:
> Keep a fundamental focus on the artist of the work, not just the elements of analysis as explained in the body.
>
> Offer a conclusion that explores the contributions of the artist in accord with your thesis statement.

Model for Argument and Persuasion Papers

If you write persuasively or argue from a set position, your paper should conform in general to this next model. Select the elements that fit your design.

Introduction:
> In one statement, establish the problem or controversial issue your paper will examine.
>
> Summarize the issues.
>
> Define the key terminology.
>
> Make concessions on some points of the argument.
>
> Use quotations and paraphrases to clarify the controversial nature of the subject.
>
> Provide background information to relate the past to the present.
>
> Write a thesis to establish your position.

Body:
> Develop arguments to defend one side of the subject.
>
> Analyze the issues, both pro and con.
>
> Give evidence from the sources, including quotations as appropriate.

Conclusion:
> Expand your thesis into a conclusion that makes clear your position, which should be one that grows logically from your analysis and discussion of the issues.

Model for Analysis of History

If you are writing a historical or political science paper that analyzes events and their causes and consequences, your paper should conform, in general, to the following plan.

Introduction:
> Identify the event.
>
> Provide the historical background leading up to the event.

Offer quotations and paraphrases from experts.

Give the thesis statement.

Body:

Analyze the background leading up to the event.

Trace events from one historic episode to another.

Offer a chronological sequence that explains how one event relates directly to the next.

Cite authorities who have also investigated this event in history.

Conclusion:

Reaffirm your thesis.

Discuss the consequences of this event, explaining how it altered the course of history.

Model for a Comparative Study

A comparative study requires that you examine two schools of thought, two issues, two works, or the positions taken by two persons. The paper examines the similarities and differences of the two subjects, generally using one of three arrangements for the body of the paper.

Introduction:

Establish A.

Establish B.

Briefly compare the two.

Introduce the central issues.

Cite source materials on the subjects.

Present your thesis.

Body (choose one):

Examine A.	Compare A and B.	Issue 1
Examine B.	Contrast A and B.	Discuss A and B.
Compare and	Discuss the central	Issue 2
contrast A and B.	issues.	Discuss A and B.
		Issue 3
		Discuss A and B.

Conclusion:

Discuss the significant issues.

Write a conclusion that ranks one side over the other, or

Write a conclusion that rates the respective genius of each side.

Remember that the models provided above are general guidelines, not ironclad rules. Adjust each as necessary to meet your special needs.

9i Writing a Formal Outline

Not all papers require a formal outline, nor do all researchers need one. A short research paper can be created from key terms, a list of issues, a rough outline, and a first draft. As noted earlier in this chapter, rough or informal outlines will help you to make sure you cover the key points and guide your research. However, a formal outline can be important because it classifies the issues of your study into clear, logical categories with main headings and one or more levels of subheadings. An outline will change miscellaneous notes, computer drafts, and photocopied materials into an ordered progression of ideas.

> **HINT:** A formal outline is not rigid and inflexible; you may, and should, modify it while writing and revising. In every case, treat an outline or organizational chart as a tool. Like an architect's blueprint, it should contribute to, not inhibit, the construction of a finished product.

You may wish to experiment with the Outline feature of your computer software, which will allow you to view the paper at various levels of detail and to highlight and drop the essay into a different organization.

Using Standard Outline Symbols

List your major categories and subtopics in this form:

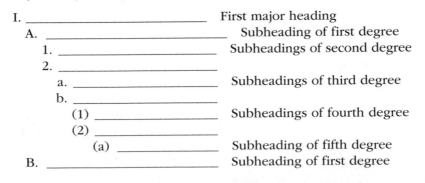

I. _____ First major heading
  A. _____ Subheading of first degree
    1. _____ Subheadings of second degree
    2. _____
      a. _____ Subheadings of third degree
      b. _____
        (1) _____ Subheadings of fourth degree
        (2) _____
          (a) _____ Subheading of fifth degree
  B. _____ Subheading of first degree

The degree to which you continue the subheads will depend, in part, on the complexity of the subject. Subheads in a research paper seldom carry beyond subheadings of the third degree, the first series of small letters.

Writing a Formal Topic Outline

If your purpose is to arrange quickly the topics of your paper without detailing your data, build a topic outline of balanced phrases. The topic outline may use noun phrases:

```
III. The senses

    A. Receptors to detect light

        1. Rods of the retina

        2. Cones of the retina
```

It may also use gerund phrases:

```
III. Sensing the environment

    A. Detecting light

        1. Sensing dim light with retina rods

        2. Sensing bright light with retina cones
```

And it may also use infinitive phrases:

```
III. To use the senses

    A. To detect light

        1. To sense dim light

        2. To sense bright light
```

No matter which grammatical format you choose, you should follow it consistently throughout the outline.

Writing a Formal Sentence Outline

The sentence outline requires full sentences for each heading and subheading. It has two advantages over the topic outline:

1. Many entries in a sentence outline can serve as topic sentences for paragraphs, thereby accelerating the writing process.
2. The subject/verb pattern establishes the logical direction of your thinking (for example, the phrase "Vocabulary development" becomes "Television viewing can improve a child's vocabulary").

Consequently, the sentence outline brings into the open any possible organizational problems rather than hiding them as a topic outline might do. The time invested in writing a complete sentence outline, like writing complete, polished notes (see 9a–9g, pages 136–148), will pay off when you write the rough draft and revise it.

A section of Jamie Johnston's sentence outline is shown in the following example. As shown here, the thesis statement should appear as a separate item in the outline. It is the main idea of the entire paper, so try not to label it as Item I in the outline. Otherwise, you may search fruitlessly for parallel ideas to put in II, III, and IV. (See also pages 200–201 on using the thesis in the opening.)

Outline

Thesis: Prehistoric humans were motived by biological instincts toward warfare rather than cultural demands for a share of limited resources.

   I. The conflict of "noble savage" versus prehistoric warriors has surfaced in recent literature.

      A. Some literature has advocated the existence of harmony and peace among early tribes.

         1. Rousseau argued for a noble savage in the 1700s.

         2. The Bible speaks of the Garden of Eden.

      B. Recent research suggests that wars have existed since the dawn of life.

         1. LaBlanc cites evidence from the Southwest Indians.

         2. Yates reports on Chinese weapons from 28,000 BC.

         3. Ferrill has examined cave paintings.

  II. The evidence points clearly to the existence of prehistoric wars.

      A. Anthropologists have uncovered skeletal remains of captives who were executed.

         1. Victims were skinned alive.

         2. Victims were decapitated.

         3. Massacres occurred in Europe, North and South America, Japan, and other parts of the world.

YOUR RESEARCH PROJECT

1. Look carefully at each of the sources you have collected so far—books, photocopies of journal articles, and Internet printouts. Try writing a summary or précis of each one. At the same time, make decisions about material worthy of direct quotation and material that you want to paraphrase or summarize.

2. Decide how you will keep your notes—and handwritten notes in a research journal or in computer files. *Note:* The computer files will serve you well because you can transfer them into your text and save typing time.

3. Write various types of notes—that is, write a few that use direct quotations, some that paraphrase, and some that summarize.

4. Conscientiously and with dedication, write as many personal notes as possible. These will be your ideas, and they will establish your voice and position. Do not let the sources speak for you; let them support your position.

5. If you have access to OneNote or some other notetaking program, take the time to consider its special features. You can create notes, store them in folders, and even search your own files by keyword, category, and reference.

6. Sketch out an outline for your project. List your general thesis and, below that, establish several divisions that will require careful and full development. Test more than one plan. Do you need several criteria of judgment? causal issues? arguments? evidence from field research? Which seems to work best for you?

7. Select one of the models, as found on pages 148–152, and develop it fully with the information in your sketch outline (see #6 immediately above).

8. Consult the research schedule outlined at the end of Chapter 1. By this time, you should have notes from sources and a plan for organizing your research project as you pull your thoughts and resources together to begin drafting your paper.

10 Drafting the Paper in an Academic Style

Chapter 10 Clear Targets

Your research project should examine a subject in depth, but it also examines *your* knowledge and the strength of *your* evidence. This chapter will help you find the style necessary to present a fair, balanced treatment of the subject:

- Focusing your argument for your field of study
- Refining the thesis statement
- Creating an academic title
- Drafting the paper from your notes
- Using visuals effectively
- Avoiding sexist and biased language

As you draft your paper, your voice should flow smoothly and logically from one idea to the next. You should adopt an academic style that presents your position with precise, supporting details. Additionally, you should offer contradictory evidence, for this will give your report something to work against, thereby strengthening your argument.

Be practical

- Write what you know and feel, not what you think somebody wants to hear.
- Write portions of the paper when you are ready, not only when you arrive there by outline sequence.
- If necessary, leave blank spots on the page to remind you that more evidence is required.
- Skip entire sections if you are ready to develop later paragraphs.

Be uninhibited

- Initial drafts must be attempts to get words on the page rather than to create a polished document.
- Write without fear or delay.

- Be conscientious about references.
- Cite the names of the sources in your notes and text.
- Enclose quotations in your notes and text.
- Preserve the page numbers of the sources.

10a Focusing Your Argument

Your writing style in a research paper should be factual, but it should also reflect your take on the topic. Your draft will evolve more quickly if you focus on the central issue(s). Each paragraph then amplifies your primary claim. Your aim or purpose is the key to discovering an argument. Do you want to persuade, inquire, or negotiate?

Persuasion means convincing the reader that your position is valid and, perhaps, asking the reader to take action. For example:

> We need to establish green zones in every city of this country to control urban sprawl and to protect a segment of the natural habitat for the animals.

Inquiry is an exploratory approach to a problem in which you examine the issues without the insistence of persuasion. It is a truth-seeking adventure. For example:

> Many suburban home dwellers complain that deer, raccoons, and other wild animals ravage their gardens, flowerbeds, and garbage cans; however, the animals were there first. Thus, we may need a task force to examine the rights of each side of this conflict.

Negotiation is a search for a solution. It means you attempt to resolve a conflict by inventing options or a mediated solution. For example:

> Suburban neighbors need to find ways to embrace the wild animals that have been displaced rather than voice anger at the animals or the county government. Perhaps green zones and wilderness trails would solve some of the problems; however, such a solution would require serious negotiations with real estate developers who want to use every square foot of every development.

Often, the instructor's research assignment will tell you whether you want to persuade, inquire, or negotiate. But if it doesn't, try to determine early in the process where your research is heading.

Maintaining a Focus on Objective Facts and Subjective Ideas

As an objective writer, you should examine the problem, make your claim in a thesis statement, and provide supporting evidence. As a subjective writer, you should argue with a touch of passion; you must believe in your position on the issues. For this reason, complete objectivity is unlikely in any research paper that puts forth an intellectual argument in the thesis statement (see pages 24–27). Of course, you must avoid being overly subjective, as by demanding, insisting, and quibbling. Moderation of your voice, even during argument, suggests control of the situation, both emotionally and intellectually.

Your objective and subjective analysis alerts the audience to your point of view in two ways:

Ethical appeal. If you project the image of one who knows and cares about the topic, the reader will recognize and respect your deep interest in the subject and your carefully crafted argument. The reader will also appreciate your attention to research conventions.

Logical appeal. For readers to believe in your position, you must provide sufficient evidence in the form of statistics, paraphrases, and direct quotations from authorities on the subject.

10b Refining the Thesis Statement

The thesis statement relates your convictions about the topic, advances your position, and limits the scope of the study. While you have worked with a preliminary thesis to direct your research, you must refine your proposition to clearly and exactly advance your viewpoint and invite the reader into the argument. The thesis statement performs three tasks:

1. It sets the argument to control and focus the entire paper.
2. It provides unity and a sense of direction.
3. It specifies to the reader the point of the research.

For example, one student started with the topic "exorbitant tuition." He narrowed his work to "tuition fees put parents in debt." Ultimately, he crafted this thesis:

> The exorbitant tuition at America's colleges is forcing out the
> poor and promoting an elitist class.

This statement, a conclusion he must defend, focuses the argument on the fees and their effects on enrollment. Without such focus, the student might have drifted into other areas, confusing himself and his readers.

RESEARCH TIP

Creating an Original Thesis

The thesis statement establishes an approach to the topic. At times the writer may assert a cause or provide an explanation while prompting a call for action. Regardless of the form it takes, a writer's original thesis establishes the possibilities, probabilities, and interpretations that are subject to review in a rational presentation. To produce original research findings and avoid a plagiarized, borrowed idea from a source, the writer must narrow and isolate one issue by finding a critical focus, such as:

> THESIS: Violence in children's programming echoes an adolescent's fascination with brutality.

This sentence advances an original idea that the writer can develop fully and defend with evidence. The writer has made a connection between the subject *television violence* and the focusing agent, *adolescent behavior.* The following thesis statements provide additional viewpoints:

> THESIS: Television cartoons can affect a child's personality because they are so violent.

> THESIS: Violence in children's programming echoes an adolescent's fascination with brutality.

These same issues apply also to the use of the enthymeme or the hypothesis, as discussed earlier (see pages 26–27).

> ENTHYMEME: America's colleges are promoting an elitist class because exorbitant tuition forces out the poor and limits their access to higher education.

> HYPOTHESIS: This study will gather evidence on this proposition: Poor students are being locked out of higher education by the rapidly rising costs of tuition and registration fees.

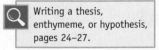
Writing a thesis, enthymeme, or hypothesis, pages 24–27.

Using Questions to Focus the Thesis

If you have trouble focusing on a thesis statement, ask yourself a few questions. One of the answers might serve as the thesis.

- What is the point of my research?

  THESIS: A delicate balance of medicine, diet, and exercise can control diabetes mellitus to offer a comfortable lifestyle for millions.

  ENTHYMEME: Because diabetes attacks the body in several ways, a person needs a careful balance of medicine, diet, and exercise.

  HYPOTHESIS: The objective of this study is to examine the effects of a balanced program of medication, diet, and exercise for a victim of diabetes.

- What do I want this paper to do?

  THESIS: The public needs to understand that advertisers who use blatant sexual images have little regard for moral scruples and ordinary decency.

- Can I tell the reader anything new or different?

  THESIS: The evidence indicates clearly that most well water in the county is unsafe for drinking.

- Do I have a solution to the problem?

  THESIS: Public support for safe houses will provide a haven for children who are abused by their parents.

- Do I have a new slant and new approach to the issue?

  THESIS: Personal economics is a force to be reckoned with, so poverty, not greed, forces many youngsters into a life of crime.

- Should I take the minority view of this matter?

  THESIS: Give credit where it is due: Custer may have lost the battle at Little Bighorn, but Crazy Horse and his men, with inspiration from Sitting Bull, *won* the battle.

- What exactly is my theory about this subject?

> THESIS: Because they have certain medicinal powers, functional foods can become an economic weapon in the battle against rising health care costs.

- Will an enthymeme serve my purpose by making a claim in a *because* clause?

> ENTHYMEME: Sufficient organ and tissue donation, enough to satisfy the demand, remains almost impossible because negative myths and religious concerns dominate the minds of many people.

- Will a hypothesis serve my purposes?

> HYPOTHESIS: An education program to dispel negative myths and religious concerns will build a greater base of organ and tissue donors.

- What are the keywords surrounding this issue that I might use in framing the thesis statement?

> HYPOTHESIS: The objective is examination of issues with regard to supply and demand, the political power struggles that are emerging, and the ethical and perhaps even moral implication engulfing the world's scattered supply of fresh water.

Adjust or Change Your Thesis During Research if Necessary

Be willing to abandon your preliminary thesis if research leads you to new and different issues. For example, one writer began research on child abuse with this preliminary thesis: "A need for a cure to child abuse faces society each day." Investigation, however, narrowed her focus: "Parents who abuse their children should be treated as victims, not criminals." The writer moved, in effect, to a specific position from which to argue that social organizations should serve abusing parents in addition to helping abused children.

CHECKLIST

Writing the Final Thesis

You should be able to answer "yes" to each question that follows. Does the thesis:

1. Express your position in a full, declarative statement that is not a question, not a statement of purpose, and not merely a topic?
2. Limit the subject to a narrow focus that grows out of research?
3. Establish an investigative, inventive edge to the discovery, interpretation, or theoretical presentation?
4. Point forward to the conclusion?
5. Conform to the title and the evidence you have gathered?

10c   Writing an Academic Title

A clearly expressed title, like a good thesis statement, will control your writing and keep you on course. Although writing a final title may not be feasible until the paper is written, the preliminary title can provide specific words of identification to keep you on track. For example, one writer began with this title: "Diabetes." Then, to make it more specific, the writer added another word: "Diabetes Management." As research developed and she realized the role of medicine, diet, and exercise for victims, she refined the title even more: "Diabetes Management: A Delicate Balance of Medicine, Diet, and Exercise." Thereby, she and her readers had a clear idea of what the paper was to do—that is, explore methods for managing diabetes. Note that long titles are standard in scholarly writing. Consider the following strategies for writing your title.

1. Name a general subject, followed by a colon and a phrase that focuses or shows your slant on the subject.

    Organ and Tissue Donation and Transplantation: Myths, Ethical Issues, and Lives Saved

    The World's Water Supply: The Ethics Of Distribution

2. Name a general subject and narrow it with a prepositional phrase.

    Gothic Madness in Three Southern Writers

3. Name a general subject and cite a specific work that illuminates the topic.

    Analysis of Verbal Irony in swift's *A Modest Proposal*

4. Name a general subject and follow it by a colon and a phrase that describes the type of study.

Black Dialect in Maya Angelou's Poetry: A Language Study

5. Name a general subject and follow it by a colon and a question.

AIDS: Where Did It Come From?

6. Establish a specific comparison.

Religious Imagery in N. Scott Momaday's *The Names* and Heronimous Storm's *Seven Arrows*

As you develop a title, be sure to avoid fancy literary titles that fail to label issues under discussion.

Poor: "Foods, Fads, and Fat"
Better: "Nutritional Foods: A Survey"
Best: "Nutritional Foods: A Powerful Step on the
               Path of Preventive Medicine"

For placement of the title, see "Title Page or Opening Page," page 222.

10d Drafting the Paper from Your Research Journal, Notes, and Computer Files

To begin writing your research essay, you may work systematically through a preliminary plan or outline. You may also begin by writing what you know at the time. Either way, keep the pieces of your manuscript under control; your notes will usually keep you focused on the subject, and your thesis statement will control the flow and direction of your argument. Yet you must let the writing find its own way, guided but not controlled by your preliminary plans. Also consult the model (see pages 148–152) that best fits your design.

Writing from Your Notes

Use your notes and research journal to

1. Transfer personal notes, with modification, into the draft.
2. Transcribe précis notes and paraphrased materials directly into the text.
3. Quote primary sources.
4. Quote secondary sources from notes.

Weave source material into the paper to support *your* ideas, not as filler. Your notes will let the essay grow, blossom, and reach up to new levels of knowledge. You can do this in several ways, and you may even have a method beyond the four mentioned here.

Method one requires separate note files within a specially named directory, as explained on pages 148–149. During the drafting stage, you can use the Insert or Copy and Paste commands to transfer your notes into your text.

Method two assumes you have placed all your notes in one file. Begin writing your paper in a new file. As you need a note, minimize this text file and maximize your file of notes, or use two windows. Find the note you want to transfer, highlight it, copy it, and then paste it into your file.

Method three assumes you have placed all your notes within one file and labeled each with a code word or title. Begin drafting your paper at the top of this file, which will push the notes down as you write. When you need a note, find it, copy it, and paste it into your text.

Method four requires the complete outline on file so you can enter information under any of the outline headings as you develop ideas (see Chapter 3 for details on outlining). You can import your notes to a specific location in the outline. This technique allows you to work anywhere within the paper to match your interest of the moment with a section of your outline. In effect, you expand your outline into the first draft of your research paper.

In the initial draft, leave plenty of space as you write. Keep the margins wide, use double spacing, and leave blank spaces between paragraphs. The open areas will invite your revisions and additions later on. The process is simplified when you use a computer because you will keyboard the paper the first time and revise directly within the file.

When working with pages copied from articles, books, or Internet sites, use caution. You will be tempted to borrow too much. Quote or paraphrase key phrases and sentences; do not quote an entire paragraph unless it is crucial to your discussion and you cannot easily reduce it to a précis. Moreover, any information you borrow should come from a credible source that has a scholarly or educational basis.

HINT: Drafting a paragraph or two by using different methods of development is one way to build the body of your paper, but only if each part fits the purpose and design of your work. Write a comparison paragraph, classify and analyze one or two issues, show cause and effect, and ask a question and answer it. Sooner than you think, you will have drafted the body of the paper. See Chapter 12 for detailed discussion of these methods of development.

Writing with Unity and Coherence

Unity refers to exploring one topic in depth to give your writing a single vision. With unity, each paragraph carefully expands on a single aspect of the narrowed subject. *Coherence* connects the parts logically by

- Repetition of keywords and sentence structures
- The judicious use of pronouns and synonyms
- The effective placement of transitional words and phrases (e.g., *also, furthermore, therefore, in addition,* and *thus*)

The next passage reads with unity (it keeps its focus) and coherence (it repeats keywords and uses transitions effectively, as shown in boldface type):

> Talk shows are spectacles and forms of **dramatic** entertainment; **therefore,** members of the studio audience are **acting** out parts in the **drama,** like a Greek chorus, just as the host, the guest, and the television viewers are **actors** as well. **Furthermore,** some sort of interaction with the "characters" in this made-for-television **"drama"** happens all the time. If we read a book or attend a play, **we question** the text, **we question** the presentation, and **we determine** for ourselves what it means to us.

Writing in the Proper Tense

Verb tense often distinguishes a paper in the humanities from one in the natural and social sciences. MLA style requires the present tense to cite an author's work (e.g., "Patel *explains*" or "the work of Scoggin and Roberts *shows*"). The CMS footnote style also asks for present tense.

> APA and CSE styles require the past tense or present perfect tense to cite an author's work. See Chapter 15, pages 290–291, and Chapter 17, pages 337–339.

MLA style requires that you use the present tense for your own comments and those of your sources because the ideas and the words of the writers remain in print and continue to be true in the universal present. Therefore, when writing a paper in the humanities, use the historical present tense, as shown here:

> "Always forgive your enemies; nothing annoys them so much," **writes** Oscar Wilde about adversaries and forgiveness.

> Yancy **argues** that sociologist Norman Guigou **has** a "fascination with the social causes rather than community solutions to homelessness" (64).

Use the past tense in a humanities paper only for reporting historical events. In the next example, past tense is appropriate for all sentences except the last:

> Great works of art had been created for ages, but Leonardo da Vinci was the first to paint the atmosphere, the air in which the subject sat and which occupied the space between the eye and the thing seen. This technique continues to influence modern paintings, which place subjects in lights and shadows as well as natural settings.

Using the Language of the Discipline

Every discipline and every topic has its own vocabulary. Therefore, while reading and taking notes, jot down words and phrases relevant to your research study. Get comfortable with them so you can use them effectively. For example, a child abuse topic requires the language of sociology and psychology, thereby demanding an acquaintance with these terms:

social worker	maltreatment	aggressive behavior
poverty levels	behavioral patterns	incestuous relations
stress	hostility	battered child
formative years	recurrence	guardians

Similarly, a poetry paper might require such terms as *symbolism, imagery, rhythm, persona,* and *rhyme.* Many writers create a terminology list to strengthen their command of appropriate nouns and verbs. However, nothing will betray a writer's ignorance of the subject matter more quickly than awkward and distorted technical terminology. For example, the following sentence uses big words, but it distorts and scrambles the language:

 Blending sources into your text, Chapter 11.

> The enhancement of learning opportunities is often impeded by a pathological disruption in a child's mental processes.

The words may be large, but what does the passage mean? Probably this:

> Education is often interrupted by a child's abnormal behavior.

Writing in the Third Person

Write your paper with third-person narration that avoids "I believe" and "It is my opinion." Rather than saying, "I think objectivity on television is nothing more than an ideal," drop the opening two words and say, "Objectivity on television is nothing more than an ideal." Readers will

---

RESEARCH TIP

Using Source Material to Enhance Your Writing

Readers want to see your thoughts and ideas on a subject. For this reason, a paragraph should seldom contain source material only; it must contain a topic sentence to establish a point for the research evidence. Every paragraph should explain, analyze, and support a thesis, not merely string together a set of quotations.

The following passage cites effectively two different sources:

> Organ and tissue donation is the gift of life. Each year many people confront health problems due to diseases or congenital birth defects. Tom Taddonia explains that tissues such as skin, veins, and valves can be used to correct congenital defects, blindness, visual impairment, trauma, burns, dental defects arthritis, cancer, and vascular and heart disease (23). Steve Barnill says, "more than 400 people each month receive the gift of sight through yet another type of tissue donationty—corneal transplants. In many cases, donors unsuitable for organ donation are eligible for tissue donation" (356). Barnill notes that tissues are now used in orthopedic surgery, cardiovascular surgery, plastic surgery, dentistry, and podiatry (358). Even so, not enough people are willing to donate organs and tissues.

This passage illustrates four points. A writer should:

1. Weave the sources effectively into a whole
2. Use the sources as a natural extension of the discussion
3. Cite each source separately, one at a time
4. Provide separate in-text citations to pages or footnote numerals

This means you will need to read carefully so that you can select the key ideas and phrasing. It also means you should be accurate and precise.

---

understand that the statement is your thought. However, attribute human functions to yourself or other persons, not to nonhuman sources:

WRONG: The study considered several findings.

CORRECT: The study reported the findings of several sources.

The study can report its findings, but it can't consider them.

Writing with the Passive Voice in an Appropriate Manner

Instructors often caution young writers against using the passive voice, which is often less forceful than an active verb. However, research writers sometimes need to shift the focus from the actor to the receiver, as shown here:

PASSIVE: Twenty-three students of a third-grade class at

Barksdale School were observed for two weeks.

ACTIVE: I observed twenty-three students of a third-grade

class at Barksdale School.

In the previous examples, the passive voice is preferred because it keeps the focus on the subject of the research, not the writer. Also, as a general rule, avoid the first person in research papers. Here are additional examples of the effective use of the passive voice:

The soil was examined for traces of mercury.

President Jackson was attacked repeatedly for his Indian policy

by his enemies in Congress.

Children with attention disorders are often targeted for drug

treatment.

As you see, the sentences place the focus on the soil, the president, and the children.

10e Using Visuals Effectively in a Research Essay

Graphics and visuals enable you to analyze trends and relationships in numerical data. Use them to support your text. Most computers allow you to create tables, line graphs, or pie charts as well as diagrams, maps, and other original designs. You may also import tables and illustrations from your sources. Place these graphics as close as possible to the parts of the text to which they relate. It is acceptable to use full-color art if your printer will print in colors; however, use black for the captions and date.

A table, as shown in the example in Figure 10.1, is a systematic presentation of materials, usually in columns. A figure is any non-text item that is not a table, such as a blueprint, a chart, a diagram, a drawing, a graph, a photograph, a photostat, a map, and so on. Figure 10.2 is a sample figure that illustrates a room layout. Use graphs appropriately. A line graph, such as the example shown in Figure 10.3, serves a different purpose than does a circle (pie) chart, and a bar graph plots different

Table 2[a]

Mean Sources of Six Values Held by College Students According to Sex

All Students		Men		Women	
Pol.	40.61	Pol.	43.22	Aesth.	43.86
Rel.	40.51	Theor.	43.09	Rel.	43.13
Aesth.	40.29	Econ.	42.05	Soc.	41.13
Econ.	39.45	Soc.	37.05	Econ.	36.85
Soc.	39.34	Aesth.	36.72	Theor.	36.50

[a]Carmen J. Finley, et al. (165).

FIGURE 10.1   Sample table with in-text citation source.

information than does a scatter graph. Figures provide a visual amplification of the text. For example, a photograph of John Keats would reinforce and augment a research paper on the British poet.

Your figures, photographs, and tables should conform to the following guidelines:

- Present only one kind of information in each one, and make it as simple and as brief as possible. Frills and fancy artwork may distract rather than attract the reader.
- Place small figures and tables within your text; place large figures, sets of figures, or complex tables on separate pages in an appendix.
- Place the figure or table as near to your textual discussion as possible, but it should not precede your first mention of it.
- In the text, explain the significance of the figure or table. Describe the item so that your reader may understand your observations without reference to the item itself, but avoid giving too many numbers and figures in your text. Refer to figures and tables by number (for example, "Figure 5") or by number and page reference ("Table 4, 16"). Avoid using vague references (such as "the table above," "the following illustration," or "the chart below").

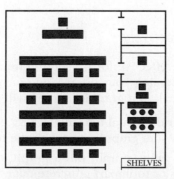

Figure 4: Audio Laboratory with Private Listening
Rooms and a Small Group Room

FIGURE 10.2   Sample figure with caption.

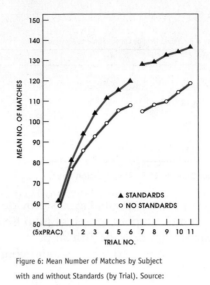

Figure 6: Mean Number of Matches by Subject
with and without Standards (by Trial). Source:
Lock and Bryan (289).

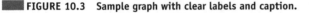**FIGURE 10.3   Sample graph with clear labels and caption.**

- Write a caption for the figure or table so that your reader can understand it without reference to your discussion.
- Number figures consecutively throughout the paper with Arabic numerals, preceded by "Fig." or "Figure" (for example, "Figure 4").
- Number tables consecutively throughout the paper with Arabic numerals, preceded by "Table" (for example, "Table 2").
- Insert a caption or number for each column of a table, centered above the column or, if necessary, inserted diagonally or vertically above it.

CHECKLIST

Using Visuals Effectively

Illustrations can be effective for presenting numerical data, analyzing trends, or reinforcing your discussion. Furnish the reader with clear, pertinent visuals and graphics if they will advance your study.

- **Introduce** Fit the visual into the text by providing and explanation of how the graphic relates to the text of your study.
- **Show** Use a table, graph, photograph, or figure to display your findings or to impart concrete data.
- **Discuss** Relate the significance of your information and how it advances the findings of your research.

- When inserting an explanatory or a reference note, place it below both a table and an illustration; then use a lowercase letter as the identifying superscript (as shown in the table in Figure 10.1), not an Arabic numeral. Sources are abbreviated as in-text citations, and full documentation must appear on the Works Cited page.

File Formats

Illustration and information graphics are usually large files, so you will need to compress them with a compression format, either JPEG or GIF, so named for their file name extensions: ".jpg" and ".gif." In general, JPEGs work best for photographs and GIFs work best for line drawings.

Making your own graphics file is complex but rewarding. It adds a personal creativity to your research paper. Use one of the following techniques:

- *Use a graphics program,* such as Adobe FreeHand MX or Adobe Illustrator. With such software you can create a graphics file and save it as a JPEG or GIF. Also useful are Adobe Photoshop and JASC Paintshop Pro, which are designed primarily for working with photographs.
- *Use a scanner* to copy your drawings, graphs, photographs, and other matter.
- *Create original photographs with a digital camera.* Consult the owner's manual to learn how to create JPEGs or GIFs from your photographs.
- *Create your own information graphics* in Microsoft PowerPoint or Excel.

As long as you create JPEG files or GIF files for your graphics, you can transport the entire research paper to a website.

10f Avoiding Sexist and Biased Language

Racial and gender fairness is one mark of the mature writer. The best writers exercise caution against words that may stereotype any person, regardless of gender, race, nationality, creed, age, or disability. If the writing is precise, readers will not make assumptions about race, age, and disabilities. Therefore, do not freely mention sexual orientation, marital status, ethnic or racial identity, or a person's disability. The following guidelines will help you avoid discriminatory language.

Age

Review the accuracy of your statement. It is appropriate to use *boy* and *girl* for children of high school age and under. *Young man* and *young woman* or *male adolescent* and *female adolescent* can be appropriate, but *teenager* carries a certain bias. Avoid *elderly* as a noun; use phrases such as *older persons,* as in "Fifteen older patients suffered senile dementia of the Alzheimer's type."

Gender

Gender is a matter of our culture that identifies men and women within their social groups. *Sex* tends to be a biological factor (see the following discussion of sexual orientation).

1. Use plural subjects so that nonspecific, plural pronouns are grammatically correct. For example, do you intend to specify that Judy Jones maintains *her* lab equipment in sterile condition or to indicate that technicians, in general, maintain *their* own equipment?
2. Reword the sentence so a pronoun is unnecessary:

   Correct: The doctor prepared the necessary surgical [not *his*] equipment without interference.

   Correct: Each technician must maintain the laboratory [not *her*] equipment in sterile condition.

3. Use pronouns denoting gender only when necessary to specify gender or when gender has been previously established.

   Larissa, as a new laboratory technician, must learn to maintain *her* equipment in sterile condition.

4. The use of *woman* and *female* as adjectives varies, as in *female athlete* and *woman athlete.* Use *woman* or *women* in most instances (e.g., *a woman's intuition*) and *female* for species and statistics, (e.g., *four female subjects, ten males and twenty-three females, a female chimpanzee*). The word *lady* has fallen from favor (i.e., avoid *lady pilot*).
5. The first mention of a person requires the full name (e.g., Ernest Hemingway, Joan Didion) and thereafter requires only the use of the surname (e.g., Hemingway, Didion). At first mention, use Emily Brontë, but thereafter use Brontë, *not* Miss Brontë. In general, avoid formal titles (e.g., Dr., Gen., Mrs., Ms., Lt., or Professor). Avoid their equivalents in other languages (e.g., Mme, Dame, Monsieur).
6. Avoid *man and wife* and *seven men and sixteen females.* Keep the terms parallel by saying *husband and wife* or *man and woman* and *seven male rats and sixteen female rats.*

Sexual Orientation

The term *sexual orientation* is preferred over the term *sexual preference.* It is preferable to use the terms *lesbians* and *gay men* rather than *homosexuals.* The terms *heterosexual, homosexual,* and *bisexual* can be used to describe both the identity and the behavior of subjects.

Ethnic and Racial Identity

Some people prefer the term *Black,* others prefer *African American,* and still others prefer *person of color.* The terms *Negro* and *Afro-American* are now dated and inappropriate. Use *Black* and *White,* not the lowercase *black* and *white.* In like manner, some individuals may prefer *Hispanic, Latino, Mexican,* or *Chicano.* Use the term *Asian* or *Asian American* rather than *Oriental. Native American* is a broad term that includes *Samoans, Hawaiians,* and *American Indians.* A good rule of thumb is to specify a person's nationality, tribe, or ethnic group when it is known (*Mexican, Korean, Comanche,* or *Nigerian*).

Disability

In general, place people first, not their disability. Rather than *disabled person* or *retarded child,* say *a person who has scoliosis* or *a child with Down syndrome.* Avoid saying *a challenged person* or *a special child* in favor of *a person with* or *a child with.* Remember that a *disability* is a physical quality, while a *handicap* is a limitation that might be imposed by nonphysical factors, such as stairs, poverty, or social attitudes.

YOUR RESEARCH PROJECT

1. Examine your own thesis statement using the Writing the Final Thesis Checklist on page 162. Modify and refine your thesis as necessary.

2. Consider your focus to determine if you will persuade, inquire, negotiate (see pages 157–162), or perhaps use a focus as explained in Chapter 1: evaluation, definition, proposal, causal argument, analogy, precedence (see pages 6–9).

3. Write an academic title for your paper—one that clearly describes the nature of your work (see pages 162–163).

4. After you draft a significant portion of the paper, review it carefully for each of these items: coherence, proper tense, third-person voice, and the language of the discipline.

Chapter 11 Clear Targets

As your research project develops and takes shape, it is vital that you provide citations for all borrowed material that you use in your paper. Your blending of in-text references should conform to standards announced by your instructor. This chapter explains MLA documentation style, as established by the Modern Language Association. It governs papers in composition courses, literature, English usage, and foreign language. Look for the following writing techniques in this chapter:

- Blending reference citations into your text
- Citing sources with no author or page number
- Identifying Internet sources
- Citing reference works and quoted matter
- Punctuating citations properly and consistently

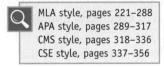

MLA style, pages 221–288
APA style, pages 289–317
CMS style, pages 318–336
CSE style, pages 337–356

The MLA style puts great emphasis on the writer of the source, asking for the full name of the scholar on first mention but last name only thereafter and last name only in parenthetical citations. Other styles emphasize the year of publication as well as the author. Still other styles use merely a number in order to emphasize the material, not the author or date.

11a Blending Reference Citations into Your Text

As you might expect, writing a research paper carries with it certain obligations. You should gather scholarly material on the topic and display it prominently in your writing. In addition, you should identify each source used with the authority's name or the title of the work with a page number, except for unprinted sources and most Internet sources, which will not require a page number. As a general policy, keep citations brief.

Remember, your readers will have full documentation to each source on the Works Cited page (see Chapter 14).

Making a General Reference without a Page Number

Sometimes you will need no parenthetical citation.

> The women of Thomas Hardy's novels are the special focus of three essays by Nancy Norris, Judith Mitchell, and James Scott.

Beginning with the Author and Ending with a Page Number

Introduce a quotation or a paraphrase with the author's name and close it with a page number, placed inside the parentheses. Try always to use this standard citation because it informs the reader of the beginning and the end of borrowed materials, as shown here:

> Herbert Norfleet states that the use of video games by children improves their hand and eye coordination (45).

In the following example, the reader can easily trace the origin of the ideas.

> Video games for children have opponents and advocates. Herbert Norfleet defends the use of video games by children. He says it improves their hand and eye coordination and that it exercises their minds as they work their way through various puzzles and barriers. Norfleet states, "The mental gymnastics of video games and the competition with fellow players are important to young children for their physical, social, and mental development" (45). Yet some authorities disagree with Norfleet for several reasons.

Putting the Page Number Immediately after the Name

Sometimes, notes at the end of a quotation make it expeditious to place the page number immediately after the name.

> Boughman (46) urges car makers to "direct the force of automotive airbags *upward* against the windshield" (emphasis added).

Putting the Name and Page Number at the End of Borrowed Material

You can, if you like, put cited names with the page number at the end of a quotation or paraphrase.

> "Each DNA strand provides the pattern of bases for a new strand to form, resulting in two complete molecules" (Justice, Moody, and Graves 462).

In the case of a paraphrase, you should give your reader a signal to show when the borrowing begins, as shown next:

> One source explains that the DNA in the chromosomes must be copied perfectly during cell reproduction (Justice, Moody, and Graves 462).

Use last names only within the parenthetical citation *unless your list contains more than one author with the same last name,* in which case you should add the author's first initial—for example, (H. Norfleet 45) and (W. Norfleet 432). If the first initial is also shared, use the full first name: (Herbert Norfleet 45).

HINT: In MLA style, do not place a comma between the name and the page number.

11b   Citing a Source When No Author Is Listed

When no author is shown on a title page, cite the title of the article, the name of the magazine, the name of a bulletin or book, or the name of the publishing organization. You should abbreviate or use an acronym (e.g., BBC, NASA).

HINT: Search for the author's name at the bottom of the opening page, at the end of the article, at an Internet home page, or in an e-mail address.

Citing the Title of a Magazine Article

Use a shorted version of the title when no author is listed:

> In the spring of 1862, the tranquil setting of Frances Chancellor's farmhouse seemed far removed from the horrors of war; however, the

civilians' impending ordeal in the midst of violent combat was fast approaching with the arrival of the Union army. According to a recent article in Hallowed Ground magazine, "Sassing Yankees seemed good sport briefly, but gave way to deadly danger when the dusty country crossroads became the focus of operations for two mighty armies" ("Dramatic Events").

The Works Cited entry would read:

> "Dramatic Events at the Chancellor House." *Hallowed Ground*.
> Spring 2013: 27.

Note: When citing a lengthy title, it is acceptable to shorten the name of the article in the in-text citation.

Citing the Title of a Report

One bank showed a significant decline in assets despite an increase in its number of depositors (*Annual Report,* 23).

Citing the Name of a Publisher or a Corporate Body

The report by the Clarion County School Board endorsed the use of Channel One in the school system and said that "students will benefit by the news reports more than they will be adversely affected by advertising" (CCSB 3–4).

11c Citing Nonprint Sources That Have No Page Number

On occasion you may need to identify nonprint sources, such as a speech, the song lyrics from a CD, an interview, or a television program. Since no page number exists, omit the parenthetical citation. Instead, introduce the type of source—for example, lecture, letter, interview—so readers do not expect a page number.

Thompson's lecture defined *impulse* as "an action triggered by the nerves without thought for the consequences."

Mrs. Peggy Meacham said in her phone interview that prejudice against young Black women is not as severe as that against young Black males.

11d Citing Internet Sources

Identify the Source with Name or Title

Whenever possible, identify the author of an Internet article. Usually, no page number is listed.

> Hershel Winthrop interprets Hawthorne's stories as the search for holiness in a corrupt Puritan society.

If you can't identify an author, give the article title or website information.

> One website claims that any diet that avoids carbohydrates will avoid some sugars that are essential for the body ("Fad Diets").

Identify the Nature of the Information and Its Credibility

As a service to your reader, indicate your best estimate of the scholarly value of an Internet source. For example, the next citation explains the role of the Center for Communications Policy:

> The UCLA Center for Communication Policy, which conducted an intensive study of television violence, has advised against making the television industry the "scapegoat for violence" by advocating a focus on "deadlier and more significant causes: inadequate parenting, drugs, underclass rage, unemployment and availability of weaponry."

Here's another example of an introduction that establishes credibility:

> Charles Bolden, NASA Administrator at the Johnson Space Center, states:
>
> > Today, 12 members of the International Space Exploration Coordination Group, of which NASA is a member, released our *"Global Exploration Roadmap,"* sending a clear signal that the global community wants to be a part of NASA's unified deep-space exploration strategic plan, with robotic and human missions to destinations that include near-Earth asteroids, the moon, and Mars.

Note: To learn more about the source of an Internet article, as in the case immediately above, learn to search out a home page. By truncating the address, you can learn about the organization that Armstrong represents.

If you are not certain about the credibility of a source—that is, it seemingly has no scholarly or educational basis—do not cite it, or describe the source so readers can make their own judgments:

> An Iowa non-profit organization, the Mothers for Natural Law, says—but offers no proof—that eight major crops are affected by genetically engineered organisms—canola, corn, cotton, dairy products, potatoes, soybeans, tomatoes, and yellow crook-neck squash ("What's on the Market").

Omitting Page and Paragraph Numbers to Internet Citations

In general, you should not list a page number, paragraph number, or screen number for an Internet site.

- You cannot list a screen number because monitors differ.
- You cannot list a page number of a downloaded document because computer printers differ.
- Unless they are numbered in the document, you cannot list paragraph numbers. Besides, you would have to go through and count every paragraph.

The marvelous feature of electronic text is that it is searchable, so your readers can find your quotation quickly with the Find or Search features. Suppose you have written the following:

> The Television Violence Report advices against making the television industry the "scapegoat for violence" by advocating a focus on "deadlier and more significant causes: inadequate parenting, drugs, underclass rage, unemployment and availability of weaponry."

A reader who wants to investigate further can consult your Works Cited page, find the Internet address (URL), use a browser to locate the article, or use "Find" for a phrase, such as "scapegoat for violence." That is much easier on you than numbering all the paragraphs and easier on the reader than counting them.

Some academic societies are urging scholars who publish on the Internet to number their paragraphs, and that practice may catch on quickly. Therefore, you should provide a paragraph number if the author of the Internet article has numbered each paragraph.

> The Insurance Institute for Highway Safety emphasizes restraint first, saying, "Riding unrestrained or improperly restrained in a motor vehicle always has been the greatest hazard for children" (par. 13).

Provide a page number only if you find original page numbers buried within the electronic article. For example, a database like JSTOR reproduces original images of works and thereby provides original page numbers, as with the article by Harold R. Walley shown in Figure 11.1. Cite these pages just as you would a printed source.

> One source says the "moralizing and philosophical speculation"
> in *Hamlet* is worthy of examination, but to Shakespeare these were
> "distinctly subsidiary to plot and stage business . . ." (Walley 778).

11e Citing Indirect Sources

Sometimes the writer of a book or article will quote another person from an interview or personal correspondence, and you will want to use that same quotation. For example, in a news release entitled "EPA Releases Agency Plans for Adapting to a Changing Climate," press agent Dale Kemery addressed the preparedness and steps taken by the agency regarding President Obama's "Climate Action Plan and Executive Order on Preparing the United States for the Impacts of Climate Change." Following is a portion of the press release:

> "To meet our mission of protecting public health and the
> environment, the EPA must help communities adapt to a changing
> climate," said EPA Administrator Gina McCarthy. "These Implementation
> Plans offer a roadmap for agency work to meet that responsibility,
> while carrying out President Obama's goal of preparing the country for
> climate-related challenges."
>
> The impacts of a changing climate—including increased extreme
> weather, floods, and droughts—affect EPA's work to protect clean air
> and water. The draft Climate Change Adaptation Implementation Plans
> recognize that EPA must integrate climate adaptation planning into its
> programs, policies, rules, and operations to ensure that the agency's
> work continues to be effective even as the climate changes.

Suppose that you want to use a portion of the quotation above by EPA Administrator Gina McCarthy. You will need to quote the words of

McCarthy and also recognize Kemery in the parenthetical citation as the primary source, as shown in the following:

> Whether it is a natural disaster or gradual climate change, towns, cities, and communities across the nation must seek guidance and assistance for balancing the needs of the people and the preservation of the environment. According to Environmental Protection Agency Administrator Gina McCarthy, "The EPA must help communities adapt to a changing climate." She goes on to say that the "Implementation Plans offer a roadmap for agency work to meet that responsibility."
>
> (qtd. in Kemery)

On the Works Cited page, you will list Kemery's name with the information for his article, but you will not list McCarthy's name there because she is not the author of the article.

In other words, in the text you need a double reference that introduces the speaker and includes a clear reference to the book or article where you found the quotation or the paraphrased material. Without the reference to Kemery, nobody could find the article. Without the reference to McCarthy, readers would assume that Kemery spoke the words.

CHECKLIST

Using Links to Document Internet Sources

If you are publishing your project on your own Web page, you have the opportunity to send your readers to other sites via hypertext links. If you do so, follow these guidelines:

1. You may activate a hot key (hypertext link) in your document that will automatically send your reader to one of your sources.

2. Identify the linked source clearly so readers know where the link will take them.

3. Be selective; don't sprinkle your document with excessive links. You want the reader to stay with you, not wander around on the Internet.

4. The links are part of your documentation, so cite these linked sources in your Works Cited list.

> ■ **HINT:** If you can locate the original source of the quotation, cite it rather than use the double reference.

11f Citing Frequent Page References to the Same Work

If you quote more than once from the same page within a paragraph and no other citations intervene, you may provide one citation at the end for all the references.

> When the character Beneatha denies the existence of God in Hansberry's *A Raisin in the Sun,* Mama slaps her in the face and forces her to repeat after her, "In my mother's house there is still God." Then Mama adds, "There are some ideas we ain't going to have in this house. Not long as I am at the head of the family" (37).

Also, when you make frequent references to the same source, you need not repeat the author's name in every instance. Note the following example:

> The consumption of "healing foods," such as those that reduce blood pressure, grows in popularity each year. Clare Hasler says that when the medicinal properties of functional food gain the support of clinical evidence, functional foods can become an economical weapon in the battle against rising health care costs. In addition, functional foods may be a promising addition to the diet of people who suffer from deadly disease. As executive director of the Functional Foods for Health Program at the University of Illinois, she claims, "Six of the ten leading causes of death in the United State are believed to be related to diet: cancer, coronary heart disease, stroke, diabetes, atherosclerosis, and liver disease" ("Western Perspective" 66).

> ■ **HINT:** If you are citing from two or more novels in your paper—let's say John Steinbeck's *East of Eden* and *Of Mice and Men*—provide both title (abbreviated) and page(s) unless the reference is clear: (*Eden* 56) and (*Mice* 12–13).

11g Citing Material from Textbooks and Large Anthologies

Reproduced below is a poem that you might find in many literary textbooks:

Love
> Love bade me welcome; yet my soul drew back,
>> Guilty of dust and sin.
> But quick-eyed Love, observing me grow slack
>> From my first entrance in,
> Drew nearer to me, sweetly questioning
>> If I lacked anything.
>>> —George Herbert, 1633

If you quote lines of the poem, and if that is all you quote from the anthology, cite the author and page in the text and put a comprehensive entry in the works cited list.

Text:

For Herbert, love "bade me welcome" and at the same time watched him "grow slack" before "sweetly questioning" if he needed something more solid and fulfilling (1094).

Works Cited entry:

Herbert, George. "Love." *Literature.* 12th ed. Ed. X. J. Kennedy and Dana Gioia. New York: Longman, 2013. 1094.

Suppose, however, that you also take quotations from other poems in the textbook.

In "The Sick Rose," William Blake observes the loss or deception found in the fading beauty of the "sick rose," for love may at one instance appear light, blithe, and beautiful yet "his dark secret love / Does they life destroy" (1069).

William Blake describes the "invisible worm" that destroyed the happiness found in the "crimson joy" of the lovely rose (1069).

More on citing anthologies, page 268.

Now, with three citations to the same anthology, you should list in your Works Cited the anthology used, as edited by Kennedy and Gioia, and also use shortened citations for Herbert and Blake, with both referring to the lead editor's name, in this case "Kennedy and Gioia."

> Blake, William. "The Sick Rose." *Literature*. 12th ed. Ed. X. J.
>
> Kennedy and Dana Gioia. New York: Longman, 2013. 1069. Print.
>
> Herbert, George. "Love." *Literature*. 12th ed. Ed. X. J. Kennedy
>
> and Dana Gioia. New York: Longman, 2013. 1094. Print.
>
> Kennedy, X. J. and Dana Gioia, eds. *Literature*. 12th ed. New York:
>
> Longman, 2013. Print.

11h Adding Extra Information to In-Text Citations

As a courtesy to your reader, add extra information within the citation. Show parts of books, different titles by the same writer, or several works by different writers. For example, your reader may have a different anthology than yours, so a clear reference, such as (*Great Expectations* 81; ch. 4), will enable the reader to locate the passage. The same is true with a reference to (*Romeo and Juliet* 2.3.65–68). The reader will find the passage in almost any edition of Shakespeare's play. Here's a reference to Herman Melville's *Moby-Dick* that shows both page and chapter:

> Melville uncovers the superstitious nature of Ishmael by stressing
>
> Ishmael's fascination with Yojo, the little totem god of Queequeg
>
> (71; ch. 16).

One of Several Volumes

These next two citations provide three vital facts: (1) an abbreviation for the title; (2) the volume used; and (3) the page number(s). The Works Cited entry will list the total number of volumes (see pages 275–276).

> In a letter to his Tennessee Volunteers in 1812 General Jackson
>
> chastised the "mutinous and disorderly conduct" of some of his troops
>
> (*Papers* 2: 348–49).

> Joseph Campbell suggests that man is a slave yet also the master
>
> of all the gods (*Masks* 2: 472).

However, if you use only one volume of a multivolume work, you need to give only page numbers in the parenthetical reference. Then include the volume number in the Works Cited entry (see page 275):

> Don Quixote's strange adventure with the Knight of the Mirrors is
>
> one of Cervantes's brilliant short tales (1,908–14).

If you refer to an entire volume, there is no need for page numbers:

> The Norton Anthology of World Literature includes masterpieces
>
> of the ancient world, the Middle Ages, and the Renaissance (Mack
>
> et al., vol. 1).

Two or More Works by the Same Writer

In this example, the writer makes reference to two novels, both abbreviated. The full titles are *Tess of the D'Urbervilles* and *The Mayor of Casterbridge.*

> Thomas Hardy reminds readers in his prefaces that "a novel is an
>
> impression, not an argument" and that a novel should be read as "a
>
> study of man's deeds and character" (*Tess* xxii; *Mayor* 1).

If the author appears in the parenthetical citation, place a comma after the name: (Hardy, *Tess* xxii; Hardy, *Mayor* 1). If anything other than a page number appears after the title, follow the title with a comma: (Worth, "Computing," par. 6).

The complete titles of the two works by Campbell referenced in the following example are *The Hero with a Thousand Faces* and *The Masks of God,* a four-volume work.

> Because he stresses the nobility of man, Joseph Campbell
>
> suggests that the mythic hero is symbolic of the "divine creative and
>
> redemptive image which is hidden within us all . . ." (*Hero* 39). The
>
> hero elevates the human mind to an "ultimate mythogenetic zone—the
>
> creator and destroyer, the slave and yet the master, of all the gods"
>
> (*Masks* 1: 472).

Several Authors in One Citation

You may want to cite several sources that treat the same topic. Put them in alphabetical order to match that of the Works Cited page, or place them in the order of importance to the issue at hand. Separate them with semicolons.

Several sources have addressed this aspect of gang warfare as a fight for survival, not just for control of the local neighborhood or "turf" (Robertson 98–134; Rollins 34; Templass 561–65).

Additional Information with the Page Number

Your citations can refer to special parts of a page—for example, footnote, appendix, graph, table—and can also specify emphasis on particular pages.

Horton suggests that Melville forced the symbolism, but Welston (199–248, esp. 234) reaches an opposite conclusion.

However, use a semicolon to separate the page number from the edition used, a chapter number, or other identifying information: (Wollstonecraft 185; ch. 13, sec. 2).

11i   Punctuating Citations Properly and Consistently

Keep page citations outside quotation marks but inside the final period, as shown here:

"The benefits of cloning far exceed any harm that might occur" (Smith 34).

In MLA style, use no comma between the name and the page within the citation (for example, Jones 16–17, *not* Jones, 16–17). Do not use *p.* or *pp.* with the page number(s) in MLA style. However, if an author's name begins a citation to paragraph numbers or screen numbers, *do* include a comma after the author's name (Richards, par. 4) or (Thompson, screens 6–7).

Commas and Periods

Place commas and periods inside quotation marks unless the page citation intervenes. The example below shows (1) how to put the mark inside the quotation marks, (2) how to interrupt a quotation to insert the speaker, (3) how to use single quotation marks within the regular quotation marks, and (4) how to place the period after a page citation.

"Modern advertising," says Rachel Murphy, "not only creates a marketplace, it determines values." She adds, "I resist the advertiser's argument that they 'awaken, not create desires'" (192).

Sometimes you may need to change the closing period to a comma. Suppose you decide to quote this sentence: "Scientific cloning poses no threat to the human species." If you start your sentence with the quotation, you will need to change the period to a comma, as shown:

"Scientific cloning poses no threat to the human species,"

declares Joseph Wineberg in a recent article (357).

However, retain question marks or exclamation marks; no comma is required:

"Does scientific cloning pose a threat to the human species?"

wonders Mark Durham (546).

Let's look at other examples. Suppose this is the original material:

The Russians had obviously anticipated neither the quick discovery of the bases nor the quick imposition of the quarantine. Their diplomats across the world were displaying all the symptoms of improvisation, as if they had been told nothing of the placement of the missiles and had received no instructions what to say about them.
—From: Arthur M. Schlesinger, Jr. *A Thousand Days.* New York: Houghton, 1965. 820.

Punctuate citations from this source in one of the following methods in accordance with MLA style:

"The Russians," writes Schlesinger, "had obviously anticipated neither the quick discovery of the [missile] bases nor the quick imposition of the quarantine" (820).

Schlesinger notes, "Their diplomats across the world were displaying all the symptoms of improvisation . . ." (820).

Schlesinger observes that the Russian failure to anticipate an American discovery of Cuban missiles caused "their diplomats across the world" to improvise answers as "if they had been told nothing of the placement of the missiles . . ." (820).

Note that the last example correctly changes the capital *T* of "their" to lowercase to match the grammar of the restructured sentence, and it does not use ellipsis points before "if" because the phrase flows smoothly into the text.

Semicolons and Colons

Both semicolons and colons go outside the quotation marks, as illustrated by these three examples:

> Zigler admits that "the extended family is now rare in contemporary society"; however, he stresses the greatest loss as the "wisdom and daily support of older, more experienced family members" (42).

> Zigler laments the demise of the "extended family": that is, the family suffers by loss of the "wisdom and daily support of older, more experienced family members" (42).

> Brian Sutton-Smith says, "Adults don't worry whether *their* toys are educational" (64); nevertheless, parents want to keep their children in a learning mode.

The third example, immediately above, shows how to place the page citation after a quotation and before a semicolon.

Use the semicolon to separate two or more works in a single parenthetical reference:

> (Roman, *Dallas* 16; Manfred 345)

> (Steinbeck, *Grapes* 24; Stuben xii)

Question Marks and Exclamation Marks

When a question mark or an exclamation mark serves as part of the quotation, keep it inside the quotation mark. Put the page citation immediately after the name of the source to avoid conflict with the punctuation mark.

> Thompson (16) passionately shouted to union members, "We can bring order into our lives even though we face hostility from every quarter!"

If you place the page number at the end of the quotation, retain the original exclamation mark or question mark, follow with the page reference, and then a sentence period outside the citation.

> Thompson passionately shouted to union members, "We can bring order into our lives even though we face hostility from every quarter!" (16).

Retain question marks and exclamation marks when the quotation begins a sentence; no comma is required.

> "We face hostility from every quarter!" declared the union leader.

Question marks appear inside the closing quotation mark when they are part of the original quotation; otherwise, they go outside.

> The philosopher Brackenridge (16) asks, "How should we order our
> lives?"

and

> The philosopher Brackenridge asks, "How should we order our
> lives?" (16).

but

> Did Brackenridge say that we might encounter "hostility from
> every quarter" (16)?

Single Quotation Marks

When a quotation appears within another quotation, use single quotation marks with the shorter one. The period goes inside both closing quotation marks.

> George Loffler (32) confirms that "the unconscious carries the
> best of human thought and gives man great dignity, but it also has
> the dark side so that we cry, in the words of Shakespeare's Macbeth,
> 'Hence, horrible shadow! Unreal mockery, hence.'"

Remember that the period always goes inside quotation marks unless the page citation intervenes, as shown below:

> George Loffler confirms that "the unconscious carries the best of
> human thought and gives man great dignity, but it also has the dark
> side so that we cry, in the words of Shakespeare's Macbeth, 'Hence,
> horrible shadow! Unreal mockery, hence'" (32).

11j Indenting Long Quotations

Set off long prose quotations of four lines or forty or more words by indenting 1 inch or 10 spaces, which is usually two clicks of the tab key. Do not enclose the indented material within quotation marks. If you quote only one paragraph or the beginning of one, do *not* indent the first line an extra five spaces. Maintain normal double spacing between your text and the quoted materials. Place the parenthetical citation *after* the final mark of punctuation. In the example below, the parenthetical citation might be a title to an Internet article rather than page numbers:

> With the fast pace of the modern world, many young people fail to realize the simplicity of previous generations. Garrett Snow, director of Roots-Web Genealogy for the Upper Cumberland, commented on the need to understand and preserve family history, especially among those of the rising generations:
>
> > With the passing of time, it is easy to forget the many individuals who have left an indelible mark on our ever-changing society. With the passing of time, it is easy to forget that for every great figure in history, there were neighbors, friends, and parents who instilled the confidence in the individual so that they could make a useful and beneficial contribution to society. With the passing of time, it is easy to forget the contribution made by our grandparents, great-grandparents, and forebears. The roll call of ancestors may not include figures of outstanding importance in history, yet this legacy is a record of men and women who lived active, useful lives, and who gave to their nation and their communities the best that was in them. ("Heritage")
>
> Whether young or old, each person must understand that heritage is not just a time designated and set aside for a day, week, or month; it is an ongoing celebration of the heirlooms, honesty, and history that has been handed down in the written, oral, and photographic traditions of our families.

If you quote more than one paragraph, indent the first line of each paragraph an extra three (3) spaces or a quarter-inch. However, if the first sentence quoted does not begin a paragraph in the original source, do not indent it an extra three spaces.

> Zigler makes this observation:
>
> > With many others, I am nevertheless optimistic that our nation will eventually display its inherent greatness and successfully correct the many ills that I have touched upon here.

Of course, much remains that could and should be done,
including increased efforts in the area of family planning, the
widespread implementation of Education for Parenthood programs,
an increase in the availability of homemaker and child care
services, and a reexamination of our commitment to doing what is
in the best interest of every child in America. (42)

11k Citing Poetry

Quoting Two Lines of Poetry or Less

Incorporate short quotations of poetry (one or two lines) into
your text.

In stanza 1 of Lord Byron's "She Walks in Beauty" (1814), the
poet extends his physical description to describe the inward, divine,
praiseworthy aspects of the woman. Beginning with an image of a dark,
clear sky to set her beauty against, he values "All that's best of dark
and bright / Meet in her aspect and her eyes" (lines 3–4). Thus, the
woman who Byron is praising holds a "tender light" (5) between her
outward beauty and the calm, soft image of her soul.

As the example demonstrates:
1. Set off the material with quotation marks.
2. Indicate separate lines by using a virgule (/) with a space before and after it.
3. Place line documentation within parentheses immediately following the quotation mark and inside the period. Do not use the abbreviations *l.* or *ll.*, which might be confused with page numbers; use *lines* initially to establish that the numbers represent lines of poetry, and thereafter use only the numbers.
4. Use Arabic numerals for books, parts, volumes, and chapters of works; acts, scenes, and lines of plays; and cantos, stanzas, and lines of poetry.

Quoting Three Lines of Poetry or More

Set off three or more lines of poetry by indenting 1 inch or 10 spaces, as shown below. Use double-spaced lines. A parenthetical citation to the lines of indented verse follows the last line of the quotation. If the parenthetical citation will not fit on the last line, place it on the next line, flush with the right margin of the poetry text.

The king cautions Prince Henry:

> Thy place in council thou has rudely lost,
>
> Which by thy younger brother is supplied,
>
> And art almost an alien to the hearts
>
> Of all the court and princes of my blood.
>
> (3.2.32–35)

Refer to act, scene, and lines only after you have established Shakespeare's *Henry IV, Part 1* as the central topic of your study; otherwise, write (IH4 3.2.32–35). If you are citing from more than one play, always add an abbreviation for the play (1H4 1.1.15–18).

Indenting Turnovers for Long Lines of Poetry

When quoting a line of poetry that is too long for your right margin, indent the continuation line three spaces or a quarter-inch more than the greatest indentation.

> Thomas Traherne opens his poem "Eden" with these lines:
>
> A learned and a happy ignorance
>
> Divided me
>
> From all the vanity,
>
> From all the sloth, care, pain, and sorrow
>
>   that advance
>
> The madness and the misery
>
> Of men. No error, no distraction I
>
> Saw soil the earth, or overcloud the sky. (lines 1–8)

For using ellipsis points with poetry, see pages 196–197.

Retaining Internal Quotations within a Block

While you should not use quotation marks around a block quotation, *do* retain any internal quotation marks:

> With his sonnet "Spring," Shakespeare playfully describes the cry of the cuckoo bird:
>
> The cuckoo then, on every tree,
>
> Mocks married men; for thus sings he, "Cuckoo!
>
> Cuckoo, cuckoo!" O word of fear,
>
> Unpleasing to a married ear! (524)

Providing Translations

When a quotation is run into the text, use double quotation marks for translations placed within parentheses but single quotations around a translation without the parentheses:

> Chaucer's setting is Spring, when "zephyrs ("west winds") have breathed softly all about . . ." (line 5).

> Chaucer's setting is Spring, when "zephyrs 'west winds' have breathed softly all about . . ." (line 5).

Do not place quotation marks around quotations and translations set off from the text in a block. Place the block of translation below the block of poetry.

> Ramon Magrans has translated this Frederico García poem in a literal manner:

> Alto pinar!
> Cuatro palomas por el aire van.

> Cuatro palomas
> Vuelan y tornan
> Llevan heridas
> sus cuatro sombras

> Bajo pinar!
> Cuatro palomas en la tierra están.

> Above the pine trees
> four pigeons fly through the air.

> Four pigeons
> fly and turn around
> Wounded, they carry
> their four shadows.

> Below the pine trees
> four pigeons lie on the earth.

11l   Handling Quotations from a Play

Set off from your text any dialog of two or more characters. Begin with the character's name, indented 1 inch and written in all capital letters. Follow the name with a period, and then start the character's lines of dialog. Indent subsequent lines of dialog an additional quarter-inch or three (3) spaces.

> At the end of *Oedipus Rex,* Kreon chastises Oedipus, reminding him
>
> that he no longer has control over his own life nor that of his children.
>
> > KREON.   Come now and leave your children.
> >
> > OEDIPUS.   No! Do not take them from me!
> >
> > KREON.   Think no longer
> >
> > > That you are in command here, but rather think
> > >
> > > How, when you were, you served your own destruction.

11m   Altering Initial Capitals in Quoted Matter

In general, you should reproduce quoted materials exactly, yet one exception is permitted for logical reasons. Restrictive connectors, such as *that* and *because,* create restrictive clauses and eliminate a need for the comma. Without a comma, the capital letter is unnecessary. In the following example, "The," which is capitalized as the first word in the original sentence, is changed to lowercase because it continues the grammatical flow of the student's sentence.

> Another writer argues that "the single greatest impediment to
>
> our improving the lives of America's children is the myth that we are a
>
> child-oriented society" (Zigler 39).

Otherwise, write:

> Another writer argues, "The single greatest . . ."

11n   Omitting Quoted Matter with Ellipsis Points

You may omit portions of quoted material with three spaced ellipsis points, as shown in the following examples.

Context

In omitting passages, be fair to the author. Do not change the meaning or take a quotation out of context.

Correctness

Maintain the grammatical correctness of your sentences—that is, avoid fragments and misplaced modifiers. You don't want your readers to misunderstand the structure of the original. When you quote only a phrase, readers will understand that you omitted most of the original sentence, so no ellipsis is necessary.

Phil Withim recognizes the weakness in Captain Vere's "intelligence and insight" into the significance of his decisions regarding Billy Budd (118).

Omission within a Sentence

Use three ellipsis points (periods) with a space before each and a space after the last.

Phil Withim objects to the idea that "such episodes are intended to demonstrate that Vere . . . has the intelligence and insight to perceive the deeper issue" (118).

Omission at the End of a Sentence

If an ellipsis occurs at the end of your sentence, use three periods with a space before each following a sentence period—that is, you will have four periods with no space before the first or after the last. A closing quotation mark finishes the punctuation.

R. W. B. Lewis (62) declares that "if Hester has sinned, she has done so as an affirmation of life, and her sin is the source of life. . . ."

However, if a page citation also appears at the end in conjunction with the ellipsis, use three periods with a space before each and put the sentence period after the final parenthesis. Thus, you will have three ellipsis points with a space before each, the closing quotation mark followed by a space, the parenthetical citation, and the period.

R. W. B. Lewis declares that "if Hester has sinned, she has done so as an affirmation of life, and her sin is the source of life . . ." (62).

Omission at the Beginning of a Sentence

Most style guides discourage the use of ellipsis points for material omitted from the beginning of a source, as shown here:

He states: ". . . the new parent has lost the wisdom and daily support of older, more experienced family members" (Zigler 34).

The passage would read better without the ellipsis points:

He states that "the new parent has lost the wisdom and daily support of older, more experienced family members" (Zigler 34).

Another option is this one, as stipulated by the *Chicago Manual of Style*: "If a quotation that is only part of a sentence in the original forms a complete sentence as quoted, a lowercase letter may be changed to a capital if appropriate."

He states: "The new parent has lost the wisdom and daily support of older, more experienced family members" (Zigler 34).

Here's another example:

R. W. B. Lewis declares, "If Hester has sinned, she has done so as an affirmation of life, and her sin is the source of life . . ." (62).

Omission of Complete Sentences and Paragraphs

Use a closing punctuation mark and three spaced ellipsis points when omitting one or more sentences from within a long quotation. Here's an omission in which one sentence ends, another sentence or more is omitted, and a full sentence ends the passage.

Zigler reminds us that "child abuse is found more frequently in a single (female) parent home in which the mother is working. . . . The unavailability of quality day care can only make this situation more stressful" (42).

Here's an omission from the middle of one sentence to the middle of another:

Zigler reminds us that "child abuse is found more frequently in a single (female) parent home in which the mother is working, . . . so the unavailability of quality day care can only make this situation more stressful" (42).

Omissions in Poetry

If you omit a word or phrase in a quotation of poetry, indicate the omission with three or four ellipsis points, just as you would with omissions in a prose passage. However, if you omit a complete line or more from the poem, indicate the omission by a line of spaced periods that equals the average length of the lines. Note that the parenthetical citation shows two sets of lines.

Elizabeth Barrett Browning asks:

Do ye hear the children weeping, O my brothers,

Ere the sorrow comes with years?

> They are leaning their young heads against their mothers,
>
>   And *that* cannot stop their tears.
>
> . . . .
>
> They are weeping in the playtime of the others,
>
> In the country of the free. (1–4, 11–12)

Avoid Excessive Use of Ellipsis Points

Many times, you can be more effective if you incorporate short phrases rather than quote the whole sprinkled with many ellipsis points. Note how this next passage incorporates quotations without the use of ellipsis:

> The long-distance marriage, according to William Nichols, "works best when there are no minor-aged children to be considered," the two people are "equipped by temperament and personality to spend a considerable amount of time alone," and both are able to "function in a mature, highly independent fashion" (54).

Ellipsis in the Original

If the original passage has ellipsis by the author, and you want to cut additional words, place brackets around your ellipsis points to distinguish them from the author's ellipsis points. If the original says:

Shakespeare's innovative techniques in working with revenge tragedy are important in *Hamlet* . . . while the use of a Senecan ghost is a convention of revenge tragedy, a ghost full of meaningful contradictions in calling for revenge is part of Shakespeare's dramatic suspense.

If you cut the middle phrase, use this form:

> One writer says, "Shakespeare's innovative techniques in working with revenge tragedy are important in *Hamlet* . . . [. . .] a ghost full of meaningful contradictions in calling for revenge is part of Shakespeare's dramatic suspense."

11o Altering Quotations with Parentheses and Brackets

You will sometimes need to alter a quotation to emphasize a point or to make something clear. You might add material, italicize an important word, or use the word *sic* (Latin for "thus" or "so") to alert readers that you have properly reproduced the material even though the logic or the spelling of the original might appear to be in error. Use parentheses or brackets according to these basic rules.

Parentheses

Use parentheses to enclose your comments or explanations that fall outside a quotation, shown in these examples:

> The problem with airbags is that children (even those in protective seats) can be killed by the force as the airbag explodes. Boughman (46) urges car makers to "direct the force of automotive airbags *upward* against the windshield" (emphasis added).

> Roberts (22) comments that "politicians suffer a conflict with honoure" (sic).

Brackets

Use brackets for interpolation, which means inserting your own comment into a text or quotation. The use of brackets signals the insertion. Note the following rules.

Use Brackets to Clarify

> This same critic indicates that "we must avoid the temptation to read it [*The Scarlet Letter*] heretically" (118).

Use Brackets to Establish Correct Grammar within an Abridged Quotation

> "John F. Kennedy [was] an immortal figure of courage and dignity in the hearts of most Americans," notes one historian (Jones 82).

> He states: "[The] new parent has lost the wisdom and daily support of older, more experienced family members" (Zigler 34).

Use Brackets to Note the Addition of Italics

> He says, for instance, that the "extended family is now rare in contemporary society, and with its demise the new parent has *lost the wisdom* [my emphasis] and daily support of older, more experienced family members" (Zigler 42).

Use Brackets to Substitute a Proper Name for a Pronoun

> "As we all know, he [Kennedy] implored us to serve the country, not take from it" (Jones 432).

Use Brackets with *Sic* to Indicate Errors in the Original

> Lovell says, "John F. Kennedy, assassinated in November of 1964 [sic], became overnight an immortal figure of courage and dignity in the hearts of most Americans" (62).

HINT: The assassination occurred in 1963. However, do not burden your text with the use of "sic" for historical matter in which outmoded spellings are obvious, as with: "Faire seemely pleasauance each to other makes."

Use Brackets with Ellipsis Points

See the example on page 198.

YOUR RESEARCH PROJECT

1. Examine your handling of the sources. Have you introduced them clearly so the reader will know when the borrowing began? Have you closed them with a page citation, as appropriate? Have you placed quotation marks at the beginning and the end of borrowed phrases as well as borrowed sentences?

2. If you have used online sources, look at them again to see if the paragraphs on the website are numbered. If so, use the paragraph numbers in your citation(s); if not, use no numbers—not the numbers on any printout and not paragraph numbers if you must count them.

3. Look at your source material to find a table, graph, figure, or photograph you might insert into your paper as additional evidence. Be certain that you have labeled it correctly (see pages 168–170 for examples).

4. Make a critical journey through your text to be certain you have made an informed choice about the documentation style you need. Normally, instructors will inform you. In general, use MLA style for papers in freshman composition and literature classes; use APA style for papers in the social sciences; use CMS note style for papers in history and the fine arts; use CSE number style for papers in the applied sciences.

12 Writing the Introduction, Body, and Conclusion

Chapter 12 Clear Targets

Your research project should adopt an academic style that presents a fair, balanced treatment of the subject. This chapter will help you establish a structure for your paper as you advance evidence from your research:

- Establishing your subject with a clear introduction
- Developing the body of the paper with your evidence
- Creating a conclusion that restates and reaches beyond your study

As you draft your paper, your voice should flow from one idea to the next smoothly and logically.

12a Writing the Introduction of the Research Paper

Use the first few paragraphs of your paper to establish the nature of your study. In brief, the introduction should establish the problem, the body should present the evidence, and the conclusion should arrive at answers, judgments, proposals, and closure. Most important, let the introduction and body work *toward* a demonstrative conclusion. The introduction should be long enough to establish the required elements described in the checklist on page 201.

> For additional discussion of thesis statement, enthymeme, and hypothesis, see pages 24–27.

How you work these essential elements into the framework of your opening will depend on your style of writing. They need not appear in this order, nor should you cram all these items into a short opening paragraph. Feel free to write two or three paragraphs of introduction, letting it run over onto the next page, if necessary. When crafting your introduction, use more than one of the techniques described in the following approaches.

Provide the Thesis Statement

Generally, the controlling statement will appear early in the introduction to establish the agenda for the paper or appear late in the introduction to

---

CHECKLIST

Writing the Introduction

Subject   Identify your specific topic, and then define, limit, and narrow it to one issue.

Background   Provide relevant historical data. Discuss a few key sources that touch on your specific issue. If writing about a major figure, give relevant biographical facts, but not an encyclopedia-type survey. (See "Provide Background Information," page 203.)

Problem   The point of a research paper is to explore or resolve a problem, so identify and explain the complications you see. The examples shown in the following sections demonstrate this technique.

Thesis   Within the first few paragraphs, use your thesis sentence to establish the direction of the study and to point your readers toward your eventual conclusions.

---

set the stage for the analysis to come in the body. For example, this opening features the thesis first:

Thesis —

> Created by an act of Congress in 1933 and signed into law by President Franklin D. Roosevelt, the Tennessee Valley Authority Act created stability on the waterways and in the lives of citizens in the mid-south. With its establishment of a series of dams, the TVA controlled the drainage of 42,000 square miles of and waterways. That same control harnessed the power of the rivers to create electricity for residents of the area.

Provide the Enthymeme

The enthymeme, as explained on page 26, uses a *because* clause to make a claim. It also determines the direction your paper will take. Notice the enthymeme that closes this opening paragraph:

> Here we are, a civilized world with reasonably educated people, yet we constantly fight with each other. These are

not sibling squabbles either; people die in terrible ways. We wonder, then, if there was ever a time when men and women lived in harmony with one another and with nature and the environment. The Bible speaks of the Garden of Eden, and the French philosopher Jean-Jacques Rousseau advanced the idea in the 1700s of the "noble savage," and that "nothing could be more gentle" than an ancient colony of people (LaBlanc 15). Wrong! There has never been a "noble savage," as such, because even prehistoric human beings fought frequent wars for numerous reasons.

Enthymeme

Provide a Hypothesis

The hypothesis, as explained on pages 26–27, is a theory that needs testing in the lab, in the literature, and/or by field research to prove its validity. Writers may list it as an objective, as in this example:

Diabetes is a disease that affects approximately 11 million people in the U.S. alone. Its complications lead to approximately 350,000 deaths per year and cost the nation $20,373 billion per year in medical care, in the direct cost of complications, and in the indirect costs of loss of productivity related to the disease (Guthrie and Guthrie 1). The condition can produce devastating side effects and a multitude of chronic health problems. Diabetes currently has no known cure, but it can be controlled. The objective of this study is to examine how well diabetes can be controlled by a combination of medication, monitoring, diet, and exercise.

Hypothesis

Relate to the Well Known

The next passage will appeal to the popular interest and knowledge of the reader:

Television flashes images into our living rooms, radios invade the confines of our automobiles, and local newspapers flash their headlines to us daily. However, one medium that has gained great popularity and influence within the past decade is the specialized magazine.

Popular appeal

Provide Background Information

Writers may trace the historical nature of a topic, give biographical data about a person, or provide a geographic description. A summary of a novel, long poem, or other work can refresh a reader's memory about details of plot, character, and so forth.

> First published in 1915, *Spoon River Anthology* by
> Edgar Lee Masters gives readers candid glimpses into the
> life of a small town at the turn of the twentieth century.

Background —
> Speaking from beyond the grave, the narrator of each poem
> gives a portrait of happy, fulfilled people or draws pictures
> of lives filled with sadness and melancholy.

This passage offers *essential* background matter, not information irrelevant to the thesis. For example, explaining that Eudora Welty was born in Jackson, Mississippi, in 1909 would contribute little to the following opening:

Background —
> In 1941 Eudora Welty published her first book of
> short stories, *A Curtain of Green*. That group of stories
> was followed by *The Wide Net* (1943) and *The Bride of the*
> *Innisfallen* (1955). Each collection brought her critical
> acclaim, but taken together the three volumes established
> her as one of America's premier short story writers.

Review the Literature

Cite a few books and articles relevant to the specific issue to introduce literature connected with the topic. This paragraph gives distinction to your introduction because it establishes the scholarship on the subject. It also distinguishes your point of view by explaining the logical connections and differences between previous research and your work:

> Throughout his novella *Billy Budd,* Herman Melville
> intentionally uses biblical references as a means of presenting
> different moral principles by which people may govern their
> lives. The story depicts the "loss of Paradise" (Arvin 294);

Review of
literature —
> it serves as a gospel story (Weaver 37–38); and it hints at a
> moral and solemn purpose (Watson 319). The story explores
> the biblical passions of one man's confrontation with good
> and evil (Howard 327–28; Mumford 248). This paper will
> examine the biblical references.

Review the History and Background of the Subject

The opening passage normally reviews the history of the topic, often with quotations from the sources, as shown below in APA style:

Autism, a neurological dysfunction of the brain which commences before the age of thirty months, was identified by Leo Kanner (1943). Kanner studied eleven cases, all of which showed a specific type of childhood psychosis that was different from other childhood disorders, although each was similar to childhood schizophrenia. Kanner described the characteristics of the infantile syndrome as:

Background information

1.   Extreme autistic aloneness

2.   Language abnormalities

3.   Obsessive desire for the maintenance of sameness

4.   Good cognitive potential

5.   Normal physical development

6.   Highly intelligent, obsessive, and cold parents

Medical studies have reduced these symptoms to four criteria: onset within thirty months of birth, poor social development, late language development, and a preference for regular, stereotyped activity (Rutter, 2013; Watson, 2012; Waller, Smith, & Lambert, 2013). In the United States, autism affects one out of 2,500 children, and is not usually diagnosed until the child is between two and five years of age (Lambert & Smith, 2013).

Take Exception to Critical Views

This opening procedure identifies the subject, establishes a basic view taken by the literature, and then differs with or takes exception to the critical position of other writers, as shown in the following example:

Lorraine Hansberry's popular and successful *A Raisin in the Sun,* which first appeared on Broadway in 1959, is a problem play of a Black family's determination to escape a Chicago ghetto to a better life in the suburbs. There is agreement that this escape theme explains the drama's conflict and its role in the Black movement (e.g., Oliver,

Archer, and especially Knight, who describes the Youngers as "an entire family that has become aware of, and is determined to combat, racial discrimination in a supposedly democratic land" [34]). Yet another issue lies at the heart of the drama. Hansberry develops a modern view of Black matriarchy in order to examine both the cohesive and the conflict-producing effects it has on the individual members of the Younger family.

Exception to prevailing views

Challenge an Assumption

This type of introduction presents a well-known idea or general theory in order to question it, analyze it, challenge it, or refute it.

Christianity dominates the religious life of most Americans to the point that many assume that it dominates the world population as well. However, despite the denominational missionaries who have reached out to every corner of the globe, only one out of every four people on the globe is a Christian, and far fewer than that practice their faith. In truth, Christianity does not dominate religious beliefs around the globe.

Challenge to an assumption

Provide a Brief Summary

When the subject is a literary work, historic event, educational theory, or similar item, a brief summary will refresh the reader's memory.

The chief legacy of the two Bush administrations might well be one of waging war. George Bush liberated Kuwait with the 1991 war against Iraq, but he withdrew after accomplishing that mission rather than overthrow Saddam Hussein and his government in Baghdad. Later, George H. Bush retaliated against the Taliban of Afghanistan in late 2001 after the 9/11 tragedy. Then, in 2003, George H. W. Bush attacked Iraq again to remove Saddam Hussein from power. This study will examine the literature to confirm the hypothesis that Bush and Bush will be remembered as war presidents.

Summary

Summary

Alice Walker's *The Color Purple* narrates the ordeal of a young Black girl living in Georgia in the early years of the twentieth century. Celie writes letters to God because she has no one else to help her. The letters are unusually strong and give evidence of Celie's painful struggle to survive the multiple horrors of her life.

Define Key Terms

Sometimes an opening passage must explain difficult terminology, as in the following example:

Definition

Occurring in one of every 3,900 babies born, cystic fibrosis remains one of the most common fatal genetic disorders in the United States. Approximately 30,000 American children and young adults have cystic fibrosis (Tariev 224). Cystic fibrosis causes the body to secrete an abnormally thick, sticky mucus that clogs the pancreas and the lungs, leading to problems with breathing and digestion, infection, and ultimately, death. Thirty years ago most infants with cystic fibrosis died in early childhood, but today more than 60 percent of babies born with cystic fibrosis reach adulthood, thanks in part to gene therapy. With continued advances in diagnosing and treating the disease, the prognosis for future generations will be significantly improved.

Supply Data, Statistics, and Special Evidence

Concrete evidence can attract the reader and establish the subject. For example, a student working with demographic data might compare the birth and death rates of certain sections of the world. In Europe, the rates are almost constant, while the African nations have birth rates that are 30 percent higher than the death rates. Such statistical evidence can be a useful tool in many papers. Just remember to support the data with clear, textual discussion.

Sample research papers with well-developed paragraphs, pages 311–314.

CHECKLIST

Avoiding Certain Mistakes in the Introduction

Avoid a purpose statement, such as "The purpose of this study is . . ." unless you are writing reports of empirical research, in which case you *should* explain the purpose of your study (see Chapter 15, "Writing in APA Style").

Avoid repetition of the title, which should appear on the first page of the text anyway.

Avoid complex language or difficult questions that may puzzle the reader. However, general rhetorical questions are acceptable.

Avoid simple dictionary definitions, such as "Webster defines *monogamy* as marriage with only one person at a time." See page 210 for an acceptable opening that features definition.

Avoid humor, unless the subject deals with humor or satire.

Avoid hand-drawn artwork, clip art, and cute lettering unless the paper's subject matter requires it (for example, "The Circle as Advertising Symbol"). *Do* use computer graphics, tables, illustrations, and other visuals that are appropriate to your subject.

12b Writing the Body of the Research Paper

Sample research paper with well-developed paragraphs, pages 228–235, and 237–248.

When writing the body of the paper, you should classify, compare, and analyze the issues. Keep in mind three key elements, as shown in the checklist on pages 208–209.

The length of your paragraphs ought to be from four sentences up to twelve or even fifteen. You can accomplish this task only by writing good topic sentences and by developing them fully. The techniques described in the following paragraphs demonstrate how to build substantive paragraphs for your paper.

Organize by Chronology

Use *chronology* and *plot summary* to trace historical events and to survey a story or novel. You should, almost always, discuss the significance of the events. This first example traces historical events.

Time Sequence established

> Following the death of President Roosevelt in April 1945, Harry S Truman succeeded to the Presidency. Although
>
> he was an experienced politician, Truman "was ill prepared

to direct a foreign policy," especially one that "called for the use of the atomic bomb to bring World War II to an end" (Jeffers 56). Consideration must be directed at the circumstances of the time, which led up to Truman's decision that took the lives of over 100,000 individuals and destroyed four square miles of the city of Hiroshima. Consideration must be given to the impact that this decision had on the war, on Japan, and on the rest of the world. Consideration must be directed at the man who brought the twentieth century into the atomic age.

The next passage shows the use of plot summary.

Quick plot summary
> John Updike's "A & P" is a short story about a young grocery clerk named Sammy who feels trapped by the artificial values of the small town where he lives and, in an emotional moment, quits his job. The store manager, Lengel, is the voice of the conservative values in the community. For him, the girls in swimsuits pose a disturbance to his store, so he expresses his displeasure by reminding the girls that the A & P is not the beach (1088). Sammy, a liberal, believes the girls may be out of place in the A & P only because of its "fluorescent lights," "stacked packages," and "checkerboard green-and-cream rubber-tile floor," all artificial things (1086).

HINT: Keep the plot summary short and relate it to your thesis, as shown by the first sentence in the previous passage. Do not allow the plot summary to extend beyond one paragraph; otherwise, you may retell the entire story.

CHECKLIST

Writing the Body of the Paper

Analysis   Classify the major issues of the study and provide a careful analysis of each in defense of your thesis.

| Presentation | Provide well-reasoned statements at the beginning of your paragraphs, and supply evidence of support with proper documentation. |
| Paragraphs | Offer a variety of development to compare, show process, narrate the history of the subject, show causes, and so forth. |

Compare or Contrast Issues, Critical Views, and Literary Characters

Employ *comparison* and *contrast* to show the two sides of a subject, to compare two characters, to compare the past with the present, or to compare positive and negative issues. The next passage compares and contrasts differences in forest conservation techniques.

When a "controlled burn" gets out of hand and burns an entire town, defenders of controlled burns have a serious public relations problem. Thus, to burn or not to burn the natural forests in the national parks is the question. The pyrophobic public voices its protests while environmentalists praise the rejuvenating effects of a good forest fire. It is difficult to convince people that not all fire is bad. The public has visions of Smokey the Bear campaigns and mental images of Bambi and Thumper fleeing the roaring flames. Perhaps the public could learn to see beauty in fresh green shoots, like Bambi and Faline do as they returned to raise their young. Chris Bolgiano explains that federal policy evolved slowly "from the basic impulse to douse all fires immediately to a sophisticated decision matrix based on the functions of any given unit of land" (22). Bolgiano declares that "timber production, grazing, recreation, and wilderness preservation elicit different fire-management approaches" (23).

Comparison and contrast

Develop Cause and Effect

Write *cause-and-effect* paragraphs to develop the reasons for a circumstance or to examine its consequences. An example is shown here that not only explains with cause and effect, but also uses the device of *analogy,* or metaphoric comparison—in this case, of bread dough and the uniform expansion of the universe.

To see how the Hubble Law implies uniform, centerless expansion of a universe, imagine that you want to make a loaf of raisin bread. As the dough rises, the expansion pushes the raisins away from each other. Two raisins that were originally about one centimeter apart separate more slowly than raisins that were about four centimeters apart. The uniform expansion of the dough causes the raisins to move apart at speeds proportional to their distances. Helen Write, in explaining the theory of Edwin Powell Hubble, says the farther the space between them, the faster two galaxies will move away from each other. This is the basis for Hubble's theory of the expanding universe (369).

Analogy

Cause and effect

Define Your Key Terminology

Use *definition* to explain and expand upon a complex subject. This next example, by Katie Hebert, defines *functional foods*:

Functional foods, as defined by the Australian National Food Authority, are:

A class of foods that have strong putative metabolic and reulatory (physiological) roles over and above those seen in a wide range of common foods; a class of foods that achieve a defined endpoint that can be monitored (e.g., reduction in blood pressure, reduction in plasma-borne risk markers); and products referred to as special dietary foods. (Head, Record, and King S17)

Definition

Explain a Process

Draft a *process* paragraph that explains, one by one, the steps necessary to achieve a desired end:

Process —

Blood doping is a process for increasing an athlete's performance on the day of competition. To perform this procedure, technicians drain about one liter of blood from the competitor about 10 months prior to the event. This time allows the "hemoglobin levels to return to normal" (Ray 79). Immediately prior to the athletic event, the blood is reintroduced by injection to give a rush of blood into the athlete's system. Ray reports that the technique produces an "average decrease of 45 seconds in the time it takes to run five miles on a treadmill" (80).

Ask Questions and Provide Answers

Framing a question as a topic sentence gives you the opportunity to develop a thorough answer with specific details and evidence. Look at how this approach is used in this example:

Question —

Does America have enough park lands? The lands now designated as national and state parks, forests, and wild land total in excess of 33 million acres. Yet environmentalists call for additional protected land. They warn of imbalances in the environment. Dean Fraser, in his book, *The People Problem,* addresses the question of whether we have enough park land:

> Yosemite, in the summer, is not unlike Macy's the week before Christmas. In 1965 it had over 1.6 million visitors; Yellowstone over 2 million. The total area of federal plus state-owned parks is now something like 33 million acres, which sounds impressive until it is divided by the total number of annual visitors of something over 400 million. . . . (33)

Answer —

We are running short of green space, which is being devoured by highways, housing projects, and industrial development.

Cite Evidence from the Source Materials

Citing evidence from authorities in the form of quotations, paraphrases, and summaries to support your topic sentence is another excellent way to build a paragraph. This next passage combines commentary by a critic and a poet to explore Thomas Hardy's pessimism in fiction and poetry.

Several critics reject the impression of Thomas Hardy as a pessimist. He is instead a realist who tends toward optimism. Thomas Parrott and Willard Thorp make this comment about Hardy in *Poetry of the Transition*:

Evidence from a source

> There has been a tendency in the criticism of Hardy's work to consider him as a philosopher rather than as a poet and to stigmatize him as a gloomy pessimist. This is quite wrong. (413)

The author himself felt incorrectly labeled, for he has written his own description:

> As to pessimism. My motto is, first correctly diagnose the complaint—in this case human ills— and ascertain the cause: then set about finding a remedy if one exists. The motto of optimists is: Blind the eyes to the real malady, and use empirical panaceas to suppress the symptoms. (*Life* 383)

Hardy is dismayed by these "optimists," so he has no desire to be lumped within such a narrow perspective.

Use a Variety of Other Methods

Many methods exist for developing paragraphs; among them are the *description* of a scene in a novel, *statistics* in support of an argument, *historical evidence* in support of a hypothesis, *psychological theory*, and others. You must make the choices, basing your decision on your subject and your notes. Employ the following methods as appropriate to your project.

- Use *classification* to identify several key issues of the topic, and then use *analysis* to examine each issue in detail. For example, you might classify several types of fungus infections, such as athlete's foot, dermatophytosis, and ringworm, and then analyze each.

- Use specific *criteria of judgment* to examine performances and works of art. For example, analyze the films of George Lucas with a critical response to story, theme, editing, photography, sound track, special effects, and so forth.
- Use *structure* to control papers on architecture, poetry, fiction, and biological forms. For example, a short story might have six distinct parts you can examine in sequence.
- Use *location* and *setting* for arranging papers in which geography and locale are key ingredients. For example, examine the settings of several novels by William Faulkner, or build an environmental study around land features (e.g., lakes, springs, sinkholes).
- Use *critical responses to an issue* to evaluate a course of action. For example, an examination of President Truman's decision to use the atomic bomb in World War II would invite you to consider several minor reasons and then to study Truman's major reason(s) for his decision.
- Dividing the body by important *issues* is standard fare in many research papers.

12c Writing the Conclusion of the Research Paper

The conclusion of a research paper should offer the reader more than a mere summary. Use the following checklist to review your conclusion.

How you work these elements into your conclusion will depend on your style of writing. They need not appear in this order, nor should you crowd all the items into one paragraph. The conclusion can extend over

CHECKLIST

Writing the Conclusion

Thesis	Reaffirm your thesis statement.
Judgment	Reach a decision or judgment about the merits of the subject, be it a work of art, an author's writing, a historical moment, or a social position.
Discussion	Discuss the implications of your findings.
Directive	Offer a plan of action or a proposal that will put into effect your ideas. (Not required of every paper.)
Ending	Use the final paragraph, especially the final sentence, to bring the paper to closure.

several paragraphs and require more than one page. When drafting the conclusion, consider using several of the techniques described here.

Restate the Thesis and Reach beyond It

As a general rule, restate your thesis statement; however, do not stop and assume that your reader will generate final conclusions about the issues. Instead, establish the essential mission of your study. In the example below, one student opens her conclusion by reestablishing her thesis statement and then moves quickly to her persuasive, concluding judgments.

Thesis restated in the conclusion —

Functional foods appear to exert a strong preventive effect on the two diseases that take most American lives than any other—coronary heart disease and cancer. High cholesterol levels cause coronary heart disease, the factor responsible for 24 percent of the fatalities that occur in the United States (Blumberg 3). Foods high in antioxidants (i.e., Vitamin C, E, and beta-carotene), omega-3 fatty acids, and soluble fiber, along with green and black tea, have been proven to be an effective form of preventive medicine for individuals at risk of developing coronary heart disease. Second only to coronary heart disease, "cancer is the cause of death in 22 percent of Americans" (4). Functional foods have exhibited similar strength in the fight for cancer prevention. By incorporating functional foods, such as insoluble fiber, garlic, and green and black tea into the diet, an individual can lower his or her risk of being diagnosed with cancer. Although this finding does not mean one should cancel all future doctor appointments, it has shown that individuals who eat functional foods are a step ahead in the battle for disease prevention.

Close with an Effective Quotation

Sometimes a source may provide a striking commentary that deserves special placement, as shown by this example:

W. C. Fields had a successful career that extended from vaudeville to musical comedy and finally to the movies. In his private life, he loathed children and animals, and he fought with bankers, landladies, and the police. Off screen, he maintained his private image as a vulgar, hard-drinking cynic until his death in 1946. On the screen, he won the hearts of two generations of fans. He was beloved by audiences primarily for acting out their own contempt for authority. The movies prolonged his popularity "as a dexterous comedian with expert timing and a look of bibulous rascality," but Fields had two personalities, "one jolly and one diabolical" (Kennedy).

Effective quotation — [bracket enclosing: The movies prolonged his popularity "as a dexterous comedian with expert timing and a look of bibulous rascality," but Fields had two personalities, "one jolly and one diabolical"]

Return the Focus of a Literary Study to the Author

While the body of a literary paper should analyze characters, images, and plot, the conclusion should explain the author's accomplishments. The following closing shows how one writer focused on the author:

As to the issues of the country versus the city and the impact of a market economy, Jonathan Swift advances the conservative position of the early eighteenth century, which lamented the loss of the rural, agrarian society, with its adherence to tradition and a stable social hierarchy. His position focused on the social outcomes: unemployment, displacement, and the disenfranchisement of a significant portion of the populace. Unlike his London contemporaries, Swift resided in the economic hinterland of Ireland, so he had a more direct view of the destructive population shifts from rural to urban.

Focus on the author — [bracket enclosing: Jonathan Swift advances the conservative position of the early eighteenth century,]

Ultimately, Swift's commentary in *A Modest Proposal* is important because it records a consciousness of a continuing problem, one that worsens with the intensification of the urban rather than rural growth. It continues to plague the twenty-first–century world, from America to Africa and from Russia to Latin America.

Focus on the author — [bracket enclosing: Ultimately, Swift's commentary in *A Modest Proposal* is important because it records a consciousness of a continuing problem, one that worsens with the intensification of the urban rather than rural growth.]

Compare the Past to the Present

You can use the conclusion rather than the opening to compare past research to the present study or to compare the historic past with the contemporary scene. For example, after explaining the history of two schools of treatment for autism, one writer switches to the present, as shown in this excerpt:

Future in contrast to the present —

> There is hope in the future that both the cause and the cure for autism will be found. For the present, new drug therapies and behavior modification offer some hope for the abnormal, SIB actions of a person with autistism. Since autism is sometimes outgrown, childhood treatment offers the best hope for the autistic person who must try to survive in an alien environment.

Offer a Directive or Solution

After analyzing a problem and synthesizing issues, offer your theory or solution, as demonstrated in the previous example in which the writer suggests that "childhood treatment offers the best hope for the autistic person who must try to survive in an alien environment." Note also this closing:

CHECKLIST

Avoiding Certain Mistakes in the Conclusion

- **Avoid** afterthoughts or additional ideas. Now is the time to end the paper, not begin a new thought. If new ideas occur to you as you write your conclusion, do not ignore them. Explore them fully in the context of your thesis and consider adding them to the body of your paper or modifying your thesis. Scientific studies often discuss options and possible alterations that might affect test results (see the next section, "Discuss Test Results").
- **Avoid** the use of "thus," "in conclusion," and "finally" at the beginning of the last paragraph. Readers can see plainly the end of the paper.
- **Avoid** ending the paper without a sense of closure.
- **Avoid** questions that raise new issues; however, rhetorical questions that restate the issues are acceptable.
- **Avoid** fancy artwork.

A directive
or solution

> All of the aspects of diabetes management can be summed up in one word: balance. Diabetes itself is caused by a lack of balance of insulin and glucose in the body. In order to restore that balance, a diabetic must juggle medication, monitoring, diet, and exercise. Managing diabetes is not an easy task, but a long and healthy life is very possible when the delicate balance is carefully maintained.

Discuss Test Results

In scientific writing (see Chapters 15 and 17), your conclusion, labeled "discussion," must explain the ramifications of your findings and identify any limitations of your scientific study, as shown:

Test results

> The results of this experiment were similar to expectations, but perhaps the statistical significance, because of the small subject size, was biased toward the delayed conditions of the curve. The subjects were, perhaps, not representative of the total population because of their prior exposure to test procedures. Another factor that may have affected the curves was the presentation of the data. The images on the screen were available for five seconds, and that amount of time may have enabled the subjects to store each image effectively. If the time period for each image were reduced to one or two seconds, there could be lower recall scores, thereby reducing the differences between the control group and the experimental group.

YOUR RESEARCH PROJECT

1. Review your opening to determine whether it builds the argument and sets the stage for analysis to come in the body. Consider adding paragraphs like those described on pages 200–207: Relate the well known, provide background information, review the literature, review the history of the subject, take exception to prevailing views, challenge an assumption, provide a summary of the issues, define key terms, and supply statistical evidence.

2. After finishing the first draft, review the body of your paper. Has your analysis touched on all the issues? Have you built paragraphs of substance, as demonstrated on pages 207–213? Judge the draft against the checklist for the body on pages 208–209.

3. Evaluate your conclusion according to the checklist on page 213. If you feel it's necessary, build the conclusion by these techniques: Elaborate on the thesis, use an effective quotation, focus on a key person, compare the past and the present, offer a directive or solution, or discuss test results (see pages 214–217 for a discussion of these techniques).

13 Revising, Proofreading, and Formatting the Rough Draft

Chapter 13 Clear Targets

After you have developed the rough draft of your paper, the serious business of editing begins. This chapter explains the necessary steps needed for refining and formatting the rough draft into a finished research project.

- Revising the paper on a global scale
- Moving blocks of material around to the best advantage and into the proper format
- Drafting with a line-by-line examination of wording and technical excellence
- Proofreading the final manuscript to assure that the text is grammatically sound

The key to having a polished, complete research paper is to revise with logic and clarity.

13a Conducting a Global Revision

For discussion of developing the introduction, see pages 200–207.

Revision can turn a passable paper into an excellent one and change an excellent one into a radiant one. First, revise the whole manuscript by performing the tasks in the checklist shown on page 220.

Revising the Introduction

Examine your opening for the presence of several items:

- Your thesis
- A clear sense of direction or plan of development
- A sense of involvement that invites the reader into your investigation of a problem

For discussion of building effective paragraphs, see pages 207–213.

Revising the Body

Use the following bulleted list as a guide for revising each individual paragraph of the body of your paper.

- Cut out wordiness and irrelevant thoughts, even to the point of deleting entire sentences that contribute nothing to the dynamics of the paper.
- Combine short paragraphs with others or build one of greater substance.
- Revise long, difficult paragraphs by dividing them or by using transitions effectively (see "Writing with Unity and Coherence," page 165).
- For paragraphs that seem short, shallow, or weak, add more commentary and more evidence, especially quotations from the primary source or critical citations from secondary sources.
- Add your own input to paragraphs that rely too heavily on the source materials.
- Examine your paragraphs for transitions that move the reader effectively from one paragraph to the next.

For discussion of writing the conclusion, see pages 214–217.

Revising the Conclusion

Examine the conclusion to see that it meets these criteria:

- It is drawn from the evidence.
- It is developed logically from the introduction and the body.
- It expresses your position on the issues.

CHECKLIST

Global Revision

1. Skim through the paper to check its unity. Does the paper maintain a central proposition from paragraph to paragraph?
2. Transplant paragraphs, moving them to more relevant and effective positions.
3. Delete sentences that do not further your cause.
4. As you cut, copy, and paste, remember to rewrite and blend the words into your text.
5. If your outline must be submitted with your draft, revise it to reflect these global revisions.

CHECKLIST

Peer Review

1. Are the subject and the accompanying issues introduced early?

2. Is the writer's critical approach to the problem presented clearly in a thesis statement? Is it placed effectively in the introduction?

3. Do the paragraphs of the body have individual unity? That is, does each one develop an important idea and only one idea? Does each paragraph relate to the thesis?

4. Are sources introduced, usually with the name of the expert, and then cited by a page number within parentheses? Keep in mind that Internet sources, in most cases, do not have page numbers.

5. Is it clear where a paraphrase begins and where it ends?

6. Are the sources relevant to the argument?

7. Does the writer weave quotations into the text effectively while avoiding long quotations that look like filler instead of substance?

8. Does the conclusion arrive at a resolution about the central issue?

9. Does the title describe clearly what you have found in the contents of the research paper?

Participating in Peer Review

Part of the revision process for many writers, both students and professionals, is peer review. This has two sides. First, it means handing your paper to a friend or classmate, asking for opinions and suggestions. Second, it means reviewing a classmate's research paper. You can learn by reviewing as well as by writing.

Since this task asks you to make judgments, you need a set of criteria. Your instructor may supply a peer review sheet, or you can use the "Peer Review" checklist provided here. Criticize the paper constructively on each point. If you can answer each question with a *yes,* your classmate has performed well. For those questions you answer *no,* you owe it to your classmate to explain what seems wrong. Make suggestions. Offer tips. Try to help!

13b   Formatting the Paper to MLA Style

The format of a research paper consists of the following parts:

1. Title page
2. Outline

3. Abstract
4. The text of the paper
5. Content notes
6. Appendix
7. Works Cited

Items 4 and 7 are required for a paper in the MLA style; use the other items to meet the needs of your research. *Note:* A paper in APA style (see Chapter 15) requires items 1, 3, 4, and 7, and the order differs for items 5–7.

Title Page or Opening Page

A research paper in MLA style does not need a separate title page unless you include an outline, abstract, or other prefatory matter. Place your identification in the upper-left corner of your opening page, as shown here:

1 inch from
top of page

1/2 inch in the header position Howell 1

Pamela Howell

Professor Magrans   Identifying
Information
English 102c

17 November 2013

Creative Marriages

Judging by recent divorce rates, it would seem that the

traditional marriage fails to meet the needs . . .

Note: APA style requires a different setup for the title page; see page 310 for an example.

If you do include prefatory matter, such as an outline, you need the title page with centered divisions for the title, the author, and the course identification.

An Interpretation of Melville's

Use of Biblical Characters

in *Billy Budd*

by

Melinda Singleton

English II, Section 108b

Dr. Crampton

April 23, 2014

Follow these guidelines for writing a title page in MLA style:

1. Use an inverted pyramid to balance two or more lines.
2. Use capitals and lowercase letters without underlining and without quotation marks. Published works that appear as part of your title require italicizing (books) or quotation marks (short stories). Do not use a period after a centered heading.
3. Place your full name below the title, usually in the center of the page.
4. Employ separate lines, centered, to provide the course information, institution, instructor, date, or program (e.g., Honors Program).
5. Provide balanced margins for all sides of the title page.

Outline

Print your outline with the finished manuscript only if your instructor requires it. Place it after the title page on separate pages and number these pages with small Roman numerals, beginning with ii (for example, ii, iii, iv, v), at the upper-right corner of the page, just after your last name (e.g., Spence iii). For information on writing an outline, see section 9i, pages 152–153, and the sample outline on page 153.

Abstract

Include an abstract for a paper in MLA style only if your instructor requires it. (APA style requires the abstract; see section 15f, pages 309–310.) An abstract provides a brief digest of the paper's essential ideas in about one hundred words. To that end, borrow from your introduction, use some of the topic sentences from your paragraphs, and use one or two sentences from your conclusion.

In MLA style, place the abstract on the first page of text one double space below the title and before the first lines of the text. Indent the abstract one-half inch as a block, and indent the first line an additonal half inch. Use quadruple spacing at the end of the abstract to set it off from the text, which follows immediately after. You may also place the abstract on a separate page between the title page and first page of text.

> For more on the abstract and examples, see pages 309–310.

Remember that the abstract is usually read first and may be the *only* part read; therefore, make it accurate, specific, objective, and self-contained (i.e., it makes sense alone without references to the main text). Note this example:

Wu 1

Child Abuse: A View of the Victims

Abstract

This study examines the problems of child abuse,

especially the fact that families receive attention after abuse occurs, not before. With abuse statistics on the rise, efforts devoted to prevention rather than coping should focus on parents in order to discover those adults most likely to commit abuse because of heredity, their own childhood, the economy, and other causes of depression. Viewing the parent as a victim, not just a criminal, will enable social agencies to institute preventive programs that may control abuse and hold together family units.

Quadruple space

Text ⎡   Family troubles will most likely affect the delicate members of our society, the children. The recognition of causal elements . . .

The Text of the Paper

Double-space throughout the entire paper except for the title page (page 222) and the separation of the abstract from the first line of text (pages 222–223). In general, you should *not* use subtitles or numbered divisions for your paper, even if it becomes twenty pages long. Instead, use continuous paragraphing without subdivisions or headings. However, some scientific and business reports require subheads (see Chapters 15 and 17).

If the closing page of your text runs short, leave the remainder of the page blank. Do not write "The End" or provide artwork as a closing signal. Do not start Notes or Works Cited on this final page of text.

Content Endnotes Page

Label this page with the word *Notes* centered at the top edge of the sheet, at least one double space below your page-numbering sequence in the upper-right corner. Double-space between the *Notes* heading and the first note. Number the notes in sequence with raised superscript numerals to match those within your text. Double-space all entries and double-space between them.

For discussion of content notes, see pages 326–328.

Appendix

Place additional material, if necessary, in an appendix preceding the Works Cited page. This is the logical location for numerous tables and illustrations, computer data, questionnaire results, complicated statistics, mathematical proofs, and detailed descriptions of special equipment.

Double-space appendixes and begin each appendix on a new sheet. Continue your page numbering sequence in the upper-right corner of the sheet. Label the page *Appendix,* centered at the top of the sheet. If you have more than one appendix, use *Appendix A, Appendix B,* and so forth.

Works Cited

See Chapter 14, "Works Cited: MLA Style," pages 250–288, and sample Works Cited on pages 235 and 249.

Center the heading *Works Cited* 1 inch from the top edge of the sheet. Continue the page-numbering sequence in the upper-right corner. Double-space throughout. Set the first line of each entry flush left and indent subsequent lines five spaces. If your software supports it, use the hanging indent.

13c Editing before Typing or Printing the Final Manuscript

For discussion of unity, coherence, and effective writing, see pages 165–167.

The cut-and-paste revision period is complemented by careful editing of paragraphs, sentences, and individual words. Travel through the paper to study your sentences and word choice. Look for ways to tighten and condense. Use the checklist provided here to guide your editing.

Note the editing by one student in Figure 13.1. As shown, this writer conscientiously deleted unnecessary material, added supporting statements, related facts to one another, rearranged data, added new ideas, and rewrote for clarity.

Using the Computer to Edit Your Text

Remember to click on Tools and use the spelling and grammar checkers to spot spelling errors and to perform several tasks related to grammar and mechanics—for example, looking for parentheses you have opened but not closed, unpaired quotation marks, passive verbs, and other items. Pay attention to these caution flags. *Caution:* The spell-checker will not discern incorrect usage of "its" and "it's." However, you must edit and adjust your paper by *your* standards with due respect to the computer analysis. Remember, it is your paper, not the computer's. You may need to use some long words and write some long sentences, or you may prefer the passive voice to emphasize the receiver of the action, not the actor.

> ### CHECKLIST
>
> #### Editing the Manuscript
>
> 1. Cut phrases and sentences that do not advance your main ideas or that merely repeat what your sources have already stated.
> 2. Determine that coordinated, balanced ideas are appropriately expressed and that minor ideas are properly subordinated.
> 3. Change most of your *to be* verbs (is, are, was) to stronger, active verbs.
> 4. Maintain the present tense in most verbs.
> 5. Convert passive structures to active if possible.
> 6. Confirm that you have introduced paraphrases and quotations so that they flow smoothly into your text. Use a variety of verbs for the instructions (*Winston argues, Thomas reminds, Morganfield offers*).
> 7. Use formal, academic style, and guard against clusters of monosyllabic words that fail to advance ideas. Examine your wording for its effectiveness within the context of your subject.

In some cases   is   see
~~One critic calls~~ television "junk food" (Fransecky

717), and ~~I think~~ excessive viewing ~~does~~ distracts
        (see esp. Paul Witty as qtd. in Postman 41)
from other activities, yet television can and does
                and shows   of our best
bring cultural programs some ~~good~~ novels. It does,
according to the evidence,
improve children's vocabularies, encourages their
                               and school
reading, and inspires their writing. Television should
                s the traditional classroom curriculum
not be ~~an~~ antagonist; ~~it should complement school~~
should seek and find harmony with the preschool television
~~work.~~
curriculum.

FIGURE 13.1 Example of editing on a manuscript page.

13d Proofreading on the Screen and on the Printed Manuscript

First, proofread your paper on the screen with a program that will check your spelling, grammar, and style, as mentioned previously. Check your formatting for double spacing, 1-inch margins, running heads, page numbers, and so forth.

CHECKLIST

Proofreading the Final Draft

1. Check for errors in sentence structure, spelling, and punctuation.

2. Check for correct hyphenation and word division. Remember that *no* words should be hyphenated at the ends of lines. If you are using a computer, turn off the automatic hyphenation option.

3. Read each quotation for the accuracy of your own wording and of the words within your quoted materials. Look, too, for your correct use of quotation marks.

4. Be certain that in-text citations are correct and that each corresponding source is listed on your Works Cited page.

5. Double-check the format—the title page, margins, spacing, content notes, and many other elements, as explained on pages 221–225 and in the glossary on pages 366–374.

Consult the "Glossary: Rules and Techniques for Preparing the Manuscript in MLA Style," pages 366–374, for instructions on handling abbreviations, margins, numbering, punctuation, and other matters.

Check the entries in your Works Cited section for precision and completeness in the citations. Also, be sure that each is formatted with a hanging indention.

After editing the text on screen to your satisfaction, print out a hard copy of the manuscript. You should proofread this final paper version with great care because the software will not have caught every error. Be sure your in-text citations are correct and confirm that you have a corresponding bibliography entry for each.

YOUR RESEARCH PROJECT

1. Examine once again the intellectual argument of your first draft. Is it clearly established in the opening and then reaffirmed in the closing?

2. Do the paragraphs of the body develop systematically the evidence to support your claim or thesis? Examine each paragraph for relevance.

3. Examine again your title. Does it meet the criteria set forth on pages 162–163?

4. If you participated in a peer review, consider carefully the recommendations and judgments of your reviewer. There's always a tendency

to dismiss words of criticism, but you need to learn that constructive criticism exists at all levels of collegiate and professional life.

5. Read aloud to yourself a portion of the paper. Does it have an academic style? If not, read pages 163–168 and begin editing.

6. Read through the two papers that follow next in this chapter, pages 228–249, to get a feel for the academic style of writing. Try to duplicate that style.

13e Sample Papers in MLA Style

Short Literary Research Paper

Ashley Irwin accepted the challenge to write a literary analysis on Sylvia Plath's poems "Daddy" and "Lady Lazarus." After establishing background information about Plath's life, she concentrated her analysis on the themes presented in each poem. Eventually, she settled her study on the "visual imagery," and the author's attitude and emotions toward her father. Her literary research paper conforms to the format specified for MLA-style research papers.

Irwin 1

Ashley Irwin

English 3440

Dr. Pasch

13 November 2013

Sylvia Plath and her "Daddy"

In photos Sylvia Plath sweetly smiles, and at first glance she appears to have been an extremely happy daughter, wife, and mother. Her writing, however, reveals a tormented life, due to the loss of her father at an early age. Her poetry, which helped her to communicate her emotions, also helped her to reconnect to her father through visual imagery. She believed that if she could find the spirit of her father in her writing, she could be free of him, and thus be free from the burden of depression that she carried each day after his death. Two of her later poems, "Daddy" and "Lady Lazarus," show the darker side of Plath's struggles that she attempted to exorcise as an adult. Although Sylvia Plath appeared

Irwin establishes the concept that she will explore.

Irwin 2

to have been happy, her happiness was false, and it is only in her poems that her true feelings toward life, her father, and her despair can be found.

The majority of Sylvia Plath's life was haunted by a feeling of depression after the death of her father when she was eight years old (Beckmann). Assuming that his fatigue and illness was cancer, her father refused to seek treatment for diabetes mellitus. Soon after the discovery of the real cause of his illness, he was hospitalized yet died a few days later (Reuben). Her mother, who believed that her children should not have to witness such a tragic event, banned them from attending the funeral (Alexander 32). Due to her absence at the funeral, Sylvia was unable to properly grieve, and for the rest of her life she struggled with the void that her father's physical absence had left.

Unable to communicate her emotions and feelings about her own feelings toward her father's death, Sylvia believed that, through his death, he had abandoned her. One critic commented that "Plath conceived of art as a compensation for loss" and that "she needed to be disloyal and loyal to her father at once" (Axelrod 25). Plath believed that she could restore herself through her writing, but that also meant that she had to kill the memories of her father and the desire that she felt to reconnect with him. For Plath, "Death is given a cruel physical allure and psychic pain becomes almost tactile" (Gilson).

Christina Britzolakis believes that Plath frequently refers to the power of her father in her poetry in order to seek approval for her own struggles. As she ages, she uses these referential terms as a form of sarcasm to destroy his authority and construct her own. Britzolakis argues that "He is linked with the figures of the oracle and the archive: cryptic repositories of literary and psychic memory in which the daughter seeks authorization for her own discourse" (62). She constantly seeks the ability to control her

Irwin cites the authorities on Plath in brief but effective ways.

father, his death, and her own thoughts and feelings about it. In the poems "Daddy" and "Lady Lazarus" Sylvia Plath finally succeeds at overcoming her father's sway as she rises to grasp her own potential.

Slightly less confrontational than "Daddy," "Lady Lazarus" expresses Plath's desire to defy and overcome society's views and constraints on death. Although Britzolakis describes this poem as "manipulative, sensationalist, or irresponsible," it is more like a transitional piece for Plath as she becomes a stronger woman in regard to the high authority of her father (152). Plath uses language in the poem to shock the reader by "using assertions and blatant statements" (Britzolakis 152). This poem is her verbal defiance and unwillingness to be what others believed she was.

"Lady Lazarus" can be read several ways, but the poem is most often viewed as a symbol of rebirth. Plath struggled with thoughts of suicide in order to reconnect with her father, and in the case of this poem, it is very likely that Plath viewed suicide as a type of rebirth. In the first three lines, she writes, "I have done it again. / One year in every ten / I manage it." By "it," Plath is referring to suicide and her ability to handle its presence in her life. One critic has noted that "the text points to the fact that maybe those scars never healed" (Connell). She does not say that she is defeated by death; instead, she states that she "manages" it. One definition of "manage" is to "control by direction or persuasion" (Morehead 440). Hence, Plath controls the direction of death in her life. It is not something that controls her, but it is something that, in the case of happening, she will take advantage of its presence in her life.

For Sylvia Plath, suicide is a type of rebirth. In "Lady Lazarus," she states, "I am only thirty. / And like the cat I have nine times to die" (lines 20–21). Plath is pleased by her age and ability to escape actual death. The death she believes that she experiences in her attempts of suicide is a type of rebirth as she

Irwin accurately cites lines of poetry.

Irwin 4

never actually terminates her life. Instead of being controlled by the memory of her father and her fear of being abandoned, Plath is declaring that she is stronger than these memories and fears, and if she wants to commit suicide, she will.

In the last half of "Lady Lazarus," Plath shows a literal defiance toward society and her relationships with men. She emphasizes her defiance in lines 57 to 64, stating that "there is a charge" for the sight of her scars, the hearing of her heart, speaking with her, touching her, hurting her, or a piece of her hair. This "charge" defies the quiet submission that society would expect her as a woman, for she is standing up for herself. Plath is tired of the concern of those around her, for she is able to take care of herself in her own way. She then shifts the direction of her words from society towards men as she writes,

Use a block quotation of lines of poetry for four or more lines.

> Herr God, Herr Lucifer
>
> Beware
>
> Beware.
>
> Out of the ash
>
> I rise with my red hair
>
> And I eat men like air. (79–84)

As Plath relates her father to God, she also associates him to "Lucifer." Axelrod noted that Plath somehow equated God with Satan (41). This relates to her conflicting view of her father as a good man and as an evil man at the same time. Hence, she warns her father that after her death, she will again be reborn and will treat men as though they do not matter. These feelings ultimately affected all other relationships with men. In "Lady Lazarus" Sylvia states that she will not be defeated even after the rebirth that will set her free from her father.

Sylvia Plath also confronts her father and the role that he has. In the poem "Daddy," Plath focuses less on society and more on her relationship with her father and the affect that he played in her relationships, her work, and in her life. She wrote this poem on the day that she agreed to divorce her husband Ted Hughes, after he had left her for another woman (Axelrod 52). This angry poem literally attacks her father as Plath dismembers her father's body piece-by-piece and finally resurrects him in the form of objects (Britzolakis 189). He is condemned to be a shoe, a tank, and a devil (2, 45, 54). Although he has died, she reincarnates him, but he is not allowed the fate that she would want if she was to be reborn. He must suffer how she has suffered, and she places this curse on him in her famous poem, "Daddy."

In "Daddy" Plath finally takes control of the situation with her father by cursing him to become an object or person who she cannot love. She initiates the poem by addressing him as a "black shoe" where she has "lived like a foot / for thirty years . . . Barely daring to breathe or Achoo" (2–5). This stanza refers to her isolation from her father due to his constant illness. As a child, Plath rarely saw her father except when she would recite poems to him before bed. These recitations were then followed by a hug, which was the only time that Otto ever touched his daughter for fear of contracting—or giving—an illness (Alexander 28). Although this might have been out of fatherly-love, Plath was never certain of her father's love; therefore, she was also wary of her own love for him.

Her love for her father was one that she never understood, for he had abandoned her by dying. She struggled with a love–hate relationship with the memories of her father and wrote in "Daddy," just as she had in "Lady Lazarus," that she wanted to kill him. Creating a "metaphorical murder" (Phillips) in the poem, she writes, "Daddy, I have had to kill you. / You died before I had time" (6–7). By using the present perfect tense, she states that he is dead, but she is still trying to kill his memory.

Irwin 6

There are constant references to Sylvia's feelings of isolation in "Daddy." She states that she never knew him and could never really talk to him, for her "tongue was stuck" and she "could hardly speak" (25, 28). This references her inability to know her father. The poem continues with, "I thought every German was you" (29). By using the word "thought," she shows that she once thought that he was "every German," but now, as a wiser adult, she knows that he is not. This, however, does not change the way that she looks at herself due to the way he treated her. She says that she began to feel like a Jew "chuffing off . . . to Dachua, Aushwitz, Belsen" (32–33). Plath viewed her father as a Nazi, and she was like a Jewish victim who had no control over her life (Britzolakis 188). If she had tried to speak to him about her life, it would not have mattered. Although he was not physically present in her life, Sylvia's father still had control of everything that had happened to her—even after his death and in her adulthood.

Added to her isolation, Plath writes, "I have always been scared of you" (41). She was frightened of him in the past, and the fear has never diminished. She then begins to describe him again and to expresses her view of him as a tank:

> With your Luftwaffe, your gobbledygoo.
>
> And your neat moustache
>
> And your Aryan eye, bright blue.
>
> Panzer-man, panzer-man, O You. (42–45)

Lines of the poem are indented, line breaks are maintained, and the line numbers are provided.

After she expresses her vulnerability, Plath attacks him again by dismembering his moustache and eye from his body and symbolizing him as a Panzer—or Nazi tank or armored vehicle (Plath, "Daddy" 1206). He again becomes an object that she cannot love, for a tank destroys scenery and landscapes. This is symbolic of the way that he destroyed her, and she, therefore, cannot love him for destroying her heart and life. She next shows that she cannot love him, for he is a man who is absolutely unlovable in her eyes.

The final lines of "Daddy" parallel the concluding themes in "Lady Lazarus." Plath writes that her father was "no less than a devil" (54). She again gives him god-like power, and, as in "Lady Lazarus," she takes an authorial voice to destroy his credibility. She writes, "I was ten when they buried you. / At twenty, I tried to die / And get back, back, back to you" (57–59). Plath uses her father as a scapegoat to blame him for her suicide attempts (Britzolakis 189). She states that she wanted to "get back" to him in order to be with him but then says, "If I've killed one man, I've killed two—/ The vampire who said he was you / And drank my blood for a year" (71–73). She is telling him that she has killed her memories of him, and he is no longer in her life. She tells him, "Daddy, you can lie back now . . . daddy, you bastard, I'm through" (75, 80). In these two lines, she is not only releasing him from her memory, but she is also telling him that he is free of her. According to Elaine Connell, "Daddy" is "a beautiful declaration of independence—a sentiment that ultimately was unable to sustain her." At the end of the poem, when she tells him that she is "through," Sylvia is also finally giving herself freedom from him. Throughout the entire poem, she expresses the idea that "love expresses itself only in terms of violence and brutality" (Hall 102). By this point, she has loved him so much, but he has not returned to her. Therefore, she is done. She is over. She is through, and she is finally free from the suicide and death of her father.

Irwin concludes with her interpretation and the implications in light of the poetic theme.

Although Plath states in "Daddy," that she is through with her father, she obviously was not done with him like she planned. Several years later, Plath was successful in her second suicide attempt. She died as a young, divorced mother, who battled the demons and memories of her father for her entire life. "Lady Lazarus" and "Daddy" show the influence and affect that her

Irwin 8

father's life and death had on her own life. When Plath evokes
images of wholeness in "Daddy" and "Lady Lazarus," she inevitably
"undercuts them, emphasizing the systematic play of elements and
the constructedness of meanings" (Narbeshuber). Never able to let
go or suppress her inner demons, she uses the symbolism of gods to
reference the power that her father had, and she also mentions that
his death caused her to seek her own. Sylvia Plath was immensely
influenced by her father's death, yet the gift and power of words
could not save her in the end.

Irwin 9

Works Cited

Alexander, Paul. *Rough Magic: A Biography of Sylvia Plath*. New York:
De Capo, 2003. Print.

Axelrod, Steven Gould. *Sylvia Plath: The Wound and the Cure of
Words*. Baltimore: Johns Hopkins UP, 1992. Print.

Beckmann, Anja. "Sylvia Plath (1932–1963): Short Biography."
2007. Web. 8 Nov. 2013.

Britzolakis, Christina. *Sylvia Plath and the Theatre of Mourning*. New
York: Oxford UP, 1999. Print.

Connell, Elaine, ed. "Daddy." *Sylvia Plath Forum*. 1 Jan. 2008. Web.
9 Nov. 2013.

---. "Lady Lazarus." *Sylvia Plath Forum*. 1 Jan. 2008. Web.
9 Nov. 2013.

Gilson, Bill. "Sylvia Plath." 2013. Web. 10 Nov. 2013.

Hall, Caroline King Barnard. *Sylvia Plath*. New York: Twayne,
1978. Print.

Citation for a
website.

Citations for
two websites
by the same
author.

Citation from
a book.

Irwin 10

Morehead, Philip D. "Manage." *The New American Webster Handy College Dictionary*. New York: New American Library, 2006. 440. Print.

Narbeshuber, Lisa. "The Poetics of Torture: The Spectacle of Sylvia Plath's Poetry." *Canadian Review of American Studies* 34.2 (2004): 185–203. Web. 11 Nov. 2013.

Phillips, Robert. "On 'Daddy.'" *Modern American Poetry*. 2013. Web. 9 Nov. 2013.

Plath, Sylvia. "Daddy." *Literature: An Introduction to Fiction, Poetry, Drama, and Writing*. 12th ed. Eds. X. J. Kennedy and Dana Gioia. New York: Pearson, 2013. 1116–1118. Print.

---. "Lady Lazarus." *Literature: An Introduction to Fiction, Poetry, Drama, and Writing*. 12th ed. Eds. X. J. Kennedy and Dana Gioia. New York: Pearson, 2013. 929–931. Print.

Reuben, Paul P. "Chapter 10: Sylvia Plath." *PAL: Perspectives in American Literature—A Research and Reference Guide*. 8 Nov. 2011. Web. 10 Nov. 2013.

Article from an academic journal.

Sample Research Paper

Kaci Holz, using MLA style for format and documentation, develops a comprehensive analysis of a communication issue: the ways men and women communicate with one another. She pinpoints several key issues, and along the way she reviews and summarizes the research literature on the subject and shares it with her readers.

Kaci Holz

Dr. Bekus

English 2230

29 April 2013

A title
page is not
required, but
provide your
name, the
instructor's
name, date,
and course.

Gender Communication

Men and women are different. Obvious enough, right? Not
so obviously, men and women have different communication
styles. During the first four weeks of existence, the human
embryo is neither male nor female (Starr, Evers, Starr, and Taggart
190). During this time, if human embryos could talk, gender
communication is not an issue. However, after the first four
weeks, the human embryo starts to develop either male or female
reproductive organs (Starr, Evers, Starr, and Taggart 190). With
these male or female developments come other differences. Men
and women develop different communication styles because of
biological and environmental differences.

The opening
statement is
followed by a
source to give
support to
the topic.

Holz
establishes
the thesis
statement as
a transition
to the
supporting
evidence.

There are numerous theories about the differences between
male and female communication styles. In her book *You Just Don't
Understand,* Professor Deborah Tannen addresses several issues
surrounding the patterns of conversation styles between men and
women. While she stresses that not all men and not all women
communicate in the same ways, she claims there are basic gender
patterns or stereotypes that can be found. In her studies of
sociolinguistics at Georgetown University, Tannen says that men
participate in conversations to establish "a hierarchical social
order" (*Don't Understand* 24), while women most often participate
in conversations to establish "a network of connections" (25). She
distinguishes the way women most often converse as "rapport-talk,"
and the way men most often converse as "report-talk" (74).

The writer
provides a
brief review
of the
literature
on the
topic in the
next three
paragraphs.

Tannen continues to differentiate between the male
communication style and the female communication style by
describing each one's purpose for communicating. She explains

Holz 2

that women often communicate to gain sympathy or understanding for a particular problem. However, men often respond to such communication with their typical "report talk" by trying to offer solutions to a woman's problems. These opposing communication styles often conflict and cause problems. The miscommunication is caused by different purposes for communicating. The woman wants sympathy, while the man thinks she wants him to solve her problems (Tannen, *Don't Understand* 49–53).

Other theorists concur with Tannen. Susan Basow and Kimberly Rubenfeld notice that "women may engage in 'troubles talk' to enhance communication; men may avoid such talk to

A line drawing, photograph, map, or graph should be labeled Figure, usually abbreviated, assigned a number, and given a caption or title.

Fig. 1 Miscommunication between men and women is often caused by the different purposes men and women have for communicating.

Holz 3

enhance autonomy and dominance" (186). In addition, Phillip
Yancey's article in *Marriage Partnership* also asserts that men and
women "use conversation for quite different purposes" (71). He
claims that women converse to develop and maintain connections,
while men converse to claim their position in the hierarchy they
see around them. Yancey asserts that women are less likely to
speak publicly than are men because women often perceive such
speaking as putting oneself on display. A man, on the other hand,
is usually comfortable with speaking publicly because that is how
he establishes his status among others (Yancey 71). Similarly,
masculine people are "less likely than androgynous individuals to
feel grateful for advice" (Basow and Rubenfeld 186).

Gender communication can be enhanced when couples focus on
interaction categories such as being trustworthy, concise, decisive,
and so on. Table 1 displays the key components to enhancing
gender communication. As this chart from Carl Brecheen and Paul
Faulkner's book *What Every Family Needs* illustrates, every couple
must remain positive to nurture and strengthen the relationship
through rapport talk. It is also telling to consider that barriers
such as commands or directions in a blunt manner inhibit true
communication that is built up through tact and sensitivity.

Table 1

Rules for Fantastic Communication

Be Knowledgeable	It takes time to truly know someone; there is no shortcut. Too often, couples refuse to spend time studying needs, thoughts, or aspirations.
Be Loving	Anyone can carry on a beautiful relationship when his or her spouse is doing all the right things. Forgiveness of faults establishes love.

(Continued)

For Table, type the table and the caption flush left on separate lines above the table, using capital letters to begin key words.

Holz 4

Be Transparent	Just as a window lets light shine through, we must also reveal our innermost thoughts and hidden feelings to develop true communication.
Be Trustworthy	Trust develops confidence, faith, and hope. At the same time, trust removes suspicion and doubt from discussions.
Be Positive	Effective communication will maximize the positive and minimize the negative. Couples must define and stress what is important.
Be Sensitive	Effective communication will balance ideas, judgments, or facts with emotions, such as joy, fear, and expectation in a relationship.
Be a Communicator	Slight clues are often enough reason to stop and check to determine whether the listener is truly understanding your message.
Be a Listener	Our culture is built on talk, not conversation. A good listener learns to listen to what is *not* said and the hidden meanings of ideas.
Be Concise	We must think and then rethink before we give a response. Words fly fast, and when not given careful consideration, our words can be hurtful.
Be Decisive	Couples will never *find* time to talk; they must instead *make* time. Effective communication is established through a resolute commitment.

Source: Brecheen, Carl, and Paul Faulkner. *What Every Family Needs*. Nashville: Gospel Advocate, 1994. 88–98. Print.

Give the source of a table below the table

    Many more differences in communication patterns of men
and women can be found. Richard L. Weaver pointed out another

Holz 5

author who identifies different communication styles for men and women. In "Leadership for the Future: A New Set of Priorities," Weaver refers to Dr. Julia T. Wood's book *Gendered Lives.* According to Weaver, Wood claims that "male communication is characterized by assertion, independence, competitiveness, and confidence, while female communication is characterized by deference, inclusivity, collaboration, and cooperation" (qtd. in Weaver 440). This list of differences describes why men and women have such opposing communication styles.

In another book, Deborah Tannen also discusses opposition in communication among men and women. In chapter six of *The Argument Culture,* entitled "Boys Will Be Boys: Gender and Opposition," Tannen addresses the issue that boys, or men, "are more likely to take an oppositional stance toward other people and the world" and "are more likely to find opposition entertaining— to enjoy watching a good fight, or having one" (*Argument* 166). Tannen goes into detail by giving examples from real life and research studies of how boys and girls play and fight differently. She claims that boys tend to cause fights, while girls try to avoid fights. A girl often tries to convince her opponent that her view would benefit the opponent. A boy, on the other hand, just argues for what is best for him (*Argument* 170–74). Tannen addresses other gender opposition factors, such as how men and women insult differently, men's negotiating status and women's forging bonds, the paradox of male and female fighting, conflict on the job, watching fights for fun, and talking in public (*Argument* 184–205).

There are numerous differences in the communication styles of men and women; moreover, there are distinct causes for these differences. Two different theories involve biological factors and/or environmental factors. Lillian Glass, another linguistics researcher, examines "the evolution of sex differences in communication" (61) in *He Says, She Says: Closing the Communication Gap between the*

Two works by the same author require an abbreviated title to the work within the parenthetical citation.

Holz reaffirms her thesis to keep the reader focused on the topic.

Sexes. Glass addresses the issue that different hormones found in men and women's bodies make them act differently and therefore communicate differently. She also discusses how brain development has been found to relate to sex differences. Glass writes extensively about how environmental factors, specifically the way we treat boy and girl infants, directly affect the ways we learn to communicate (64–73). Added to this research, one additional source states: "The way men and women are raised contributes to differences in conversation and communication" (James and Cinelli 41).

In "Parental Influence on Children's Socialization to Gender Roles," Susan Witt discusses the various findings that support the idea that parents have a great influence on their children during the development of their self-concept. She states, "Children learn at a very early age what it means to be a boy or a girl in our society" (253). Things that affect a child's idea of self-concept are the things they encounter early and throughout life such as: "parent-child interactions, role modeling, reinforcement for desired behaviors, parental approval or disapproval, friends, school, those around them, media, television" (Witt 253). Witt sums her theory up by saying, "Through all these socialization agents, children learn gender stereotyped behavior. As children develop, these stereotypes become firmly entrenched beliefs, and thus, they are a part of the child's self-concept" (253).

To further demonstrate the environmental factor that influences learned gender characteristics, Witt discusses how parents treat sons and daughters differently from the time they are babies. She says that parents "dress infants in gender-specific colors, give gender-differentiated toys, and expect different behavior from boys and girls" (Witt 254). At play and in chores, parents tend to "encourage their sons and daughters to participate in sex-typed activities" (Witt 254). Witt claims that women have even admitted a preference to having male children over female

The writer clarifies the influence of environment on gender characteristics.

Holz 7

children in order to "please their husbands, to carry on the family name, and to be a companion to the husband" (254). Conversely, Witt found that women want daughters "to have a companion for themselves and to have fun dressing a girl and doing her hair" (254). These choices affect a child's learned patterns of communication. The environmental factors around a child help determine how a child will act and how he or she will communicate with others.

Discussing the environmental factor, Phillip Yancey explores the fact that many times a communication difference between genders exists simply because of their different roots (69). Two people who come from two different families often have different ideas of how men and women should communicate. Different families have different conversation styles, different fighting styles, and different communication styles overall. Yancey addresses the communication problems between genders as a cultural gap, defining culture as "shared meaning" (68). "Some problems come about because one spouse enters marriage with a different set of 'shared meanings' than the other" (69).

Yancey goes into detail about the issue "that boys and girls grow up learning different styles of communicating" (70). So not only does the cultural gap between families sometimes pose a problem, the gender gap between the way boys and girls are raised can also impair efficient communication. Yancey points out:

> Boys tend to play in large groups that are hierarchically
> structured, with a leader who tells the others what to do
> and how to do it. Boys reinforce status by giving orders and
> enforcing them; their games have winners and losers and are
> run by elaborate rules. In contrast, girls play in small groups
> or in pairs, with 'best friends.' They strive for intimacy, not
> status. These gender patterns continue into adulthood. (70)

The page reference for an indented quotation goes outside the final period.

Holz 8

The different ways that boys and girls play help to explain different ways that boys and girls, or men and women, communicate.

Most of us have heard of the "Battle of the Sexes" as seen in conflict between men and women. Reverting back to his "childhood gender pattern" theory, Yancey claims that "men, who grew up in a hierarchical environment, are accustomed to conflict. Concerned more with relationship and connection, women prefer the role of peacemaker" (71). Men often use and value criticism, but women avoid and dislike outright criticism for fear of offending (Yancey 71–72).

Like Yancey, Deborah Tannen also addresses the fact that men and women often come from different worlds, or from different influences. Men are taught to be masculine and women are taught to be feminine. She says, "Even if they grow up in the same neighborhood, on the same block, or in the same house, girls and boys grow up in different worlds of words" (*Don't Understand* 43). Tannen distinguishes between the way boys are talked to and the way girls are talked to, and she addresses the differences between the way boys play and the way girls play (*Don't Understand* 43–47).

Though Tannen often addresses the nurture, or environmental issue in much of her research, she also looked at the nature, or biological issue in her book *The Argument Culture*. Tannen states, "Surely a biological component plays a part in the greater use of antagonism among men, but cultural influence can override biological inheritance" (205). She sums up the nature versus nurture issue by saying, "The patterns that typify women's and men's styles of opposition and conflict are the result of both biology and culture" (207).

Numerous authorities believe that the causes of different styles of gender communication are biological, while others attribute causes to environmental factors. Still more people contend that men and women have different communication styles

Holz 9

because of a combination of biological and environmental factors. With these differences in the styles of gender communication and possible causes of gender communication, one must consider the possible results.

Let us look briefly at a hypothetical situation that will demonstrate different gender communication styles. We will examine the results of this situation to grasp an understanding of possible results in life. Consider the following scenario. A husband and wife have just arrived home after a long day of work in the business world. The wife asks her husband, "How was your day?" And the husband replies, "Fine." The wife is offended by this simplistic response and expresses her hurt by saying, "That's it? 'Fine'? Why don't you ever talk to me?" In confusion as to where this statement has come from, the husband defends himself declaring, "What are you talking about? I do talk to you. I'm talking to you right now!" They both blow each other off and refuse to talk to each other for the rest of the night. What went wrong in this conversation? The resulting failure of communication happened because men and women have different communication styles that directly affect intentional and perceived meaning from one to the other. Perhaps the communication failure above can be explained when backed by an understanding of the differences between the purposes and the ways that men and women communicate. Let us take this specific example and examine the results as compared to theories about gender communication.

In this scenario, the husband and wife are exhibiting different communication styles that directly relate to their own gender. Through various studies, Tannen has concluded that men and women have different purposes for engaging in communication. In *You Just Don't Understand,* Tannen states, "For girls, talk is the glue that holds relationships together" (85). Boys, on the other hand, use language when "they feel the need to impress, or when they are in

Holz provides a scenario to illustrate the validity of her research.

situations where their status is in question" (85). Tannen goes on to explain the different ways men and women handle communication throughout the day. She explains that a man constantly talks during his workday in order to impress those around him and to establish his status in the office. When a man comes home from work, he is tired of talking. He expects to be able to be silent in his home where he does not have to impress anyone or establish his status (86).

On the other hand, a woman is constantly cautious and guarded about what she says during her workday. Women try hard to avoid confrontation and avoid offending anyone with their language. So when a woman comes home from work, she expects to be able to talk freely without having to guard her words. Can we see the controversy that the man's expectation to be silent and the woman's expectation to talk can cause?

With Tannen's input, hopefully we can begin to see the differences in the communication styles of the wife and the husband. When the wife asked, "How was your day?" she expected a detailed response because her purpose of communication was to strengthen her relationship with her husband. She honestly wanted to know what specific things happened during her husband's workday so that she would be able to sympathize with what he was feeling and become closer to him. She wanted to talk freely because she had been busy guarding her words all day.

The husband's response of "fine" was direct and to the point because he felt no need to communicate further. At home with his wife, he was not in a situation in which he needed to impress anyone or establish status. He simply answered the question that was asked of him and was willing to leave it at that. He wanted to be silent because he had been working hard at communication all day.

Though the intentions of both husband and wife seem innocent enough when looking at them with the thought of

The scenario is analyzed and conclusions are presented to the reader.

different communication styles in mind, the husband and wife obviously didn't see the other's response as innocent. Because the wife didn't receive the in-depth description she was expecting, she was disappointed. Tannen says that "when a woman who expects her partner to talk to her is disappointed that he doesn't, she perceives his behavior as a failure of intimacy: He's keeping things from her; he's lost interest in her; he's pulling away" (*Don't Understand* 83). Can we imagine the wife's pain now?

The husband did not sense her pain. When his wife came back with "That's it? 'Fine?' Why don't you ever talk to me?" this just triggered anger and defense. Because the wife and the husband had different purposes for and different ways of communicating, they misinterpreted each other. This misinterpretation led to anger, and the anger led to frustration and the abandonment of communication.

The results of gender communication can look bleak. What can we do about this apparent gap in communication between genders? Some researchers have offered several solutions. In his article published in *Leadership,* Jeffrey Arthurs has the suggestion that women should make an attempt to understand the male model of communication and that men should make an attempt to understand the female model of communication (49). Having men who can better understand women and having women who can better understand men cannot be a bad thing. Even a general study of the different communication styles could benefit men and women by helping them understand possible misinterpretations before cross-gender communication is abandoned.

In his article "Speaking across the Gender Gap," David Cohen mentions that experts did not think it would be helpful to teach men to communicate more like women and women to communicate more like men. This attempt would prove unproductive because it would go against what men and women have been taught since birth. Rather than change the genders to be more like one another, we could simply try to understand each other better. By doing a little research and a little thoughtful consideration about the differences in gender communication styles, men and women would be able to communicate more successfully.

Richard Weaver has observed, "The idea that women should translate their experiences into the male code in order to express themselves effectively is an outmoded, inconsistent, subservient notion that should no longer be given credibility in modern society" (439). He suggests three things we can change: (1) Change the norm by which leadership success is judged, (2) Redefine what we mean by power, and (3) Become more sensitive to the places and times when inequity and inequality occur (Weaver 439). Phillip Yancey also offers advice to help combat "cross-cultural" fights. He suggests: (1) Identify your fighting style, (2) Agree on rules of engagement, and (3) Identify the real issue behind the conflict (71). In truth, men and women must understand one another, communicate honestly and respectfully, and manage conflict in a way that maintains the relationship to get the job done. Moreover, we must acknowledge the differences that do exist, understand how they develop, and discard dogma about what are the "right" roles of women and men.

By acknowledging that there are differences between the way men and women communicate, whether caused by biological and/or environmental factors, we can be on the watch for circumstances that might lead to miscommunications, as well as consider the possible causes, results, and solutions discussed previously. Using this knowledge, we should be able to more accurately interpret communication between genders. The next cross-gendered misinterpretation we face, we should stop for a moment to consider the differing gender before we make things worse or abandon communication all together.

Holz reaffirms her thesis in the final paragraph.

Holz 13

Works Cited

Arthurs, Jeffrey. "He Said, She Heard: Any Time You Speak to Both

Men and Women, You're Facing Cross-Cultural Communication."

Leadership 23.1 (Winter 2002): 49. Print.

Basow, Susan A., and Kimberly Rubenfeld. "'Troubles Talk': Effects

of Gender and Gender Typing." *Sex Roles: A Journal of Research*

48 (2003): 183–87. *EBSCOhost*. Web. 24 Apr. 2013.

Brecheen, Carl, and Paul Faulkner. *What Every Family Needs*.

Nashville: Gospel Advocate, 1994. 88–98. Print.

Cohen, David. "Speaking across the Gender Gap." *New Scientist* 131

(1991): 36. *InfoTrac*. Web. 23 Apr. 2013.

Glass, Lillian. *He Says, She Says: Closing the Communication Gap*

between the Sexes. New York: Penguin, 1993. Print.

James, Tammy, and Bethann Cinelli. "Exploring Gender-Based

Communication Styles." *Journal of School Health* 73 (2003):

41–42. Abstract. Web. 25 Apr. 2013.

Starr, Cecie, Christine Evers, Lisa Starr, and Ralph Taggart. *Biology:*

The Unity and Diversity of Life. 13th ed. Florence: Cengage,

2012. Print.

Tannen, Deborah. *The Argument Culture: Moving from Debate to*

Dialogue. New York: Random House, 1998. Print.

———. *You Just Don't Understand: Women and Men in Conversation*.

New York: HarperCollins. 2007. Print.

Weaver, Richard L. "Leadership for the Future: A New Set of

Priorities." *Vital Speeches of the Day* 61 (1995): 438–41.

Access My Library. Web. 22 Apr. 2013.

Witt, Susan D. "Parental Influence on Children's Socialization to

Gender Roles." *Adolescence* 32 (1997): 253–59. *Questia*. Web.

22 Apr. 2013.

Yancey, Phillip. "Do Men and Women Speak the Same Language?"

Marriage Partnership 10 (1993): 68–73. *EBSCOhost*. Web. 24

Apr. 2013.

Begin the
Works Cited
on a new
page.

A source from
an electronic
database.

An article
from an
academic
journal
found on the
Internet.

Internet
sources
require the
word "Web"
preceding
the date of
access.

Chapter 14 Clear Targets

T he final step to completing your research project is to finalize your Works Cited page. Preparing the Works Cited list will be relatively simple if you have carefully developed your working bibliography as a computer file with detailed publication data for each source cited in the paper (see pages 66–67). The following components discussed in this chapter will help to accurately document your research paper:

- Writing Works Cited references in MLA style
- Formatting Works Cited entries for online and print sources
- Creating Works Cited entries for special sources

The MLA documentation style gives all scholars in the field a consistent way to consult the sources that are cited in your project. Keep in mind that on occasion somebody might use your Works Cited listing for research of his or her own. Inaccurate records might prevent an easy retracing of your steps. List only those materials actually used in your manuscript, including works mentioned within content endnotes and in captions to tables and illustrations.

Select a heading that indicates the nature of your list.

Works Cited for a list of works including books, articles, films, recordings, Internet sources, and so on that are quoted or paraphrased in the research paper.

Works Consulted if your list includes works not cited in your research paper.

Annotated Bibliography for a list of references that includes a description of the contents of each source (see pages 125–127).

Selected Bibliography for a list of readings on the subject.

For examples of Works Cited pages, see pages 235–236 and 249. For an example of an annotated bibliography, see pages 125–127.

The title *Works Cited* is usually most appropriate, because it lists scholarly works of printed books and articles, Web sources, and non-print items.

Works pertinent to the paper but not quoted or paraphrased, such as an article on related matters, can be mentioned in a content endnote (see pages 326–328) and then listed in the Works Cited.

14a Formatting the Works Cited Page

Arrange items in alphabetic order by the surname of the author using the letter-by-letter system. Ignore spaces in the author's surname. Consider the first names only when two or more surnames are identical. Note how the following examples are alphabetized letter by letter. When no author is listed, alphabetize by the first important word of the title. Imagine lettered spelling for unusual items. For example, "#2 Red Dye" should be alphabetized as though it were "Number 2 Red Dye."

> Dempsey, Morgan
> "Facing Your Failures"
> Lawrence, Jacob
> Lawrence, Melissa
> McPherson, James Alan
> "Miracles and Tragedies in West Virginia Coal Mines"
> Saint-Exupéry, Antoine de
> St. James, Christopher

When two or more entries cite coauthors that begin with the same name, alphabetize by the last names of the second authors:

> Huggins, Marjorie, and Devin Blythe
> Huggins, Marjorie, and Stephen Fisher

The list of sources may also be divided into separate alphabetized sections for primary and secondary sources, for different media (articles, books, Internet sources), for different subject matter (biography, autobiography, letters), for different periods (Neoclassic period, Romantic period), and for different areas (German viewpoints, French viewpoints, American viewpoints).

Place the first line of each entry flush with the left margin and indent succeeding lines one-half inch, usually one tab space. Double-space each entry as well as between all entries. Use one space after periods and other marks of punctuation.

HINT: MLA style uses italics in place of underlining for titles.

Set the title *Works Cited* 1 inch down from the top of the sheet and double-space between it and the first entry. The following example illustrates a sample Works Cited page.

Karhu 11

Works Cited

Bry, Dave. *Public Apology.* New York: Grand Central, 2013. Print.

Cannadine, David. *The Undivided Past: Humanity beyond Our*
    Differences. New York: Knopf Doubleday, 2013. Print.

Cooper, Christopher A. and H, Gibbs Knotts. "Overlapping Identities
    in the American South." *Social Science Journal* 50.1 (Mar. 2013):
    6–12. *EBSCOHost.* Web. 19 Oct. 2013.

Farah, Joseph. "Hollywood Getting Something Right." *WorldNetDaily.* 7
    Apr. 2013. Web. 15. Sept. 2013.

---. "If All Kids Really Belong to Everyone . . . " *WorldNetDaily.* 17
    Apr. 2013. Web. 15. Sept. 2013.

Kugelman, Michael. "The 21st-Century Land Rush." *Issues in Science*
    and Technology Online. (Winter 2013). Web. 16 Sept. 2013.

Martin, Thomas R. "Religion, Myth, and Community." *An Overview of*
    Classical Greek History from Homer to Alexander. 2013. Web. 18
    Sept. 2013.

Petruzzi, J. David. "A Bloody Summer for Horsemen." *Civil War Times.*
    June 2013: 30–37. Print.

Werner, Erica. "Labor, Business Agree to Principles on Immigration."
    Denver Post Online. 21 Feb 2013. Web. 28 Mar. 2013.

Williamson, Peter, Megan Mercurio, and Constance Walker. "Songs of
    the Caged Birds: Literacy and Learning with Incarcerated Youth."
    English Journal 102.4 (Mar. 2013): 31–37. Print.

Index to Works Cited Models: MLA Style

Index to Works Cited Models: MLA Style

(continued on page 254)

(continued from page 253)

Index to Works Cited Models: MLA Style

Index to Works Cited Models: MLA Style

(continued on page 256)

(continued from page 255)

Index to Works Cited Models: MLA Style

14b   Works Cited Form—Online Sources

The Internet gives us access to a cornucopia of information from millions of sources. Because of the fluid nature of online addresses, the *MLA Handbook for Writers of Research Papers,* 7th edition, no longer recommends the inclusion of URLs in Works Cited entries. Instead, researchers may document the medium of access by providing the word "Web," followed by a period, just before the date of access. Rather than typing the URL, readers are more likely to find resources on the Web by searching for the name of the author or the title of the article.

Citing Sources Found Online

For further discussion of how to cite online sources, see pages 257–262. For making judgments about the validity of online sources, see pages 45–46.

Include these items as appropriate to the source:

1. Author/editor name.
2. Title of the article within quotation marks, or the title of a posting to a discussion list or forum followed by the words *online posting,* followed by a period.
3. If the document has a printed version, provide the publication information and the date. Titles of books and journals should be formatted in italics.
4. Information on the electronic publication, such as the title of the site, the date of the posting, and the sponsoring organization, followed by a period.

5. The medium of publication—"Web."

6. Date of your access, followed by a period.

> Bellis, Mary. "History of Observing Small Things." *About: Inventors.* 6 Apr.
>
> 2013. Web. 13 May 2013.

Following is a detailed breakdown of the components found in the entry
found above:

> Author's Name. "Title of Article." *Name of Sponsoring Organization.*
>
> Website posting date. Medium of Publication—"Web." Your date of
>
> access to the website.

NOTE: Do not include page numbers unless the online article
shows original page numbers from the printed version of the
journal or magazine. Do not include the total number of paragraphs nor specific paragraph numbers unless the online article
has provided them.

Abstract

> Aderka, Idan M., et al. "Information-Seeking Bias in Social Anxiety
>
> Disorder." Abstract. *Journal of Abnormal Psychology* 122.1 (2013): 7.
>
> Web. 10 May 2013.

Advertisement

> "Legends of Flight 3D." Advertisement. Arizona Science Center, 2013.
>
> Web. 4 Aug. 2013.

Anonymous Article

> "In Large-Truck Crashes, Most Fatalities Occur in Other Vehicles." *National*
>
> *Highway Traffic Safety Administration.* NHTSA, 15 Apr. 2013 Web. 23
>
> Nov. 2013.

Archive or Scholarly Project

> *Victorian Women Writers Project.* Indiana U Digital Library Program. 2013.
>
> Web. 19 Oct. 2013.

Article from an Online Magazine

> Neustadt, Robert. "Looking Beyond the Wall: Encountering the
>
> Humanitarian Crisis of Border Politics." *UTNE Reader.* May/June
>
> 2013. Web. 19 June 2013.

Article from a Scholarly Journal

Goldstein, Abby L., et al. "Childhood Maltreatment, Alcohol Use Disorders, and Treatment Utilization in a National Sample of Emerging Adults." *Journal of Studies on Alcohol and Drugs* 74.2 (2013): 185–194. Web. 12 July. 2013.

Article Written for the Internet

"The Beaches of Elba Island." *Elba Online.* 2013. Web. 16 Oct. 2013.

Audio Program Online

See the entry for "Television or Radio Program."

Blogs and Tumblrs

Bursack, Carol Bradley, narr. "Minding Our Elders Together: Joining a Community of Caregivers." *Minding Our Elders Blog,* 17 Apr. 2013. Web. 28 Oct. 2013.

Cartoon

Coverly, Dave. "Before We Begin." Cartoon. *Speed Bump.* 13 Apr. 2013. Web. 29 Apr. 2013.

Chapter or Portion of a Book

Add the name of the chapter after the author's name:

Dewey, John. "Waste in Education." *School and Society.* Chicago: U of Chicago P, 1907. Web. 14 Mar. 2013.

Database

Most libraries have converted their computer searches to online databases, such as Lexis-Nexis, ProQuest Direct, EBSCOhost, Electric Library, InfoTrac, and others. Omit the identifying numbers for the database or the key term used in the search. Following are examples:

"America's Children: Key National Indicators of Well-Being, 2013." Federal Interagency Forum on Child and Family Statistics. July 2013. *ERIC.* Web. 8 Dec. 2013.

Bonanno, Rina A., and Shelley Hymel. "Cyber Bullying and Internalizing Difficulties: Above and beyond the Impact of Traditional Forms of Bullying." Journal of Youth and Adolescence 42.5 (May 2013): 685–97. *MasterFILE Elite.* Clarksville Montgomery County Library, Clarksville, TN. Web. 17 Aug. 2013.

"Culture: Top 50 Films for Architects." *Building Design* 25 Jan. 2013:
    19. *General OneFile*. Web. 17 Apr. 2013.

Esslin, Martin. "Theater of the Absurd." *Grolier Multimedia*
    Encyclopedia. 2013 ed. Web. 22 Oct. 2013.

Kutzscher, Lia. "Management of Irritant Contact Dermatitis and
    Peripherally Inserted Central Catheters." *Clinical Journal of Oncology*
    Nursing 16.2 (Apr. 2012): 48. *InfoTrac*. Web. 3 Oct. 2013.

Editorial

Crisp, David. "Wasteful College Spending Has Its Advantages." Editorial.
    Billings Outpost Online 14 Mar. 2013. Web. 30 Apr. 2013.

E-mail

Wright, Ellen. "Online Composition Courses." Message to the author. 24
    May 2013. E-mail.

Encyclopedia Article Online

"Kurt Vonnegut, Jr." *Encyclopedia Britannica Online.* Encyclopedia
    Britannica, 2012. Web. 9 Mar. 2013.

Film or Video Online

"Epiphany: Festival of Lights." *Greek Orthodox Archdiocese of America.*
    Leadership 100, 2013. Web. 8 Jan. 2014.

Home Page for an Academic Course

"Science and Society." College of Liberal Arts & Sciences, Arizona State U,
    2013. Web. 12 Nov. 2013.

Home Page for an Academic Department

"Dakota and Native American Studies." Home page. College of Arts,
    Humanities and Social Sciences, North Dakota State U, 17 Apr. 2013.
    Web. 17 Apr. 2013.

Home Page for an Academic Site

"Robert Penn Warren: 1905–1989." Home page. *Modern American Poetry,*
    Dept. of English, U of Illinois, Urbana–Champaign. Web. 2 Apr. 2013.

Home Page for a Personal Website

Giovanni, Nikki. Home Page. Dept. of English, Virginia Tech U, 2013. Web.
21 Nov. 2013.

Interview

Turow, Scott. Interview by Kacey Kowars. *Kacey Kowars Show*. June 2010.
Web. 24 Oct. 2013.

Journal Article

Vrtis, Mary C. "Preventing and Responding to Acute Kidney Injury."
American Journal of Nursing 113.4 (2013): 38–47. Web. 9 Nov. 2013.

Sosteric, Michael. "Isolation and Connection in a Digital Village."
Socjournal 1 Mar. 2013: n.pag. Web. 22 Sept. 2013.

Manuscript

Montague, Mary Katherine. *Of Old Barns and Bridges*. Southern Tech. U.
MS. 2013. Web. 24 Aug. 2013.

Map

"Virginia—1735." Map. *U. S. County Formation Maps, 1643–Present*.
Genealogy, Inc. 1999. Web. 30 Sept. 2013.

Newsletter

Meagher, Sharon M. "Pushing the Boundaries of Philosophy." *APA Online.*
American Psychological Association, 9.2 (Spring 2010). Web. 30
Sept, 2010.

Newspaper Article, Column, Editorial

Whitefield, Mimi. "Port Executives Say a Funding Gap for Port Upgrades
Could Hurt U.S. Competitiveness." Miamiherald.com. Miami Herald,
17 Apr. 2013. Web. 17 Apr. 2013.

Novel

Conrad, Joseph. "Chapter 1." *Heart of Darkness. 1902.* Web. 26 Jan. 2014.

Online Posting for E-mail Discussion Groups

Supply the list's moderator the Internet site if known; otherwise show
the e-mail address of the list's moderator.

Worthen, Rena. "Floyd County Cemeteries." Online Posting. *VaGenWeb,* 23

May 2010. Web. 16 Oct. 2013.

Photo, Painting, or Sculpture

MLA style does not require you to label the type of work, as shown in the first example of a photograph. Usually, the text will have established the nature of the work. However, if you feel that clarification is necessary, as in the case of "The Blessed Damozel," which is both a painting and a poem, you may want to designate the form.

Bauer, Jerry. "Robert Penn Warren." Photograph. Google, 2013. Web. 11

Oct. 2013.

"Boy and Bear." Bronze Sculpture. Marshall M. Fredericks Sculpture

Museum, 2013. Web. 29 Apr. 2013.

Rossetti, Dante. "The Blessed Damozel." 1875–78. Painting. *Liverpool*

Museum, 2013. Web. 3 Feb. 2013.

Poem, Song, or Story

Dylan, Bob. "Tangled Up in Blue." 1975. Song lyrics. BobDylan.com, 2013.

Web. 13 Nov. 2013.

Hardy, Thomas. "Her Death and After." *Wessex Poems and Other Verses.*

1898. Bartleby.com. Great Books Online, 2013. Web. 10 May 2013.

Report

"Fighting Back against Identity Theft." Federal Trade Commission, 2013.

Web. 4 Nov. 2013.

Serialized Article

Lippincott-Schwartz, Jennifer. "Breakthroughs in Imaging Using

Photoactivatable Fluorescent Proteins." The Discovery Lecture Series.

Vanderbilt Medical Center, 18 Apr. 2013. Web. 20 Jan. 2014.

Song

See "Poem, Song, or Story."

Sound Clip, Speech, or Recording

See "Television or Radio Program."

Story

See "Poem, Song, or Story."

Television or Radio Program

Gleiser, Marcelo. "Defining Our Place in the Universe." *Morning Edition*.

National Public Radio, 17 Apr. 2013. Web. 24 Apr. 2013.

University Posting, Online Article

Goodman, Herb. "Weaving That Originated at Family Nature Day Now

Graces Maywoods." Online Posting. Eastern Kentucky U, 1 Mar. 2013.

Web. 13 Feb. 2014.

Video

See "Film or Video Online."

14c Works Cited Form—Citing Database and CD-ROM Sources

Databases provide information in four different ways, and each method of transmission requires an adjustment in the form of the entry for your Works Cited page.

Full-Text Articles with Publication Information for the Printed Source

Full-text articles are available from national distributors, such as ProQuest, ERIC, InfoTrac, EBSCOhost, and others. Conform to the examples that follow:

"Animals in the Front Seat." *Insurance Advocate* 4 Mar. 2013: 26.

EBSCOhost. Web. 18 Apr. 2013.

Babcock, Hope M. "Putting a Price on Whales to Save Them: What Do

Morals Have to Do with It?" *Environmental Law* Winter 2013: 1+.

InfoTrac. Web. 18 Apr. 2013.

Muhlhausler, Beverly S., Frank H. Bloomfield, and Matthew W. Gillman.

"Whole Animal Experiments Should Be More Like Human Randomized

Controlled Trials." *PLOS Biology* 11.2 (2013). *Academic OneFile*. Web.

18 Apr. 2013.

HINT: Complete information may not be readily available; for example, the original publication data may be missing. In such cases, provide all available information.

Abstracts to Articles and Books Provided by the National Distributors

As a service to readers, the national distributors have members of their staff write abstracts of articles and books if the original authors have not provided such abstracts. As a result, an abstract that you find on InfoTrac and ProQuest may not be written by the original author, so you should not quote such abstracts. You may quote from abstracts that say, "Abstract written by the author." Some databases *do* have abstracts written by the original authors. In either case, conform to the example that follows, which provides name, title, publication information, the word *abstract,* the name of the database italicized, the medium (CD-ROM), the name of the vendor, and—if available to you—the electronic publication date (month and year).

> Fandrey, Joachim. "Highlight: Sensing Hypoxia in the Cell and the
>
> Organism." *Biological Chemistry* 394.4 (2013): 433+. *Academic*
>
> *OneFile.* Web. 18 Apr. 2013.

Full-Text Articles with No Publication Information for a Printed Source

Sometimes the original printed source of an article or report will not be provided by the distributor of the CD-ROM database. In such a case, conform to the examples that follow, which provide limited data.

> "Faulkner Biography." *Discovering Authors.* CD-ROM. Detroit: Gale, 2012.
>
> "U.S. Population by Age: Urban and Urbanized Areas." 2012 *U.S. Census*
>
> *Bureau.* CD-ROM. US Bureau of the Census. 2013.

Complete Books and Other Publications on CD-ROM

Cite this type of source as you would a book, and then provide information to the electronic source that you accessed.

> *English Poetry Full-Text Database.* Re. 2. CD-ROM. Cambridge, UK.:
>
> Chadwyck, 2013.
>
> "John F. Kennedy." *InfoPedia.* CD-ROM. N.p.: Future Vision, n.d.
>
> Olesberg, Lindsay. *Ephesians: Studying with the Global Church.* CD-ROM.
>
> Peabody, MA: Hendrickson, 2013.

Nonperiodical Publication on CD-ROM

Cite a CD-ROM or DVD-ROM as you would a book, with the addition of a descriptive word. If relevant, show the edition (3rd ed.), release (Rel. 2), or version (Ver. 3). Conform to the examples that follow.

> Lester, James D., Jr. *Introduction to Greek Mythology: Computer Slide*
>
> *Show.* Clarksville: Austin Peay State U, 2013. 12 lessons on CD-ROM.

2011 Statistics on Child Abuse—Montgomery County, Tennessee. Rel. 2.

Clarksville: Harriett Cohn Mental Health Center, 2012. Diskette.

Encyclopedia Article

For an encyclopedia article on a CD–ROM, use the following form:

"Abolitionist Movement." *World Book Encyclopedia.* CD-ROM. Mac Kiev, 2013.

Multidisc Publication

When citing a multidisc publication, follow the term *CD-ROM* with the total number of discs or with the disc that you cited from:

Springer, Alice G. *Barron's AP Spanish.* 7th ed. Hauppauge: Barron's, 2011.

CD-ROM. Disc 3.

Other Electronic Sources

Some distributors issue packages that include different media, such as CD-ROM or a book with accompanying DVD. Cite such publications as you would a nonperiodical CD-ROM with the addition of the media available with this product.

Collins, Mary B. "Prologue." *The Canterbury Tales : A Unit Plan.* Clayton:

Teacher's Pet, 2010. CD-ROM, print.

14d Works Cited Form—Books

Enter information for books in the following order. Items 1, 3, 7, and 10 are required; add other items according to the circumstances explained in the text that follows.

1. Author(s)
2. Chapter or part of book
3. Title of the book
4. Editor, translator, or compiler
5. Edition
6. Volume number of book
7. Place, publisher, and date
8. Page numbers
9. Number of volumes
10. Medium of publication—"Print."

The following example provided shows three primary divisions of a Works Cited entry for a book, Author's Name. *Title of the Book.* Publication information.

Allison, Dorothy. "This Is Our World." *The Writer's Presence.* Eds. Donald

McQuade and Robert Atwan. 7th ed. Boston: Bedford/St. Martins,

2011. 633–41. Print.

Soffer, Jennifer. *Tomorrow There Will Be Apricots*. Boston: Houghton Mifflin

Harcourt, 2013. Print.

Following is a detailed breakdown of the components found in the entry found above:

Author Name. "Title for section of the book." *Book Title in Italics*. Name

of the editors. Edition. City, State of publication: Name of Publisher,

Year of Publication. Page Numbers. Medium of Publication.

Author's Name

List the author's name, surname first, followed by given name or initials, and then a period:

Follett, Ken.

Always give authors' names in the fullest possible form, for example, "Jimmerson, Aundra V." rather than "Jimmerson, A. V." unless, as indicated on the title page of the book, the author prefers initials. If you spell out an abbreviated name, put square brackets around the material added.

Tolkien, J[ohn] R[onald] R[euel].

With pseudonyms you may add the real name, enclosing the addition in brackets.

Carroll, Lewis [Charles Lutwidge Dodgson].

Omit a title, affiliation, or degree that appears with the author's name on the title page.

If the title page says:	*In the Works Cited use:*
Sir John Gielgud	Gielgud, John
Sister Margaret Grayson	Grayson, Margaret
Barton O'Connor, Ph.D.	O'Connor, Barton

However, do provide an essential suffix that is part of a person's name:

Justin, Walter, Jr.
Peterson, Robert J., III.

Title of the Book

State the title of the book, including any subtitle. Use italics for the entire title, including any colon, subtitle, or punctuation. Place a period after the entire title, unless it ends in another punctuation mark.

Follett, Ken. *Winter of the World*.

Publication Information

Provide the city of publication, the publisher's name, the year of publication, and the medium of publication. The word *Print* is given as the medium of publication for books and periodicals.

> Follett, Ken. *Winter of the World.* New York: Dutton, 2013. Print.

Include the abbreviation for the state or country only if necessary for clarity.

If more than one place of publication appears on the title page, the first city mentioned is sufficient. If successive copyright dates are given, use the most recent (unless your study is specifically concerned with an earlier, perhaps definitive, edition). A new printing does not constitute a new edition.

If the place, publisher, date of publication, or pages are not provided, use one of these abbreviations:

n.p.	No place of publication listed
n.p.	No publisher listed
n.d.	No date of publication listed
pag.	No pagination listed

> Lewes, George Henry. *The Life and Works of Goethe.* 2 vols. 1855. Rpt. as
>
>   vols. 13 and 14 of *The Works of J. W. von Goethe.* Ed. Nathan Haskell
>
>   Dole. 14 vols. London: Nicolls, n.d. Print.

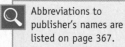
> Abbreviations to publisher's names are listed on page 367.

Provide the publisher's name in a shortened form, such as "Bobbs" rather than "Bobbs-Merrill Co., Inc." A publisher's special imprint name should be joined with the official name, for example, Anchor-Doubleday.

The following list provides examples and explains the correct form for books listed on a Works Cited page.

Author, Anonymous

Begin with the title. Do not use *anonymous* or *anon.* Alphabetize by the title, ignoring initial articles, *A, An,* or *The.*

> *The Song of Roland.* Trans. Arthur S. Way. New York: Cambridge U P,
>
>   2013. Print.

Author, Pseudonymous but Name Supplied

> Slender, Robert [Freneau, Philip]. *Letters on Various and Important*
>
>   *Subjects.* Philadelphia: Hogan, 1799. Print.

Author, Listed by Initials with Name Supplied

> Rowling, J[oanne] K[athleen]. *The Casual Vacancy.* Boston: Little, Brown,
>
>   2013. Print.

Authors, Two

Bennett, William J., and John T. E. Cribb. *The American Patriot's Almanac.*

Nashville: Nelson, 2013. Print.

Authors, Three

Katz, Lilian G., Sylvia C. Chard, and Yvonne Kogan. *Engaging Children's Minds:*

The Project Approach. 3rd ed. Westport, CT: Greenwood, 2013. Print.

Authors, More Than Three

Use "et al.," which means "and others," or list all the authors. See the two examples that follow:

Garrod, Andrew C., et al. *Adolescent Portraits: Identity, Relationships, and*

Challenges. 7th ed. Boston: Allyn, 2011. Print.

Orlich, Donald C., Robert J. Harder, Richard C. Callahan, Michael S.

Trevisan, and Abbie H. Brown. *Teaching Strategies: A Guide to*

Effective Instruction. 10th ed. Stamford, CT: Cengage, 2009. Print.

Author, Corporation or Institution

A corporate author can be an association, a committee, or any group or institution when the title page does not identify the names of the members.

American Medical Association. *Health Care Careers Directory 2012–2013.*

40th ed. New York: Random, 2012. Print.

List a committee or council as the author even when the organization is also the publisher, as in this example:

Consumer Reports. *Consumer Reports Buying Guide 2013.* New York:

Consumer Reports, 2013.

Author, Two or More Books by the Same Author

When an author has two or more works, do not repeat his or her name with each entry. Rather, insert three hyphens flush with the left margin, followed by a period. Also, list the works alphabetically by the title (ignoring *a, an,* and *the*), not by the year of publication. In the following example, the *Wi* of *Winter* precedes the *Wo* of *World*:

Follett, Ken. *Fall of Giants.* New York: Dutton, 2012. Print.

---. *Winter of the World.* New York: Dutton, 2013. Print.

---. *World Without End.* New York: Signet, 2010. Print.

The three hyphens stand for exactly the same name(s) as in the preceding entry. However, do not substitute three hyphens for an author who has two or more works in the Works Cited when one is written in collaboration with someone else:

Gaiman, Neil. *Fortunately, the Milk.* New York: HarperCollins, 2013. Print.

---. *Stardust.* New York: HarperCollins, 2012. Print.

Gaiman, Neil, and Michael Reaves. *InterWorld.* New York: Harper, 2013. Print.

If the person edited, compiled, or translated the work that follows on the list, place a comma after the three hyphens and write *ed., comp.,* or *trans.* before you give the title. This label does not affect the alphabetic order by title.

Finneran, Richard J., ed. *The Collected Poems of W. B. Yeats Volume I:*

   The Poems. New York: Simon, 2010. Print.

---, ed. *The Tower: A Facsimile Edition.* New York: Simon, 2004. Print.

Author, Two or More Books by the Same Multiple Authors

When you cite two or more books by the same authors, provide the names in the first entry only. Thereafter, use three hyphens, followed by a period.

Axelrod, Rise B., and Charles R. Cooper. *St. Martin's Guide to Writing.* 10th

   ed. Boston: St. Martin's, 2013. Print.

---. *Sticks and Stones: And Other Student Essays.* 8th ed. Boston:

   St. Martin's, 2013. Print.

Anthology, or a Compilation

In general, works in an anthology have been published previously and collected by an editor. Supply the names of authors as well as editors. Many times the prior publication data on a specific work may not be readily available; therefore, use this form:

> If you use several works from the same anthology, you can shorten the citation by citing the short work and by making cross-references to the larger one; see "Cross-References to Works in a Collection," page 270.

Wolfe, Thomas. "The Far and the Near." *The Scope*

   of Fiction. Eds. Cleanth Brooks and Robert

   Penn Warren. New York: Appleton-Century-

   Crofts, 1960. 292–95. Print.

Provide the inclusive page numbers for the piece, not just the page or pages that you have cited in the text.

The Bible

Do not italicize the word Bible or the books of the Bible. Common editions need no publication information, but do italicize special editions of the Bible.

The Bible. Print. [Denotes King James version]

The Geneva Bible. 1560. Facsim. rpt. Madison: U of Wisconsin P, 1961.

 Print.

NASB [New American Standard Bible] The MacArthur Study Bible. Nashville:

 Thomas Nelson, 2013. Print.

A Book Published before 1900

For older books that are now out of print, you may omit the name of the publisher and use a comma, instead of a colon, to separate the place of publication from the year. If it has no date listed, use "n.d." If it has no publisher or place of publication mentioned, use "n.p."

Dewey, John. *The School and Society.* Chicago, 1899. Print.

Chapter or Part of the Book

List the chapter or part of the book on the Works Cited page only when it is separately edited, translated, or written, or when it demands special attention. For example, if you quote from a specific chapter of a book, let's say Chapter 6, "When You Believe in God but Won't Forgive," of Craig Groeschel's book, the entry should read:

Groeschel, Craig. *The Christian Atheist: Believing in God, but Living as If*

 He Doesn't Exist. Grand Rapids, MI: Zondervan, 2010. Print.

> If you cite from an anthology or collection, list the title of the specific story, poem, essay, and so on. See "Anthology, or a Compilation," page 268, or "Collection, Component Part," page 269.

Your in-text citation will have listed specific page numbers, so there is no reason to mention a specific chapter, even though it is the only portion of Groeschel's book that you read.

Classical Works

Homer. *The Odyssey.* Trans. Stephen Mitchell. New

 York: Atria, 2013. Print.

You are more likely to find a classic work in an anthology, which would require this citation:

Sophocles. *Oedipus the King. Literature.* 12th Edition. Ed. X. J. Kennedy

 and Dana Gioia. New York: Longman, 2013. 1207–244. Print.

Collection, Component Part

If you cite from one work in a collection of works by the same author, provide the specific name of the work and the corresponding page numbers. This next entry cites one poem from a collection of poetry by the same author:

Mueller, Lisel. "Not Only the Eskimos." *Good Poems.* Ed. Dani Shapiro. New

 York: Viking, 2002. 316–18. Print.

Cross-References to Works in a Collection

If you are citing several selections from one anthology or collection, provide a full reference to the anthology (as explained on pages 183–184) and then provide references to the individual selections by providing the author and title of the work, the last name of the editor of the collection, and the inclusive page numbers used from the anthology.

Dartt, Victoria. "The Bee Keeper's Love Song." Sutton 131–38.

Furman, Sarah J. "Of Polecats and Egg Salad." Sutton 18–27.

Sutton, Martin B., ed. *Reading on the Sly*. Clarksville, TN: Warioto,

2013. Print.

Wilmer, Donald. "MeMaw's Ironing Board." Sutton 112–16.

Edition

Indicate the edition used, whenever it is not the first, in Arabic numerals ("3rd ed."), by name ("Rev. ed.," "Abr. ed."), or by year ("2013 ed."), without further punctuation:

Brinkerhoff, David, Rose Weitz, and Suzanne Ortega. *Essentials of*

Sociology. 9th ed. Florence, KY: Cengage, 2013. Print.

Indicate that a work has been prepared by an editor, not the original author:

Crane, Stephen. *Maggie: A Girl of the Streets and Other Selected Stories*.

Ed. and Introd. Alfred Kazin. New York: Signet, 2006. Print.

If you want to show the original date of the publication, place the year immediately after the title, followed by a period. *Note:* The title of an edition in a series is capitalized.

Hardy Thomas. *Far from the Madding Crowd*. 1874. Ed. Joslyn T. Pine.

Mineola, NY: Dover, 2007. Print.

Editor, Translator, Illustrator, or Compiler

If the name of the editor or compiler appears on the title page of an anthology or compilation, place it first:

Pollack, Harriet, ed. *Eudora Welty, Whiteness, and Race*. Athens:

U Georgia P, 2013. Print.

If your in-text citation refers to the work of the editor, illustrator, or translator (e.g., "The Ciardi edition caused debate among Dante scholars"), use this form with the original author listed after the work, preceded by the word *By:*

Raffel, Burton, trans. *Beowulf*. Glendale, CA: Bibliotech, 2012. Print.

Dore, Gustave, illus. *Don Quixote*. By Miguel Cervantes. Raleigh, NC: Lulu,

2013. Print.

Otherwise, mention an editor, translator, or compiler of a collection *after* the title with the abbreviations Ed., Trans., or Comp., as shown here:

Sophocles. *Oedipus at Colonus.* Eds. Mark Griffith, Glenn W. Most, David

Greene, and Richard Lattimore. 3rd ed. Chicago: U Chicago P, 2013.

Print.

Encyclopedia, Dictionary, or Reference Book

Treat works arranged alphabetically as you would an anthology or collection, but omit the name of the editor(s), the volume number, place of publication, publisher, and page number(s). If the author is listed, begin the entry with the author's name; otherwise, begin with the title of the article. If the article is signed with initials, look elsewhere in the work for a complete name. Well-known works, such as the two examples that follow, need only the edition and the year of publication.

"Tumult." *The American Heritage College Dictionary.* 2013. Print.

Ward, Norman. "Saskatchewan." *Encyclopedia Americana.* 2012 ed. Print.

If you cite a specific definition from among several, add *Def.* (Definition), followed by the appropriate number/letter of the definition.

"Level." Def. 4a. *The American Heritage College Dictionary.* 2013. Print.

Less-familiar reference works need a full citation, as shown in the next examples:

"Probiotics." *Dictionary of Medical Terms.* 6th ed. Eds. Rebecca E. Sell,

M.D., Mikel A. Rothenberg, M.D., and Charles F. Chapmen. New York:

Barrons, 2013. Print.

"Clindamycin." *Nursing 2013 Drug Handbook.* Ed. Karen D. Comerford.

Philadelphia: Lippincott Williams & Wilkins, 2013. Print.

If you cite material from a chapter of one volume in a multivolume set, you must include the volume number. Although not required, you may also provide the total number of volumes. Conform to the following entry format:

Saintsbury, George. "Dickens." *The Cambridge History of English Literature.*

Ed. A. W. Ward and A. R. Waller. Vol. 13. New York: Putnam's, 1917.

Print. 14 vols.

Introduction, Preface, Foreword, or Afterword

If you are citing the person who has written the introduction to a work by another author, start with the name of the person who wrote the preface or foreword. Give the name of the part being cited, neither italicized nor enclosed within quotation marks. Place the name of the author in normal order after the title preceded by the word *By.* Follow with publication information and end with the inclusive page numbers.

Hyman, Mark, M.D.. Foreword. *The Immune System Recovering Plan*. By

Susan Blum, M.D., M.P.H. New York: Scribner, 2013. ix–xii. Print.

Schilling, Curt. Introduction. *The Best Kind of Different*. By Shonda

Schilling. New York: William Morrow, 2010. 1–5. Print.

If the author has written the prefatory matter, not another person, use only the author's last name after the word *By*.

O'Reilly, Bill. Afterthoughts. *Pinheads and Patriots*. By O'Reilly. New York:

Harper, 2010. 241–42. Print.

Use this form only if you cite from the introduction and not the main text.

Manuscript or Typescript

> For more details about this type of citation, see "Chapter or Part of the Book," page 269, and "Anthology, or a Compilation," page 268.

Chaucer, Geoffrey. *The Canterbury Tales*. 1400–

1410. MS Harley 7334. British Library,

London.

Tabares, Miguel. "Voices from the Ruins of

Ancient Greece." Unpublished essay, 2014.

Play, Classical

Shakespeare, William. *Macbeth*. Ed. Jesse M. Lander. Rpt. of the 1623 ed.

Shakespeare's Great Tragedies. New York: Barnes, 2010. Print.

Today, classical plays are usually found in anthologies, which will require this form:

Shakespeare, William. *Othello*. *Literature*. Ed. X. J. Kennedy and Dana

Gioia. 12th ed. New York: Longman, 2013. 1290–390. Print.

Play, Modern

Contemporary plays may be published independently or as part of a collection.

Shepard, Sam. *Heartless: A Play*. New York: Knopf, 2013. Print.

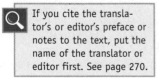

> If you cite the translator's or editor's preface or notes to the text, put the name of the translator or editor first. See page 270.

Poem, Classical

Classical poems are usually translated, so you will often need to list a translator and/or editor. If the work is one part of a collection, show which anthology you used.

Alighieri, Dante. *Inferno*. *The Divine Comedy*. Trans. John Ciardi. *The*

Norton Anthology of World Masterpieces. Ed. Sarah Lawall et al. New

York: Norton, 1999. 1303–429. Print.

Clive, James, trans. *Divine Comedy*. By Dante Alighieri. New York:

Liveright, 2013. Print.

Poem, Modern Collection

Use this form that includes the inclusive page numbers if you cite one short poem from a collection:

Plath, Sylvia. "Pheasant." *Bright Wings*. New York: Columbia U P, 2012.

63–64. Print.

Use this next form if you cite from one book-length poem:

Eliot, T. S. *Four Quartets*. *The Complete Poems and Plays 1909–1950*. New

York: Harcourt, 1952. 115–45. Print.

Do not cite specific poems and pages if you cite several different poems of the collection. Your in-text citations should cite the specific poems and page numbers (see pages 191–193). Your Works Cited entry would then list only the name of the collection.

Eliot, T. S. *The Complete Poems and Plays 1909–1950*. New York: Harcourt,

1952. Print.

Reprinted Works

Use the following form if you can quickly identify original publication information.

Allenda, Isabel. "Enamored with Shakespeare." *Folger Magazine* Spring

2013: n. pag. Rpt. in *Living with Shakespeare*. Ed. Susannah Carson.

New York: Vintage, 2013. 489–92. Print.

Republished Book

If you are citing from a republished book, such as a paperback version of a book published originally in hardback, provide the original publication date after the title and then provide the publication information for the book from which you are citing.

Stevenson, Robert Louis. *Treasure Island*. 1883. New York: Cambridge UP,

2013. Print.

Although it is not required, you may want to give facts about the original publication if the information will serve the reader. In this next example the republished book was originally published under a different title.

Arnold, Matthew. "The Study of Poetry." *Essays: English and American*.

Ed. Charles W. Eliot. 1886. New York: Collier, 1910. Print.

Rpt. of the General Introduction to *The English Poets*. Ed.

T. H. Ward. 1880.

Screenplay

> Boal, Mark. *Zero Dark Thirty: The Shooting Script.* Screenplay. New York:
>
> HarperCollins, 2013. Print.

Series, Numbered and Unnumbered

If the work is one in a published series, show the name of the series, abbreviated, without quotation marks or italics, the number of this work in Arabic numerals and a period:

> Wallerstein, Ruth C. *Richard Crashaw: A Study in Style and Poetic*
>
> *Development.* Madison: U of Wisconsin P, 1935. Print. U of
>
> Wisconsin Studies in Lang. and Lit. 37.

> If you cite more than one article from a casebook, use cross-references. See page 270.

Sourcebooks and Casebooks

If you can identify the original facts of publication, include that information:

> Ellmann, Richard. "Reality." *Yeats: The Man and the Masks.* New York:
>
> Macmillan, 1948. Rpt. in *Yeats: A Collection of Critical Essays.*
>
> Ed. John Unterecker. Twentieth Century Views. Englewood Cliffs:
>
> Prentice, 1963. 163–74. Print.

Title of the Book

Show the title of the work italicized, followed by a period.

> Hood, Ann. *The Obituary Writer.* New York: Norton, 2013. Print.

Separate any subtitle from the primary title by a colon and one space even though the title page has no mark of punctuation or the card catalog entry has a semicolon.

If an italicized title to a book incorporates another title that normally receives italics, do not italicize the shorter title nor place it within quotation marks. In the title below, *Absalom and Acidophil* is the shorter title; it does not receive italics.

> Schilling, Bernard N. *Dryden and the Conservative Myth: A Reading of*
>
> Absalom and Acidophil. New Haven: Yale UP, 1961. Print.

Title of a Book in Another Language

In general, use lowercase letters for foreign titles except for the first major word and proper names. Provide a translation in brackets if you think it necessary (e.g., *Étranger* [*The Stranger*] or *Praha* [*Prague*]).

Coelho, Paulo. Manuscrito encontrado en accra. New York: Knopf

　　Doubleday, 2013. Print.

Allende, Isabel. El cuaderno de maya. New York: Knopf Doubleday,

　　2012. Print.

Translator

List the translator's name first only if the translator's work (preface, foreword, afterword, notes) is the focus of your study.

Neruda, Pablo. *Sublime Blue: Selected Early Odes by Pablo Neruda.*

　　Trans. William Pitt Root. San Antonio: WingsPress, 2013. Print.

Volumes

If you are citing from only one volume of a multivolume work, provide the number of that volume in the Works Cited entry with information for that volume only. In your text, you will need to specify only page numbers, for example, (Borgese 45–51).

Chircop, Aldo, Moira L. McConnell, and Scott Coffen-Smout, eds. *Ocean*

　　Yearbook. Vol. 27. Chicago: U of Chicago P, 2013. Print.

Although additional information is not required, you may provide the inclusive page numbers, the total number of volumes, and the inclusive dates of publication:

Lauter, Paul, ed. "New Generations: Postmodernity and Difference." *The*

　　Heath Anthology of American Literature. 7th ed. Vol. E. Boston:

　　Houghton Mifflin, 2013. 2345–54. Print. 5 vols.

If you are citing from two or more volumes of a multivolume work, your in-text citation will need to specify volume and page (2: 120–21); then the Works Cited entry will need to show the total number of volumes in Arabic numerals, as shown here:

Thomas, Jay C., and Michel Hersen, eds. *Handbook of Clinical Psychology*

　　Competencies. 2 vols. New York: Springer-Verlag, 2013. Print.

If you are citing from volumes that were published over a period of years, provide the inclusive dates at the end of the citation. Should the volumes still be in production, write *to date* after the number of volumes and leave a space after the dash that follows the initial date.

Walsch, Neale Donald. *Conversations with God: An Uncommon Dialogue.* 3

　　vols. New York: Penguin, 2007–08. Print.

Cassidy, Frederic, ed. *Dictionary of American Regional English.* 3 vols. to

　　date. Cambridge: Belknap-Harvard UP, 1985–. Print.

If you are using only one volume of a multivolume work and the volume has an individual title, you can cite the one work without mentioning the other volumes in the set.

Crane, Stephen. *Wounds in the Rain. Stephen Crane: Tales of War.*

Charlottesville: UP of Virginia, 1970. 95–284. Print.

As a courtesy to the reader, you may include supplementary information about an entire edition.

Crane, Stephen. *Wounds in the Rain. Stephen Crane: Tales of War.*

Charlottesville: UP of Virginia, 1970. Print. 95–284. Vol. 6 of

The University of Virginia Edition of the Works of Stephen Crane.

Ed. Fredson Bowers. 10 vols. 1969–76.

14e Works Cited Form—Periodicals

For journal or magazine articles, use the following order:

1. Author(s)
2. Title of the article
3. Name of the periodical—*italicized*
4. Series number (if it is relevant)
5. Volume and issue number (for journals)—(e.g., 70.4)
6. Date of publication
7. Page numbers
8. Medium of publication—"Print."

Lidz, Franz. "Kon-Tiki Sails Again." *Smithsonian* Apr. 2013: 62–65. Print.

Following is a detailed breakdown of the components found in the entry found above:

Author's Name. "Title of Article." *Title of Periodical.* Publication Date:

Page Numbers. Medium of Publication.

Give the name of the journal or magazine in full, underscored or italicized, and with no following punctuation. Omit any introductory article, such as *The*.

Hooker, Morna D. "Artemis of Ephesus." *Journal of Theological Studies*

64.1 (Apr. 2013): 37–46. Print.

Be sure to include the volume as well as issue number for journals immediately after the title of the journal. In this example, the volume and issue number is 64.1. If no issue number is provided, then simply give the volume number, 64. Magazine entries on the Works Cited page do not need to mention the volume or issue number.

The formatting of Works Cited entries for periodicals are explained and illustrated in the following examples.

Abstract

If you cite from an abstract found in a journal, be sure to designate that you are citing only from the overview information found in the abstract.

Kozuch, Sebastian, and Jan M. L. Martin. "Halogen Bonds: Benchmarks and

Theoretical Analysis." *Journal of Chemistry Theory and Computation*

9.4 (2013): 1918–31. Abstract. Print.

Author(s)

Show the author's name flush with the left margin, without a numeral and with succeeding lines indented five spaces. Enter the surname first, followed by a comma, followed by a given name or initials, followed by a period:

Downes, Alexander B., and Jonathan Monten. "Forced to Be Free?: Why

Foreign-Imposed Regime Change Rarely Leads to Democratization."

International Security 37.4 (Spring 2013): 90–131. Print.

Author, Anonymous

"Protecting Puget Sound's Species." *Nature Conservancy* Apr. 2013: 22. Print.

Interview, Published

Roark, John. Interview with Ric Burns. "Challenging the Numbers." *Civil*

War Times 52.1 (Feb. 2013): 8. Print.

Journal, with All Issues for a Year Paged Continuously

Baker, Raymond W. "The Paradox of Islam's Future." *Political Science*

Quarterly 127.4 (Winter 2012-13): 519–66. Print.

Journal, with Each Issue Paged Anew

Add the issue number after the volume number because page numbers alone are not sufficient to locate the article within a volume of six or twelve issues when each issue has separate pagination. Adding the month or season with the year will also serve the researcher.

Townsend, Jane S., et al. "An Online Writing Partnership: Transforming

Classroom Writing Instruction." *English Journal* 102.4 (Mar. 2013):

74–80. Print.

Note: If a journal uses only an issue number, treat it as a volume number:

Shore, Robert. "Post-Photography: The Unknown Image." *Elephant* 13

(Winter 2012–13): 66+. Print.

Magazine

With magazines, the volume number offers little help for finding an article. For example, one volume of *Time* (52 issues) will have page 16 repeated fifty-two times. For this reason, you need to insert an exact date (month and day) for weekly and fortnightly (every two weeks) publications. Do not list the volume and issue numbers.

> McGrath, Ben. "The White Wall." *New Yorker* 22 Apr. 2013: 80–95. Print.

The month suffices for monthly and bimonthly publications:

> Murphy, Marielle. "A Knockout Story." *Writer's Digest* May/June 2013:
>
>   47–48. Print.

Notes, Editorials, Queries, Reports, Comments, Letters

Magazine and journals publish many pieces that are not full-fledged articles. Identify this type of material if the title of the article or the name of the journal does not make clear the nature of the material (e.g., "Letter" or "Comment").

> Greenman, John. "Lady Oscar." Puzzle. *People* 29 Apr. 2013: 96. Print.
>
> Williams, Christian. "When I Was Growing Up." Editor's note. *UTNE*
>
>   *Reader* Mar.–Apr. 2013: 5. Print.
>
> Mark, Jason. "Arrogance Is Bliss." Editorial. *Earth Island Journal* Spring
>
>   2013: 2. Print.

Review, in a Magazine, Newspaper, or Journal

Name the reviewer and the title of the review. Then write *Rev. of* and the title of the work being reviewed, followed by a comma, and the name of the magazine or journal. If necessary, identify the nature of the work within brackets immediately after the title.

> Purewal, Sarah Jacobsson. "Digital Storm x17: A More Portable Gaming
>
>   Option." Rev. of Digital Storm x17. *PC World* May 2013: 49. Print.

If the name of reviewer is not provided, begin the entry with the title of the review.

> "Creative Compact" Rev. of Nikon 1 JZ. *Photography Monthly* Feb. 2013:
>
>   106–107. Print.

If the review has no title, omit it from the entry.

Skipped Pages in an Article

Supply inclusive page numbers (202–09, 85–115, or 1112–24), but if an article is paged here and there throughout the issue (for example, pages 74, 78, and 81–88), write only the first page number and a plus sign with no intervening space:

> Rosin, Hanna. "The Touch-Screen Generation." *Atlantic* Apr. 2013: 57+. Print.

Special Issue

If you cite one article from a special issue of a journal, you may indicate the nature of this special issue, as shown next:

Howard, Beth. "Don't Just Sit There." *Best Hospitals.* Spec. Issue of *U.S.*
News and World Report 2013: 74–76. Print.

If you cite several articles from the special issue, begin the primary citation with the name of the editor:

Johns, Chris, ed. *125 Years of Great Explorations.* Spec. Issue of *National*
Geographic 2013: 1–128. Print.

Once that entry is established, cross-reference each article used in the following manner:

Skerry, Brian. "Open Blue: Going Green." Photograph. *Johns,* 119.

Title of the Article

Show the title within quotation marks followed by a period inside the closing quotation marks:

Moss, Marissa R. "Dawes: America's Favorite New Band Expand Their
Horizons." *American Songwriter* Mar.–Apr. 2013: 40–49. Print.

Title, within the Article's Title

Wicker, Alan. "From Humble Roots to *Divine Identities*: A Review Essay."
Prairie Poets Quarterly 25.3 (Fall 2013): 93–94. Print.

 Note: See also "Title of a Book in Another Language," page 274.

Title, Foreign

Rosas, Blanca González. "La intolerancia artística del
Papa Francisco." *Proceso* 17 Mar. 2013: 68. Print.

Volume, Issue, and Page Numbers for Journals

Some journals are paged continuously through all issues of an entire year, so listing the month of publication is unnecessary. For clarity, provide the volume and issue number, as well as the page numbers. Give the issue number following the volume number, separated by a period.

Stiles, William B. "The Variables Problem and Progress in Psychotherapy
Research." *Psychotherapy* 50.1 (Mar 2013): 33–41. Print.

14f Works Cited Form—Newspapers

Provide the name of the author, the title of the article, and the name of the newspaper as it appears on the masthead, omitting any introductory article (e.g., *Wall Street Journal,* not *The Wall Street Journal*).

If the city of publication is not included in the name of a newspaper published locally, add the city in square brackets, not italicized, after the name: "*Times-Picayune* [New Orleans]." Provide the complete date—day, month (abbreviated), and year. Omit any volume and issue numbers.

Provide a page number as listed (e.g., 21, B-7, 13C, D4). For example, *USA Today* uses "6A" but the *New York Times* uses "A6." There is no uniformity among newspapers on this matter, so list the page accurately as an aid to your reader. If the article is not printed on consecutive pages, for example, if it begins on page 1 and skips to page 8, write the first page number and a plus (+) sign (see the entry below). Finally, provide state the medium of publication—"Print."

Newspaper in One Section

McTague, Jim. "A GOP House?" *Barron's* 27 Sept. 2010: 27–29. Print.

Newspaper with Lettered Sections

Mitchell, Kirk. "Time to Rethink 'Time Earned' Policy." *Denver Post* 21 Apr.

2013: 1A+. Print.

Newspaper with Numbered Sections

Guerrero, Rafael. "Tanning Beds in Cross Hairs." *Chicago Tribune* 6 Apr.

2013, sec. 1: 1. Print.

Newspaper Editorial with No Author Listed

"The High Cost of Free Speech." Editorial. [Nashville] *Tennessean* 15 May.

2013: A16. Print.

Newspaper Column, Cartoon, Comic Strip, or Advertisement

Add a description to the entry to explain that the citation refers to something other than a regular news story.

Robnison, Eugene. "Margaret Thatcher, a Bold, Decisive Leader." Column.

Washington Post 8 Apr. 2013: A3. Print.

Newspaper Article with City Added

In the case of locally published newspapers, add the city and state in square brackets.

Leiser, Satcy. "Face-to-Face in a Digital World." *Leaf Chronicle* [Clarksville, TN]

21 Apr. 2013: D1+. Print.

Newspaper Edition or Section

When the masthead lists an edition, add a comma after the date and name the edition (*late ed., city ed.*), followed by a colon and then the page number.

> Salzer, James, and Aaron Gould Sheinin. "Tax Breaks Sought Amid
>
> > Budget Cuts." *Atlanta Journal-Constitution* 21 Feb. 2013, home ed.:
> >
> > A1+. Print.

Newspaper in a Foreign Language

> "Pour resoudre les problemes d'alimentation." *Eurotec* Jan. 2013:
>
> > 41. Print.

14g Works Cited Form—Government Documents

Since the nature of public documents is so varied, the form of the entry cannot be standardized. Therefore, you should provide sufficient information so that the reader can easily locate the reference. As a general rule, place information in the Works Cited entry in this order (but see below if you know the author, editor, or compiler of the document):

1. Government
2. Body or agency
3. Subsidiary body
4. Title of document
5. Identifying numbers
6. Publication facts
7. Medium of publication

When you cite two or more works by the same government, substitute three hyphens for the name of each government or body that you repeat:

> United States. Cong. House.
>
> ---. ---. Senate.
>
> ---. Dept. of Justice.

Congressional Papers

Senate and House sections are identified by an S or an H with document numbers (e.g., S. Res. 16) and page numbers (e.g., H2345-47).

> United States. Cong. House. Cybersecurity Enhancement Act of 2013.
>
> > 113th Cong., 1st sess. H. Bill 2042. Washington, DC: GPO,
> >
> > 2013. Print.

> ---. ---. ---. Congressional Earmarks, Limited Tax Benefits, or Limited Tariff
>
> Benefits. 1st sess. H. Bill 951. Washington, DC: GPO, 2013. Print.

If you provide a citation to the *Congressional Record,* you should abbreviate it and provide only the date and page numbers.

> *Cong. Rec.* 17 Apr. 2013: S2697–2774. Print.

Executive Branch Documents

> United States. Dept. of State. *Foreign Relations of the United States:*
>
> *Diplomatic Papers, 1943.* 5 vols. Washington: GPO, 1943–44. Print.
>
> ---. President. *2013 Economic Report of the President.* Washington:
>
> GPO, 2013. Print.

Documents of State Governments

Publication information on state papers will vary widely, so provide sufficient data for your reader to find the document.

> *2012–2013 Statistical Report.* Nashville: Tennessee Board of Regents,
>
> 2013. TBR A-001-03. Print.
>
> *Tennessee Election Returns, 1796–1825.* Microfilm. Nashville: Tennessee
>
> State Library and Archives, n.d. M-Film JK 5292 T46. Print.
>
> "Giles County." *2012–13 Directory of Public Schools.* Nashville: State Dept.
>
> of Educ., n.d. 61. Print.

Legal Citations and Public Statutes

Use the following examples as guidelines for developing your citations, which can usually appear as parenthetical citations in your text, but not on the Works Cited page.

> Illinois. Illinois Recycled Newsprint Use Act. (415 *ILCS* 110) 2013. Print.
>
> Noise Control Act of 2013. Pub. L. 92-574. 2013. Stat. 86. Print.
>
> People v. McIntosh. California 321 P.3d 876, 2001-6. 1970. Print.
>
> State v. Lane. Minnesota 263 N. W. 608. 1935. Print.
>
> U.S. Const. Art 2, sec. 1. Print.

14h Works Cited Form—Other Sources

Advertisement

Provide the title of the advertisement, within quotation marks, or the name of the product or company, not within quotation marks, the label *Advertisement,* and publication information.

"Peru: Empire of Hidden Treasures." Advertisement. *Smithsonian* Apr.

2013: 101. Print.

OnStar. Advertisement. CNN. 14 Jan. 2013. Television

Art Work

If you actually experience the work itself, use the following form:

Remington, Frederic. *Mountain Man*. 1903 Bronze. Metropolitan Museum

of Art, New York.

If the art work is a special showing at a museum, use the form of the next examples.

Gruber, Aaronel deRoy. "Aaronel deRoy Gruber: Art(ist) in Motion."

Art Exhibition. Westmoreland Museum of American Art, Greensburg,

PA 14 May 2013. Visual Art.

"Blues for Smoke." Whitney Museum of American Art, New York.

28 Mar. 2013. Visual art.

Use this next form to cite reproductions in books and journals.

Raphael. *School of Athens*. Fresco. The Vatican, Rome. *The World Book-*

Encyclopedia, 2013 ed. Print.

If you show the date of the original, place the date immediately after the title.

Raphael. *School of Athens*. 1510–11. Fresco. The Vatican, Rome. *The World*

Book-Encyclopedia. 2012 ed.

Broadcast Interview

Cooper, Anderson. "Victim: I Saw Things I Wish I Didn't See." Interview.

CNN. Cable News Network, 17 Apr. 2013. Television.

Bulletin

"Winter Bee Losses 'Normal,' According to State Agriculture Department."

The Market Bulletin. Charleston, WV: West Virginia Department of

Agriculture, 22 Mar. 2013. Print.

Maryland State Bar Association's Public Awareness Committee.

Appointing a Guardian. Baltimore: Maryland State Bar Association.

2013. Print.

Cartoon

If you cannot decipher the name of the cartoonist and cannot find a title, use this form:

"When Did People Start Inventing Things in the Garage?" Cartoon. *Popular*

Science May 2013: 71. Print.

Sometimes you will have the artist's name but not the name of the cartoon:

Garland, Nicholas. "All the Iron Ladies: Nicholas Garland on Drawing

Thatcher over Five Decades. Cartoon. *Spectator* 13 Apr. 2013:

xv. Print.

Computer Software

Publisher Deluxe 2012. Redmond, WA: Microsoft, 2012. CD-ROM.

Conference Proceedings

Biller, Alia K., Esther Y. Chung, and Amelia E. Kimball. *BUCLD-36:*

Proceedings of the Thirty-fourth Boston University Conference

on Language Development. Apr. 2012. Somerville, MA:

Cascadilla, 2012. Print.

Dissertation, Published

Caudill, Sarah E. *Searches for Gravitational Waves from Perturbed Black*

Holes in Data from Ligo Detectors. Diss. Louisiana State U, 2012.

Baton Rouge: Louisiana State U, 2012. Print.

Dissertation, Unpublished

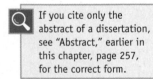

If you cite only the abstract of a dissertation, see "Abstract," earlier in this chapter, page 257, for the correct form.

Patel-McCune, Santha. "An Analysis of Homophone

Errors in the Writing of 7th Grade Language

Arts Students: Implications for Middle School

Teachers." Diss. Southern Tech. U, 2014. Print.

Film or DVD

Cite the title of a film, the director, the distributor, and the year.

The Lone Ranger. Dir. Gore Verbinski. Walt Disney Studios, 2013. DVD.

If relevant to your study, add the names of performers, writers, or producers after the name of the director.

The Last of the Mohicans. Dir. Michael Mann. Perf. Daniel Day-Lewis.

Twentieth Century Fox, 1992. DVD.

If the film is a DVD, videocassette, filmstrip, slide program, or video-disc, add the type of publication medium after the date. You can also add the date of the original film, if relevant.

Citizen Kane. Dir. Orson Welles. 1941. Warner, 2010. DVD.

If you are citing the accomplishments of the director or a performer, begin the citation with that person's name.

Caird, John, and Gavin Taylor, dir. *Les Miserables*. 1995. Perf. Colm

   Wilkinson, Philip Quast, Ruthie Henshall, and Jenny Galloway. BBC,

   2008. DVD.

Interview, Unpublished

See also "Published Interview," page 277, and "Broadcast Interview," page 283.

For an interview that you conduct, name the person interviewed, the type of interview (e.g., telephone interview, personal interview, e-mail interview), and the date. Include TS as the medium of publication if the interview was transcribed into a written document.

Carter, Luella. "Growing Georgia Greens." Personal Interview. 5 Oct. 2013. TS.

Letter, Personal

Knight, Charles. Letter to the author. 21 Oct. 2013. TS.

Letter, Published

Eisenhower, Dwight. "Letter to Richard Nixon." 20 April 1968. *Memoirs of*

   Richard Nixon. By Richard Nixon. New York: Grosset, 1978. 178–79

   Print.

Manuscript (MS) and Typescript (TS)

Moss, Millicent. Journal 3. N.d. MS. Millicent Moss Private Papers,

   Emporia, KS. 2012.

Williams, Ralph. "Walking on the Water." 2013. TS.

Map

Treat a map as you would an anonymous work, but add a descriptive label, such as *map, chart,* or *survey,* unless the title describes the medium.

County Boundaries and Names. United States Base Map GE-50, No. 86.

   Washington: GPO, 2010. Print.

Pennsylvania. Map. Chicago: Rand, 2013. Print.

Miscellaneous Materials (Program, Leaflet, Poster, Announcement)

"Earth Day." Poster. Louisville. 22 Apr. 2013. Print.

"Parent's Association—Family Weekend." Program. Knoxville: U of

Tennessee, 28 Sept. 2013. Print.

Musical Composition

For a musical composition, begin with the composer's name, followed by a period. Italicize the title of an opera, ballet, or work of music identified by name, but do not italicize or enclose within quotation marks the form, number, and key when these are used to identify an instrumental composition.

Mozart, Wolfgang A. *Jupiter.* Symphony No. 41. London: n.p., 2012. CD.

Treat a published score as you would a book.

Legrenzi, Giovanni. *La Buscha.* Sonata for Instruments. *Historical*

Anthology of Music. Ed. Archibald T. Davison and Willi Apel.

Cambridge: Harvard UP, 1950. 70–76. Print.

Pamphlet

Treat pamphlets as you would a book.

Federal Reserve Board. *Consumer Handbook to Credit Protection Laws.*

Washington: GPO, 2013. Print.

Westinghouse Advanced Power Systems. *Nuclear Waste Management:*

A Manageable Task. Madison, PA: Westinghouse, n.d. Print.

Performance

Treat a performance (e.g., play, opera, ballet, or concert) as you would a film, but include the site (normally the theater and city) and the date of the performance.

Under the Cherokee Moon. Cherokee Heritage Center, Tahlequah, OK. 28

May 2013. Performance.

Twelfth Night. By William Shakespeare. Folger Theatre, Washington. 9 June

2013. Performance.

If your text emphasizes the work of a particular individual, begin with the appropriate name.

Frisell, Bill. "Gershwin & Beyond." The Allen Room, New York. 20 Sept.

2013. Performance.

Public Address or Lecture

Identify the nature of the address (e.g., Lecture, Reading) and include the site (normally the lecture hall and city) and the date of the performance.

Anson, Chris. "Climate Change." Conf. on Coll. Composition and

Communication Convention. The Riviera, Royale Pavilion,

Las Vegas. 14 Mar. 2013. Address.

Recording on Record, Tape, or Disk

Indicate the medium you are citing (e.g., audiocassette, audiotape [reel-to-reel tape], or LP [long-playing record]).

"Chaucer: The Nun's Priest's Tale." *Canterbury Tales.* Narr. in Middle English

by Alex Edmonds. London, 2005. Audiocassette.

Dylan, Bob. "The Times They Are A-Changin'." *Bob Dylan's Greatest Hits.*

CBS, 1967. LP.

Do not italicize or enclose within quotation marks the title of a private recording or tape. However, you should include the date, if available, as well as the location and the identifying number.

Drake, Marc. Early Settlers of the Smokey Mountains. Rec. Feb. 2013. U of

Knoxville. Knoxville, TN. UTF.34.82. Audiotape.

Cite a libretto, liner notes, or booklet that accompanies a recording in the form shown in the following example.

Turner, Frank. Liner Notes. *Tape Deck Heart.* By Frank Turner. Xtra Mile,

2013. Print.

Report

Unbound reports are placed within quotation marks; bound reports are treated as books:

United Nations Office on Drugs and Crime. *2012 Annual Report.* Vienna:

UNODC, 15 Apr. 2012. Print.

Brodeur, Andre, and Martin Pergler. "Risk Oversight Practices." The

Conference Board. New York: CBS/Broadcast Group, Sept. 2013. Print.

Reproductions, Photographs, and Photocopies

Blake, William. *Comus.* Plate 4. "Blake's *Comus* Designs." *Blake Studies* 4

(Spring 1972): 61. Print.

Michener, James A. "Structure of Earth at Centennial, Colorado." Line drawing

in *Centennial.* By Michener. New York: Random, 1974. 26. Print.

Table, Illustration, Chart, or Graph

Tables or illustrations of any kind published within works need a detailed label (chart, table, figure, photograph, and so on):

"Pop-up Glossaries in Computerized Tests." Figure. *English Journal* 102.3

(Jan. 2013): 128. Print.

Alphabet. Chart. Columbus: Scholastic, 2011. Print.

Television or Radio Program

If available or relevant, provide information in this order: the episode (in quotation marks), the title of the program (italicized), title of the series (not italicized nor in quotation marks), name of the network, call letters and the broadcast date. Add other information (such as narrator) after the episode or program narrated or directed or performed. Place the number of episodes, if relevant, before the title of the series.

Burlingame, Michael, and Brooks Simpson. "Abraham Lincoln's War

Policies." C-SPAN. 21 Apr. 2013. Television.

The Abolitionists. 3 episodes. American Experience. Dir. Rob Rapley.

NPT, Nashville. 8 Jan. 2013. Television.

"Sonia Sotomayor." *Anderson Cooper 360°*. Host Anderson Cooper. CNN. 7

Mar. 2013. Television.

Thesis

See "Dissertation, Unpublished," page 284.

Transparency

Sharp, La Vaughn, and William E. Loeche. *The Patient and Circulatory*

Disorders: A Guide for Instructors. 54 transparencies, 99 overlays.

Philadelphia: Lorrenzo, 2011. Print.

Unpublished Paper

Schuler, Wren. "Prufrock and His Cat." Unpublished essay, 2013. Print.

15 Writing in APA Style

Chapter 15 Clear Targets

Governed by *The Publication Manual of the American Psychological Association,* 6th edition, APA style has gained wide acceptance in the social sciences, and versions similar to it are used in the biological sciences, business, and the earth sciences. The following components discussed in this chapter will help to accurately document your research paper:

- Writing theory, reporting test results, or reviewing literature
- Writing in the proper tense for an APA research paper
- Using in-text citations in APA style
- Preparing a list of references
- Formatting an APA paper

Research is paramount in the social sciences; you will need to execute your project with accuracy and precision.

15a Writing Theory, Reporting Test Results, or Reviewing Literature

In the sciences, you may choose between three types of articles, or your instructor will specify one of these:

- Theoretical articles
- Reports of empirical studies
- Review articles

For a sample theoretical article, see the student paper on pages 310–317, which examines the trend of eliminating recess in elementary schools to gain more instructional time.

Theoretical Article

The theoretical article draws on existing research to examine a topic. This is the type of paper you will most likely write as a first-year or second-year student. You will need to trace the development of a theory or compare theories by examining the literature to arrive at the

289

current thinking about topics such as autism, criminal behavior, dysfunctional families, and learning disorders. The theoretical article generally accomplishes four aims:

1. Identifies a problem or hypothesis that has historical implications in the scientific community.
2. Traces the development and history of the evolution of the theory.
3. Provides a systematic analysis of the articles that have explored the problem.
4. Arrives at a judgment and discussion of the prevailing theory.

Report of an Empirical Study

For additional details about field research, consult Chapter 6, pages 84–94.

When you conduct field research and perform laboratory testing, you must report the details of your original research. The empirical report accomplishes these four purposes:

1. Introduces the problem or hypothesis investigated and explains the purpose of the work.
2. Describes the method used to conduct the research.
3. Reports the results and the basic findings.
4. Discusses, interprets, and explores the implications of the findings.

You will need to work closely with your instructor to accomplish each of these stages.

Review Article

See pages 128–134 for a sample review of literature.

You may be required to write a critical evaluation of a published article, a book, or a set of articles on a common topic. The purpose is to examine the state of current research—and, in some cases, to determine if additional work might be in order. A review article sets out to accomplish several goals:

1. Define a problem or issue that is the subject of discussion.
2. Summarize the article(s) or book(s) under review.
3. Analyze the literature to discover strengths, weaknesses, or inconsistencies in the research.
4. Recommend additional research that might grow logically from the work under review.

15b Writing in the Proper Tense for an APA Paper

Verb tense is an indicator that distinguishes papers in the humanities from those in the natural and social sciences. MLA style, as shown in previous chapters, requires you to use present tense when you refer to a cited work ("Jeffries *stipulates*" or "the work of Mills and Maguire *shows*"). In contrast, APA style requires you to use past tense or present perfect tense ("Jeffries *stipulated*" or "the work of Mills and Maguire *has demonstrated*"). The APA style does require present tense when you discuss the results (e.g., "*the results confirm*" or "*the study indicates*") and when you mention established knowledge (e.g., "*the therapy offers some hope*" or "*salt contributes to hypertension*"). The following paragraphs, side by side, show the differences in verb tenses for MLA and APA styles.

MLA style:	**APA style:**
The scholarly issue at work here is the construction of reality. Cohen, Adoni, and Bantz label the construction a social process "in which human beings act both as the creators and products of the social world" (34). These writers identify three categories (34–35).	The scholarly issue at work here is the construction of reality. Cohen, Adoni, and Bantz (2013) labeled the construction a social process "in which human beings act both as the creators and products of the social world" (p. 34). These writers have identified three categories.

APA style, shown on the right, requires that you use the present tense for generalizations and references to stable conditions, but it requires the present perfect tense or the past tense for sources cited (e.g., the sources *have tested* a hypothesis or the sources *reported* the results of a test). This next sentence uses tense correctly for APA style:

> The danger of steroid use exists for every age group, even youngsters. Lloyd and Mercer (2013) reported on six incidents of liver damage to 14-year-old swimmers who used steroids.

For updates to APA style, consult the association's Internet site: http://www.apastyle.org/.

As shown in this example, use the present tense (*exists*) for established knowledge and the present perfect (*has reported*) or the past tense (*reported*) for a citation.

15c Using In-Text Citations in APA Style

APA style uses the following conventions for in-text citations:

- Cites last names only.
- Cites the year, within parentheses, immediately after the name of the author. Include only the year in the text citation even if the reference includes a month.

- Cites page numbers with a direct quotation but not with a paraphrase.
- Uses "p." or "pp." before page numbers.

Citing Last Name Only and the Year of Publication

An in-text citation in APA style requires the last name of the author and the year of publication.

> Nguyen (2012) has advanced the idea of combining the social sciences and mathematics to chart human behavior.

If you do not use the author's name in your text, place the name(s) within the parenthetical citation.

> One study has advanced the idea of combining the social sciences and mathematics to chart human behavior (Nguyen, 2012).

Providing a Page Number

If you quote the exact words of a source, provide a page number and use "p." or "pp." Place the page number in one of two places: after the year (2012, p. B4) or at the end of the quotation.

> Nguyen (2012) has advanced the idea of "soft mathematics," which is the practice of "applying mathematics to study people's behavior" (p. B4).

Citing a Block of Material

Present a quotation of forty words or more as a separate block, indented five spaces or one-half inch from the left margin. (*Note:* MLA style uses ten spaces or 1 inch). Because it is set off from the text in a distinctive block, do not enclose it with quotation marks. Do not indent the first line an extra five spaces; however, *do* indent the first line of any additional paragraphs that appear in the block an extra five spaces—that is, ten spaces or one inch from the left margin. Set parenthetical citations outside the last period.

> Albert (2013) reported the following:
>
> > Whenever these pathogenic organisms attack the human body and begin to multiply, the infection is set in motion. The host responds to this parasitic invasion with efforts to cleanse itself of the invading agents. When rejection efforts of the host become visible (fever, sneezing, congestion), the disease status exists. (pp. 314–315)

Citing a Work with More Than One Author

When one work has two or more authors, use *and* in the text but use *&* in the citation.

> Werner and Throckmorton (2013) offered statistics on the toxic
>
> levels of water samples from six rivers.

but

> It has been reported (Werner & Throckmorton, 2013) that toxic
>
> levels exceeded the maximum allowed each year since 2009.

For three to five authors, name them all in the first entry (e.g., Torgerson, Andrews, Smith, Lawrence, & Dunlap, 2013), but thereafter use "et al." (e.g., Torgerson et al., 2013). For six or more authors, employ "et al." in the first and in all subsequent instances (e.g., Fredericks et al., 2012).

Citing More Than One Work by an Author

Use lowercase letters (a, b, c) to identify two or more works published in the same year by the same author—for example, (Thompson, 2013a) and (Thompson, 2013b). Then use "2013a" and "2013b" in your References. If necessary, specify additional information:

> Horton (2012; cf. Thomas, 2013a, p. 89, and 2013b, p. 426)
>
> suggested an intercorrelation of these testing devices, but after
>
> multiple-group analysis, Welston (2011, esp. p. 211) reached an
>
> opposite conclusion.

Citing Indirect Sources

Use a double reference to cite a person who has been quoted in a book or article—that is, use the original author(s) in the text and cite your source for the information in the parenthetical citation.

> In other research, Massie and Rosenthal (2013) studied home
>
> movies of children diagnosed with autism, but determining criteria was
>
> difficult due to the differences in quality and dating of the available
>
> videotapes (cited in Osterling & Dawson, 2012, p. 248).

Citing from a Textbook or Anthology

If you make an in-text citation to an article or chapter of a textbook, casebook, or anthology, use the in-text citation to refer only to the person(s) you cite:

> One writer stressed that two out of every three new jobs in this
>
> decade will go to women (Ogburn 2013).

Citing Classical Works

If an ancient work has no date of publication, cite the author's name followed by n.d. within parentheses.

> Seeing psychic emotions as . . . (Sophocles, n.d.).

Cite the year of any translation you have used, preceded by *trans.*, and give the date of the version used, followed by *version*.

> Plato (trans. 1963) offered a morality that . . .
>
> Plato's *Phaedrus* (1982 version) explored . . .

If you know the original date of publication, include it before the date of the translation or version you have used.

> In his "Poetics," Aristotle (350 B.C.E. 2012) viewed the structure of the plot as a requisite to a good poem.

Note: Entries on your References page need not cite major classical works and the Bible. Therefore, identify in your text the version used and the book, chapter, line, verse, or canto.

> In Exodus 24:3–4 Moses erects an altar and "twelve pillars according to the twelve tribes of Israel" (King James version).

> The *Epic of Gilgamesh* shows, in part, the search for everlasting life (Part 4).

> In the *Iliad,* Homer takes great efforts in describing the shield of Achilles (18:558–709).

Abbreviating Corporate Authors in the Text

The names of groups that serve as authors, such as corporations, associations, and government agencies, are usually spelled out each time they appear. The names of some corporate authors may be abbreviated after a first, full reference:

> One source questioned the results of the use of aspirin for arthritis treatment in children (American Medical Association [AMA], 2013).

Thereafter, refer to the corporate author by initials: (AMA, 2013). It is important to give enough information in the text citation for the reader to locate the entry in the reference list without difficulty.

Citing a Work with No Author

When a work has no author listed, cite the title as part of the in-text citation (or use the first few words of the material).

> The cost per individual student has continued to rise rapidly ("Tuition Crises," 2012, p. B-3).

Citing Personal Communications

E-mail, telephone conversations, memos, and in-person conversations do not provide recoverable data, so APA style excludes them from the References. Consequently, you should cite personal communications in the text only. In so doing, give the initials as well as the last name of the source, provide the date, and briefly describe the nature of the communication.

> M. Gaither (personal communication, January 11, 2014) described the symptoms of Wilson's disease.

Citing Online Sources in Your Text

In general, citations for electronic sources include the same basic information as for print sources, with the following qualifications.

Omit a page or paragraph number. The marvelous feature of electronic text is that it is searchable, so your readers can find your quotation quickly with the Find feature. Suppose you have written the following:

> The Internet Report presented by the University of South Carolina (2013) advised policy makers with "a better understanding of the impact the Internet is having in our society."

A reader who wants to investigate further will find your complete citation, including the Internet address or digital object identifier (DOI) of the article, in your References list. After finding the article via a browser (e.g., Safari or Internet Explorer), the investigator can press Edit, then Find, and type in a key phrase, such as *better understanding of the impact.* The software will immediately move the cursor to the passage shown above. That is much easier than counting through forty-six paragraphs.

Provide a paragraph number. Some scholars who write on the Internet number their paragraphs. Therefore, if you find an online article that has numbered paragraphs, by all means supply that information in your citation.

> The Insurance Institute for Highway Safety (2012) has emphasized restraint first, and said, "A federal rule requiring special attachments to

anchor infant and child restraints in vehicles is making installation easier, but not all child restraints fit easily in all vehicles" (para. 1).

Recommendations for treating non-insulin-dependent diabetes mellitus (NIDDM), the most common type of diabetes, include a diet that is rich in carbohydrates, "predominantly from whole grains, fruit, vegetables, and low-fat milk." (Yang, 2013, para. 3).

Provide a page number. In a few instances, you will find page numbers buried within brackets here and there throughout an article. These refer to the page numbers of the printed version of the document. In these cases, you should cite the page just as you would a printed source. Here is the Internet source with the page numbers buried within the text to signal the break between page 17 and page 18:

What is required is a careful reading of Chekhov's subtext, that elusive [pp 17–18] literature that lingers in psychological nuances of the words, not the exact words themselves.—Ward

The page number may be included in the citation:

One source argued the merits of Chekhov's subtext and its "psychological nuances of the words" (Ward, 2013, p. 18).

Online Sources

Internet article

Commenting on the distinction between a Congressional calendar day and a legislative day, Dove (2014) stated that "a legislative day is the period of time following an adjournment of the Senate until another adjournment."

"Reports of abuses in the interrogation of suspected terrorists raise the question of how—or whether—we should limit the interrogation of a suspected terrorist when our national security may be at stake" (Parry & White, 2014, abstract).

Online newspaper article

Ochberg (2013) commented on the use of algae in paper that "initially has a green tint to it, but unlike bleached paper which turns yellow with age, this algae paper becomes whiter with age."

Online magazine

BusinessWeek Online (2013) reported that the idea of peer-to-peer computing is a precursor to new Web applications.

Government document

The website *Thomas* (2013) has outlined the amendments to the *American Geothermal Exploration and Technology Act of 2013,* which promotes the mapping and development of United States geothermal resources to improve technology and demonstrate the use of geothermal energy in large-scale thermal applications, and for other purposes.

Other Electronic Sources

E-mail. The *Publication Manual of the American Psychological Association* stipulates that personal communications, which others cannot retrieve, should be cited in the text only and not mentioned at all in the bibliography.

One technical writing instructor (March 8, 2014) has bemoaned the inability of hardware developers to maintain pace with the ingenuity of software developers. In his e-mail message, he indicated that educational institutions cannot keep pace with the hardware developers. Thus, "students nationwide suffer with antiquated equipment, even though it's only a few years old" (dplattner@cscc.edu).

Electronic mailing list posting. Some listserv groups have gained legitimacy in recent years, so in your text you might want to give an exact date and provide the e-mail address *only* if the citation has scholarly relevance and *only* if the list has an academic sponsor, such as an instructor of an online class.

R. D. Brackett (online discussion, May 7, 2013) has identified the book *Echoes of Glory* for those interested in detailed battlefield maps of the American Civil War.

A. G. Funder (January 5, 2014) argued against the "judgmental process."

CD-ROM

Grolier's Multimedia Encyclopedia (2013) explained that in recent decades huge swaths of the rain forest have been toppled; as the trees disappeared, so, too, did the flora and fauna that thrived under their canopy.

15d Preparing the List of References

Use the title *References* for your bibliography page. Like the body of the paper, your reference list should be double-spaced throughout. Alphabetize the entries letter by letter—remembering, for example, that Adkins, Y. R., precedes Adkinson, A. G., even though *o* precedes the *y* for the first entry. Every reference used in your text, except personal communications and major classical works, should appear in your alphabetical list of references at the end of the paper. Type the first line of each entry flush left and indent succeeding lines five spaces. Italicize names of books, periodicals, and volume numbers.

Index to Bibliographic Models: APA Style

Book

Turney, C. (2013). *1912: The Year the World Discovered Antarctica.*

Berkeley, CA: Counterpoint.

List the author (surname first and then initials for given names), year of publication within parentheses, title of the book italicized and with only first word of the title and any subtitle capitalized (but do capitalize proper nouns), place of publication (including state abbreviation or country name), and publisher. In the publisher's name omit the words *Publishing, Company,* and *Inc.,* but otherwise give a full name: Florida State University Press; Pearson Longman; HarperCollins.

List chronologically, not alphabetically, two or more works by the same author—for example, Fitzgerald's 2012 publication would precede the 2013 publication.

Fitzgerald, R. A. (2012). Crimson glow . . .

Fitzgerald, R. A. (2013). Walking . . .

References with the same author in the same year are alphabetized and marked with lowercase letters—*a, b, c*—immediately after the date:

Craighead, T. B. (2013a). Marketing trends . . .

Craighead, T. B. (2013b). Maximizing sales . . .

Entries of a single author precede multiple-author entries beginning with the same surname without regard for the dates:

Watson, S. M. (2012). Principles . . .

Watson, S. M., & Wheaton, A. F. (2013). Crimes . . .

References with the same first author and different second or third authors should be alphabetized by the surname of the second author:

> Bacon, D. E., & Smithson, C. A. (2013). Arctic explorers . . .
>
> Bacon, D. E., & Williamson, T. (2014). Seasons in . . .

If, *and only if,* the work is signed *Anonymous,* the entry begins with the word *Anonymous* spelled out, and the entry is alphabetized as if *Anonymous* were a true name. If no author is given, the title moves to the author position, and the entry is alphabetized by the first significant word of the title.

Part of a Book

List author(s), date, chapter or section title, editor (with name in normal order) preceded by "In" and followed by "(Ed.)" or "(Eds.)," the name of the book, (italicized), page numbers to the specific section of the book cited (placed within parentheses), place of publication, and publisher.

> Kahlenberg, R. D. (2013). Unions and the public interest: Is collective
>
>   bargaining for teachers good for students?—Pro. In N. Berlatsky
>
>   (Ed.). *At issue series: Are unions still relevant?* (pp. 133-138).
>
>   Farmington Hills, MI: Greenhaven.

If no author is listed, begin with the title of the article.

> Mount of Olives. (2011). *Holman concise Bible dictionary.* Nashville,
>
>   TN: B & H.

Encyclopedia or Dictionary

> Rubin, H. W. (2013). *Dictionary of insurance terms* (6th ed.). New York,
>
>   NY: Barrons.
>
> Moran, J. M. (2013). Weather. *World Book encyclopedia* (2013 ed., Vol. 21,
>
>   pp. 166-174). Chicago, World Book.

Book with Corporate Author

> Mayo Clinic. (2013). *Mayo Clinic diabetes diet.* Intercourse, PA: Good.

Periodical

Journal

List author(s), year, title of the article without quotation marks and with only the first word (and any proper nouns) capitalized, name of the journal underscored or italicized and with all major words capitalized, volume number underscored or italicized, and inclusive page numbers *not* preceded by "p." or "pp."

Busby, J. W., Smith, T. G., White, K. L., & Strange, S. M. (2013). Climate

change and insecurity: Mapping vulnerability in Africa. *International*

Security, 37(4), 132–172.

Article Retrieved from a Database

Collins-Sowah, P. A., Kuwornu, J. K. M., & Tsegai, D. (2013). Willingness

to participate in micro pension schemes: Evidence from the informal

sector of Ghana. *Journal of Economics and International Finance,*

5 (1), 21–34. Retrieved from InfoTrac database.

Magazine

List author, the date of publication—year, month without abbreviation, and the specific day for magazines published weekly and fortnightly (every two weeks)—title of the article without quotation marks and with only the first word capitalized, name of the magazine in italics with all major words capitalized, the volume number if it is readily available, and inclusive page numbers if you do not provide the volume number. If a magazine prints the article on discontinuous pages, include all page numbers.

Petruzzi, J. D. (2013, June). A bloody summer for horsemen. *Civil War*

Times, 30–37.

Curry, A. (2013, April). The secret life of dirt. *Smithsonian,* 40–45.

Newspaper

List author, date (year, month, and day), title of article with only first word and proper nouns capitalized, complete name of newspaper in capitals and underlined, and the section with all discontinuous page numbers. Unlike other periodicals, p. or pp. precedes page numbers for a newspaper reference in APA style. Single pages take p., while multiple pages take pp., as shown below.

Few, J. (2013, April 21). New hope for foreign teachers. *Savannah*

Morning News, pp. 1A, 6A.

Abstract
Abstract as the Cited Source

Stauffer, G. E., Rotella, J. J., & Garrott, R. A. (2013, May). Variability

in temporary emigration rates of individually marked female

Weddell seals prior to first reproduction [Abstract]. *Oecologia, 172,*

129–140.

Abstract of an Unpublished Work

Darma, J. (2013). Political institutions under dictatorship [Abstract].

Knoxville, TN: University of Tennessee.

Review

Purewal, S. J. (2013). Digital storm x17: A more portable gaming option.

[rev. article]. *PC World*, 49.

Report

Gorman, L. (2013). Reporting insurance fraud (No. 2013-2). Hartford,

CT: Insurance Institute.

Nonprint Material

Computer Program

Adobe Photoshop (CS3) [Computer software]. San Jose, CA: Adobe

Systems.

DVD, Film

Edwards, B. (Director). (1961). *Breakfast at Tiffany's* [DVD].

Hollywood, CA: Paramount.

Interviews, Letters, and Memos

Kramer, S. R. (2013, April 7). "Palm reading as prediction"

[Interview]. Chattanooga, TN.

Unpublished Raw Data from a Study, Untitled Work

Barstow, I. (2013, May 22). [Homophone errors in essays of 100 9th

grade writers]. Unpublished raw data.

Sources Accessed Online

When citing electronic sources in your APA references, include the following information if available:

1. Author/editor last name, followed by a comma, the initials, and a period.
2. Year of publication, followed by a comma, then month and day for magazines and newspapers, within parentheses, followed by a period.

3. Title of the article, not within quotations and not italicized, with the first word and proper nouns capitalized. *Note:* This is also the place to describe the work within brackets, as with [Abstract] or [Letter to the editor].
4. Name of the book, journal, or complete work, italicized, if one is listed.
5. Volume number, if listed, italicized.
6. Page numbers only if you have that data from a printed version of the journal or magazine. If the periodical has no volume number, use "p." or "pp." before the numbers; if the journal has a volume number, omit "p." or "pp.").
7. Give the DOI (Digital Object Identifier) if available.
8. If no DOI is available, then use the words "Retrieved from" followed by the URL. Line breaks in URLs should come before punctuation marks such as slashes. Include the date of access only for material that changes over time (e.g., Wikis).

Article from an Online Journal

Ellis, C. (2012). Dualism and progress in Kant and Nietzsche. *Minerva: An Internet Journal of Philosophy.* Retrieved from http://www.minerva.mic.ul.ie/vol16/Dualism.pdf

Article with DOI Assigned

Todd, P., & Binns, J. (2013). Work-life balance: Is it now a problem for management? *Gender, Work and Organization, 20*(3), 219–231. DOI: 10.1111/j.1468-0432.2011.00564.x

Article from a Printed Journal, Reproduced Online

Many articles online are the exact duplicates of their print versions, so if you view an article in its electronic form and are confident that the electronic form is identical to the printed version, add within brackets the words *Electronic version.* This allows you to omit the URL.

Douven, I., Decock, L., Dietz, R., & Égré, P. (2013). Vagueness: A conceptual spaces approach. [Electronic version]. *Journal of Philosophical Logic, 42*(1), 137–160.

Add the URL if page numbers are not indicated, as shown in the following entry:

Beckett, L. R. (2013, May). Mounting your own turkey tail, beard, and spurs. *Missouri Conservationist, 74*(5). Retrieved from http://mdc.mo.gov/sites/default/files/magazine/2013/04/20130501.pdf

Article from an Online-Only Newsletter

Hart, R. (2013, March 4). No joke: Humor helps in the hospital. *Rush University Medical Center Newsletter.* Retrieved from http://www.rush.edu/rumc/page-1298330519221.html

Document from a University Program or Department

Henry, S. (2011). *Department of Language and Literature writing guidelines.* Retrieved from Clayton State University, Department of Arts & Sciences site: http://a-s.clayton.edu/langlit/guidelines/default.html

Report from a University, Available on a Private Organization's Website

University of Illinois at Chicago, Institute for Health Research and Policy (2013, May 1). *An endgame for tobacco.* Retrieved from the Robert Wood Johnson Foundation website: http://www.rwjf.org/en/research-publications/find-rwjf-research/2013/05/an-endgame-for-tobacco-.html

Abstract

Clasen, P. C., Wells, T. T., Ellis, A. J., & Beevers, C. G. (2013). Attentional biases and the persistence of sad mood in major depressive disorder [Abstract]. *Journal of Abnormal Psychology, 122.* Retrieved from http://psycnet.apa.org/index.cfm?fa=browsePA.volumes&jcode=abn

Article from a Printed Magazine, Reproduced Online

Neustadt, G. (2013, May/June). Looking beyond the wall: Encountering the humanitarian crisis of border politics. *Utne.* Retrieved from http://www.utne.com/politics/humanitarian-crisis-of-border-politics-zm013mjzbla.aspx

Article from an Online Magazine, No Author Listed

How a psychologist can help you control anger. (2013). *APA Online.* Retrieved from http://www.apa.org/topics/anger/help.aspx

Note: Avoid listing page numbers for online articles.

Article from an Online Newspaper

> Charles, J. (2013, April 23). Disease, hunger rise as donors' aid falls
>
> off. *Miami Herald*. Retrieved from http://www.newseum.org/
>
> todaysfrontpages/hr.asp?fpVname=FL_MH&ref_pge=lst

Blog (Web Log)

Include the title of the message or video and the URL. Please note that titles for items in online communities (e.g. blogs, newsgroups, forums) are not italicized. If the author's name is not available, provide the screen name. Distinguish between blog posts and comments.

> Kilpi, E. (2013, March 10). Emergence and self-organization. [Web log
>
> comment]. Retrieved from http://eskokilpi.blogging.fi/2013/03/10/
>
> emergence-and-self-organization/

Bulletin

> Doctors health press reports on study: Fiber found to help control the
>
> progression of prostate cancer. (2013, January 20). Doctor's Health
>
> Press. Retrieved from http://www.prweb.com/releases/2013/1/
>
> prweb10337555.htm

Government Document

> U.S. Cong. House. (2013, January 3). *Cybersecurity Enhancement Act*
>
> *of 2013.* H. Resolution 756. Retrieved from http://thomas.loc.gov/
>
> cgi-bin/query/z?c113:H.R.756:

Message Posted to an Online Discussion Group or Forum

> Smith, M. (2013, April 22). Earth Day every day. Environmental Discussion
>
> Group. Retrieved from http://greenreview.blogspot.com/2013/04/
>
> earth-day-every-day.html

Newsgroup, Message

> Clease, G. V. (2014, November 5). Narrative bibliography [Msg. 41].
>
> Message posted to jymacmillan@mail.csu.edu

Online Forum or Discussion Board Posting

Include the title of the message and the URL of the newsgroup or discussion board. Titles for items in online communities (e.g., blogs, newsgroups, forums) are not italicized. If the author's name is not available, provide the screen name. Place identifiers like post or message numbers, if available, in brackets. If available, provide the URL where the message is archived (e.g., "Message posted to. . . , archived at. . . ").

> Wainwright, R. (2012, May 31). What if the Internet collapsed? World Economic Forum. Message posted to http://forumblog.org/2012/05/what-if-the-internet-collapsed/

Podcast

For all podcasts, provide as much information as possible. Possible addition identifiers may include Producer, Director, and so on.

> Next-generation space ambitions keep rolling. (2012, November 28). NASA—Beyond Earth Video Podcast. Podcast retrieved from http://www.nasa.gov/mp4/710079main_ksc_112812_ccp_future-pod.mp4

Symposium or Virtual Conference, Report

> Tully, T. N. (2013, March 22). *Integrating foundations of medicine to multiple species.* Paper presented at the SAVMA Symposium 2013, Baton Rouge, Louisiana. Abstract retrieved from http://www.savmasymposium2013.com/wordpress/wp-content/uploads/2012/11/SAVMA2013-Lectures.pdf

Wikis

Please note that wikis are collaborative projects that cannot guarantee the verifiability or expertise of their entries.

> House of Isenburg. (n.d.). Retrieved April 30, 2013, from the History Wiki: http://history.wikia.com/wiki/House_of_Isenburg

Article from a Library Database

University libraries, as well as public libraries, feature servers that supply articles in large databases, such as InfoTrac, EBSCOhost, ERIC, and others. For most common databases, APA no longer requires the database name as part of the citation.

> America's children: Key national indicators of well-being. (2012). Federal Interagency Forum on Child and Family Statistics. Retrieved from ERIC database. (ED533560)

Wood, C. L., Mustain, A. L., & Lo, Y. (2013, February). Effects of
supplemental computer-assisted reciprocal peer tutoring on
kindergarteners' phoneme segmentation fluency. *Education &
Treatment of Children, 36*(1), 33–36.

CD-ROM

Material cited from a CD-ROM requires slightly different formatting.

Encyclopedia Article

African American history: Abolitionist movement [CD-ROM]. (2012).
Encyclopedia Britannica 2012 Deluxe. Chicago, IL: Encyclopedia
Britannica Educational.

Full-Text Article

Marieb, E. N., & Hoehn, K. (2012). Thyroid gland [CD-ROM]. *Human
anatomy and physiology.* (9th ed.). San Francisco, CA: Benjamin
Cummings.

15e Formatting an APA Paper

APA style applies to three types of papers: theoretical articles, reports
of empirical studies, and review articles (as explained in section 15a).
Each requires a different arrangement of the various parts of the paper.

Theoretical Paper

The theoretical paper should be arranged much like a typical research
paper, with the additional use of side heads and italicized side heads to
divide the sections.

The introduction should:

- Establish the problem under examination.
- Discuss its significance to the scientific community.
- Provide a review of the literature (see pages 128–134 for more
  information).
- Quote the experts who have commented on the issue.
- Provide a thesis sentence that gives your initial perspective on the
  issue.

The body of the theoretical paper should:

- Trace the various issues.
- Establish a past-to-present perspective.

- Compare and analyze the various aspects of the theories.
- Cite extensively from the literature on the subject.

The conclusion of the theoretical paper should:

- Defend one theory as it grows from the evidence in the body.
- Discuss the implications of the theory.
- Suggest additional work that might be launched in this area.

Report of Empirical Research

The design of a report of original research, an empirical study, should conform to the following general plan.

The introduction should:

- Establish the problem or topic to be examined.
- Provide background information, including a review of literature on the subject.
- Give the purpose and rationale for the study, including the hypothesis that serves as the motivation for the experiment.

The body of the report of empirical research should:

- Provide a methods section for explaining the design of the study with respect to subjects, apparatus, and procedure.
- Offer a results section for listing in detail the statistical findings of the study.

The conclusion of a report of empirical research should:

- Interpret the results and discuss the implications of the findings in relation to the hypothesis and to other research on the subject.

Review Article

The review article is usually a shorter paper because it examines a published work or two without extensive research on the part of the review writer.

The introduction of the review should:

- Identify the problem or subject under study and its significance.
- Summarize the article(s) under review.

The body of the review should:

- Provide a systematic analysis of the article(s), the findings, and the apparent significance of the results.

The conclusion of the review should:

- Discuss the implications of the findings and make judgments as appropriate.

15f Writing the Abstract

You should provide an abstract with every paper written in APA style. An abstract is a quick but thorough summary of the contents of your paper. It is read first and may be the only part read, so it must be:

1. *Accurate,* in order to reflect both the purpose and content of the paper
2. *Self-contained,* so that it (1) explains the precise problem and defines terminology, (2) describes briefly both the methods used and the findings, and (3) gives an overview of your conclusions—but see item 4 following
3. *Concise and specific,* in order to remain within a range of 80 to 120 words
4. *Nonevaluative,* in order to report information, not to appraise or assess the value of the work
5. *Coherent and readable,* in a style that uses an active, vigorous syntax and that uses the present tense to describe results (e.g., the findings confirm) but the past tense to describe testing procedures (e.g., I attempted to identify)

For theoretical papers, the abstract should include:

- The topic in one sentence, if possible
- The purpose, thesis, and scope of the paper
- A brief reference to the sources used (e.g., published articles, books, personal observation)
- Your conclusions and the implications of the study

For a report of an empirical study (see also 6e, pages 92–93), the abstract should include the four items listed above for theoretrical papers, plus three more:

- The problem and hypothesis in one sentence if possible
- A description of the subjects (e.g., species, number, age, type)
- The method of study, including procedures and apparatus

15g Sample Paper in APA Style

The following paper demonstrates the format and style of a paper written to the standards of APA style. The paper requires a title page that establishes the running head, an abstract, in-text citations to name and year of each source used, and a list of references. Marginal notations explain specific requirements.

Running Head: MORE ACADEMICS   1

Page
header

Title

More Academics for the Cost of Less Engaged Children

Byline

Caitlin Kelley

Affiliation

English 4010, Austin Peay State University

MORE ACADEMICS   2

Abstract

The abstract
provides a
quick but
thorough
summary of
the context
of your paper.

The elimination of elementary school recess periods was
investigated to examine the theoretical implications of depriving
learners of these important mental and physical stimuli. The goal
was to determine the effect of the modern trend to use recess
time for longer academic periods. The social and psychological
implications were determined by an examination of the literature,
including comments from educational leaders. Results are mixed, as
the end result of an increased emphasis on standardized testing will
not be realized for several years. The social implications affect the
mental and physical lives of school-aged children who are learning
less about cooperation with their peers and more about remaining
stagnant with little activity for lengthy periods of time.

MORE ACADEMICS   3

More Academics for the Cost of Less Engaged Children

Everyone remembers the days out on the playground
when "you got skinned knees and bruises and sand in your
eyes" (DeGregory, 2005). Growing up in the 1990s I remember
the days when classes walked to the cafeteria for lunch, and
students could sit next to whomever they wanted. When they
were finished, they were free to play outside for 30 to 40
minutes on the playground. However, times are changing, and
so are the rules. Not all school children have the luxury of free
play on the hard top.

In Pinellas County, Florida, in an elementary school
of 800 students, one boy did not know what recess was. For
a class newspaper, this first grade student wrote that his
favorite day to have gym class was Friday because the children
were allowed "Open Court" because they were allowed to play
whatever they wanted without the instruction of the teacher.
Lane DeGregory (2005), the journalist who wrote the article,
mentioned, "It sounds just like recess. He's 7 years old and he
doesn't know what recess is." Because this elementary school
does not have recess, the children in Pinellas County only have
25 minutes every Friday to play with one another, explore and
make their own rules to games. However, this school is not
alone; according to Education World, "40 percent of schools in
the United States have cut recess or are considering dropping
it" (Poynter, 2008).

The question is why are nearly half of the elementary
schools around the country dropping free play and expression
from the daily lives of young children? The two prevailing
reasons are that eliminating free play reduces the risk of

Establish the topic along with social and/or psychological issues that will be examined.

A theoretical study depends heavily on the literature, which must be cited correctly in APA form.

MORE ACADEMICS   4

accidents and by eliminating recess, students have more time
in their day for academics, mostly reading and math (Chen,
2011). Contradicting these arguments are mostly parents
and doctors who feel that "recess provides children with the
opportunity to develop friendships, negotiate relationships and
build positive connections" (DeGregory, 2005). The elimination
and reduction of recess in elementary schools to allow more
time for academics is detrimental to the student's mental and
physical well-being.

Posing a
question in
the paper
helps to
reemphasize
the thesis.

So who is to say what is best for the children? The
process of eliminating or limiting recess is the decision of the
principal of the elementary school. According to Greg Toppo
(2007, p. 1-A), "the principal of each school respectively
decides whether his or her children need that extra time for
play, or whether it would be better spent on academics."

According to Patti Caplan, spokeswoman for the
Howard County schools in Washington, DC, principals stated,
"shortening recess by five minutes daily provides 25 minutes

Use present
tense verbs
(take, proves)
for what
happens or
can happen
now.

of additional instruction time each week" (Matthews, 2004,
p. B1). Most schools take their students straight from lunch
back to the classroom and start a lecture right away. This lack
of a break often proves to be a problem because the students
are restless and fidgety (Adelman & Taylor, 2012). In some
schools, however, "with the principal's permission, a teacher
can take his or her class outside for 15 minutes. For the
kids, it's like a jailbreak" (DeGregory, 2005). In the typical
classroom, children sit in their seats for up to 6 hours each
day. With academics and curriculum becoming harder, schools
need those extra 25 minutes each day to teach students
everything they will need to know in preparation for the

MORE ACADEMICS   5

ever-increasing glut of standardized tests. Schools are

completely focused on academics, not only so that the

students pass the standardized tests, but because "the federal

government expects schools to have all children testing at

the proficient level in science, language arts and math by

the year 2014" (Nussbaum, 2006, p. C1). Unfortunately,

these expectations are unable to be reached because of the

bell curve; an average will be formulated by the low and

high scores, illuminating the possibility of a perfect score.

Specifically, not every student can learn and comprehend

information in the same way. With the pressure of standardized

tests and a more challenging curriculum, "parents worry about

the strain on their children" (Matthews, 2004, p. B1). For this

reason, recess for children is even more important than ever.

Ginny Mahlke, the principal of Wolftrap Elementary School in

Fairfax, Virginia, summed up the shift in a more stringent,

performance-based curriculum:

> The increased demands on schools mean it is even more
>
> important now for students to get outside, relax, and
>
> get some exercise, for every minute spent at school is
>
> instructional time, right down to learning the skills of
>
> negotiating by deciding whose turn it is on the swing.
>
> (Matthews, 2004, p. B1)

Sharing the opinion of Mahlke are 60 percent of principals who

believe that their students do not learn well without a break

because they are fidgety and cannot pay attention sitting in a

chair for six hours at a time (Adelman & Taylor, 2012). Before

the limitations of recess started in the 1980s, students enjoyed

breaks for 10 to 20 minutes at a time in the morning, after

lunch, and in the afternoon (Nussbaum, 2006, p. C1). In order

Use the present perfect tense (will be formulated) for actions completed and for actions continued into the present time.

Indent block quotations 1 full tab.

to give students the recess and the healthy break they need in the middle of the day, some parents argue that if the school days were longer, there would be enough time for a recess break and enough time for the teaching required for the year. (Hill & Turner, 2012, p. 8). Then parents would not be forced to choose between recess and instruction.

The problems with eliminating recess do not just stop on an academic level. Cutting out play time for young children affects their social skills and their physical skills. Students need to learn to make up their own rules and play their own games. With recess, students can experience uninstructed play in contrast to being constantly directed all day. On the playground, with adults serving only as supervisors, children learn to work through altercations, to make decisions, and also how to make friends. It is essential to have physical contact with other children in a world of technology where students often play with themselves. Scientists have concluded that children who are glued to their computers interact less with other children, become passive learners, and read less (Hayashi & Baranauskas, 2013).

Recess is a physical activity for most children, which is constructive toward their health and well-being. Research studies have shown that between more schools eliminating recess and after-school programs, the amount of time kids spend being physically active is dwindling significantly. When children are taken outside for recess after lunch, they are exposed to and become used to playing outdoors, an activity that can be repeated in the home environment. Because of the stagnant environment of school, too many children would rather play inside with electronics than go outside. Even worse than children not getting the exercise they need is that schools are contributing to childhood obesity. Results from

MORE ACADEMICS   7

recent research revealed that "36% of schools sell treats such
as chips, candy and ice cream in the school cafeteria" (Toppo,
2007, p. 1-A). If children had recess as an outlet to run around
and play, the rates of childhood obesity would be cut because
the children would be burning calories.

The other speculation as to why recess is being eliminated
in schools is that children are being injured and schools are
being sued by parents because of the injuries ("Tag—You're
Illegal!" 2006). This reason brings up the debate of whether
or not children are being nurtured too much and whether they
are being made into weaker human beings because of it. "An
elementary school in Massachusetts that banned tag, dodge ball
and all other 'contact' or 'chase' games" ("Tag—You're Illegal!"
2006) has joined the bandwagon with many other schools that
worry about the scratches and scrapes of its young children.
Another town even "outlawed touching altogether" ("Tag—
You're Illegal!" 2006). It is no wonder why childhood obesity is
such a prevalent issue in American society today. Children are
not given the opportunity to exercise and have fun, even when
they are allowed onto the playground.

Amazingly, only 60 percent of the nation's elementary
schools still have a full 20 to 40 minute recess period
after lunch (Poynter, 2008). Students in the 40 percent of
elementary schools that are neglecting the benefits and needs
of recess are suffering from it. Children need recess to exercise
their bodies and their minds, especially at such a young age
when they are still growing and developing. Principals have
reasons to back up their decisions for doing away with recess;
however, there is more evidence that proves students need
the time and exercise that a recess period provides. How will
the elimination of recess affect that 40 percent of children
in the United States who do not have play time during the day?

Use the
past tense
(outlawed,
banned)
to express
actions at a
specific time
in the past.

The
conclusion
can include
a statement
on the state
of research
in the area of
study as well
as questions
for further
research.

MORE ACADEMICS   8

Will it stunt their mental growth and become detrimental in
the long run? At the present time it is too early to tell because
these eliminations are so new; however, the more important
question is whether elementary school children today can reach
their full potential after being deprived of the mental and
physical stimuli that can be experienced on the playground.

MORE ACADEMICS   9

References

Adelman, H., & Taylor, L. (2012). *Attention problems: Intervention and
    resources.* UCLA Center for Mental Health in Schools. Retrieved
    from http://smhp.psych.ucla.edu/

Chen, G. (2011, April 14). Who killed recess? The movement to
    resuscitate recess. *Public School Review.* Retrieved from http://
    www.publicschoolreview.com/articles/317

DeGregory, L. (2005, March 29). Boulevard of dreams. *St. Petersburg
    Times.* Retrieved from http://www.sptimes.com/2005/03/29/
    Floridian/Out_of_play.shtml

Hayashi, E. C. S., & Baranauskas, M. C. C. (2013). Affectibility in
    educational technologies: A socio-technical perspective for
    design. *Educational Technology & Society, 16*(1), 57–59. Retrieved
    from Academic OneFile database.

Hill, G. M., & Turner, B. (2013). A system of movement and motor
    skill challenges for children. *Strategies: A Journal for Physical
    and Sport Educators, 25*(8), 8–10. Retrieved from http://www
    .aahperd.org/naspe/publications/journals/strategies/

Matthews, J. (2004, April 9). Federal education law squeezes out
    recess. *Washington Post,* p. B1.

References
begin on a
new page.

Citation for
an online
article from
a research
center at an
institution.

Citation for
an online
newspaper
article.

Internet
sources
require
the word
"Retrieved"
preceding the
URL.

Nussbaum, D. (2006, December 10). Before children ask, what's recess? *New York Times*, p. C1.

Poynter, A. (2008). *The end of recess*. Retrieved from http://www.poynter.org/column.asp?id=2&aid=80426

Tag—you're illegal! (2006, October 28). *Los Angeles Times*. Retrieved from http://www.latimes.com/news/opinion/la-ed-tag28oct28,0,59791.story?coll=la-opinion-leftrail

Toppo, G. (2007, May 16). School recess isn't exactly on the run. *USA Today*, p. 1-A. Retrieved from EBSCOhost database.

Citation of an article from a library database.

16 The Footnote System: CMS Style

Chapter 16 Clear Targets

Directed by the standards of *The Chicago Manual of Style,* CMS style has gained wide acceptance in the fine arts and some fields in the humanities, except literature. When using the footnote system, you must place superscript numerals within the text (like this[15]) and place documentary footnotes on corresponding pages. This chapter will help to accurately document your research paper:

- Inserting superscript numerals in the text
- Formatting and writing footnotes
- Writing endnotes rather than footnotes
- Preparing a Bibliography page for a paper that uses footnotes
- Formatting a paper using CMS style

The following discussion assumes that notes will appear as footnotes; however, some instructors accept endnotes—that is, all notes appear together at the end of the paper, not at the bottom of individual pages (shown later in this chapter; see pages 326–339).

There are two types of footnotes: One documents your sources with bibliographic information, but the other can discuss related matters, explain your methods of research, suggest related literature, provide biographical information, or offer information not immediately pertinent to your discussion.

To see examples of content notes as opposed to documentation notes, see pages 326–330.

If available, use the footnote or endnote feature of your computer software. It will not only insert the raised superscript number but also keep your footnotes arranged properly at the bottom of each page or keep your endnotes in a correct list. In most instances, the software will insert the superscript numeral, but it will not write the note automatically; you must type in the essential data in the correct style.

16a Inserting a Superscript Numeral in Your Text

Use Arabic numerals typed slightly above the line (like this[12]). In both Microsoft Word and WordPerfect, go to Font and select Superscript or go to Insert and select Footnote. Place a superscript numeral at the end of each quotation or paraphrase, with the number following immediately without a space after the final word or mark of punctuation, as in this sample:

> Steven A. LeBlanc, an archeologist at Harvard University, along with several other scholars, argues instead that "humans have been at each others' throats since the dawn of the species."[1] Robin Yates, for example, says the ancient ancestors of the Chinese used "long-range projectile weapons" as long ago as 28,000 B.C. for both hunting and "intrahuman conflict."[2] Arthur Ferrill observes, "When man first learned how to write, he already had war to write about."[3] Ferrill adds, "In prehistoric times man was a hunter and a killer of other men. The killer instinct in the prehistoric male is clearly attested by archeology in fortifications, weapons, cave paintings, and skeletal remains."[4]

The footnotes that relate to these in-text superscript numerals will appear at the bottom of the page, as shown here:

> 1. See Steven A. LeBlanc, *Constant Battles: The Myth of the Peaceful, Noble Savage* (New York: St. Martin's, 2004), 15; and also L. D. Cooper, *Rousseau, Nature, and the Problem of the Good Life* (University Park: Pennsylvania State University Press, 2000).
>
> 2. Steven A. LeBlanc, "Prehistory of Warfare," *Archaeology* (May/June 2003): 18.
>
> 3. Robin Yates, "Early China," in *War and Society in the Ancient and Medieval Worlds,* ed. Kurt Raaflaub and Nathan Rosenstein (Cambridge, MA: Center for Hellenic Studies, 2001), 9.
>
> 4. Arthur Ferrill, "Neolithic Warfare," accessed April 6, 2013, http://eserver.org/history/neolithic-war.txt.

However, you may place the notes at the back of your paper, so you should usually include a source's name in your text. The first example below implies a source that will be found in the footnote; the second expresses the name in the text. Some writers prefer the first approach, others the second.

Implied reference:

The organic basis of autism is generally agreed upon. Three possible causes for autism have been identified: behavioral syndrome, organic brain disorder, or a range of biological and psychosocial factors.[9]

Expressed reference:

Martin Rutter has acknowledged that the organic basis of autism is generally agreed upon. Rutter named three possible causes for autism: behavioral syndrome, organic brain disorder, or a range of biological and psychosocial factors.[10]

Writing Full or Abbreviated Notes

CMS Style permits you to omit a bibliography page as long as you give full data to the source in each of your initial footnotes.

1. Michael Moran, *The Reckoning: Debt, Democracy, and the Future of American Power* (New York: Palgrave Macmillan, 2013), 49.

However, you may provide a comprehensive bibliography to each source and abbreviate all footnotes, even the initial ones, since full data will be found in the bibliography.

1. Moran, *The Reckoning*, 49.

The bibliography entry would read this way:

Moran, Michael. *The Reckoning: Debt, Democracy, and the Future of American Power*. New York: Palgrave Macmillan, 2013.

Consult with your instructor on this matter if you are uncertain about the proper format for a specific course.

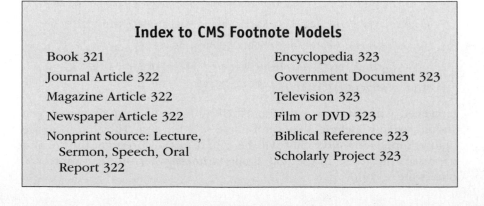

16b Formatting and Writing the Footnotes

Place footnotes at the bottom of pages to correspond with superscript numerals (as shown in section 16a). Some papers will require footnotes on almost every page. Follow these conventions:

1. **Spacing.** In academic papers not intended for publication, footnotes are commonly typed single-spaced and placed at the bottom of the page, usually with a line space between each note. Drafts and manuscript intended for publication in print or on the Web should have all notes double-spaced and placed together on one page at the end of the paper. The student example on page 331 shows single-spaced footnotes. A Notes page with double spacing can be found on page 326.
2. **Indention.** Indent the first line of the note five spaces or one-half inch (usually one click of the tab key).
3. **Numbering.** Number the footnotes consecutively throughout the entire paper with an indented number, a period, and space, as shown in the examples throughout this chapter.
4. **Placement.** Collect at the bottom of each page all footnotes to citations made on that page.
5. **Distinguish footnotes from text.** Separate footnotes from the text by triple spacing or, if you prefer, by a twelve-space line from the left margin.
6. **Footnote form.** Basic forms of notes should conform to the following styles.

Book

List the author, followed by a comma, the title underlined or italicized, the publication data within parentheses (city: publisher, year), followed by a comma and the page number(s). Unless ambiguity would result, the abbreviations *p.* and *pp.* may be omitted.

1. Emerson Eggerichs, *Love & Respect in the Family: The Transforming Power of Love and Respect between Parent and Child* (Nashville: Thomas Nelson, 2013), 20–23.

List two authors without a comma:

> 2. Barrie Levy and Patricia O. Giggans, *When Dating Becomes Dangerous: A Parent's Guide to Preventing Relationship Abuse* (Center City, MN: Hazelden, 2013), 18.

🔍 See page 325 for further details about subsequent references and the use of Latinate phrases.

Note: Publisher's names are spelled out in full but the words *Company* or *Inc.* are omitted. Reference to an edition follows the title or the editors, if listed (see footnote 3).

For more than three authors, use *et al.* after mention of the lead author:

> 3. Andrew C. Garrod et al., eds., "Introduction," *Adolescent Portraits: Identity, Relationships, and Challenges,* 7th ed. (Boston: Allyn & Bacon, 2011), 3.

For a subsequent reference to an immediately preceding source, use "Ibid." in the roman typeface, not in italics and not underscored:

> 4. Ibid.

Journal Article

> 5. Gedeon O. Deák and Alexis J. Toney, "Young Children's Fast Mapping and Generalization for Words, Facts, and Pictograms," *Journal of Experimental Child Psychology* 115 (2013): 273–296.

Note: Use a colon before the page number of a journal but a comma before page numbers for magazines and books.

Magazine Article

> 6. Allen C. Guelzo, "George Meade's Mixed Legacy," *Civil War Times,* June 2013, 38–45.

Newspaper Article

> 7. John Kirkenfeld, "Digging for More Dirt," *Mill City Daily News,* July 23, 2013, 1A.

Nonprint Source: Lecture, Sermon, Speech, Oral Report

> 8. Dick Weber, "The Facts about Preparing Teens to Drive" (lecture, Morrow High School, Morrow, GA, October 16, 2013).

Encyclopedia

9. *World Book Encyclopedia,* 2012 ed., s.v. "Raphael."

Note: "s.v." means *sub verbo,* "under the word(s)."

Government Documents

10. US Department of the Treasury, "Social Media: Consumer Compliance Risk Management Guidance," *Federal Register,* 78, no. 15 (2013) Washington, DC, 4848–54.

11. U.S., *Constitution,* art. 1, sec. 4.

12. United Kingdom, *Coroner's Act, 1954,* 2 & 3 Eliz. 2, ch.31.

Television

13. Bob Schieffer, *CBS News,* June 13, 2013.

Film or DVD

14. *Breakfast at Tiffany's,* directed by Blake Edwards (1961; Hollywood, CA: Paramount, 2009), DVD.

Biblical Reference

15. Matt. 10:5.

16. 1 Pet. 5:1–3 (New Revised Standard Version).

16c Writing Footnotes for Electronic Sources

To cite electronic sources, *The Chicago Manual of Style* includes a publication date, the URL, and the date of access. The models below show these requirements. Adjust your sources accordingly.

Scholarly Project

17. *The Byron Chronology,* ed. Ann R. Hawkins (Univ. of Maryland, 2013), accessed March 12, 2013, http://www.rc.umd.edu/reference/chronologies/byronchronology/index.html.

Article Online, Limited Information

18. Arthur Ferrill, "Neolithic Warfare Frontline Educational Foundation," accessed February 19, 2014, http://eserver.org/history/neolithic-war.txt.

Magazine Article Reproduced Online

19. James Wood, "Becoming Them," *The New Yorker,* 21 January 2013, accessed April 27, 2013, http://www.newyorker.com/reporting/2013/01/21/130121fa_fact_wood.

Journal Article Reproduced Online

20. Jakob Demant and Signe Ravn, "Communicating Trust between Parents and Their Children: A Case Study of Adolescents' Alcohol Use in Denmark," *Journal of Adolescent Research* 28 (2013): 325–47, accessed September 28, 2013, doi:10.1177/0743558413477198.

Article from a Database

At a minimum, provide the name of the database, a descriptive phrase or record locator number to indicate the part of the database being cited, the access date, and the URL or DOI designation.

21. Fulvio Scarano, Sina Ghaemi, and Stefan Probsting, "Data Reduction from Time-Resolved Tomographic PIV for Unsteady Pressure Evaluation." Aerospace Research Central Database, accessed January 27, 2014, DOI: 10.2514/6.2013-771.

Article Accessed from a Database through the Library System

22. "Emancipators Descend on a Virginia Woman's Farm: America's Civil War." *American History,* 48 (2013), General OneFile (A325891848).

Book Online

23. Sarah Morgan Dawson, *A Confederate Girl's Diary,* (Chapel Hill, NC: University of North Carolina, 2013), accessed November 3, 2013, http://docsouth.unc.edu/fpn/dawson/menu.html.

CD-ROM Source

24. The Old Testament, The Bible, Bureau Development, CD-ROM.

Article from an Online Service

25. Rossella Lorenzi, "Gold-Adorned Skeleton Could Be First Windsor Queen," *Discovery News,* April 23, 2013, accessed September 9, 2013, http://news.discovery.com/history/archaeology/ancient-gold-adorned-skeleton-found-130423.htm

16d Writing Subsequent Footnote References

After a first full footnote, references to the same source should be shortened to the author's last name and page number. When an author has two works mentioned, employ a shortened version of the title, e.g., "3. Jones, *Paine,* 25." In general, avoid Latinate abbreviations such as *loc. cit.* and *op. cit.*; however, whenever a note refers to the source in the immediately preceding note, you may use "Ibid." alone or "Ibid." with a page number, as shown in the next examples. If the subsequent note does not refer to the one immediately above it, do not use "Ibid." Instead, repeat the author's last name (note especially the difference between notes 2 and 4):

1. Tracey Tokuhama-Espinosa, *Making Classrooms Better: 50 Practical Applications of Mind, Brain, and Education Science* (New York: Norton, 2013), 23.

2. Ibid., 27.

3. Bruce A. VanSledright, *Assessing Historical Thinking and Understanding: Innovative Designs for New Standards* (New York: Taylor & Francis, 2013), 91.

4. Tokuhama-Espinosa, 24.

5. Ibid., 27.

Note: In academic papers not intended for publication, footnotes are commonly typed single-spaced and placed at the bottom of the page with extra space between the notes.

16e Writing Endnotes Rather Than Footnotes

With the permission of your instructor, you may put all your notes together as a single group of endnotes to lessen the burden of typing the paper. Most computer software programs will help you with this task by inserting the superscript numerals and by allowing you to type the endnotes consecutively at the end of the text, not at the bottom of each page. Follow these conventions:

1. Begin notes on a new page at the end of the text.
2. Entitle the page "Notes," centered, and placed 2 inches from the top of the page.
3. Indent the first line of each note one-half inch or five spaces. Type the number of the note followed by a period.
4. Double-space the endnotes.
5. Triple-space between the heading and the first note.

Conform to the following example:

Notes

1. Sebastien Chartrand and John Philpot, eds., *Justice Belied: The Unbalanced Scales of International Criminal Justice* (Montreal: Baraka Books, 2013), 24.

2. Ibid., 27.

3. Michael L. Perlin, *A Prescription for Dignity: Rethinking Criminal Justice and Mental Disability Laws* (Burlington, VT: Ashgate Publishing, 2013), 91.

4. Erin Murphy, "The Politics of Privacy in the Criminal Justice System: Information Disclosure, the Fourth Amendment, and Statutory Law Enforcement Exemptions," *Michigan Law Review* 111.4 (2013): 485–88, accessed September 30, 2013, http://www.michiganlawreview.org/issues/79.

5. Chartrand and Philpot, 28.

6. Mark M. Lanier and Lisa T. Briggs, *Research Methods in Criminal Justice and Criminology: A Mixed Methods Approach* (New York: Cambridge University Press, 2013), 133.

7. Ibid., 134.

8. Murphy, 486.

9. Chartrand and Philpot, 28.

10. Murphy, 486.

16f Writing Content Footnotes or Content Endnotes

As a general rule, put important matters in your text. Use a content note to explain research problems, conflicts in the testimony of the experts, matters of importance that are not germane to your discussion, interesting tidbits, credit to people and sources not mentioned in the text, and other matters that might interest readers.

HINT: After you have embedded most of your computer files in your draft, check the remaining files to find appropriate material for a few content endnotes.

Content notes should conform to these rules:

1. Content notes are *not* documentation notes; a full citation to any source mentioned in the note will appear elsewhere—in a documentation note or on the Bibliography page (see item 4.)
2. Content notes may be placed on a separate page(s) following the last page of text, but generally they appear as footnotes mixed among the documentation footnotes.
3. Content footnotes should be single-spaced, like your documentation footnotes. Content endnotes should be double-spaced, as shown in the next few examples.
4. Full information on sources mentioned in content notes must appear elsewhere in a footnote or in a separate Bibliography page at the end of the paper.
5. Unless ambiguity might result without them, do not use *p.* or *pp.* with page numbers.

The following samples demonstrate various types of content endnotes.

Related Matters Not Germane to the Text

1. The problems of politically correct language are explored in Adams, Tucker (4–5), Zalers, as well as Young and Smith (583). These authorities cite the need for caution by administrators who would impose new measures on speech and behavior.

Blanket Citation

2. On this point see Giarrett (3–4), de Young (579), Kinard (405–07), and Young (119).

3. Cf. Campbell (*Masks* 1: 170–225; *Hero* 342–45), Frazer (312), and Baird (300–44).

Note: Cf. means *compare.*

Literature on a Related Topic

4. For additional study of the effects of alcoholics on children, see especially the *Journal of Studies on Alcohol* for the article by Wolin et al. and the bibliography on the topic by Orme and Rimmer (285–87). In addition, group therapy for children of alcoholics is examined in Hawley and Brown.

Major Source Requiring Frequent In-Text Citations

5. All citations to Shakespeare are to the Fogler Library edition.

Reference to Source Materials

6. See also James Baird, who argues that the whiteness of Melville's whale is "the sign of the all-encompassing God" (257). Baird states: "It stands for what Melville calls at the conclusion of the thirty-fifth chapter of *Moby-Dick* 'the inscrutable tides of God'; and it is of these tides as well that the great White Whale himself is the quintessential emblem, the iconographic representation" (257).

NOTE: Either list Baird in the bibliography or include full bibliographic information with this footnote.

Explanation of Tools, Methods, or Testing Procedures

7. Water samples were drawn from the identical spot each day at 8 a.m., noon, 4 p.m., and 8 p.m., with testing done immediately on site.

8. The control group continued normal dietary routines, but the experimental group was asked to consume nuts, sharp cheeses, and chocolates to test acne development of its members against that of the control group.

NOTE: A report of an empirical study in APA style would require an explanation of tools and testing procedures in the text under "Methods." See section 15e, pages 307–308.

Statistics

See also "Using Visuals Effectively in a Research Essay," pages 168–170.

9. Database results show 27,000 pupil-athletes in 174 high schools with grades 0.075 above another group of 27,000 non-athletes at the same high schools.

Variables or Conflicts in the Evidence

10. The pilot study at Dunlap School, where sexual imbalance was noticed (62 percent males), differed sharply with test results of other schools. The male bias at Dunlap thereby caused the writer to eliminate those scores from the totals.

16g Using the Footnote System for Papers in the Humanities

Several disciplines in the humanities—history, philosophy, religion, and theology—use footnotes. The following list demonstrates the format for the types of notes you might need to write. They are shown as endnotes, which should be double-spaced.

Notes

1. Frank Sheed, *Knowing God: God and the Human Condition* (San Francisco: Ignatius Press, 2013), 23–27.

2. Linda Woodhead, *Christianity: A Brief Insight* (New York: Sterling, 2010), 114–17.

3. Claude Levi-Strauss, *The Savage Mind* (Chicago: University of Chicago Press, 1966), chap. 9, esp. p. 312.

4. Ibid., 314.

5. Humphries, P. T., "Marriage as Inspiration," Sermon (Bowling Green, KY: Mt. Hope Primitive Baptist Church, 2013).

6. Sheed, *Knowing God*, 26.

7. Romans 6:2.

8. P. Sommerville, "The Church and Religion," accessed February 19, 2013, http://history.wisc.edu/sommerville/367/367-023.htm.

16h Writing a Bibliography Page for a Paper That Uses Footnotes

In addition to footnotes or endnotes, you may be requested to supply a separate bibliography page that lists sources used in developing the paper. Use a heading that represents its contents, such as Selected Bibliography, Sources Consulted, or Works Cited.

See page 336 for a sample of a complete bibliography for a research paper.

If your initial footnotes are completely documented, the bibliography is redundant. Check with your instructor before preparing one because it may not be required.

Separate the title from the first entry with a triple space. Type the first line of each entry flush left; indent the second line and other succeeding lines five spaces or one-half inch. Alphabetize the list by last names of authors. Double-space the entries as shown. List alphabetically by title two or more works by one author. The basic forms are:

Book

Haslam, Rein, ed. *Estonian Studies in the History and Philosophy of Science.* New York: Springer-Verlag, 2013.

Journal Article

Murdie, Amanda. "The Bad, the Good, and the Ugly: The Curvilinear Effects of Civil-Military Conflict on International Crisis Outcome." *Armed Forces & Society* 39 (April 2013): 233–54.

Newspaper

Kanell, Michael E. and Nisha Giridharan. "Jobless Rate Falls, But Worries Persist." *Atlanta Journal-Constitution* 26 April 2013, 1A+.

Internet Article

"Biography." Paul Laurence Dunbar Website. Accessed February 23, 2012. http://www.dunbarsite.org/biopld.asp.

If the author is known, provide the date when the page was "last modified."

Grose, Thomas K. "Reshaping Flight for Fuel Efficiency: Five Technologies on the Runway." *National Geographic News.* Last modified April 23, 2013. http://news.nationalgeographic.com/news/ energy/2013/04/130423-reshaping-flight-for-fuel-efficiency/

16i Sample Research Paper in the CMS Style

The essay that follows demonstrates the format and documentation style you should use for a research paper when the instructor asks that you use "footnotes," the Chicago style, or the CMS style, all of which refer to *The Chicago Manual of Style.* If permitted, notes may be placed at the end of the paper as double-spaced endnotes rather than at the bottom of the pages.

In the paper that follows, Clare Grady has researched the history of the space race that began in the late 1950s. The student offers solid references to the time period and how the competition between the United States and the Soviet Union was as much about the Cold War arms race as it was about reaching for the new horizons of space. Ultimately, she poses the key issue—the competitiveness between the United States and the Soviet Union, although sometimes tense, signaled an age of optimism as "one small step" moved the world toward a deeper sense of cooperation and understanding.

```
                The Space Race: One Small Step—One Giant Leap




                                Clare Grady




                         U.S. History II - 2020
                           Professor Gregory
                            April 21, 2013
```

```
                                                        Grady 1


        I believe that this nation should commit itself to achieving

        the goal, before the decade is out, of landing a man on the

        moon and returning him safely to the earth. No single space

        project will be more exciting, or impressive to mankind, or

        more important and none will be so difficult or expensive to

        accomplish.

        —John F. Kennedy[1]
        _____

            1. John F. Kennedy, "Special Message to Congress on Urgent
        National Needs" (speech presented to Congress, Washington, DC, May
        25, 1961). The American Presidency Project, accessed April 13, 2013,
        http://www.presidency.ucsb.edu/ws/?pid=8151.
```

Grady 2

In 1961, President John F. Kennedy delivered a challenge to the United States of America—to be the first nation to land a man on the moon and successfully return him to Earth. This momentous goal was reached on July 20, 1969, when Neil Armstrong spoke his famous line upon successfully landing on the moon, "That's one small step for man, one giant leap for mankind."[2] However, without the hard work, profound technological advances, and pure dedication put forth in the 1960s, the United States may have never reached its goal. After World War II, tensions mounted between the world's two major superpowers, the U.S. and the U.S.S.R. Known as the Cold War, the hostility between the United States and the Soviet Union from 1957–1975 resulted in an arms race and a push for space exploration. This new philosophy to explore the vast unknown was fueled by both the necessity for national security and a symbolic superiority over an adversary. If the United States could achieve its goal, it would signify the technological, economic, and ideological dominance that the U.S. had over the Soviet Union. The opposing superpower presented a challenge, and the Space Race had started.

The Soviets stunned every American when they launched *Sputnik 1* into orbit on October 4, 1957.[3] Not only was this viewed as competition, many American citizens and government officials worried it was a military threat and danger to national security. The U.S. government responded to this threat by creating the National Aeronautics and Space Administration, otherwise known as NASA. Established in 1958, this new organization focused on the technological aspect and challenges that came with entering the

---

2. Ned Potter, "Neil Armstrong: How 'One Small Step' Became First Words on the Moon," *ABC News*, January 2, 2013, accessed April 15, 2013, http://abcnews.go.com/Technology/neil-armstrong-small-step-words-moon-apollo-11/story?id=18115402.

Grady 3

Space Race.[4] Soon after the Russian launch of *Sputnik 1,* the U.S. followed with its first, unmanned satellite, *Explorer 1,* on January 31, 1958.[5] The launches of these two satellites marked the official beginning of the Space Race. Americans realized the intensity of the competition as national pride and patriotism swelled throughout the country. Sadly, and shockingly, the Soviets beat the United States once again by putting the first man into space, Yuri Gagarin on April, 12, 1961.[6] America had been too slow once again and desperately needed a boost in morale.

    Kennedy used politics as one of the driving forces behind the space program by supporting an all out effort in defeating the Soviets. At first Kennedy was skeptical about the program, but later backed it as a mechanism to gain popularity and votes before being elected President.[7] Upon being elected, he continued to support the efforts put forth toward the Space Race. In an inspiring speech made to Congress and Americans, the President declared that the U.S. would be the first to land a man on the moon; moreover, this feat would be accomplished by the end of the decade. This became the ultimate goal of the United States and would signify the final defeat of the Soviets in the Space Race. Through his pressing

---

    3. Gina Holland. *A Cultural History of the United States: Through the Decades. The 1960s* (San Diego: Lucent Books, 1999), 112.

    4. Andre Balogh. "Above and Beyond: In 1969 Men Set Foot on the Moon for the First Time," *History Today,* July 2009, accessed April 14, 2013, http://www.questia.com/library/1G1-202918955/above-and-beyond-in-1969-men-set-fo-on-the-moon.

    5. Holland, *A Cultural History,* 112.

    6. Ibid.

    7. John N. Wilford, "Sputnik: A Tiny Sphere That Changed Everything—For a While," *New York Times,* September 25, 2007, accessed April 14, 2013, http://www.nytimes.com/2007/09/25/health/25iht-sputnik.1.7629111.html?pagewanted=all&_r=0.

insistence, Kennedy was able to rally Americans and garner the support of Congress with funding for the massive project.[8]

In a letter written by President Kennedy to Lyndon B. Johnson, who was then Chairman of the Space Council, Kennedy asked his vice president questions pertaining to the status of the space program. These questions include whether the goal of putting a man on the moon was actually attainable, how much it would cost, how many hours a day men would be required to work on the program if maximum effort was put forth to achieve the goal.[9]

His questions were soon answered when the U.S. matched the Soviet's latest feat on February 20, 1962, by making John H. Glenn the first American in orbital flight in *Friendship 7*.[10] This accomplishment made the nation once again confident and willing to go forth in space exploration. NASA began its next step in the race to the moon by creating the Apollo human spaceflight program. Apollo mission planners attempted to design a safe and reliable vehicle that would carry the astronauts to the moon and back. They suggested several approaches to accomplish a safe moon landing, but eventually agreed upon creating a spacecraft composed of modular parts. A command module would stay in orbit around the moon while a lunar module would detach from the command ship and land on the moon's surface. The rocket needed to boost both parts into space was the massive Saturn V.[11] However, a race brings haste, and haste is often followed by tragedy.

---

8. John F. Kennedy. "Special Message to Congress on Urgent National Needs."

9. John F. Kennedy. "Letter from John F. Kennedy to Lyndon Johnson" (Washington, DC, April 20, 1961). *Letters of Note,* September 7, 2010, accessed April 16, 2013, http://www.lettersofnote.com/2010/09/is-there-space-program-which-which-we.html

10. Holland, *A Cultural History,* 115.

11. Andre Balogh. "Above and Beyond."

Grady 3

The first manned test flight began with Apollo 1 on February 21, 1967. The test turned to horror when the cabin caught fire due to the 100% oxygen atmosphere inside. All three crew members, Virgil I. "Gus" Grissom, Edward H. White II, and Roger Bruce Chaffee, were killed. Although this disaster set the manned phase of the Apollo program back twenty months, the country worked diligently to get back on track.[12] By July 20, 1969, the ultimate goal was achieved.

Broadcast on live television, people all over the world watched the Apollo 11 mission play out. Crew members Buzz Aldrin, Neil Armstrong, and Michael Collins launched from the Kennedy Space center on July 16, 1969. Four days later, Aldrin and Armstrong landed on the moon at 4:18 EDT in the landing module while Michael Collins orbited the moon in the command module. A billion viewers witnessed the first man to set foot on the moon when Neil Armstrong stepped off the ladder onto its surface at 10:56 EDT.[13] With the simple yet profound words, "That's one small step for man, one giant leap for mankind," Armstrong delivered to every American and to every world citizen the promise made by President Kennedy eight years earlier.[14] The Space Race was over, and the United States had won.

The space program was the high point in the age of optimism.[15] The competitiveness between the United States and the Soviet Union, although sometimes tense, promoted friendship and cooperation. It also fueled the American desire to achieve its goals. The U.S. threw safety out of the window and accepted a risky and adventurous view on space exploration that eventually paid off. The Apollo project inspired Americans and showed the country almost anything is possible with skill, courage, and a little luck.

---

12. Ibid.

13. Holland, *A Cultural History*, 117–18.

14. Potter, "Neil Armstrong."

15. Balogh, "Above and Beyond."

Bibliography

Balogh, Andre. "Above and Beyond: In 1969 Men Set
    Foot on the Moon for the First Time." *History
    Today,* July 2009. Accessed April 14, 2013. http://
    www.questia.com/library/1G1-202918955/
    above-and-beyond-in-1969-men-set-foot-on-the-moon.

Holland, Gina. *A Cultural History of the United States: Through
    the Decades. The 1960s.* San Diego: Lucent Books, 1999.

Kennedy, John F. "Letter from John F. Kennedy to Lyndon
    Johnson," (April 20, 1961). *Letters of Note,* September 7,
    2010. Accessed April 16, 2013. http://www.lettersofnote.
    com/2010/09/is-there-space-program-which-which-we.html.

---. "Special Message to Congress on Urgent National Needs"
    (May 25, 1961). The American Presidency Project.
    Accessed April 13, 2013, http://www.presidency.ucsb.edu/
    ws/?pid=8151.

Potter, Ned. "Neil Armstrong: How 'One Small Step'
    Became First Words on the Moon." *ABC News,*
    January 2, 2013. Accessed April 15, 2013.
    http://abcnews.go.com/Technology/neil-
    armstrong-small-step-words-moon-apollo-11/
    story?id=18115402.

Wilford, John N. "Sputnik: A Tiny Sphere That Changed
    Everything—For a While." *New York Times,* September
    25, 2007. Accessed April 14, 2013. http://www.nytimes.
    com/2007/09/25/health/25iht-sputnik.1.7629111.
    html?pagewanted=all&_r=0.

17 CSE Style for the Natural and Applied Sciences

Chapter 17 Clear Targets

The Council of Science Editors has established two separate forms for citing sources in scientific writing. One is the **citation-sequence** system for writing in the applied sciences, such as chemistry, computer science, mathematics, physics, and the medicine sciences. This system uses numbers in the text rather than a name and year. The second style format is the **name-year** system for use in the biological and earth sciences. The elements discussed in this chapter will assist with the CSE documentation style for your research paper:

- Writing in-text citations using the citation-sequence or name-year sequence
- Preparing a References page
- Formatting a paper in CSE style

There are advantages and disadvantages to each system. The citation-sequence system saves space, and the numbers make minimal disruption to the reading of the text, yet this style seldom mentions names, so readers must refer to the bibliography for the names of authors.

Citation-Sequence

The original description (3) contained precise taxonomic detail that differed with recent studies (4–6).

Name-Year

The original description (Roberts 2014) contained precise taxonomic detail that differed with recent studies (McCormick 2012a, 2012b, and Tyson and others 2013).

The name-year system mentions authors' names in the text with the year to show timely application and historical perspective. Citations can be deleted or added without difficulty. But a long string of citations in the text can be more disruptive than numbers. In truth, the decision is usually not yours to make. The individual disciplines in the sciences have adopted one form or the other, as shown in the chart below.

Index to Bibliographic Models: CSE Style

Guide by Discipline

17a Writing In-Text Citations Using the CSE Citation-Sequence System

This system employs numbers to identify sources. Use this style with these disciplines: chemistry, computer science, engineering, mathematics, physics, and the medical sciences (medicine, nursing, and general health). In simple terms, the system requires an in-text *number,* rather than the year, and a list of References that are numbered to correspond to the in-text citations.

After completing a list of references, assign a number to each entry. Use one of two methods for numbering the list: (1) arrange references in alphabetical order and number them consecutively (in which case the numbers will appear in random order in the text) or (2) number the references consecutively as you put them into your text, interrupting that order when entering references cited earlier.

The number serves as the key to the source, as numbered in the References. Conform to the following regulations:

1. Place the number within parentheses (1) or as a raised index numeral, like this.[5] A name is not required and is even discouraged, so try to arrange your wording accordingly. Full information on the author and the work will be placed in the References list.

   > It is known (1) that the DNA concentration of a nucleus doubles during interphase.

   > A recent study (1) has raised interesting questions related to photosynthesis, some of which have been answered (2).

   > In particular, a recent study[1] has raised many interesting questions related to photosynthesis, some of which have been answered.[2]

2. If you include the authority's name, add the number after the name.

   > Additional testing by Cooper (3) included alterations in carbohydrate metabolism and changes in ascorbic acid incorporation into the cell and adjoining membranes.

3. If necessary, add specific data to the entry:

   > "The use of photosynthesis in this application is crucial to the environment" (Skelton,[8] p 732).

   > The results of the respiration experiment published by Jones (3, Table 6, p 412) had been predicted earlier by Smith (5, Proposition 8).

17b Writing a References Page

Supply a list of references at the end of your paper. Number the entries to correspond to sources as you cite them in the text. An alternate method is to alphabetize the list and then number it. Label the list *References*. The form of the entries should follow the examples provided here.

Book

Provide a number and then list the author, title of the book, place of publication, publisher, year, and total number of pages (optional).

> 1. Gribbin J. Edwin Schrodinger and the quantum revolution. New
>   York: Wiley; 2013. 336 p.

Article in a Journal

Provide a number and then list the author, the title of the article, the name of the journal, the year and month if necessary, volume number and issue number if necessary, and inclusive pages. The month or an issue number is necessary for any journal that is paged anew with each issue.

> 2. Busby JW, Smith TG, White KL, Strange SM. Climate change
>   and insecurity: Mapping vulnerability in Africa. Intl. Security
>   2013;37(4): 132–172.

Online Articles and Other Electronic Publications

Add at the end of the citation an availability statement as well as the date you accessed the material. Use the form in number 4 for an article published online. Use the form in number 4 for a periodical article that has been reproduced online. Number 3 is online and number 4 is a printed journal [serial online].

> 3. Ben-Joseph EP. Do my kids need vaccines before traveling?
>   [Internet]. 2013. [cited 2013 Oct 3]; Available from: http://
>   kidshealth.org/parent/question/safety/travel-vaccinations.
>   html#cat20290
>
> 4. Pérez-Gil J, Rodríguez-Concepción M. Metabolic plasticity for
>   isoprenoid biosynthesis in bacteria. Biochemical J. [Internet]
>   2013 [cited 2013 Nov 18]; 452:19–25. Available from: http://www
>   .biochemj.org/bj/431/bj4310023.htm.

Magazine or Newspaper Article

Add a specific date and, for newspapers, cite a section letter or number.

> 5. McGrath B. The white wall. New Yorker 2013 Apr 22: 80–95.

6. [Anonymous]. What are mesenchymal stem cells? Chattanooga

Times Free Press 2013 Apr 28; Sect A:1.

Proceedings and Conference Presentations

 For a sample of a "References" page using the number system, see pages 355–356.

After supplying a number, give the name of the author or editor, the title of the presentation, name of the conference, type of work (report, proceedings, proceedings online, etc.), name of the organization or society, the date of the conference, and the place. If found on the Internet, add the URL and the date you accessed the information.

7. Barbose G, Connelly P, Kenney R. The future of renewable energy.

NCSL Energy, Transportation and Agriculture Committee: National

Conference of State Legislatures [Internet]; 2013 May 2–4 [cited

2013 Sept 27]; Denver, CO. Available from http://comm.ncsl.org/

MeetingAgenda/tabid/193/s/2/mpid/63770312/Default.aspx

17c Writing In-Text Citations with Name and Year

The CSE name-year style applies to these disciplines:

Agriculture	Anthropology	Archeology
Astronomy	Biology	Botany
Geography	Geology	Zoology

When writing research papers in accordance with the name-year system, conform to the following rules:

1. Place the year within parentheses immediately after the authority's name:

Stroyka (2012) ascribes no species-specific behavior to man.

However, Adamson (2013) presents data that tend to be contradictory.

2. If you do not mention the authority's name in your text, insert the name, year, and page numbers within the parentheses:

One source found some supporting evidence for a portion of the

questionable data (Marson and Brown 2013, pp 23–32) through point

bi-serial correlation techniques.

3. For two authors, employ both names in your text and in the parenthetical citation:

> Torgerson and Andrews (2014)

or

> (Torgerson and Andrews 2014)

For three or more authors, use the lead author's name with "and others" in the written text of the paper.
Note: CSE style prefers English terms and English abbreviations in the text, but use Latin words and abbreviations, such as *et al.* for in-text citations.

In the text:	Torgerson and others (2014)
In the parenthetical citation:	(Torgerson et al. 2014)

4. Use lowercase letters (a, b, c) to identify two or more works published in the same year by the same author—for example, "Thompson (2013a)" and "Thompson (2013b)." Then use "2013a" and "2013b" in your list of references.

5. If necessary, supply additional information:

> Alretta (2009a, 2009b; cf. Thomas 2010, p 89) suggests an
> intercorrelation of these testing devices. But after multiple-group
> analysis, Welston (2013, esp. p 211) reached an opposite conclusion.

6. In the case of a reference to a specific page, separate the page number from the year with a comma and a space. Do not use a period after the "p."
   a. A quotation or paraphrase in the middle of the sentence:

> Jones stated, "These data of psychological development suggest
> that retarded adolescents are atypical in maturational growth"
> (2013, p 215), and Jones attached the data that were accumulated
> during the study.

   b. A quotation or paraphrase that falls at the end of a sentence:

> Jones (2013) found that "these data of psychological
> development suggest that retarded adolescents are atypical in
> maturational growth" (p 215).

c. A long quotation, indented with the tab key and set off from the text in a block (and therefore without quotation marks):

> Tavares (2014) found the following:
>
> > Whenever these pathogenic organisms attack the human body and begin to multiply, the infection is set in motion. The host responds to this parasitic invasion with efforts to cleanse itself of the invading agents. When rejection efforts of the host become visible (fever, sneezing, congestion), the disease status exists. (pp 314–315)

7. Punctuate the citations according to the following stipulations:

a. Use a comma followed by a space to separate citations of different references by the same author or authors in same-year or different-year references:

> Supplemental studies (Johnson 2013a, 2013b, 2012) have
> shown . . .
> Supplemental studies (Randolph and Roberts 2013, 2014) have
> shown . . .

b. Use a comma to separate two authors of the same work.

> (Ramirez and Montoya 2013)

Use commas with three or more authors:

> (Smith, Jones, Thompson, and others 2012)

c. Use a semicolon followed by a space to separate citations to different authors:

> Supplemental studies (Smith 2012; Barfield 2011, 2013; Barfield
> and Smith 2013; Wallace 2014) have shown . . .

17d Using Name-Year with Bibliography Entries

Alphabetize the list and label it *References*. Double-space the entries and use hanging indention. When there are two to ten authors, all should be named in the reference listing. When there are eleven or more authors, the first ten are listed, followed by "and others." If the author is anonymous, insert "[Anonymous]." Place the year immediately after the author's name.

Article in a Journal

List the author, year, article title, journal title, volume number, and inclusive pages. Add an issue number for any journal that is paged anew with each issue.

Chesney, RW. 2013. The disappearance of diseases, conditions, and

disorders of childhood. J Pediatrics 162(5): 903–905.

Book

List the author, year, title, place of publication, publisher, and total number of pages (optional).

Zhang Y, Wen F, Xiao M. 2013. Quantum control of multi-wave mixing.

New York: Wiley. 430 p.

Online Articles and Other Electronic Publications

Add at the end of the citation an availability statement as well as the date you accessed the material.

[Anonymous]. 2013. Chemical Activity Barometer: Economic Growth

Remains Slow. Chem. Proc. [Internet]. [cited 2014 Jan 14] Available

from: http://www.chemicalprocessing.com/industrynews/2013/

chemical-activity-barometer-economic-growth-remains-slow/

Journal Article Reprinted Online

Provide original publication data as well as the Internet address and the date you accessed the material.

Forte, A, Lampe, C. 2013. Defining, understanding and supporting

open collaboration: Lessons from the literature [abstract]. Am.

Behav. Sci. [Internet], [cited 2013 Aug 30]; 54(5). 535–547.

Available from: http://abs.sagepub.com/content/57/5/535

Magazine and Newspaper Article

Add a specific date and, if listed, a section letter or number.

Gray C. 2013 May. Clear as a bell. Smithsonian 44(2): 58–59.

Bailey T. 2013 Apr 28. How many restaurants can Memphis support? The

[Memphis] Commercial Appeal 1+.

Proceedings and Conference Publications

Give author, date, title of the presentation, name of conference, type of work (report, proceeding, proceedings online, etc.), name of the organization or society, and place of the conference. If found on the Internet, add the URL and the date of your access.

Samuels A, Fishman J, Williams P. 2012. Effective use of partnerships, tools, and coalitions to improve outreach [abstract online].

In: Abstracts: 2012 National Conference on Health Communication Marketing and Media [Internet]; 2012 Aug 7–9; Atlanta, GA.

[cited 2013 Feb 19]. Available from: http://www.cdc.gov/nchcmm/ pdf/2012nchcmmconferenceprogram.pdf

Arranging the References List

The list of references should be placed in alphabetical order, as shown next.

References

Allender, TY. 2013 June. Analysis of perchlorates in water intended for human consumption. Midwest Sci. Qtr. 31(6): 47–49.

[Anonymous]. 2012. Final regulatory determination for perchlorate in drinking water [Internet]. Environmental Protection Agency. [cited 2013 Nov 8]. Available from: http://water.epa.gov/drink/ contaminants/unregulated/perchlorate.cfm

[Anonymous]. 2012. Perchlorate in drinking water [Internet]. California Department of Health Services. [cited 2013 Nov 7]. Available from http://www.cdph.ca.gov/certlic/drinkingwater/pages/Perchlorate. aspx

Kemsley J. 2013 Apr 8. Archaea feed on perchlorate. Chem. & Eng. News. [Internet]. [cited 2013 Nov 8]; 91(14): 8. Available from: http://cen.acs.org/articles/91/i14/Archaea-Feed-Perchlorate.html

Zhang T, Wu Q, Sun HW, Rao J, Kannan K. 2010. Perchlorate and iodide in whole blood samples from infants, children, and adults in Nanchang, China. [abstract]. 44(18):6947–6953. Chem. Engr. News. [Internet]. [cited 2013 Nov 6]. Available from http://pubs.acs.org/ doi/abs/10.1021/es101354g

17e Sample Paper Using the CSE Citation-Sequence System

Student Sarah Bemis has researched problems with managing diabetes and presented the paper using the CSE citation-sequence system. As she cites a source in the text, she uses a number that also reappears on her References page. Accordingly, the references are not in alphabetical order. As is standard with writing in the sciences, an abstract is provided.

Balance the
title, name,
and
affiliation.

Diabetes Management:

A Delicate Balance

By

Sarah E. Bemis

English 103: College Writing

Sister Winifred Morgan, O.P.

5 March 2013

An abstract
of 100–200
words states
the purpose,
scope, and
major
findings of
the report.

Abstract

Bemis ii

Diabetes affects approximately 11 million people in the
U.S. alone, leading to $350 billion in medical costs. Two types,
I and II, have debilitating effects. The body may tolerate
hyperglycemia for a short time, but severe complications can
occur, such as arterioscleroses, heart disease, nerve damage, and
cerebral diseases. New drugs continue to improve the lifestyle
of a person with diabetes, but controlling blood sugar requires
three elements working together—medication, diet, and exercise.
This study examines the importance of each of the three.
Patients need a controlled balance of the medication, diet, and
exercise program.

Bemis 1

Diabetes Management: A Delicate Balance

Diabetes is a disease that affects approximately 11 million people in the United States alone (1), and its complications lead to hundreds of thousands of deaths per year and cost the nation billions in medical care for the direct cost of complications and for indirect costs of lost productivity related to the disease. The condition can produce devastating side effects and a multitude of chronic health problems. For this reason, it can be very frightening to those who do not understand the nature and treatment of the disease. Diabetes currently has no known cure, but it can be controlled. Diabetes research has made great advancements in recent years, but the most important insights into the management of this disease are those which seem the most simplistic. By instituting a healthy, balanced lifestyle, most persons with diabetes can live free of negative side effects.

Diabetes mellitus, according to several descriptions, is a disorder in which the body cannot properly metabolize glucose or sugar. The body's inability to produce or properly use insulin permits glucose to build up in the bloodstream. The excess sugar in the blood, or hyperglycemia, is what leads to the side effects of diabetes (2,3,4).

There are actually two types of diabetes. Type 1, or juvenile diabetes, is the name given to the condition in which the pancreas produces very little or no insulin. It is normally discovered during childhood, but can occur at any age (3). Adult onset, or Type II diabetes, occurs when the pancreas produces usable insulin, but not enough to counteract the amount of glucose in the blood. This often results from obesity or poor diet.

In both Type I and Type II diabetes, the problem has been identified as hyperglycemia (5). This buildup of glucose in the

---

Margin notes:

Use a number to register the use of a source.

The thesis or hypothesis is expressed at the end of the introduction.

Scientific writing requires careful definition, as shown here.

More than one source can be listed for one idea or concept.

Bemis 2

bioodstream leads to a number of dangerous side effects. The initial effects and indicators of hyperglycemia are frequent urination, intense thirst, increased hunger and fatigue. When glucose begins to build up in the blood, the kidneys begin to filter out the excess sugar into the urine. The amount of glucose the kidneys can filter varies with each person. In this process, all the water in the body's tissues is being used to produce urine to flush glucose from the kidneys. This is what leads to the intense thirst and frequent urination associated with hyperglycemia (5).

Causal analysis, as shown here, is a staple of scientific writing.

Because the body lacks the insulin needed to allow glucose into the cells, the glucose cannot be processed to produce energy. The cells signal the brain that they are not getting sugar and this causes hunger. However, no matter how much a victim of hyperglycemic diabetes eats, the cells will not be producing energy (6).

It has been shown (4) that with hyperglycemia the kidneys try to compensate for the excess of sugar and lack of energy. While the kidneys attempt to filter the sugar from the blood, the liver tries to produce energy by burning fat and muscle to produce ketones, a protein that the body attempts to burn in place of glucose. Ketones do not provide the energy the body requires but do produce chemicals toxic to the body. When too many ketones are present in the blood, ketoacidosis occurs (4).

Refer to the sources with the past tense verb or the present participle.

Guthrie and Guthrie (1) have demonstrated that ketoacidosis is a condition caused by high levels of hydrogen in the blood. This leads initially to a high blood pH, depleted saline fluids and dehydration. If untreated it can lead to a shut down of the central nervous system, coma or even death. In fact, many diabetes-related deaths are caused by ketoacidosis that has reached a comatose state. Ketoacidosis is characterized by

In addition to the number, you may mention the name(s) of your sources.

frequent urination, dry mouth, extreme thirst, headache, rapid and deep respiration, increased heart rate, nausea, vomiting, disorientation and lethargy (1).

The American Academy of Family Physicians (4) has reported that hyperglycemia can cause other, more subtle, side effects. Because the body is not receiving the nourishment it requires, a victim of hyperglycemic diabetes often experiences poor tissue growth and repair. This can cause problems with growth and development in children and wound healing in adults as well as children. It has also been reported (7) that the immune system is also affected and that victims experience infection more often and more severely than a person without diabetes. Other conditions that frequently occur in conjunction with hyperglycemia in its early stages are depression and chronic fatigue (8). Many patients who experience hypoglycemia have difficulties controlling gain and loss of weight as well.

It has been shown (Guthrie and Guthrie 1) that the body may tolerate hyperglycemia over a short time period. However, if untreated, it leads to other chronic and often fatal health conditions. Arterioscleroses occurs in hyperglycemic diabetics over time, resulting in decreased circulation and eyesight. This also may lead to heart disease, angina and heart attack, the most prevalent causes of death among diabetics (1). Also common is diabetic neuropathy, a degeneration of the nerves. This condition causes pain and loss of function in the extremities (1).

A person with diabetes is also at risk for many cerebral diseases. Both the large and small cerebral arteries of victims are prone to rupture, which can cause cerebral hemorrhage, thrombosis or stroke. Blockages in the carotid arteries can decrease blood flow to the brain, causing episodes of lightheadedness and fainting (1, pp 201–202).

You may add page numbers to the reference as a courtesy to the reader.

Bemis 4

Diabetic nephropathy occurs when the kidneys are overloaded with glucose. Eventually, they begin to shut down. The kidneys of a person with uncontrolled diabetes are also susceptible to infection, resulting in decreased kidney function (1).

With all the complications victims experience, the outlook for a long and healthy life does not seem good for those diagnosed with the disease. However, all of these effects can be reduced, delayed, and even prevented with proper care and control. By monitoring blood sugar and reacting accordingly with medication, by special diets, and by exercise and a controlled lifestyle, persons with diabetes can avoid these serious health conditions (Hu and others 9).

Process analysis, as shown here, is often a staple of scientific writing.

The first aspect of diabetes care is blood sugar monitoring and medication. The two go hand in hand in that the patient must have the appropriate type and dosage of medication and must know blood sugar values and patterns in order to determine the correct regimen. Two main types of monitoring are necessary for diabetes control. Patients must perform home glucose monitoring on a daily basis. Advancements in this area in recent years have made this relatively effortless. Several glucose monitoring kits are available to the general public. These consist of a small, electronic machine that measures the amount of glucose in the blood, as well as the equipment necessary to obtain a small sample. With such equipment, patients can test and record blood sugars several times per day. This gives both short-term and long-term information by which they and their physicians can determine insulin dosages and meal plans.

In addition to daily monitoring, victims should visit their physician regularly. Doctors usually perform a test called a hemoglobin AIC, which gives a better indication of blood sugar control over a longer period of time than a home test. This

Bemis 5

should be done approximately every ninety days, as that is the time period over which blood cells are renewed. This test along with consideration of daily glucose values can help the physician determine overall control and effectiveness of the patient's routine. Regular visits also give the physician an opportunity to monitor the general health of the patient, including circulation, eyesight, infections, and organ infections.

The treatment of diabetes usually involves medication. Since Type I diabetics produce very little or no insulin, insulin injections will always be necessary. For Type II, the treatment may be strictly dietary, dietary with oral hypoglycemic agents, or insulin therapy.

> The writer explores control element number one: methods of administering medication.

When insulin therapy is required, it is very important that the appropriate type and dosage is implemented. Many types of insulin are available. The main distinction among these types is in their action time, onset, peak-time, and duration. Different types of insulin begin to act at different rates. They also continue to act for different periods of time and hit peak effectiveness at different intervals (1). This is why it is important to have records of blood sugars at regular intervals over several weeks. From this it can be determined when and what type of insulin is needed most. Once it is determined what insulin regimen is appropriate, the patient must follow it closely. Routine is very important in controlling diabetes.

Patients with diabetes now have a few options when it comes to injection method. One may chose traditional manual injection, an injection aid, or an insulin pump. Injection aids can make using a needle easier and more comfortable or actually use air pressure to inject. The insulin pump is a device that offers convenience as well as improved control. The pump is a small battery-operated device that delivers insulin 24 hours a day through a small needle worn under the skin. The pump contains

Bemis 6

a computer chip that controls the amount of insulin delivered according to the wearer's personalized plan (10). The pump is meant for patients who do not wish to perform multiple injections, but are willing to test blood sugars frequently. The pump can help patients who have some trouble controlling their blood sugars by providing insulin around the clock. It also provides an element of freedom for persons with busy schedules.

Some Type II patients can control the disease with a combination of diet, exercise and an oral hypoglycemic agent. These drugs themselves contain no insulin. They traditionally lower blood glucose levels by stimulating the pancreas to produce insulin (1). Therefore, they are only appropriate for patients whose pancreas is still producing some insulin. Diabetes research has advanced in recent years, however. Some new drugs are coming available in the new millennium. Creators of the pharmaceuticals are able to increase sensitivity to insulin and suppress the secretion of hormones that raise blood sugar. A number of new drugs that are aimed at taking the place of insulin therapy are currently in the final stages of research and development. Glucovance has been advanced as a valuable new medication (11). For now, the oral medications that are available can aid in keeping better control when properly paired with an effective diet and exercise plan.

The writer now explores control element number two: methods of diet management.

While it is important to have the proper medication, the backbone of diabetes management is the meal plan. By making wise choices in eating, persons with diabetes can reduce stress on the body and increase the effectiveness of their medication. The basis of a good meal plan is balanced nutrition and moderation. Eating a low fat, low sodium, low sugar diet is the best way for a diabetic to ensure longevity and health. It is important for everyone to eat balanced meals on a routine schedule. For victims

Bemis 7

of diabetes, it can help in blood sugar control and in preventing heart disease and digestive problems.

Two established meal plans are recommended for patients: the Exchange Plan and carbohydrate counting (12, 13). Both are based on the Diabetes Food Pyramid (Nutrition). The Food Pyramid divides food into six groups. These resemble the traditional four food groups, except that they are arranged in a pyramid in which the bottom, or largest, section contains the foods that should be eaten most each day. The top, or smallest, section contains the foods that should be eaten least, if at all. With any diabetic meal plan, the patient should eat a variety of foods from all the food groups, except the sweets, fats, and alcohol group. New directives by the American Diabetes Association offer helpful and authoritative guidance to help victims cope with their meal planning (14, 15).

The Exchange Plan provides a very structured meal plan. Foods are divided into eight categories, which are more specific than those of the Food Pyramid are. A dietician or physician determines a daily calorie range for the patient and, based on that range, decides how many servings she or he should eat from each category per meal. Portion sizes are determined and must be followed exactly. The patient then has the option to either choose foods that fit into the groups recommended for each meal or exchange foods from one group for foods from another.

Another meal plan patients can utilize is carbohydrate counting. This plan is less structured and gives the patient more flexibility in making meal choices. It also involves less planning. Once again, food is categorized, but into only three groups. The largest food group, carbohydrates, encompasses not only starches, but dairy products, fruits, and vegetables as well. The dietician or physician again assigns a calorie range. With this plan, however, only the number of carbohydrates per meal are assigned, and even this is flexible. This plan is recommended for those who know how to make balanced meal choices, but need to keep track of their food intake. Once again, portion sizes are important, and the patient must remember to eat the recommended amount of foods from each pyramid category (5, 11, 12).

The writer now explores control element number three: methods of exercise.

The final element in successfully managing diabetes is exercise. It has been shown (16) that exercise can help stimulate the body to use glucose for energy, thus taking it out of the blood. Diabetic patients need regular exercise programs that suit their personal needs. Something as simple as a walking routine can significantly reduce blood glucose levels (16). Some patients may require as little as a fifteen-minute per day walk, where some may need a more involved workout. In each case, an exercise schedule works with meal plans, medication, and lifestyle. Also crucial to the success of an exercise routine is close monitoring of blood sugar. If glucose levels are too high or too low, exercise will have negative effects.

All of the aspects of diabetes management can be summed up in one word: balance. Diabetes itself is caused by a lack of balance of insulin and glucose in the body. In order to restore that balance, a person with diabetes must juggle medication, monitoring, diet, and exercise. Managing diabetes is not an easy task, but a long and healthy life is very possible when the delicate balance is carefully maintained.

Bemis 9

References

1. Guthrie DW, Guthrie RA. Nursing management of diabetes mellitus. New York: Springer, 2008. 500 p.

2. [Anonymous]. Diabetes insipidus [Internet]. American Academy of Family Physicians. [cited 2013 Feb 20]. Available from http://familydoctor.org/familydoctor/en/diseases-conditions/diabetes-insipidus/symptoms.html.

3. Fowler, MJ. Diabetes treatment, part 1: Diet and exercise. Clin Diabetes 2007; 25(3): 105–109.

4. [Anonymous]. Diabetes: Monitoring your blood sugar level [Internet]. American Academy of Family Physicians. [cited 2013 Feb 22]. Available from http://familydoctor.org/familydoctor/en/diseases-conditions/diabetes/treatment/monitoring-your-blood-sugar-level.html

5. Peters AL. Conquering diabetes. New York: Penguin, 2006. 368 p.

6. Arangat AV, Gerich JE. Type 2 diabetes: postprandial hyperglycemia and increased cardiovascular risk. Vasc. Health and Risk Manag. 2010 Mar 6; 145–155.

7. Milchovich SK, Dunn-Long B. Diabetes mellitus. Boulder, CO: Bull, 2011. 240 p.

8. Davile A. Complications [Internet]. Diabetes Hands Foundation 2013. [cited 2013 Feb 21]. Available from http://www.tudiabetes.org/notes/Complications.

9. Hu FB, Li TY, Colditz GA, Willett WC, Manson JE. Television watching and other sedentary behaviors in relation to risk of obesity and type 2 diabetes mellitus in women. JAMA 2003; 289; 1785–1791.

10. [Anonymous]. Insulin pump therapy [Internet]. Children with Diabetes 2013. [cited 2013 Feb 24]. Available from http://www.childrenwithdiabetes.com/pumps/.

11. [Anonymous]. Glucophage [Internet]. Diabetes Healthsource. 2013. [cited 2013 Feb 28]. Available from http://www.glucophage.com.

Citations on this page demonstrate the citation-sequence method, as explained on pages 340–341. For details on the name-year system, see pages 343–345.

Bemis 10

12. McDermott MT. Endocrine secrets. New York: Elsevier, 2009. 448 p.

13. Bittencourt JA. The power of carbohydrates, proteins, and lipids. Charleston, SC: Createspace, 2011. 196 p.

14. American Diabetes Association. The American Diabetes Association complete guide to diabetes. Alexandria, VA: ADA, 2013. 576 p.

15. American Diabetes Association. The diabetes comfort food cookbook. Alexandria, VA: ADA, 2013. 192 p.

16. American Diabetes Association. Ideas for exercise [Internet]. American Diabetes Association 2013. [cited 2013 Feb 25]. Available from http://www.diabetes.org/food-and-fitness/fitness/ideas-for-exercise/?loc=DropDownFF-exerciseideas.

18 Creating Electronic and Multimedia Research Projects

Chapter 18 Clear Targets

Digital and online media have become an increasingly important source of research information, while electronic environments provide key components for presenting investigative analysis. To that end, this chapter suggests ways to create and publish your research project electronically or online:

- Developing electronic documents and slide shows
- Creating Web pages with hypertext markup language (HTML)
- Using graphics in your digital or multimedia research paper
- Preparing a writing portfolio

Creating your research paper electronically has a number of advantages:

- **It is easy.** Creating research projects can be as simple as saving your paper in a file and publishing it online or e-mailing it to your instructor.
- **It offers multimedia potential.** Unlike paper documents, electronic documents enable you to include anything available in digital form—including text, illustrations, sound, and video.
- **It can link your reader to more information.** Your readers can click a hyperlink to access additional sources of information. (A **hyperlink** is a word or image that, when clicked, links readers to another relevant source or location.) Links allow readers to jump from one place to another—for example, from your research paper to an online article or a related image or video.

18a Beginning the Digital Project

Before you decide to create your research paper electronically, consider three questions to assist the development of the presentation:

1. **What support is provided by your school?** Most institutions have made investments in technology and the personnel to support it.

Investigate how your college will help you publish in an electronic or online medium.

2. **Is electronic publishing suitable for your research topic?** Ask yourself what your readers will gain from reading a digital text rather than the traditional paper version. Will an on-screen electronic format help you to better convey your ideas to readers?

3. **What form will it take?** Electronic research papers appear generally in one of the following forms:

   - A word-processed document
   - A slide show presentation (see section 18b)
   - A website (see section 18c)

18b Building Digital Presentations

If you plan an oral presentation, a slide show can help illustrate your ideas. Commonly referred to as PowerPoint presentations (for the popular software program), electronic presentations differ from word-processed documents in that each page, or slide, comprises one screen. By clicking or setting timers between screens, you can move from slide to slide.

Figure 18.1 shows the opening slide for a presentation based on a research project about the writings of American playwright August Wilson.

August Wilson

American playwright August Wilson (1945–2005) created an impressionistic account of the African-American experience throughout the twentieth century, setting each of his plays in a different decade.

FIGURE 18.1 Slide #1 from a research paper slide presentation.

As you create your electronic presentation, consider the following suggestions:

- Since each slide can hold only limited information, condense the content of each slide and fill in the details orally.
- Use the slide show to support your oral presentation.
- If appropriate, include graphics from your research project in your slide show.

18c Research Project Websites

A website can be an exciting and flexible way to convey your research. It is also the easiest way to get your work out to a large audience. Like an electronic presentation, a research paper website can include graphics, sound, and video.

Creating a Web page or a website involves collecting or making a series of computer files—some that contain the basic text and layout for your pages, and others that contain the graphics, sounds, or video that go in your pages. These files are assembled together automatically when you view them in a Web browser.

Creating a Single Web Page

If you want to create a single Web page from your research paper, the easiest but most limited method is to save your word-processed research paper in HTML (hypertext markup language, the computer language that controls what websites look like). Different word-processing programs perform this process differently, so consult your software's help menu for specific instructions.

When the word-processing software converts your document to HTML, it also converts any graphics you have included to separate graphics files. Together, your text and the graphics can be viewed in a Web browser like any other Web page.

Your research paper will look somewhat different in HTML format than in its word-processed format. In some ways, HTML is less flexible than word processing, but you can still use word-processing software to make changes to your new HTML-formatted paper.

NOTE: The reader will need to scroll down the screen to continue to read the document.

Importing, Entering, and Modifying Text

You can create your text within the Web page editor or outside it. To import text, simply copy it from your word processor and paste it into your Web page editor. You can also specify fonts, font sizes, font styles (such as bold), alignment, lists with bullets, and numbered lists. Here are a few tips for entering text into a Web page:

- **Use bold or italics rather than underlining for emphasis and titles.** On a website, links are often underlined, so any other underlining can cause confusion.
- **Do not use tabs.** HTML does not support tabs for indenting the first line of a paragraph. You also will not be able to use hanging indents for your bibliography.
- **Do not double-space.** The Web page editor automatically single spaces lines of text and double spaces between paragraphs.
- **Make all lines flush left** on the Works Cited Page; HTML does not support hanging indention.

Citing Your Sources in a Web-Based Research Paper

For an online research paper, include parenthetical citations in the text itself. Create and link to a separate Web page for references; remember to include hyperlinks that direct readers to any online works cited in the paper.

18d Using Graphics in Your Electronic Research Paper

Graphics will give your electronic text some exciting features that are usually foreign to the traditional research paper. They go beyond words on a printed page to pictures, sound, video clips, animation, and a vivid use of full-color art.

Decorative graphics make the document look more attractive but seldom add to the paper's content. Most clip art, for example, is decorative. Most academic writing projects should not make use of merely decorative graphics.

Illustration graphics provide a visual amplification of the text. For example, a photograph of Thomas Hardy could augment a research paper on the British poet and novelist. Graphics like cartoons, illustrations, and photographs can also make strong visual arguments of their own, or can provide examples.

Information graphics, such as charts, graphs, diagrams, or tables, provide data about your topic. They can serve as powerful forms of evidence, and they can help you to communicate complex information to readers.

Graphic File Formats

For more information on securing permission for borrowed material on your website, see Chapter 7, pages 97–102.

Graphics usually take up a lot of space, but you can save them as either JPEG or GIF files to make them smaller. In fact, websites can use only graphics saved in these formats. Both formats compress redundant information in a file, making it smaller while retaining most of the image quality. You can recognize the file format by looking at the extension to the file name—GIFs have the extension .gif, and JPEGs have the extension .jpg or .jpeg. GIF stands for Graphical Interchange Format, which develops and transfers digital images. JPEG stands for Joint Photographic Experts Group, which compresses color images to smaller files for ease of transport.

In general, JPEGs work best for photographs and GIFs work best for line drawings. To save a file as a GIF or JPEG, open it in an image-editing program like Adobe Photoshop and save the file as one of the two types (for example, thardy.jpg or thardy.gif).

Creating Your Own Digital Graphics

Making your own graphics file is complex but rewarding. It adds a personal creativity to your research paper. Use one of the following techniques:

- **Use a graphics program,** such as Macromedia Freehand or Adobe Illustrator. With such software you can create a graphic file and save it as a JPEG or GIF file.
- **Use a scanner** to copy your drawings, graphs, photographs, and other matter. Programs such as Adobe Photoshop and JASC Paintshop Pro are useful for modifying scanned photographs.
- **Create original photographs with a digital camera.** Digital cameras usually save images as JPEGs, but the files may be very large and require compression. However, you will not need to convert the files into another format.

As long as you create JPEG files or GIF files for your graphics, you can transport the entire research paper to a website.

18e Using Sound and Video in Your Electronic Research Paper

Because it usually requires additional hardware and software, working with sound and video can be complicated—but linking to sound files posted online or to videos hosted or YouTube or Vimeo is an option.

Including actual files in your work may make your research paper large and difficult to compress and transfer. Before attempting to use digital audio or video, check into your own resources as well as those of your instructor and school. Some institutions have invested heavily in multimedia technology, while others have not. If your paper is posted online—or is a Web page itself—it may be simpler to insert sound or video. Host sites like Word Press and Blogger offer easy ways to post and integrate multimedia content. If you are using work created by someone else, be sure to credit that source and properly cite it.

CHECKLIST

Delivering Your Electronic Research Paper

- **High-speed USB flash drive.** These devices hold large amounts of data, so they work well for transmitting graphics, sound, or video files. Their compact size and plug-and-play operation allow easy access to your instructor's laptop or desktop computer with a USB port.

- **E-mail.** E-mailing your file as an attachment is the fastest way to deliver your electronic research paper; however, it works best if you have a single file, like a word-processed research paper, rather than a collection of related files, like a website.

- **Drop Box or other file sharing services.** Many schools are now utilizing online sharing folders. Students can select the class and subject online and then submit their research paper to the teacher's "Drop Box." Check with your college for specific guidance and details for this submission process. You may also be given access to shared FTP sites, Google Drive, or similar file sharing locations.

- **Website.** If you have created a website or Web page, you can upload your work to the server and readers can access your work online. Procedures for uploading websites vary from school to school and server to server; work closely with your instructor and within school policy to perform this process successfully. Regardless of what method you choose, be sure to follow your instructor's directions and requirements.

18f Preparing a Writing Portfolio

Over the past decade, writing portfolios have become a choice assessment tool for many instructors. As a result, most students who have participated in writing projects, from high school to PhD programs, have assembled portfolios of some kind. Writing portfolios provide a tangible demonstration of talent and experience. Your portfolio will include selected previous written works in a class, plus any additional assignments that the instructor requests. The writing portfolio has several benefits:

- It provides clear objectives and evaluative criteria for writing assignments.
- It provides a real audience as you learn to direct your writing to an unknown reader.
- It provides informed feedback from your instructor, peers, and writing associates.

Specifically, the writing portfolio is a purposeful collection of writing assembled to demonstrate specified writing capabilities to an audience.

At first, selecting folio material may seem like an overwhelming task, especially if you are starting from scratch. The truth is that most writers have many writing samples available, however. Listed here are some potential places to begin looking for folio material:

- Coursework from your classes, not just writing courses. Hanging on to class notebooks and assignments is beneficial and provides writing examples from a number of subject areas.
- Previous essays and research projects. These are great because they usually contain the writer's "best" work and include self-analysis essays regarding strengths and weaknesses as a writer.
- Journals and personal writing. Unconstrained writing reveals a lot about a writer's style and preferred voice.

Although the portfolio philosophy is to save everything, you need not feel pressured to hoard every scrap of writing. Instead, a light screening of portfolio materials should be conducted to prevent an unmanageable collection of samples from forming. Use the following criteria to help select folio material:

- Select materials that clearly demonstrate your abilities.
- Select materials based on quality. Choose documents that demonstrate audience analysis, grammar, clarity, conciseness, technical information, instructions, page layout and design, organization, group or independent work, diversity, and variety.
- Select materials that demonstrate learning. For instance, if a particular piece demonstrates your understanding of persuasive methods, include it.
- Select materials that will have long-term value and usefulness.

NOTE: The safest and most dependable way to store your materials is backed up in at least two places electronically or on a network, on printed hard copy, and on a flash drive.

Begin creating a collection of any and all materials that you might want to place in your writing portfolio. Remember, the portfolio philosophy is SAVE EVERYTHING! The more material you collect in your portfolio, the broader the selection and greater the flexibility you will have when pulling together a presentation of your writing talents.

18g   Presenting Research in Alternative Formats

Current technology provides various options for presenting your research project. Desktop publishing programs such as Microsoft Publisher, Adobe InDesign, or Broderbund Print Shop provide templates for the effective design of newsletters and brochures. Consider an alternative format for your findings when it includes information that can inform or assist a broad array of readers.

Often printed on both sides of a sheet of paper, **newsletters** usually contain multiple pages. **Brochures** are formatted with columns or "panels" that are designed to fit on the front and back of one single sheet of paper so that it can easily be folded. You can also present either of these document types as Web page or as PDFs for electronic distribution. Both newsletters and brochures follow certain conventions of style:

- Place your information in a logical order.
- Use a type size, font style, and color of text that is easy to read.
- Use left-justified formatting that leaves a "ragged" right-hand margin. This is a style that is easier for readers to follow.
- Avoid distracting gaps between words and awkward hyphens dividing words at the end of lines.
- Keep paragraphs short when information is presented in columns.

For most class projects, print newsletters and brochures from your personal computer. For documents in the workplace or for a social group, you may choose to consider using a professional printer; however, remember that a print agency will charge for its services. More and more, brochures and newsletters are distributed electronically.

Alternative formats for the presentation of your research should be chosen carefully to stimulate interest and highlight the key components of the project.

CHECKLIST

Publishing Alternative Documents

- Decide on the purpose of the document and the response that you want the audience to have about the information.
- Sketch out or visualize how each section or panel will look.

- Determine whether the document should be printed or distributed and published online. If the former, select a paper size, binding, or folding that presents your research in a straightforward, clear method.

- Consider graphics, colors, and formatting that add to the clarity of your document.

- Use a distinctive font in the masthead or title as well as headlines for the sections of the document that emphasize their importance.

- Make each section or panel an independent item that can be understood if the brochure is folded or turned to a secondary page.

- Limit information to what readers can comprehend in a brief reading, while informing them where more information can be found.

YOUR RESEARCH PROJECT

1. If you are interested in producing an electronic or multimedia research paper, consult with your instructor for advice and to learn about the support system provided by your school.

2. Begin by building a basic model with word processing, one that might include graphics and other elements as described in section 18d.

3. If the assignment includes an oral presentation, consider building a slide show as described in section 18b.

4. Try building a Web page and then a website. Consult with your instructor before publishing it, and before determining privacy settings.

5. Make yourself comfortable about your knowledge of technical terms such as USB flash drive, masthead, and HTML.

Glossary
Rules and Techniques
for Preparing the Manuscript
in MLA Style

The alphabetical glossary that follows will answer most of your questions about matters of form, such as margins, pagination, dates, and numbers. For matters not addressed here, consult the index, which will direct you to appropriate pages elsewhere in this text.

Abbreviations

Employ abbreviations often and consistently in notes and citations, but avoid them in the text. In your citations, but not in your text, always abbreviate these items:

- technical terms and reference words (anon., e.g., diss.)
- institutions (acad., assn., Cong.)
- dates (Jan., Feb.)
- states and countries (OH, CA, U.S.A.)
- names of publishers (McGraw, UP of Florida)
- titles of well-known religious and literary works

See also "Names of Persons," page 371, for comments on abbreviations of honorary titles. A few general rules apply:

1. With abbreviations made up of capital letters, use neither periods nor spaces:
   MS   JD   CD-ROM   AD
2. Do use periods and a space with initials used with personal names:
   W. E. B. DuBois   J. K. Rowling   T. S. Eliot

Abbreviations Commonly Used for Technical Terms

abr.	abridged
anon.	anonymous
art., arts.	article(s)
bibliog.	bibliography, bibliographer, bibliographic
bk., bks.	book(s)
ca., c.	*circa* "about"; used to indicate an approximate date, as in "ca. 1812"
cf.	*confer* "compare" (one source with another); not, however, to be used in place of "see" or "see also"
ch., chs.	chapter(s), also shown as chap., chaps.
doc.	document
ed., eds.	editor(s), edition, or edited by
et al.	*et alii* "and others"; "John Smith et al." means John Smith and other authors
ibid.	*ibidem* "in the same place," i.e., in the immediately preceding title, normally capitalized as in "Ibid., p. 34"
i.e.	*id est* "that is"; preceded and followed by a comma
ms., mss.	manuscript(s) as in "(Cf. the mss. of Glass and Ford)"
narr.	narrated by
n.d.	no date (in a book's title or copyright pages)
n.p.	no place (of publication)

n. pag.	no page
op. cit.	*opere citato* "in the work cited"
p., pp.	page(s); do not use "ps." for "pages"
proc.	proceedings
qtd.	quoted
rev.	revised, revised by, revision, review, or reviewed by
rpt.	reprint, reprinted
ser.	series
sic	"thus"; placed in brackets to indicate an error has been made in the quoted passage and the writer is quoting accurately.
supp.	supplement(s)
trans., (tr.)	translator, translated, translated by, or translation
vol., vols.	volume(s) (e.g., vol. 3)

Abbreviations of Publishers' Names

Use the shortened forms below as guidelines for shortening all publishers names for MLA citations (but *not* for APA, CMS, or CSE styles).

Abrams	Harry N. Abrams, Inc.
Barnes	Barnes and Noble Books
Farrar	Farrar, Straus and Giroux
MIT P	The MIT Press
U of Chicago P	University of Chicago Press

Abbreviations of Biblical Works

Use parenthetical documentation for biblical references in the text—that is, place the entry within parentheses immediately after the quotation. For example:

> He hath shewed thee, O man, what is good; and what doth the LORD
> require of thee, but to do justly, and to love mercy, and to walk humbly with thy
> God? (Mic. 6:8).

Do not italicize titles of books of the Bible. Abbreviate books of the Bible, except some very short titles, such as Ezra and Mark, as shown in these examples.

Acts	Acts of the Apostles	Matt.	Matthew
1 and 2 Chron.	1 and 2 Chronicles	Num.	Numbers
1 and 2 Cor.	1 and 2 Corinthians	Obad.	Obadiah
Deut.	Deuteronomy	Ps. (Pss.)	Psalm(s)

Abbreviations for Literary Works

Shakespeare

In parenthetical documentation, use italicized abbreviations for titles of Shakespearean plays, as shown in this example:

> MIRANDA O, wonder!
> How many goodly creatures are there here!
> How beauteous mankind is! O brave new world,
> That has such people in't! (*Tmp.* 5.1.181–184).

Abbreviate as shown by these examples:

Ant.	*Antony and Cleopatra*	*JC*	*Julius Caesar*
AWW	*All's Well That Ends Well*	*Lr.*	*Lear*
F1	*First Folio Edition (1623)*	*Mac.*	*Macbeth*
H5	*Henry V*	*MND*	*A Midsummer's Night Dream*

Chaucer

Abbreviate in parenthetical documentation as shown by these examples. Italicize the book but not the individual tales:

CkT	The Cook's Tale	NPT	The Nun's Priest's Tale
CT	*The Canterbury Tales*	PardT	The Pardoner's Tale

Other Literary Works

Wherever possible in your in-text citations, use the initial letters of the title. A reference to page 00 of Melville's *Moby-Dick: The White Whale* could appear as (*MD* 18). Use the following italicized abbreviations as guidelines:

Aen.	*Aeneid* by Vergil	*Lys.*	*Lysistrata* by Aristophanes
Beo.	*Beowulf*	*Med.*	*Medea* by Euripides

Accent Marks

When you quote, reproduce accents exactly as they appear in the original. You may need to use the character sets embedded within the computer software. Write the mark in ink on the printout if your typewriter or word processor does not support the mark.

"La tradición clásica en españa," according to Romana, remains strong and vibrant in public school instruction (16).

Acknowledgments

Generally, acknowledgments are unnecessary. Nor is a preface required. Use a superscript reference numeral to your first sentence and then place any obligatory acknowledgments or explanations in a content endnote (see pages 326–328). Acknowledge neither your instructor nor word processor for help with your research paper, though such acknowledgments are standard with graduate theses and dissertations.

Ampersand

MLA Style

Avoid using the ampersand symbol "&" unless custom demands it (e.g., "A&P"). Use *and* for in-text citations in MLA style (e.g., Smith and Jones 213–14).

APA Style

Use "&" within citations (e.g., Spenser & Wilson, 2014, p. 73) but not in the text (Spenser and Wilson found the results in error.)

Annotated Bibliography

An annotation describes the essential details of a book or article. Place it just after the facts of publication. Provide enough information in about three sentences for a reader to have a fairly clear image of the work's purpose, contents, and special value. See pages 125–127 for a complete annotated bibliography.

Arabic Numerals

Both the MLA style and the APA style require Arabic numerals whenever possible: for volumes, books, parts, and chapters of works; acts, scenes, and lines of plays; cantos, stanzas, and lines of poetry.

Bible

Use parenthetical documentation for biblical references in the text (e.g., 2 Chron. 18.13). Do not italicize the books of the Bible. For abbreviations, see page 367.

Clip Art

Pictures, figures, and drawings are available on many computers, but avoid the temptation to embed them in your document. Clip art, in general, conveys an informal, sometimes comic effect, one that is inappropriate to the serious nature of most research papers.

Copyright Law

"Fair use" of the materials of others is permitted without the need for specific permission as long as your purpose is noncommercial for purposes of criticism, scholarship, or research. Under those circumstances, you can quote from sources and reproduce artistic works within reasonable limits. The law is vague on specific amounts that can be borrowed, suggesting only the "substantiality of the portion used in relation to the copyrighted work as a whole." In other words, you should be safe in reproducing the work of another as long as the portion is not substantial.

To protect your own work, keyboard in the upper-right corner of your manuscript, "Copyright © 20__ by _____." (Fill the blanks with the proper year and your name.) Then, to register a work, order a form from the U.S. Copyright Office, Library of Congress, Washington, DC 20559. This office can also be found online.

Covers and Binders

Most instructors prefer that you submit manuscript pages with one staple in the upper-left corner. Unless required, do not use a cover or binder.

Definitions

For definitions and translations within your text, use single quotation marks without intervening punctuation. For example:

> The use of *et alii* "and others" has diminished in scholarly writing.

Electronic Presentations

If you have the expertise, many instructors will allow you to submit the research paper in electronic form. See Chapter 18 for more information.

Endnotes for Documentation of Sources

An instructor or supervisor may prefer traditional superscript numerals within the text and documentation notes at the end of paper. If so, see Chapter 16, pages 326–328.

Fonts

Most computers offer a variety of typefaces. Use a sans serif typeface like Arial (**Arial**) or a serif typeface like Times Roman (**Times Roman**). Use the same font consistently throughout for your text. Use 12-point type size.

Footnotes for Documentation

If your instructor requires you to use footnotes, see Chapter 16, pages 321–325, for discussion and examples.

Foreign Cities

In general, spell the names of foreign cities as they are written in original sources. However, for purposes of clarity, you may substitute an English name or provide both with one in parentheses:

Braunschweig (Brunswick)   München (Munich)

Köln (Cologne)   Praha (Prague)

Foreign Languages

Italicize foreign words used in an English text:

> Like his friend Olaf, he is *aut Caesar, aut nihil,* either overpowering perfection or ruin and destruction.

Do not italicize quotations of a foreign language:

> Obviously, he uses it to exploit, in the words of Jean Laumon, "une admirable mine de themes poetiques."

Do not italicize foreign titles of magazine or journal articles, but *do* italicize the names of the magazines or journals themselves:

> Arrigoitia, Luis de. "Machismo, folklore y creación en Mario Vargas Llosa." *Sin nombre* 13.4 (1983): 19–25. Print.

Headings

Begin every major heading on a new page (title page, opening page, notes, appendix, Works Cited or references). Center the heading in capital and lowercase letters one inch from the top of the sheet. Use a double space between the heading and your first line of text. Number *all* text pages, including those with major headings.

Indention

Indent the first line of paragraphs one tab or a half-inch. Indent long quotations (four lines or more) ten spaces or one inch from the left margin.

Italics

If your word-processing system and your printer can reproduce italic lettering, use it in place of underscoring if you prefer that style.

Margins

A one-inch margin on all sides of each page is recommended. Place your page number one-half inch down from the top edge of the paper and one inch from the right edge. Your software will provide a ruler, menu, or style palette that allows you to set the margins. *Tip:* If you create a header, the running head may appear one inch from the top, in which case your first line of text will begin one and one-half inches from the top.

Names of Persons

As a general rule, the first mention of a person requires the full name (e.g., Ernest Hemingway, Margaret Mead) and thereafter requires only usage of the surname (e.g., Hemingway, Mead). *Note:* APA style uses last name only in the text. Omit formal titles (Mr., Mrs., Dr., Hon.) in textual and note references to distinguished persons, living or dead.

Numbering

Pagination

Use a header to number your pages in the upper-right corner of the page. Depending on the software, you can create the head with the Page Numbering or Header feature. It may appear one-half inch or a full inch down from the top edge of the paper and one inch from the right edge. Precede the number with your last name unless anonymity is required, in which case you may use a shortened version of your title rather than your name, as in APA style (see page 310). Otherwise, type the heading and then double-space to your text.

Use lowercase Roman numerals (ii, iii, iv) on any pages that precede the main portion of your text. If you have a separate title page, count it as page i, but do not type it on the page. You *should* put a page number on your opening page of text, even if you include course identification (see page 228).

Paper

Print on one side of white bond paper, 16- or 20-pound weight, 8½ by 11 inches. Use the best-quality paper available; avoid erasable paper. Staple the pages of your manuscript together with one staple in the upper-left corner. Do not enclose the manuscript within a cover or binder unless your instructor asks you to do so.

Proofreader Marks

Be familiar with the most common proofreading symbols so you can correct your own copy or mark your copy for a typist or keyboarder. Some of the most common proofreading symbols are shown on the next page.

Roman Numerals

Use capital Roman numerals in titles of persons as appropriate (Elizabeth II) and major sections of an outline (see pages 152–155). Use lowercase Roman numerals to number the preliminary pages of a text or paper, as for a preface or introduction (iii, iv, v). Otherwise, use Arabic numerals (e.g., Vol. 5, Act 2, Ch. 17, Plate 21, 2 Sam. 2.1–8, or *Iliad* 2.121–30), *except* when writing for some instructors in history, philosophy, religion, music, art, and theater, in which case you may need to use Roman numerals (e.g., III, Act II, I Sam. ii.1–8, *Hamlet* I.ii.5–6).

Running Heads

Repeat your last name in the upper-right corner of every page just in front of the page number (see the sample paper, pages 228–236). APA style differs, see page 310.

Short Titles in the Text

Use abbreviated titles of books and articles mentioned often in the text after a first full reference. For example, after initially citing *Backgrounds to English as Language*, shorten the title to *Backgrounds* in the text, notes, and in-text citations (see also pages 191–192), but not in the bibliography entry. Mention *The Epic of Gilgamesh* and thereafter use *Gilgamesh*. (*Note:* Be certain to italicize it when referring to the work.)

Common Proofreading Symbols

ι   error in spelling (m/stake) with correction in margin

lc   lowercase (mis/ake)

⌒   close up (mis take)

I   delete and close up (misstake)

⊢—⊣   delete and close up more than one letter (the mistakes and errors continue)

∧   insert (mi̧take)

∿ (tr)   transpose elements (th(eir))

⬭   material to be corrected or moved, with instructions in the margin, or material to be spelled out, (corp.)

caps or ☰   capitalize (Huck finn and Tom Sawyer)

¶   begin a paragraph

No ¶   do not begin a paragraph

∧   insert

℮   delete (a mistakes)

add space

⊙   add a period

⌃   add a comma

⌃   add a semicolon

⌄   add an apostrophe or single closing quotation mark

⌄   add a single opening quotation mark

⌄ ⌄   add double quotation marks

(bf)   change to boldface

stet   let stand as it is; ignore marks

Slang

Avoid the use of slang. When using it in a language study, enclose in double quotation marks any words to which you direct attention. Words used as words, however, require italics.

Spacing

As a general rule, double-space the body of the paper, all indented quotations, and all reference entries. Footnotes, if used, should be single spaced, but endnotes should be double spaced (see pages 326–328). APA style (see Chapter 15) requires double-spacing after all headings and before and after indented quotes and figures.

Spelling

Spell accurately. Always use the computer to check spelling if the software is available. When in doubt, consult a dictionary. If the dictionary says a word may be spelled two ways, employ one way consistently (e.g., accessory *or* accessary).

Statistical and Mathematical Copy

Use the simplest form of equation that can be made by ordinary mathematical calculation. If an equation cannot be reproduced entirely by keyboard, type what you can and fill in the rest with ink on the printout. As a general rule, keep equations on one line rather than two:

$(a + b)/(x + y)$

APA style requires quadruple line spacing above and below an equation.

Theses and Dissertations

The author of a thesis or dissertation must satisfy the requirements of the college's graduate program. Therefore, even though you may use MLA style or APA style, you must abide by certain additional rules with regard to paper, typing, margins, and introductory matter such as title page, approval page, acknowledgment page, table of contents, abstract, and other matters. Use both the graduate school guidelines and this book to maintain the appropriate style and format.

Titles within Titles

For an article title within quotation marks that includes a book title, as indicated by italics, retain the italic lettering.

"*Great Expectations* as a Novel of Initiation"

For an article title within quotation marks that includes another title indicated by quotation marks, enclose the internal title within single quotation marks.

"A Reading of O. Henry's 'The Gift of the Magi' "

For an italicized book title that incorporates another title that is normally italicized, do not italicize the internal title nor place it within quotation marks.

Interpretations of Great Expectations

Using Shakespeare's Romeo and Juliet *in the Classroom*

Typing

Submit the paper in typed 12-point form. Use no hyphens at the ends of lines. Avoid widows and orphans, which are single lines at the top of a page and single words at the bottom of a paragraph, respectively; some computers will help you correct this problem. Use special features—boldface, italics, graphs, color—with discretion. Your writing, not your graphics, will earn the credits and the better grades. You are ultimately responsible for correct pagination and accuracy of the manuscript. See also Chapter 13, "Revising, Proofreading, and Formatting the Rough Draft," pages 219–227.

Underscoring (Italicizing)

Do not italicize sacred writings (Genesis, Old Testament); series (The New American Nation Series); editions (Variorum Edition of W. B. Yeats); societies (Victorian Society); courses (Greek Mythology); divisions of a work (preface, appendix, canto 3, scene 2); or descriptive phrases (Nixon's farewell address or Reagan's White House years).

Underscoring (Italicizing) Individual Words for Emphasis

Italicizing words for emphasis is discouraged. A better alternative is to position the word in such a way as to accomplish the same purpose. For example:

Graphical emphasis: Perhaps an answer lies in *preventing* abuse, not in makeshift remedies after the fact.

Linguistic emphasis: Prevention of abuse is a better answer than makeshift remedies after the fact.

Some special words and symbols require italicizing.

- Species, genera, and varieties:

  Penstemon caespitosus subsp. *thompsoniae*

- Letters, words, and phrases cited as a linguistic sample:

  the letter *e* in the word *let*

- Letters used as statistical symbols and algebraic variables:

  trial *n* of the *t* test or $C(3, 14) = 9.432$

Word Division

Avoid dividing any word at the end of a line. Leave the line short rather than divide a word.

Finding Reference Works for Your General Topic

We have tried to make this list as user-friendly as possible, which will enable you to select rather quickly a few basic references from one of ten general categories. Three or four items from a list will be more than sufficient to launch your investigation. Each category has two lists:

1. *Library reference books and electronic databases.* The books will require you to make a trip to the library, but the academic databases can be accessed anywhere by logging into your library's network—from your dorm room, computer lab, or at the library itself.
2. *Reputable Internet sources accessed by a browser,* such as Google, Lycos, AltaVista, and others, as listed on pages 43–46.

Remember, too, that the library gives you an electronic catalog to all books in the library as well as access to general-interest databases, such as:

Gale Cengage
NewsBank
LexisNexis Academic
netLibrary
Oxford Reference Online

Here are the ten sections and the page number that begins each:

1. Historic Issues of Events, People, and Artifacts, page 375
2. Scientific Issues in Physics, Astronomy, and Engineering, page 376
3. Issues of Health, Fitness, and Athletics, page 377
4. Social and Political Issues, page 377
5. Issues in the Arts, Literature, Music, and Language, page 378
6. Environmental Issues, Genetics, and the Earth Sciences, page 379
7. Issues in Communication and Information Technology, page 380
8. Issues in Religion, Philosophy, and Psychology, page 380
9. Issues in Business and Economics, page 381
10. Popular Culture, Current Events, and Modern Trends, page 382

By no means are the ten lists definitive, but one of them should serve as your launching pad at the beginning of the project. These works will carry you deeper and deeper toward specific material for collecting your summaries, paraphrases, and quotations.

Historic Issues of Events, People, and Artifacts

If you are interested in events of the past, classical architecture, famous people, and ancient artifacts, you need sources in history, biography, art history, architecture, anthropology, and similar sources. Listed here are important reference works in the library and on the Internet that can launch your investigation.

At the library, investigate these books and academic databases:

Abstracts in Anthropology. Farmingdale: Baywood, 1970–date. This reference guide gives brief descriptions of thousands of articles on the cultural development of human history.

American National Biography. 24 vols. New York: Oxford, 2002. Online or in print, this source is the place to start for a study of most historical figures in American history.

Dictionary of American History. 3rd ed. 10 vols. New York: Scribner's, 2003. This set of books offers a well-documented, scholarly source on the people, places, and events in U.S. history and includes brief bibliographies to recommended sources.

Historical Abstracts. Santa Barbara: ABC-CLIO, 1955–date. This set of abstracts provides a quick overview of historical issues and events worldwide.

Primary Sources in U.S. History. Sponsored by the Library of Congress, this database is wide-ranging and gives, for example, excellent sources on American women's studies.

American Historical Association. Provides an effective index to articles in *American Historical Review, Perspectives on History,* and many others.

On the Internet, investigate these sites:

Annual Reviews: Anthropology
Anthropology Internet Resources
Archiving Early America
Best History Sites
History Best Information on the Net
The History Guide: Resources for Historians
NPS Archeology Program

Scientific Issues in Physics, Astronomy, and Engineering

If you are interested in the heavens (the stars, moon, and planets), the laws of supersonic flight, nuclear energy, plasma television screens, and similar topics, you need to begin your investigation with some of the reference works listed here, which you will find in the library and on the Internet.

At the library, investigate these books and academic databases:

American Chemical Society Publications (ACS). This database offers searchable access to online archives of chemistry journals dating back to 1879.

Astronomy Encyclopedia. Ed. Patrick Moore. New York: Oxford UP, 2002. This source suggests possible topic ideas for research in the field; good starting point for students.

Applied Science and Technology Index. New York: Wilson, 1958–date. This major reference work indexes recent articles in all areas of the applied sciences, engineering, and technology.

Engineering Index. New York: Engineering Index Inc., 1884–date. This work is available in versions ranging from books to electronic databases.

General Science Index. New York: Wilson, 1978–date. This index covers about 100 science periodicals, including many in the applied sciences.

Physics Abstracts. Surrey: Institute of Electrical Engineers, 1898–date. Using keywords, this reference helps you choose a topic and find abstracts to articles on that topic.

On the Internet, investigate these sites:

American Astronomical Society
American Institute of Physics
Mount Wilson Observatory
National Academy of Sciences
Physics World
PhysLink
Planet Quest

Issues of Health, Fitness, and Athletics

If you have an interest in sports medicine, jogging, dieting, good health, nutrition, and similar topics, you should begin your investigation with some of the reference works listed here, which you will find in the library and on the Internet.

At the library, investigate these books and academic databases:

Atlas of Human Anatomy. 5th ed. Frank H. Netter. Teterboro: ICON, 2010. This reference work contains wonderful illustrations of the human body, extensively labeled.

Consumer Health and Nutrition Index. Phoenix: Oryx, 1985–date. This reference work contains an index to sources for consumers and scholars.

Cumulated Index Medicus. Bethesda, MD: U.S. Department of Health and Human Services, 1959–date. This reference work is an essential starting point for most papers in medical science.

Cumulated Index to Nursing and Allied Health Literature. Glendale: CINAHL, 1956–date. This reference work offers nursing students an index to *Cancer Nurse, Journal of Practical Nursing, Journal of Nursing Education,* and many more journals; may be listed as *CINAHL.*

Encyclopedia of Human Nutrition. 4 vols. San Diego: Academic, 2005. This reference work offers a good starting point for a paper on nutrition.

Miller-Keane Encyclopedia and Dictionary of Medicine, Nursing, and Allied Health. 7th ed. Philadelphia: Saunders, 2005. This reference work offers practical applications as well as explanations of concepts and terminology. The reference is now offered in an electronic version also.

Physical Education Index. Cape Giradeau, MO: BenOak, 1978–date. This reference work indexes most topics in athletics, sports medicine, and athletics.

On the Internet, investigate these sites:

Healthfinder
IDEA—Health and Fitness Association
MedWeb
National Institute of Health
PubMed
SIRC—Sports Information Research Center
Strive—Fitness, Athletics, Nutrition

Social and Political Issues

If you have an interest in social work at nursing homes, current events such as rap music or rave parties, congressional legislation on student loans, education, and the SAT examinations, gender issues, and similar topics, you should begin your investigation with some of the reference works listed here, which you will find in the library and on the Internet.

At the library, investigate these books and academic databases:

ABC: Pol Sci. Santa Barbara: ABC-CLIO, 1969–date. This reference work indexes the tables of contents of about 300 international journals in the original language.

CQ Researcher. This reference work provides access to a database containing documents covering hundreds of hot-topic issues such as social networking, election reform, and civil liberties.

Education Index. New York: Wilson, 1929–date. This reference work indexes articles in such journals as *Childhood Education, Comparative Education, Education Digest,* and *Journal of Educational Psychology.*

Encyclopedia of Sociology. Ed. Edgar F. Borgatta et al. 2nd ed. 5 vols. Detroit: Macmillan, 2000. This encyclopedia offers a starting point for research, giving you terms, issues, and theories to motivate your own ideas.

Social Sciences Index. New York: Wilson, 1974–date. This reference work provides a vital index to all aspects of topics in sociology, social work, education, political science, geography, and other fields.

Westlaw. This database contains federal and all state court cases and statutes (laws).

On the Internet, investigate these sites:

Bureau of the Census
FedStats: One Stop Shopping for Federal Statistics
Internet Legal Resources Guide
Political Science Research Guide
Thomas—Library of Congress
Women's Studies Databases

Issues in the Arts, Literature, Music, and Language

If you have an interest in Greek drama, the films of Alfred Hitchcock, the postcolonial effects on languages in the Caribbean, the music of Andrew Lloyd Webber, the poetry of Dylan Thomas, and similar topics, you should begin your investigation with some of the reference works listed here, which you will find in the library and on the Internet.

At the library, investigate these books and academic databases:

Art Index. New York: Wilson, 1929–date. This reference work indexes most art journals, including *American Art Journal, Art Bulletin, and Artforum.*

Avery Index to Architectural Periodicals. Boston: Hall, 1973–date. This reference work is a good source for periodical articles on ancient and modern edifices.

Bibliographic Guide to Art and Architecture. Boston: Hall, 1977–date. Published annually, this reference work provides bibliographies on most topics in art and architecture—an excellent place to begin research in this area.

Bibliographic Guide to Music. Boston: Hall, 1976–date. This reference work provides an excellent subject index to almost every topic in the field of music and gives the bibliographic data for several articles on most topics in the field.

Contemporary Literary Criticism (CLC). This database provides an extensive collection of full-text critical essays about novelists, poets, playwrights, short story writers, and other creative writers who are now living or who died after December 31, 1959.

Humanities Index. New York: Wilson, 1974–date. This reference work indexes all of the major literary magazines and journals; it may be listed as *Wilson Humanities Index*.

Music Index. Warren: Information Coordinators, 1949–date. This reference work indexes music journals such as *American Music Teacher, Choral Journal, Journal of Band Research,* and *Journal of Music Therapy*.

On the Internet, investigate these sites:

American Musiological Society
Artspan
The English Server
Project Gutenberg
Voice of the Shuttle
Worldwide Arts Resources
Worldwide Internet Music Resources

Environmental Issues, Genetics, and the Earth Sciences

If you have an interest in cloning, abortion, the shrinking rain forest in Brazil, sinkholes in Florida, the Flint Hills grassland of Kansas, underground water tables in Texas, and similar topics, you should begin your investigation with some of the reference works listed here, which you will find in the library and on the Internet.

At the library, investigate these books and academic databases:

AGRICOLA. This database, produced by the National Agricultural Library, provides access to articles, books, and websites in agriculture, animal and plant sciences, forestry, and soil and water resources.

Bibliography and Index of Geology. Alexandria: American Geological Institute, 1933–date. Organized monthly, with annual indexes, this reference work indexes excellent scholarly articles.

Biological and Agricultural Index. New York: Wilson. 1916–date. This reference work is a standard index to periodicals in the field.

Biological Abstracts. Philadelphia: Biosis, 1926–date. This reference work contains abstracts useful to review before locating the full articles at the library's computer.

Ecological Abstracts. Norwich: Geo Abstracts, 1974–date. This reference work offers a chance to examine the brief abstract before finding and reading the complete article.

Geographical Abstracts. Norwich: Geo Abstracts, 1972–date. This reference work provides a quick overview of articles that can be searched for full text later.

On the Internet, investigate these sites:

Academy of Natural Sciences
Biology Online
EnviroLink Network
Environmental Protection Agency
Genetics Home Reference
National Agricultural Library
Nature Conservancy

Issues in Communication and Information Technology

If you have an interest in talk radio, television programming for children, bias in print journalism, developing computer software, the glut of cell phones, and similar topics, you should begin your investigation with some of the reference works listed here, which you will find in the library and on the Internet.

At the library, investigate these books and academic databases

Computer Abstracts. London: Technical Information, 1957–date. This work provides short descriptions of important articles in the field.

Computer Literature Index. Phoenix: ACR, 1971–date. This index identifies articles on computer science in a timely fashion, with periodic updates.

Encyclopedia of Computer Science and Technology. Ed. J. Belzer. 22 vols. New York: Dekker, 1975–91. Supplement 1991–date. This reference work provides a comprehensive source for launching computer investigations.

Information Technology Research, Innovation, and E-Government. Washington: National Press Academy, 2002. This site focuses on the use of the Internet in government administration.

The Elements of Style. William Strunk, Jr., and E. B. White. Boston: Allyn, 1999. A classic book that teaches and exhorts writers to avoid needless words, urges them to use the active voice, and calls for simplicity in style.

On Writing Well. 30th anniversary ed. William K. Zinsser. New York: Harper, 2006. This book is a well-written text on the art of writing, especially on the best elements of nonfiction prose.

Style: Ten Lessons in Clarity and Grace. 11th ed. Joseph M. Williams. New York: Longman, 2013. This book provides an excellent discussion of writing style and the means to attain it.

On the Internet, investigate these sites:

Communication Institute for Online Scholarship
Computer Science
Meta-guides to Mass Communications Resources on the Web
InfoTech Spotlight
Internet Resources for Technical Communicators
National Communication Association
Society for Technical Communication

Issues in Religion, Philosophy, and Psychology

If you have an interest in human values, moral self-discipline, the ethics of religious wars, the power of religious cults, the behavior of children with single parents, the effect of the environment on personality, and similar topics, you should begin your investigation with some of the reference works listed here, which you will find in the library and on the Internet.

At the library, investigate these books and academic databases:

Cambridge Dictionary of Philosophy. Ed. R. Audi. 2nd ed. New York: Cambridge, 1999. This reference work provides an excellent base for launching your investigation into philosophical issues.

Encyclopedia of Psychology. Ed. Alan E. Kazdin. 8 vols. New York: Oxford, 2000. This reference work contains the most comprehensive basic reference work in the field; published under the auspices of the American Psychological Association.

Psychological Abstracts. Washington: APA, 1927–date. This reference work provides brief abstracts to articles in such psychology journals as *American Journal of Psychology, Behavioral Science,* and *Psychological Review.* On the library's network, look for *PsycINFO.*

Religion: Index One: Periodicals, Religion and Theological Abstracts. Chicago: ATLA, 1949–date. This reference work indexes religious articles in such journals as *Biblical Research, Christian Scholar, Commonweal,* and *Harvard Theological Review.*

Routledge Encyclopedia of Philosophy. Ed. E. Craig. 10 vols. New York: Routledge, 1999. This work is the most comprehensive, authoritative, and up-to-date reference work in the field.

On the Internet, investigate these sites:

American Philosophical Association
American Psychological Association
Episteme Links: Philosophy Resources on the Internet
Humanities: Religion Gateway
Philosophy Index
Virtual Religion Index
Vanderbilt Divinity School

Issues in Business and Economics

If you want to write about the impact of rising tuition costs, the effect of credit cards for college students, the marketing success of discount stores, the economic impact of federal tax cuts, the stock market's effect on accounting practices, and similar topics, you should begin your investigation with some of the reference works listed here, which you will find in the library and on the Internet.

At the library, investigate these books and academic databases:

Business Abstracts. New York: Wilson, 1995–date. This reference work provides short descriptions of business, economic, and marketing articles.

Business Periodicals Index. New York: Wilson, 1958–date. This reference work indexes most journals in the field, such as *Business Quarterly, Business Week, Fortune,* and *Journal of Business.* See also on the library's network *Reference USA, Business Dateline,* and *Business and Company.*

Business Publications Index and Abstracts. Detroit: Gale, 1983–date. This reference work provides a place to launch searches on almost any topic related to business.

General Business File. This database lists citations and summaries of articles and the entire text of some articles in business, management, and economic periodicals.

Index of Economic Articles. Nashville: American Economic Association, 1886–date. This reference work, arranged as both a topic and an author index, provides a good start for the student and professional alike.

Journal of Economic Literature. Nashville: American Economic Association, 1886–date. This reference work offers articles followed by bibliographies for further research.

World Economic Survey. 1945–date. An annual publication originally from the League of Nations and currently from the United Nations, this reference work offers varying topics each year to researchers.

On the Internet, investigate these sites:

Business Insider
The Economist
FDIC—Federal Deposit Insurance Corporation
Financial Web
Forbes
The Incidental Economist
International Business Web

Popular Culture, Current Events, and Modern Trends

If you are interested in current events and popular culture as well as modern trends, consult sources that provide recent facts and details about famous people, developments in society, and changes in human customs. Listed here are important reference works in the library and on the Internet that can launch your investigation.

At the library, investigate these books and academic databases:

American National Biography. 24 vols. New York: Oxford, 1999. This resource is the place to start for a study of most historical figures in American history.
CQ Researcher. This reference works provides access to a database containing documents covering hundreds of "hot topic" issues such as social media, election reform, or civil liberties.
Illustrated Encyclopedia of Mankind. 22 vols. Freeport: Marshall Cavendish, 1989. This massive work has been a standard in the field for some time.
NewsBank. NewsBank provides searchable full text articles appearing in local publications.

On the Internet, investigate these sites:

Bookwire
Freedom Center
Gallup Organization
The Internet Movie Database
Multi-Channel News
Newser
Popular Culture

Credits

Index

Note: Page number followed by the letter *f* indicates figure.